BEHIND THE SCENES:

The Politics of a Constitutional Convention

BEHIND THE SCENES:

The Politics of a Constitutional Convention

Philip G. Schrag

GEORGETOWN
UNIVERSITY
PRESS

WASHINGTON, D.C.

Library of Congress Cataloging in Publication Data

Schrag, Philip G., 1943——
  Behind the scenes.

  1. Washington (D.C.). Statehood Constitutional
Convention (1982)   2. Washington (D.C.)—Politics and
government—1967-   . I. Title.
JK2716.S37   1984   342.753′0292   84-21120
ISBN 0-87840-413-9   347.5302292

Design & production by Graphics Associates, Inc. / Reston, Va.

TO

David and Zachary

CONTENTS

LIST OF TABLES

ACKNOWLEDGMENTS

The author is grateful to Hilda and Charles Mason, James Baldwin, Edward Guinan, Barbara Maguire, Deborah Hanrahan, and Richard Bruning for the interviews granted him; to Professor Bruce Ackerman for his frequent encouragement; to Professor David Koplow for his intellectual support throughout the convention and the writing of this history; to Emily Schrag for her patience and her comments on the manuscript; to Terry Hoopes and Sal Mungia for their help in tracking down elusive published sources; to the Georgetown University Library and Secretariat (and particularly to Mary Ann De Rosa) for their extraordinary assistance in obtaining documents and helping to prepare the manuscript; to Marilyn Taylor-Berry for her technical support over a two-year period; to Lisa G. Lerman for the jacket photograph; to his seminar students Sara Blackwell, Keith Fischler, Janet Forsyth, Martin Kobren, Cyrus Vance, Jr., and Yvette Taylor for their wise counsel.

* * *

This work appeared originally, in a different format, as an article in Volume 72 of the *Georgetown Law Journal*. The author appreciates the outstanding editorial assistance of the *Journal's* editors and staff, and particularly of executive editor Mark D. Schneider.

BEHIND THE SCENES:

The Politics of a Constitutional Convention

*　　*　　*

The following sources will be cited extensively throughout the chapter notes and have been given these short citation forms:

Committee Tape Recordings (the author's transcripts of his unofficial tape recording of constitutional convention committee meetings) [cited as CTR, and followed by the name of the committee, the date, and the transcript page number].

Constitution of the State of New Columbia set forth in Appendix B [cited as Const. and followed by the article and section number].

Minutes of the District of Columbia Statehood Constitutional Convention [cited as Minutes and followed by the date].

Robert's Rules of Order (rev. ed. 1981) [cited as Robert's, and followed by the page].

Unofficial Rules of the District of Columbia Statehood Constitutional Convention (adopted Feb. 18, 1982, and distributed to delegates Feb. 27, 1982) [cited as Rules and followed by section number].

Revised Rules of the District of Columbia Statehood Constitutional Convention (adopted April 24, 1982) [cited as Revised Rules and followed by the section number].

Transcript of the District of Columbia Statehood Constitutional Convention [cited as Transcript and followed by the date and page].

District of Columbia Self-Government and Governmental Reorganization Act, Pub. L. No. 93-198, 87 Stat. 774. 813 (1973) [cited as Pub. L. No. 93-198, and followed by the section number].

Petition for Initiative No. 3, filed with the D.C. Board of Elections and Ethics, July 10, 1979 [cited as Initiative No. 3, and followed by the section number].

*　　*　　*

The notes to each chapter have been arranged so that the text is not frequently interrupted by citation numbers. For a set of references keyed more particularly to individual quotations and assertions, the reader may wish to consult the earlier version of this work in Volume 72 of the Georgetown Law Journal.

INTRODUCTION

On the day that Ronald Reagan was first elected President of the United States, the voters of the District of Columbia began the process of turning the District into the fifty-first state. By a sixty-forty margin, they approved an initiative to call a Constitutional Convention; when ratified by the people, the charter written by the delegates to this convention would be submitted to Congress as part of a statehood application. Under the United States Constitution, a simple majority in each House of Congress would be sufficient to admit the new state to the Union.[1]

The Constitutional Convention that resulted sixteen months later was, in many ways, similar to other postwar state constitutional conventions. Delegates were elected from geographical districts; they organized politically; they formed committees, wrote drafts and reports, and held hearings and floor debates. In some other respects, however, the District of Columbia's Convention was unusual or even unprecedented. The first striking difference, of course, lay in the fact that the delegates in the District of Columbia were establishing a *new* state. In modern history, only Alaska and Hawaii had written constitutions from scratch; other conventions had set about to revise existing state constitutions. Second, the District's Convention emerged, through the initiative process, from a grass-roots movement that was never encouraged or supported by the commercial or political establishments of Washington. The power structure remained aloof while ordinary citizens—most of them political amateurs, who had either never held elective office or who had at most been neighborhood organizers—built the structure for a future state government. Third, because the establishment was so cool to the enterprise, the operation was run on a shoestring. The District's Council appropriated only $150,000 for the Convention, compared to $1,500,000 for the Hawaii Convention of 1967 and $2,000,000 for the Maryland Convention of 1968, and the Convention lacked the services of an expert Preparatory Commission, traditionally regarded as essential for such conventions.[2]

Fourth, the one-party nature of District politics resulted in very few Republicans serving as delegates, and party loyalties consequently played almost no role in the Convention. Fifth, because the political profile of the

District is more liberal than that of any existing state, and because the District's senior public officials and business leaders did not participate, the delegates tended to reflect varying degrees of progressivism. The delegates spanned a somewhat unusual political spectrum for United States politics. Four Republicans and a Communist aside, they ranged from liberal Democrats to Socialists, and thus the draft constitution that emerged from the Convention was as much a manifesto for social reform (including clauses guaranteeing the rights to employment, abortion, and strike) as an outline for a form of governmental structure. Finally, seventy percent of the District's residents are black.[3] For the first time in history, members of what is nationally a minority group constituted a majority of delegates to a state constitutional convention. Inevitably, race played an especially significant role in the Convention's politics.

Constitutional conventions are significant events in the life of a polity, and they merit academic attention. Such conventions are occasions for expressing ultimate public aims and concepts of democratic government: They reflect the aspirations of people and their views on the use of public power to achieve their goals. Because any subject that can be addressed in legislation can be treated in a constitution, conventions also tend to be cauldrons into which social issues of significant controversy are thrust. Conventions can be occasions on which the people themselves, setting their elected legislators at a distance, employ an alternate and perhaps equally legitimate political device for making law with respect to major public policies.[4]

Scholars have, of course, recognized the importance of these conventions and have produced valuable literature on their process. Books have been written on many of the major state constitutional conventions between 1943 and 1975; they chronicle the efforts, some of which were rejected by the voters in subsequent referenda, to develop new constitutions for Missouri, Alaska, New Jersey, Rhode Island, Hawaii, New York, Pennsylvania, Maryland, and Illinois.[5]

These books, most of which were written under the sponsorship of the National Municipal League's State Constitutional Convention Project as a result of a Carnegie Corporation grant, have much to offer the student of the convention process. They typically describe how the convention was called, the backgrounds of the delegates, the roles played by convention officers, the types of proposals suggested, and the major substantive issues addressed. They are very useful as general descriptions of what conventions do and as guides to the reasons given by the delegates to explain the outcomes on particular constitutional issues.

But these prior studies of constitutional conventions are incomplete. Written largely from public records, newspaper accounts, and occasional memoirs, they describe the conventions as though they had been performances on the stages of public auditoriums, as viewed from the last row or, at best, the front row. The outcomes of political conflicts often appear to result exclusively from rational public debate and the persuasiveness of argument. In a sense, of course, this perspective is fair; conventions are official public meetings, and part of what happens is the formal debate and the final result. I would contend, however, that these studies fail to present a complete picture of constitutional conventions because they do not capture what it is like to be *on* the stage, extemporizing the lines, or behind the scenes, hunting for the missing props.

More particularly, I served as an elected delegate to the District of Columbia Constitutional Convention, and not having found a history that comes close to revealing the quality of a convention as I experienced it, I set out to write one. In doing so, I had three objectives.

First, I desired to write about this convention in the format of the traditional political histories of state constitutional conventions. The founding of a new state merits such a history, even if it turns out that many years and false starts separate this particular convention from the District's entry into the Union. In addition, the "grass roots" nature of this particular convention makes the event a small but important episode in the ragged history of American populism.

Second, I sought to capture the elements missing from the traditional accounts, the political and personal aspects of convention routine. No constitutional convention can possibly be as dry and stuffy as most of the literature implies—the one that I attended certainly was not. Like a legislature, a constitutional convention is a swirl of personal rivalries and power plays, political battles and deals, alliances and treacheries, missed meals and missed families, raging emotions, strategic plotting, tense roll calls, procedural maneuvers, surprising reversals, and lucky or unlucky breaks. In trying to convey these less visible aspects of the process of constitution-making, I have tried to follow the trail blazed by Eric Redman, whose classic study *The Dance of Legislation*[6] has given the public access to some of the realities of the federal legislative process.

My third objective involves the relationship between the other two. I have sought to suggest something about the limits of any one mode of reporting, and to imply that neither type of account can alone do justice to a legislative process. Each provides merely one perspective from which to view an event that can never be recaptured in its totality and which, indeed, was never glimpsed in that totality even by those who participated in it. The point has been made before, particularly in Graham Allison's leading book, *The Essence of Decision*,[7] but it is worth applying to a lawmaking context. I am acutely aware that although I have set forth my own story of the Convention at some great length, each of the forty-four other delegates could also provide his or her personal perspective. Each of these perspectives would be different from mine, in major as well as minor ways; these other viewpoints would focus on aspects of which I am nearly unaware, contradict my observations, reach different conclusions, resolve some of my still unanswered questions and, surely, view me in ways altogether different from the way I view myself. Not only the other delegates, but every research assistant, every court reporter, every secretary could write a book about the Convention, and all would be different, all valid, all a fraction of understanding.[8]

The structure of this work reflects my third objective. I have sought to heighten the contrast between the perspective of the observer whose duty is defined only in terms of reporting and commenting on publicly observable political events, and that of the participant observer who is enmeshed in those events. I have therefore divided each aspect of Convention history into two parts. By perusing only the odd-numbered chapters, the reader will absorb an overview of the Convention, much as if he or she had happened upon a history of the traditional type. Such a history cannot conceal the author's own political stance, and this one does not, but it attempts to steer clear of the highly personal reporting that characterizes participant journalism. By working through only the even-numbered chapters, the reader will see the Convention as I saw it: charged, fragmented, a storm that developed quickly and did not abate until the final fall of the gavel. By going through the entire work, chapter by chapter, the reader may be able to share my sense of how much is happening at once in a political arena, and of just how limiting a single perspective can be.

*   *   *

This history of the District of Columbia Statehood Constitutional Convention was written during the year and a half after the convention ended in May 1982. It is based both on the documentary record of the convention and on notes made by the author, a delegate to the convention, during the proceedings. It was the author's practice to take detailed contemporaneous notes in longhand, particularly in organizational and committee meetings for which no transcripts were made, and also to dictate additional notes immediately after a meeting, conversation, or other event. The author did not systematically inform other delegates that he intended to write about the convention, but he did not conceal this intent, and he revealed it to all who asked about his note-taking. The fact that he was considering publication became so well-known within a few weeks that one of the running jokes of the convention was "better not say that; Schrag will put it in his book." Several other delegates also revealed that they eventually intended to write about the process of the convention.

1. U.S. Const. art. IV, § 3.

2. D.C. Council Act 4-250 (D.C. Register, Sept. 18, 1981, at 4062) ($150,000 appropriation for District of Columbia Constitutional Convention); Norman Meller, *With an Understanding Heart: Constitution Making in Hawaii* (New York: National Municipal League, 1971), p. 82 ($1,500,000 appropriation for Hawaii Convention); John Wheeler & Melissa Kinsey, *Magnificent Failure—The Maryland Constitutional Convention of 1967-68* (New York: National Municipal League, 1970), p. 47 ($2,000,000 appropriation for Maryland Convention).

3. 1980 Census of Population Characteristics, District of Columbia, Table 15, 10-8 (1982).

4. *See The Federalist No. 40*, pp. 256-59 (James Madison) (Modern Library ed. 1937).

5. Martin Faust, *Constitution Making in Missouri: The Convention of 1943-44* (New York: National Municipal League, 1971); Victor Fischer, *Alaska's Constitutional Convention* (Fairbanks: University of Alaska Press, 1975); Richard Connors, *The Process of Constitutional Revision in New Jersey: 1940–47* (New York: National Municipal League, 1970); Elmer Cornwell & Jay Goodman, *The Politics of the Rhode Island Constitutional Convention* (New York: National Municipal League, 1969); Norman Meller, *With an Understanding Heart: Constitution Making in Hawaii* (New York: National Municipal League, 1971); Donna Shalala, *The City and the Constitution: The 1967 New York Convention's Response to the Urban Crisis* (New York: National Municipal League, 1972); George Wolf, *Constitutional Revision in Pennsylvania* (New York: National Municipal League, 1969); John Wheeler & Melissa Kinsey, *Magnificent Failure—The Maryland Constitutional Convention of 1967-68* (New York: National Municipal League, 1970); Samuel Gove & Thomas Kitsos, *Revision Success: The Sixth Illinois Constitutional Convention* (New York: National Municipal League, 1974).

6. Eric Redman, *The Dance of Legislation* (New York: Simon & Schuster, 1973).

7. Graham Allison, *The Essence of Decision* (Boston: Little, Brown & Co., 1971).

8. I am reminded of the main point that D.M. Thomas makes at the end of *The White Hotel* (1981). Although he tells the story of only one life, the lives and stories of each of those who died at Babi Yar would be as unique, as rich, and as important as the one he details.

CHAPTER 1:

The Campaign for Statehood

Somewhere on this planet, there is an island whose territory comprises sixty-seven square miles. The island is a colony, owned by one of the world's great powers. The natives are mostly black. The colonial rulers are almost exclusively white.

Bowing to the twentieth century, the colonial power has permitted its colony a limited amount of self-government. The natives are allowed to elect their own council, but the council's law-making powers are limited in two ways. First, no law passed by this council can go into effect without review by the colonial power's legislature, which has the power to veto any such law within thirty days after enactment.[1] For laws that might affect the colonial power's officials, such as revisions to the local criminal code, a veto by even one House of the colonial power's bicameral legislature will prevent the law's enactment.[2] Second, even after the thirty days have expired, the colonial power's legislature still reserves the right to amend or repeal the council's laws. Indeed, the colonial power even reserves the right to rescind, at any time, the council's law-making power altogether.[3]

The limited self-government that has been granted to the colony does not extend to the budget; the natives cannot be trusted to look after their money. The local council may recommend a budget, but the power to authorize expenditures of local tax revenues is exclusively the province of the colonial power's legislature.

Many of the colonial power's rulers have bought homes in the colony. In order to protect themselves and their investment, they have taken special care to see to it that the natives do not control the systems of criminal or civil justice. The leader of the colonial power appoints the prosecutor for the colony, usually a white. He also appoints all of the colony's judges, civil and criminal.

These rulers enjoy the life style in the colony, and have taken care to insure that certain aspects of it are not disrupted. The local council, for example, has been forbidden to pass any laws permitting the erection of tall buildings.[4] Although such buildings might expand the local tax base, they would spoil the long vista enjoyed by the colonial rulers. Similarly, the colonial rulers have communicated effectively that they expect taxicab rates to be kept much lower than they are on the mainland of the colonial power.[5]

The natives are required to pay, in addition to their local taxes, a tax to the colonial power. This tax, on income, is at the same rate that citizens of the colonial power are themselves obliged to pay. Unlike the citizens of the colonial power, however, the natives are not permitted to vote for the colonial legislators who impose the tax or determine its rate.[6]

The colonial power is the United States of America. The colony is Washington, D.C. The perspective is that of many residents of the nation's capital.

* * *

Washington's appeal for statehood is rooted in long-term dissatisfaction with the relationship between the city, actually a "federal district" and the national government—a relationship which has changed many times during the nearly 200 years of the District's history.[7] The District was born as the result of a national political compromise in the early days of the Republic. The South, fearful that Northern states would have too much influence if the federal capital were located in a Northern city such as Philadelphia, demanded that it be placed in the South. At the same time, the Northern states, which had incurred the largest part of the Revolutionary War debts, were pressing, over Southern resistance, for the federal government to assume those obligations.[8] Alexander Hamilton struck a compromise: To induce the South to accept federal assumption of the debt, the national capital would remain in Philadelphia for only ten years, after which it would be moved to the Potomac River, near Georgetown. The states of Maryland and Virginia ceded land to the federal government for the creation of the new capital.[9]

The capital city that came into being in 1800 was, in reality, a few federal buildings surrounded by thinly populated swampland, on which a few marginal farms were maintained. The towns of Georgetown and Alexandria were included in the District, but even Georgetown was, to Abigail Adams, "the very dirtyest Hole I ever saw for a place of any trade or respectability of inhabitants."[10]

The residents of the new District were required to give up the franchise that they had enjoyed as inhabitants of Maryland and Virginia, but the expectation was that Congress, to which the Constitution gave exclusive but delegable powers over the District, would grant them some form of local self-government. Madison had said in the Federalist Papers that a "municipal legislature for local purposes, derived from their own suffrages, will of course be allowed them."[11]

In 1802 Congress began to make good on this expectation; a new charter provided for a Presidentially-appointed Mayor and an elected Council. In 1812 election of the Mayor by the Council was authorized, and popular election of the Mayor was permitted eight years later.

This form of home rule continued until 1871, when Congress established a territorial form of government for the District. The people continued to elect the lower house of the legislature, but the upper house, the Governor, and a Board of Public Works with independent assessment power were appointed by the President. At the same time, the District was given a non-voting Delegate in Congress.[12]

President Grant appointed one of his loyalists, Alexander Shepherd, as Commissioner of Public Works. Shepherd's actions in office were to affect the political life of the District for a hundred years. Congress had never invested adequately in the physical plant of the city, which had become particularly filthy and slum-ridden in the years after the Civil War. Streets were unpaved and unsightly, and animals ran through them. Shepherd set out to make up for decades of neglect, undertaking a massive program of building sewers, planting trees, paving streets, and installing gas lights. In the process, he expended three times as much money as had been projected, and substantial sums could not be accounted for in the records of the Public Works Commission.[13]

Congress reacted sharply. As a result of the ensuing investigation, Shepherd fled to Mexico, and in 1874 Congress concluded that limited self-government for the District had been a mistake. It abolished the territorial form of government, and rather than returning power to an elected Mayor, it determined to govern the District itself. From 1874 until 1974, Congress made all legislation for the District, and the House and Senate District Committees, comprised entirely of people responsible to voters in other areas of the country, became the District's *de facto* City Council. Executive power was vested in an appointed three-member Board of Commissioners.[14]

The significance of the Shepherd scandal in the history of District government is difficult to overestimate. In the late 1960's, lobbyists for home rule were being told by Congressmen that "the city of Washington isn't ready for home rule; just look what happened last time we tried it."[15]

At first, the political responsibility that Congress had assumed for District affairs led it to accept a large measure of financial responsibility as well. In 1878 it approved a formula under which the federal government would pay for fifty percent of local expenditures. The fifty percent federal contribution, however, was gradually reduced to about one-third by 1913, a percentage not since exceeded.[16]

Meanwhile, the District became more and more heavily populated as the federal government grew and required manpower and ancillary services. People looking for work flooded into the capital after the Civil War and Washington's population increased from 61,000 to 109,000 in a single decade.[17] As Washington became more populous, it also became poorer and blacker. Blacks, four-fifths of them slaves, had constituted about a quarter of the population of the District in 1800, but 40,000 blacks, including many emancipated slaves, migrated to the District during the Civil War. Blacks continued to arrive in subsequent decades, and by 1900 they constituted about a third of the District's population. This ratio of blacks to whites held steady until a major migration of blacks to the District took place after World War II, when in two decades the ratio was reversed, and the District became about seventy percent black.[18]

During the twentieth century, gradually deteriorating race relations, exacerbated by congressional indifference to the needs of what was becoming a larger proportion—and eventually a majority—of the District's population, made the 1874 system of local government seem increasingly unsatisfactory. Many blacks worked in local government jobs in the early 1880's, but these jobs disappeared within a decade. Citizen associations and the Board of Trade discouraged or barred black membership. Civil rights laws were disregarded, railroads and buses to Maryland and Virginia were segregated, and unions refused to admit blacks to membership. In 1919 a band of white servicemen attacked a group of blacks, leading to five days of rioting in which thirty-nine people were killed. The federal government itself tolerated segregation in the nation's capital, hired few blacks in the federal service (except in custodial jobs), and did nothing to improve conditions in the ever-growing slums. In the 1930's the chairman of the House Subcommittee on District Appropriations turned down the District's request for welfare assistance by explaining to the city's welfare director that "if I went along with your ideas . . . I'd never keep my seat in Congress. My constituents wouldn't stand for spending all that money on niggers."[19]

* * *

All this is a form of ancient history, known to many District residents but not itself the source of the emotionally felt grievances which led to the call for statehood. The modern counterpart—the history within the living memory of those active in District politics—dates from the 1950's and 1960's, and particularly from the civil rights activism born in that period. Increasing national sensitivity to issues of black power during this period was not reflected in the actions of the congressional committees that governed the District. The House District Committee was dominated throughout this period by Southern whites who viewed the District as above all else a fine opportunity for patronage. Only rarely was a black appointed as one of the District's three Commissioners, and most of the managerial jobs in city government also went to whites. Nor were the white managers Washingtonians: Judges, for example, were imported by the White House and the District Committee from all over the country to serve in the nation's capital.[20]

In all kinds of minor ways that rankled District residents, Congress suited itself and made life more difficult for the local population. Its white appointees set up a taxicab rate system, for example, in which payment depended not on distance or time of the ride, but on the number of zones that a rider traveled through—and rides between Georgetown and Capitol Hill were much less costly than shorter ones between two of the city's black communities. Noise from planes landing at National Airport became a matter of local concern—and members of Congress, pleased to have a close-in airport for trips back to their districts, largely ignored residents' complaints. District police officers were permitted to live in the white suburbs in Maryland and Virginia, and the emerging black majority in the District found the police increasingly unresponsive to their problems. Even such mundane matters as traffic regulation became a source of annoyance, as members of Congress took it to be part of their daily routine to fix tickets for constituents who were visiting Washington.[21]

By the late 1960's, national consciousness about civil rights was reaching a peak, and the treatment of black District residents by Southern white Congressmen became an issue on the civil rights agenda. President Lyndon Johnson tried to obtain congressional approval of a home rule bill for the District in 1966. When he failed, he cleverly turned to the District's advantage the fact that it was a ward of the federal government. The President had the authority to reorganize federal agencies by Executive Order, and, declaring the District of Columbia to be a federal agency—a not unrealistic view in the light of how it was being treated—he abolished the three Commissioners, authorized himself to appoint a Mayor and Council for the District, and selected a black District resident, Walter Washington, as the District's first Mayor in a century. The District's non-voting delegate in Congress was restored, and as the indirect result of a lawsuit, the District was also permitted to elect its own Board of Education.[22]

This move, however, did little to satisfy the growing sense among Washingtonians that they required full self-determination. There was grumbling because Mayor Washington had been selected by the President without significant citizen participation.[23] More important, the Mayor was not permitted, politically, to remove senior officials of his government who were holdovers from Commission rule, and many of these officials demonstrated their loyalty to the congressional District Committees who had originally selected them as patronage appointees, rather than to the Mayor. There was a famous incident, for example, involving the Three Sisters Bridge, the approaches for which were slated to go through a black neighborhood, destroying homes in the process. The community opposed the bridge, and the appointed Council voted against it. Nevertheless, Tom Ayres, the holdover Highway Commissioner, testified in Congress in favor of building the bridge, and when a leading Member of Congress was asked about the discrepancy between the views of the Mayor and Council, on one hand, and the Highway Commissioner, on the other, he is reported to have replied that he listened to the Commissioner.[24]

Frustration with Congress mounted, as did pressure for autonomy. The key obstacle to a greater degree of home rule was Representative John McMillan of South Carolina, Chairman of the House District Committee and one of the most powerful men in the political life of the District. The Voting Rights Act of 1965, however, was changing the nature of McMillan's constituency. In 1972 the District's non-voting Delegate, Walter Fauntroy, traveled to South Carolina to campaign against him among the newly registered blacks of his home district, explaining how McMillan was treating blacks in Washington. McMillan was defeated, and it became possible to pass legislation providing home rule for District residents.[25]

There were still important pockets of congressional resistance to home rule, and the bill that eventually passed the Congress did not provide for full self-governance. For the first time since 1870, Washington was to have an elected Mayor and an elected Council that could legislate. But the Council's powers were severely restricted. It was forbidden altogether from passing laws on a variety of subjects, including taxation of commuters from Maryland and Virginia, the selection of judges and prosecutors (who were to remain federal appointees), the structure of the judiciary and the maximum height of buildings. On all other matters, local legislation could not become effective until it lay before Congress for thirty working days, during which it could be vetoed by Congressional resolution.[26] At first such vetoes were rarely exercised, but their threat was an ever-present deterrent to progressive legislation. In 1981 the House, perhaps responding to national right-wing pressure, vetoed a long-overdue reform of the criminal code for sexual offenses that had the strong support of the Council and of the District generally.[27]

Although the Council and Mayor could recommend annual budgets, they could not implement them through taxes and appropriations like the governing bodies of other cities. The Council and Mayor had to act like federal agencies, justifying each line item to the House and Senate Committees on Appropriations. Furthermore, Congress often used the federal appropriation process to pass legislation for the District, either in the form of a rider or as an instruction in the conference report accompanying an appropriation bill. In 1981, for example, the House "barred the city from buying more than 25 new police cars, hiring more than 32,608 employees, charging patients more than $12 a visit at public health clinics, . . . boycotting any state that has not passed the Equal Rights Amendment, . . . [or] installing meters in city taxicabs."[28]

Three general aspects of the new system also continued to distress the District's inhabitants. First, the law did not provide for voting representation in Congress, so the District continued to lack political clout with which to bargain and log-roll for its needs. Second, the *form* of the home rule system (most notably, the fact that the Council had thirteen members—eight elected from wards and five, including a president, chosen at large) was congressionally dictated, and was beyond the people's power to change. Finally, the permanence of the new system was no more assured than that of the 1871-1874 territorial government. The ever-present possibility remained that a future Congress might further restrict or even abolish the home rule that had been granted.[29]

Many district residents continued to feel powerless, but now they were developing, as a result of elections for School Board and then for Council and Mayor, a politically active and sophisticated cadre. Political parties and non-partisan civic associations flourished, encouraged greatly by a provision in the Home Rule Act that established Advisory Neighborhood Commissions throughout the city. These regional Commissions, while relatively weak in legal terms, were to become the training ground for future candidates for higher office. Because an Advisory Neighborhood Commissioner was to be chosen from among each 2,000 residents, there was soon no shortage of people who knew the ills of the city and who had both a platform and an incentive for demanding more resources, more power, and increased autonomy for the District. A city with no tradition of local politics suddenly had hundreds of active local politicians.[30]

The new class of political activists had plenty to complain about. Washington was becoming a city increasingly divided between an affluent white minority and a poor black majority, as the middle class, both black and white, fled to the suburbs. Crime increased, the schools deteriorated, and the riots after the assassination of Martin Luther King frightened people away. The city lost nearly 200,000 residents, a fourth of its former population, between 1950 and 1980. In 1982 nineteen percent of Washingtonians had incomes below the poverty level (compared with less than thirteen percent nationwide), a fifty-one percent illegitimacy rate (compared with sixteen percent nationally), the sixth highest crime rate in the nation, ten percent unemployment, a sixth of its population receiving food stamps, and as a result of white flight, a school system ninety-four percent black, a percentage far higher than that of black residents generally. At the same time, Washington had the fifth highest cost of living for a metropolitan area in the nation, and had the third highest tax rate.[31]

The great majority of the new politicians took the view—in public, at least—that limited home rule could be made to work, and that in a new, cooperative spirit, the District and Congress could eventually solve the obvious problems.[32] These politicians easily dismissed occasional talk of statehood for the District: The District was too small to be credibly thought of as a state, and Congress would never accept a small, predominantly black, entirely urbanized state into the Union. Even if it did, statehood would bring economic ruin because the District, which lacked an industrial revenue base, would lose the fraction of its budget that was annually contributed by Congress in recognition of the large amount of federally owned tax-exempt land in the District.[33]

One particularly visible local politician took a different line. Julius Hobson was well known as a local civil rights firebrand. As head of the Washington branch of the Committee on Racial Equality (CORE) in the early 1960's, he had accomplished more than anyone to break segregation in what was then a very "Southern" city. He had used every tactic in the book. He had picketed more than a hundred stores in the downtown area, leading to employment for thousands of blacks, led protest marches, and organized effective mass demonstrations against housing discrimination. He was a frequent plaintiff in the courts, and won a famous lawsuit that outlawed rigid tracking and teacher assignment systems in the public schools. By drawing attention to the non-accountability of the School Board, which was then appointed by the Presidentially-appointed United States District Judges for the District of Columbia, his suit, combined with protest and political action, led to the creation of the District of Columbia's elected School Board. But he did not limit his protests to lawful means; like other civil rights leaders of the time, he engaged in civil disobedience, such as sit-ins, when necessary, and he went to jail on more than one occasion.

In the early 1970's, when it became possible to run for office in the District of Columbia—for School Board, then non-voting Delegate in Congress, then Mayor and Council Member—Hobson added political campaigns to his kit of tactics for reform. But unlike the overwhelming majority of his fellow activists, Hobson did not rush to leadership in the Democratic Party. As usual, he followed a more lonely, visionary, and difficult path, declaring that the home rule system was inherently flawed and that only statehood, on a basis equal to that of other states, would give Washingtonians control over their own fate. He collected the few who would follow him, many of them Marxists like himself, founded the Statehood Party, and led this splinter organization into a series of campaigns for office.[34]

A few months before founding the Statehood Party in 1969, Hobson had been elected, in a nonpartisan race, to the first elected School Board, winning an at-large seat for a one-year term. At the end of the year, he chose to run for re-election from his own ward, rather than at large, so that his friends and fellow Statehood Party members Bardyl Tirana and Charles Cassell, who did not have vacancies in their wards, could run for the two available at-large seats.[35] He lost in his ward, however, and so served on the School Board for only a year. In 1971 he ran another race, this time for non-voting Delegate in Congress, declaring that "if elected, they can't isolate me from the House District Committee. I'll break up their goddamn meeting. What's going on up there anyway? Nothing but theft." Hobson lost again, badly.[36]

Then, when Congress established the elected Council for the District in 1973, Hobson got a lucky break. In order to obtain Republican votes for home rule, the Democrats drafted into the home rule bill a provision designed to ensure that despite overwhelming Democratic Party advantage among District voters, there would be at least some Republicans on the Council. At every biennial Council election, two at-large members would be elected, but each party could run only one candidate.[37]

Leadership of a small but official political party suddenly became, for Hobson, a significant political asset. He did not need to come in first to win the election: A second place finish, ahead of the Republican candidate, would give him a seat on the Council. And Hobson did finish second, many Democrats voting for him strategically because they knew that election of the official Democratic candidate was assured.[38]

Almost simultaneously with his victory, Hobson was stricken with incurable cancer of the spine. Much of his three years on the Council were spent in a wheel chair that had to be carried up the steps of the District Building by attendants, because a ramp commissioned to accommodate his needs was not completed until shortly after his death.

While on the Council, Hobson pressed for a gamut of progressive bills, his voice sometimes only a lone cry from the left. One cause which he never abandoned was statehood. He repeatedly introduced bills calling for referenda on the convening of a statehood constitutional convention. The Council took no action, however, and the bills languished.

After an initial surge of membership to a peak of 2500 registrants, the Statehood Party also seemed to languish. More and more, the District's local politicians were caught up in the daily routine of running the city, or running against those who were running the city. Active membership in the Statehood Party dwindled to a stable core who turned out each fall to work on election campaigns. Apart from occasional speeches by Hobson, statehood disappeared as a public issue.[39]

There was, however, enough energy in the Statehood Party to maintain it as a minor political force. The law barring the Democratic Party from simultaneously winning two at-large seats remained on the books, which was reason enough for the Statehood Party to remain in existence and to be prepared to supply a successor when Hobson died. In addition, School Board races, nonpartisan by law, were wide open, and the biennial race for Delegate to Congress offered a ready forum for raising statehood issues. In fact, when Hobson died in March of 1977, the party was ready not merely with a single successor, but with a husband and wife team: Hilda and Charles Mason.[40]

* * *

By the late 1960's Hilda Mason had been a school teacher and counselor for fifteen years, and was serving, temporarily, as Assistant Principal of one of the public schools in the District. She had always been active in the Unitarian Church, and through her church, which permitted community groups to use its meeting rooms, she became involved in the civil rights movement and met Julius Hobson. She participated, increasingly, in the protests and demonstrations that Hobson led, but always as a follower, never a leader. She joined the Statehood Party when it was founded and became one of its hardest workers. In 1971 Hobson needed a Statehood Party member with experience in the educational system to run for the School Board. He encouraged her to run, and she won.

Charles Mason

From the beginning of her service on the Board, Hilda Mason had more influence than ordinarily enjoyed by a junior member. She brought to the task not only her considerable skill and such minor staff assistance as members were entitled to, but also the services of a full-time volunteer lawyer. This lawyer was not only one of the most punctilious craftsmen in the service of the District's government but was also, as her husband, totally devoted to her interests.

Hilda Mason is black. Charles Mason is as Massachusetts Yankee as they come. One of his grandfathers, as the Chief Justice of the Massachusetts Superior Court, presided at the trial of Lizzie Borden in the famous axe-murder case of the nineteenth century. The other grandfather, whom Charles remembers well, graduated from Harvard in 1855. Charles Mason got his own B.A. there seventy-seven years later.

When he left college in the middle of the Depression, he took the only jobs he could get. He taught math at a junior college and worked for a couple of years as an engineer in the inspection department of a fire insurance company. Finally, after taking the civil service examination for college graduates, he was given a job in the Civil Service Commission itself, helping to classify jobs of scientists and engineers in the Boston area. Poor eyesight prevented him from serving in World War II, and at the end of the war, returning veterans had preference over him in civil service assignments. Mason therefore was transferred to the personnel office of the Naval Research Laboratory in Washington where, as time went on, he became less and less interested in his work. In 1965 he met Hilda at church, and was married for the first time at the age of fifty-four. Three years later, he retired from the civil service after thirty years of service, and with his federal pension secured, he entered Howard Law School, one of four or five whites in a class of 120.

Just when Mason, then sixty, had passed the bar, his wife left teaching as a result of her election to the School Board. From then on, he devoted his legal efforts to a single client.

Hilda Mason was re-elected to the School Board in 1975 and was half-way through her term when the dying Julius Hobson approached her and asked that she try to succeed him on the Council. The Statehood Party gave her the designation, and she was elected, first to fill the remainder of his term and then, in 1978, for a full four-year term. Within a few years, she became chair of the Committee on Education and had become a visible public figure in the District, addressing meetings almost every night on disarmament, women's rights, and, of course, statehood. Charles did not speak out, but was always there with her—taking notes, drafting speeches and legislation, planning legislative strategy. They were known throughout the District as the Bobbsey Twins of Washington politics.

By the late 1970's, when the effort that led to the District's Constitutional Convention was born, the District's economic and social problems were long-standing and severe, particularly for many among the black majority. A political party that believed statehood to be the answer was reasonably well established—the Statehood Party. It had been in existence for about ten years and apparently had a lock on at least one of the thirteen seats on the Council. Over the years, it had also elected several members to the School Board, despite its nearly insignificant enrollment.[41] But the lightning bolt that struck was not sent by blacks, or by the Statehood Party, or by its top office holder, Hilda Mason. It came from two Irish Catholic radicals who were relative newcomers to Washington.

*   *   *

Ed Guinan looks like a kindly gentleman, with sparkling blue eyes and neatly combed white hair.[42] He is often quiet, but those who have worked with him describe him as a charismatic man of unbounded energy.

He grew up in a working class family in Denver, entered the Navy, and put himself through the University of Colorado by driving an ambulance. Afterwards he became a successful San Francisco stockbroker, with an apartment in the city, a house on the beach, and a sports car.

Through a close friend who was a Paulist priest, Guinan began to do volunteer work with children. After a time, the service work became increasingly satisfying, and the purchase and sale of securities became less so. Guinan made the kind of change in his life that is almost unheard of in the twentieth century. He gave up his wealth and his career and moved to Washington to study for the priesthood at St. Paul's College. After completing his studies at the Paulist center, he was ordained.

During the war in Viet Nam he was a chaplain at George Washington University. The war pushed him further and further to the left, and he became involved with the Berrigans and other Catholic radicals. He founded, in Washington, the Center for Creative Non-Violence, a hub of anti-war activity. He also periodically attended workshops on nonviolence at a farm called Oak Ridge, in New Jersey.

At one such workshop, Guinan concluded that his anti-war activities were of no relevance to the poor. He announced to the others in his workshop that he was returning to the District of Columbia and would commit himself to open a soup kitchen in the poorest neighborhood of Washington. He asked whether anyone would join him. The woman who responded later became his wife.

Within a few months, the Zacchaeus Soup Kitchen was collecting funds from individuals and community organizations and serving soup to

600 people a day in the Shaw neighborhood, one of the District's most desperate slums. The kitchen was followed by an overnight shelter and then by the Community Pretrial House, where homeless people who had been arrested could go to establish a residence, therefore becoming eligible for bail while awaiting trial.

By 1977 Guinan's network of services for the impoverished was firmly established, but managing it was exhausting him. Guinan applied to Friends World College for an intern to help him; the College, located on Long Island, is an alternative educational institution that offers its students placements in various service settings. Barbara Maguire arrived in Washington pursuant to Guinan's request.[43]

Barbara Maguire

Maguire had grown up in Philadelphia with two sisters, two brothers, a mother, and a father who was determined that his children, particularly his daughters, be assertive and make their mark upon the world. Every night at dinner, he forced them to debate with him, and he screamed at them until they took positions and defended them. Her older sister was very bright, and she won scholarships easily. Wanting to avoid a competition with her sister which she feared she would lose, Maguire selected what she regarded as a pose: the role of an offbeat rebel. After her sophomore year she transferred from a 6000-student Catholic high school to the Parkway Program, an all-black Philadelphia high school which prided itself on alternative, experiential education. She studied Poe at Poe's house in Philadelphia and learned history at Independence Hall. In her valedictory address, she commented on the fact that the only white woman in the class was valedictorian: Did this prove Parkway to be a non-racist environment, or was her emergence in that position racist? In her own mind she wondered: "Have I hustled this school?"

Still in flight from the prospect of competition with her sister, Maguire enrolled in Friends World College. There she sought a placement that would enable her to work with a family court judge, as she had done as part of her course of study in the Parkway Program. The school was unable to find such a setting for her. She settled for the next best thing, a placement at the Community Pretrial House in Washington, D.C.

Arriving in the District in December 1977, Maguire tried to understand what was happening in her new surroundings. She recalls that her first impression was that President Carter's nearest neighbors were utterly destitute people who, to keep warm, slept on subway gratings near the White House. She involved herself in all of Guinan's charitable enterprises; her daily routine, like that of Guinan and his wife, involved cooking huge quantities of soup and serving it to hundreds of the kitchen's clients. Maguire listened to the hopeless life stories, stories filled with poverty, illness, emotional misery, and the certainty that life could not become any better.

In the evenings, after the kitchen had been cleaned, Maguire and the Guinans sat in the Guinans' living room and talked about the politics of poverty and the unwillingness or inability of governments to improve the lives of those driven to the Soup Kitchen by near-starvation. Gradually they came to the conclusion that their clients were doomed to a lifetime of poverty because they had no dignity and no political power. The Guinans were experienced political organizers, but it had proved impossible to organize the poorest of the poor because there was no power to be exercised even if they were organized. Home rule notwithstanding, even those in public office in Washington had little control over the distribution of wealth and income in their city.

Statehood seemed the obvious answer. It combined a share of national power, through voting representation in the House and Senate, with the principle of self-determination, a necessary precondition for increased dignity. The Guinans knew that statehood bills regularly had been introduced unsuccessfully in the Council by Julius Hobson, and after his death, by Hilda Mason. But by this time the legal environment had changed in one critical respect.

The Council had just passed a law permitting statutes to be passed by the people themselves, if, through an arduous petition drive, a sufficient number of District voters asked that the proposed law be put to the electorate for a vote.[44] A statehood initiative campaign was, to community organizers like the Guinans, a perfect opportunity; it combined the highly desirable goal of statehood with an opportunity to build a political network out of the processes of petitioning and campaigning for voter approval.

It was not, however, Ed Guinan's style to begin an organizing campaign by assembling all the people who might be interested and seeking consensus among them. Instead, in August 1979 he sat down in his living room and wrote out the statute that he wanted enacted. He typed it up, took it to the Board of Elections, and filed it.[45]

The proposed law that Ed Guinan wrote did not simply call for a popular vote for or against the concept of statehood. He chose a more complex route, one that could build a political infrastructure to support statehood and lobby it through Congress.

Under Guinan's proposal, the people would vote on whether to call a statehood constitutional convention. If they approved the call, delegates would be elected at the following election, five from each of the District's eight wards and five at large. The delegates would draft a state constitution, which would be submitted to the voters for ratification. If the constitution were ratified, it would be presented to Congress as part of a statehood application.

Drafting a state constitution before applying to Congress for admission to the Union is not a necessary part of the statehood admission process. The United States Constitution is silent on the procedure for statehood, except to say that only an Act of Congress is necessary.[46] Having a constitution in hand, however, would give the potential state at least the psychological advantage of demonstrating the seriousness of its effort, particularly if the constitution was drafted through a process broadly representative of the citizenry. The convention itself could build support for the effort; at least the forty-five delegates and their supporters would have a major stake in persuading Congress to follow through on what they had done. Several other states—most recently Alaska—had followed this very procedure of drafting a proposed constitution before engaging Congress.[47]

Guinan's draft had some other features as well. It called for the election of potential United States Senators and a Representative in

Congress at the same time as the vote on ratification of the constitution. Until Congress agreed to admit the proposed state, these three officials would be paid by the District of Columbia and would serve as lobbyists for statehood. A similar role had been played, with great effect, by Alaska's potential Representative and Senators while that state sought admission to the Union.[48]

Another feature of Guinan's bill was that if the proposed constitution were to be rejected by the voters when it was submitted for ratification, the Mayor of the District would be required to reassemble the convention at once to draft a new constitution. No limit was set on the number of times that the convention could redraft and resubmit a proposed constitution.

The proposed initiative authorized the creation of two commissions in addition to the convention. A Statehood Commission, comprised of three persons from each ward selected by the convention, would be formed "for purposes of educating, advocating, promoting and advancing the statehood position," and a Statehood Compact Commission, consisting of some of the members of the Statehood Commission and "an equal number of representatives from the Federal government as may be authorized by the President and/or the United States Congress" would study what legislation and administrative action might be necessary to transfer authority to the new state.

Recognizing that admission of the proposed state would be made much more difficult, politically, by any claim that the major federal buildings—particularly the White House and the Capitol—were to be included within it, Guinan specified that the purpose of his initiative was "the calling of a state constitutional convention . . . for purposes of producing a state constitution (excluding the federal area)." He did not try, however, to specify the boundaries that would separate the bulk of the District, which was to become a state, from the much smaller enclave that would remain purely federal territory.

Finally, Guinan recognized that the Council that had refused to pass a bill putting statehood to a referendum might also sabotage his effort by refusing to appropriate the funds necessary to hold the convention. He therefore provided that "there is hereby authorized an appropriation from the general fund of the District of Columbia a sum not in excess of $400,000 to the Constitutional Convention." An additional $300,000 was to be allocated to the two commissions.[49]

*   *   *

The Statehood Party first learned of Guinan's filing when Josephine Butler, its chair, received a courtesy call from Bill Lewis, the Board of Elections' General Counsel. Neither she nor any of the other Statehood Party activists had ever heard of Ed Guinan. She invited him to a meeting in the living room of Deborah Hanrahan, a party stalwart.

"The whole thing was fantastic," says Hanrahan. "He had done the whole thing by himself, all the research and writing, with no legal help, and no consultation at all with the Statehood Party. He said to us, essentially, 'Join me or dissolve!'"

"We had been considering running an initiative campaign in a couple of years," says Richard Bruning, the Statehood Party's Secretary. "But we figured that it would be necessary to reorganize the party first, on a precinct-by-precinct basis, if possible. Then, with the machinery in place, we could mount an initiative campaign and have a chance of success."

Guinan's filing shocked the party and divided it deeply. "There was a big debate as to whether to let it die or get behind it," Bruning recalls. "Half of the party's Central Committee walked away," Hanrahan says. "They said that the city wasn't ready, that the initiative wouldn't pass."

The party temporized by investigating Guinan. "We did some probing and digging to find out where he was coming from. We couldn't figure out his motivations. We were all miffed because he hadn't consulted us," Bruning says. "We checked his registration, of course, and were surprised to find that he was a member of the Statehood Party."

Despite deep reservations, party leaders eventually decided to back the initiative campaign. "We really had no choice," Bruning says. "We had to get on board. If it failed, it would seem a repudiation of statehood as a concept. We couldn't successfully separate Ed from the party in the mind of the public. If we tried to divorce ourselves from the initiative campaign, many party members would take a role anyway and we would be unable to deny that key party people were working on it."

"No one was very enthusiastic," Hanrahan adds. "We were just stuck with Ed's filing."[50]

*   *   *

Guinan set up a headquarters in the basement of his house, and he and Maguire contacted friends and Statehood Party members, encouraging them to gather signatures. Guinan formed a Statehood Initiative Committee to bring Democrats, Independents, and any Republicans that could be found together with those from the Statehood Party who were active in the project. Signature solicitors fanned out to busy street corners. Under the initiative procedure statute, 12,451 voters' signatures collected within a six-month period would be needed to trigger a vote on the proposed law.[51]

As the Initiative Committee developed, Guinan was increasingly troubled by the racial ratio of its membership. It was overwhelmingly white. "We knew that we would lose at the polls if this initiative were seen as a project of Dupont Circle whites," Maguire says. "But our contacts were all white, and most of the Statehood Party activists were white too. Still, the Statehood Party had a few blacks in its leadership, particularly Jo Butler and Hilda Mason, and we asked them for more names. Through them, a few others participated, but whites got most of the signatures, even in black neighborhoods. Eight people, all of them white, collected about three-fourths of the signatures. But dozens of people, black and white, collected at least some signatures, and we eventually did have a real city-wide organization." Expansion of the organization had to be accomplished entirely through personal contacts, because the campaign was not yet taken seriously by the press, and it received no media attention whatsoever.[52]

Once the manpower had been secured, the actual process of gathering signatures proved easy. As is true with almost any political petition campaign, few voters, even those opposed to statehood, refused to give the question a chance to appear on the ballot. On February 11, 1980, Guinan filed petitions with 21,928 signatures, more than enough to protect the petition campaign from successful challenge by anyone tempted to check individual signers' names against the registration lists.[53]

The Board of Elections' General Counsel, William Lewis, recommended to the Board that the statehood initiative be certified for inclusion on the ballot at the time of the next primary elections, in September.[54] Guinan and Maguire paid a casual visit to the weekly meeting of the Board of Elections to observe the official recognition of their months of work.

To their horror, the Board disagreed with its Counsel and voted down the motion to put the initiative on the ballot. The Board ruled that because Washington was a federal district, it could not become a state: The "initiative is unconstitutional and . . . this Board has an obligation not to permit unconstitutional measures to go to the public."[55]

Guinan quickly contacted lawyers who had joined the Statehood Initiative Committee, and they immediately brought suit. When the case was heard late in June, Superior Court Judge William E. Stewart ruled from the bench that the Board had erred.[56] Several months had been lost, however, and the initiative had to be moved to the November ballot.

Guinan's next task was to build up votes for the initiative. The Initiative Committee continued to grow slowly, aided somewhat by publicity associated with the filing of the petitions and the successful lawsuit. The city's newspaper and public figures began taking positions. The *Washington Star*, the District's evening newspaper, became an early opponent. "Statehood is neither appropriate nor likely," the paper editorialized. "The District of Columbia is not and should not be a state; it was created as the seat of national government, and that was and remains its character—and pride."[57]

A second source of opposition was the District's non-voting Delegate in Congress, Walter Fauntroy. Fauntroy had, in 1978, successfully pushed through Congress a constitutional amendment to permit the District to have two Senators and a Representative in Congress—all with votes.[58] This had been an impressive achievement, since it had required a two-thirds vote in each House.[59] Fauntroy and his supporters claimed that the Voting Rights Amendment had succeeded in Congress because of the threat of black votes in the South; even South Carolina's conservative Republican Senator Strom Thurmond had ultimately voted for it. Fauntroy's detractors claimed, however, that members of Congress had voted for the amendment only because they were certain that it would not be ratified by the requisite three-fourths of state legislatures.[60] Indeed, the Amendment had encountered heavy opposition, even in Northern industrial states, and had been accepted by only seven states in the two years since it had been available for ratification. On the weekend that the statehood petitions were filed, the *Washington Post* noted that the Voting Rights Amendment was "faltering badly."[61]

Still, Fauntroy had staked his reputation on the amendment, and he saw that the statehood initiative offered state legislators an easy excuse to vote it down. He believed the amendment could still be passed, while statehood would be nearly impossible to achieve. He also thought that a successful statehood effort would eventually lead to the city's bankruptcy.

In September he sent his constituents a letter opposing the statehood initiative. "If statehood were sought, the District would face the prospect of a severe cutback in federal aid, a situation that could mark financial disaster to an already unstable District budget. . . . I have not and do not today support the Statehood Initiative."[62]

Gradually, though, the initiative picked up the endorsement of some of the District's officials. Although only Hilda Mason campaigned actively for an affirmative vote, several officeholders, including Mayor Marion Barry, Jr., stated their support. It was clear, however, that the support was grudgingly given, in recognition of the potential voting power of the thousands who had signed the statehood petitions. Politicians complained to the press that they disliked the idea but were afraid of appearing to oppose full home rule for the city. "You cannot speak out against self-determination," Council Chair Arrington Dixon said as he endorsed the initiative. "As a statement of self-determination, we cannot not support it. We almost have to support it." "It's a damned-if-you-do, damned-if-you-don't situation," complained Council Member David A. Clarke, another endorser.[63] Eventually, the initiative was supported by nine of the thirteen Council Members.[64]

The major citizens' organizations played little role in the election, with the notable exception of the League of Women Voters. The League declared the initiative "poorly drafted." As an example, it noted that the initiative specified no time limit on the period during which the District would pay the two Senators-elect and the Representative-elect as statehood lobbyists. "These costs may go on year after year," it noted. The League also criticized the provision in the initiative for creation of the Statehood and Statehood Compact Commissions, which could become "a new alternative layer of government . . . who could go out and say they speak for the people of the District, yet they are responsible and accountable to no one . . . you can't vote them out of office, you can't get rid of them."[65]

The core of the League's constituency lay in Ward Three, west of Rock Creek Park, the most affluent area of the city.[66] Ward Three was suburban in character, and nearly all white in racial composition; the names of some of its neighborhoods, Georgetown and Cleveland Park, were recognizable nationally. It was also more conservative than most other parts of the District, and it housed the bulk of the District's Republicans as well as a large number of people who registered as Democrats in order to have influence in the only primaries that counted, but who voted Republican in general elections.[67] Ward Three was also of special political significance because the percentage of its citizens who regularly voted was higher than the corresponding percentage elsewhere.[68] Candidates almost never won city-wide office without carrying Ward Three. To the Initiative Committee, this was more an opportunity than a problem. "We wanted to win without Ward Three," Barbara Maguire recalls, "because it hadn't been done before. We thought we could do it because we had the issue."[69]

By election day, even Delegate Fauntroy conceded that the Initiative Committee indeed had the issue. "I think it's going to pass," Fauntroy told reporters. "Everybody's against sin and for motherhood."[70]

The initiative did pass, easily. On election day 1980, the District of Columbia produced a large turnout which voted, contrary to most states, for the re-election of President Jimmy Carter. It approved the statehood initiative by a three-to-two margin, voting it up by substantial percentages in every ward except Ward Three, where it lost two-to-one.[71] Table I reflects the vote.

TABLE I: District Vote by Ward in 1980 for the Statehood Initiative

	Negative Votes	Affirmative Votes	Affirmative Percentage
Ward 1	5,196	10,387	67%
Ward 2	6,980	9,979	59
Ward 3	20,256	12,404	38
Ward 4	7,625	15,118	66
Ward 5	6,074	11,946	66
Ward 6	5,674	10,306	64
Ward 7	5,181	11,215	68
Ward 8	2,236	6,484	74
TOTAL:	59,222	87,839	60%

*   *   *

Ed Guinan knew, as soon as the polls had closed and the results had been announced, that his organization would fail and his control would slip away. Suddenly, his project had been magnified; there would be public offices to run for, money to be spent. People who had been active in the Initiative Committee would disappear to organize their own campaigns or those of friends for delegate, and new people who had played no role in getting to this point would intrude. Still, he determined to do his best to provide some overall leadership and direction to the next stage of activity, stimulating candidates to run in every ward, and increasing public awareness that a real statehood movement was under way.[72]

The initiative having passed, it became appropriate to change the name of the organizing vehicle, and Guinan restructured the Statehood Initiative Committee as the 51st State Committee. Guinan realized that in the District, a white president of the organization could not help with recruiting where it was most needed, so the Committee was structured, like a corporation, to have two chief officers. The president, Hilda Mason, would chair membership meetings and speak to the public on behalf of the Committee. Guinan, who had far more time to devote to Committee activities, would do the day-to-day work as chair of the board. By-laws were drawn up, and elections were held. Mason and Guinan were unopposed for the leadership of the Committee. Lillian Huff, a former D.C. member of the Democratic Party's National Committee, was elected vice-chair. Barbara Maguire became treasurer.[73]

As an organizing device, the Committee held a day-long public conference on the statehood process. The meeting was held in April 1981, at a public school, and Guinan hoped that in the wake of the election victory, press releases about the meeting would be widely carried.

attracting many newcomers to the 51st State Committee. In fact, the meeting received no publicity, either before or after it was held. On the day of the meeting an auditorium capable of holding several hundred participants held only about seventy-five conferees, most of them veterans of the petition drive, for whom a recitation of the reasons for statehood, a history of the effort to date, and an assertion of the desirability of generating public interest in races for delegates was wasted repetition. As a result of the poor publicity, only a sprinkling of new faces emerged at this meeting.

Meanwhile, three new problems emerged for the Committee. First, a new danger threatened the initiative itself. The initiative was law, and like all District of Columbia laws, it could not take effect until it lay before Congress for thirty working days. The initiative was certified to Congress on December 1, 1980, but the Ninety-sixth Congress, to which it was submitted, adjourned for the final time before thirty working days had elapsed. Staff members in the Ninety-seventh Congress, elected in 1980, took the view that the initiative had to be resubmitted, and the D.C. government was persuaded not to put up a fight, because Congress could retaliate by cutting the District's budget.[74] When the initiative was resubmitted, Representative Robert W. Daniel, Jr., of Virginia (a state which stood to lose were the District to become a state and thereby gain the power to tax commuters) introduced a resolution of disapproval.[75]

Fortunately, an initiative legalizing a lottery had passed at the same election and had been simultaneously submitted to Congress; this other initiative attracted most of the fire. In addition, the House District Committee had changed significantly since the days of its domination by Southern whites and now was chaired by a liberal black, Representative Ron Dellums of Oakland and Berkeley, California, who was sympathetic to the desires of those in the District. Fauntroy was also a member of the committee, and by this time he was adept at counting the votes in favor of statehood. With help from other Northern liberals, Dellums was able to kill Daniel's resolution in his committee on a vote of five to four.[76]

The second crisis erupted a few days later when the Board of Elections again raised a problem. Its counsel notified Guinan that, read literally, the text of the initiative that passed would require the Board to hold a new referendum the following fall on whether to hold a constitutional convention. The delegates who would be elected simultaneously would actually assume office only if the new referendum called for a convention.[77]

Guinan conceded that the text of the initiative was faulty, but he blamed the Board's own staff which, pursuant to the D.C. initiative procedure law, had rewritten the words he had originally submitted. The League of Women Voters announced that in the new election, it would again bring up the issues that had concerned it.[78] Statehood advocates had reason for concern, because turnout would be much smaller in an off-year election, but would remain large in Ward Three where a lively race to replace a retiring School Board incumbent had developed.[79]

Eventually, the 51st State Committee appealed to the Council for help. The Council resolved the issue by amending the initiative (which it could do because the initiative had the legal status of any District law) to make it clear that no further vote on whether to have a convention was necessary. The Council's consideration of the initiative legislation, however, gave critics the opportunity to amend the law in other ways as well. Ward Three Council Member Polly Shackleton succeeded in making a critical change in the law that would influence the entire life of the convention: At her suggestion, the Council limited the working life of the convention to ninety days. Also at Shackleton's insistence, the Council provided that if the voters rejected the proposed constitution, the convention could attempt a single redraft, but that if the voters rejected the constitution a second time, the effort would come to an end.[80]

The third and most serious problem developed two months later, and it involved money. Mayor Marion Barry, Jr. had proposed to appropriate the full $700,000 authorized by the initiative for the convention and its two statehood commissions. Council Member Betty Ann Kane, who had nominally supported the initiative, proposed cutting this figure to $10,000, because the District could not afford to appropriate the funds. The 51st State Committee tried to neutralize Kane by asking the Council to authorize and appropriate $1,600,000. Ultimately, the Council approved only $150,000 for the convention, and none (in the fiscal year about to begin) for the ancillary commissions.[81]

The need to fight these defensive battles diverted Guinan and other 51st State Committee leaders from what they saw as a real priority: The development of position papers and research reports so that the convention would be able to begin with a running start. These were never written, but it is doubtful whether they would have been produced even if the defensive battles had not been waged. The election season in the District of Columbia is a long one, and nominating petitions for a November election begin to circulate early in July, requiring candidates to organize in June.[82] By late spring, the most able members of the 51st State Committee leadership were already beginning to concentrate their efforts and spare hours on their personal candidacies for delegate; by summer, the troops had gone. Among the candidates from the committee were Guinan, Maguire, both Masons, Lillian Huff, and Wesley Long, a white member of the District's Public Utilities Commission who had organized and chaired the educational conference in April. No one was left to keep an eye on the project as a whole. Meetings of the committee's board and membership were held with less and less frequency. A bitter squabble over a year-old loan split the organization. Within a few weeks, Guinan resigned as chair of the board; Lillian Huff was elected to the vacancy. She inherited a shell of an organization with no meetings, no program, a ledger full of debts, no cash and, as a result of Guinan's view that dues would interfere with freedom of political association, no regular income.

* * *

Candidates ran, elections were held, but it is hard to say that there was a campaign. One hundred and three men and women filed petitions for the forty-five delegate positions.[83] Few of them were known outside their immediate neighborhoods or the organizations in which they worked. The only candidates who were very well known in the District were three Council members, Hilda Mason, David Clarke, and the Council's only Republican, Rev. Jerry Moore, and School Board member Barbara Lett

Simmons. All of these well known candidates ran for at-large seats. A few other candidates may have enjoyed somewhat less name recognition, notably Charles Cassell, a black who had once been a Statehood Party member of the School Board, and who had played a minor role in the proceedings of the 51st State Committee; James Coates and Victoria Street, who had also served on the School Board at one time; and Wesley Long. Most of the other candidates started near zero, or, if they served on an Advisory Neighborhood Commission, with a political base equal to one-fortieth of a ward, but fortunately for them, so did their competition.[84]

Few of the candidates had money to spend or the ability to raise it, particularly in a race for such a minor office, carrying no patronage. Several had coteries of friends or political associates who could be called upon to help distribute literature, but only the Council members had anything like political machines that could be cranked up.

The media gave the candidates no help at all. From the start of the election through election day, only one story about the campaign graced the pages of the *Washington Post*, which in August became the District's only daily newspaper. That one story, far from an introduction of the candidates to the voters, was essentially a warning that most of the candidates were overly liberal activists who were likely to push causes favored by special interest groups. "The campaign has drawn little interest from the city's top elected leaders, political establishment and business community, largely leaving the contests to a potpourri of liberal community activists, a few elected or appointed officials and a sprinkling of political unknowns," the *Post* complained.[85]

Although the *Post* had done nothing to stimulate wider interest in the election (it had not, for example, reported the early election calendar or the availability of nominating petition forms at the Board of Elections), its analysis was not inaccurate. Had Mayor Barry run for delegate, for example, or even arranged for a close political associate to do so, he would instantly have legitimated the convention. His failure to do so was a signal that he was warily keeping his distance from what many regarded as a quixotic venture. Similarly, the relatively small percentage of major officeholders who sought to participate in the convention, and the total absence from the race of members of the business community, contributed to a general sense that the convention was not a serious political event. Thus, a cycle developed in which the absence from the race of the community's established leadership made the venture seem flaky, while the seeming flakiness of the enterprise helped to deter the establishment from participating.

Shortly before election day, Guinan and Huff held a press conference to publicize "the news media blackout of voter information" about the candidates and the election. The result, however, was only a sarcastic feature on one television station focusing on the fact that almost no reporters attended the conference. The final blow to public awareness of the election was the *Washington Post*'s decision not to pick up from the fallen *Star* the burden of reprinting the League of Women Voters' Annual Voters Guide. Of course, publicity at this stage could have given voters some familiarity with the candidates, but because the filing date for nominating petitions had passed in August, only news coverage during the spring and summer would have contributed to stimulating candidacies by those who were not already involved in statehood or local politics and therefore aware of the elections for delegate at an early date.

It was, for all these reasons, a very quiet election. Simultaneous School Board elections were far more visible because the candidates and their offices were far more familiar and they spent far more money. In the absence of coverage by the *Post* and the electronic media, campaigning by would-be delegates was limited, in most instances, to posting leaflets on trees and lamp posts, neighborhood house parties, and word-of-mouth recommendations. The candidates had to put virtually all of their efforts into enabling the voters to pick their names from a list. Platforms consisted of lists of what the candidates had done for the ward and the local committees on which they had served. When issues existed at all, they were phrased generally and debated little. Who could argue with a pledge to develop an effective structure for government or a strong bill of rights?

The campaigning for the office of delegate to the constitutional convention did little to alert the public to the task ahead, or to the various paths that might be followed. There were no slates, no clashes of opposing philosophies—not even on the issue of statehood itself, because except in Ward Three, only people who supported statehood bothered to run for delegate.

As might be expected under these circumstances, voter participation in the election for delegates was extraordinarily low. To begin with, only forty-three percent of the population of the District was eligible and registered to vote.[86] Only thirty-one percent of the registered voters (thirteen percent of the population) went to the polls. And of those who went to the polls, fewer than half—only six percent of the District's population—cast votes for delegates to the convention. In the ward with the lowest percentage of registered voters, only three percent of the population participated in choosing the ward's constitutional framers. Table II (*overleaf*) records voter participation by ward.

But election laws being what they are, a sleepy election produces officeholders just as surely as an exciting one. On November 4, 1981, forty-five delegates were elected, many of them as unknown to each other as they continue to be to the public. All of them were eager to work, but few if any had a program, a vision of a constitution, or an idea of how prior constitutional conventions had proceeded. Other state constitutional conventions, called by the acts of state or territorial legislatures, had been preceded by months or years of staff work, so that the delegates could be briefed on arrival and could make policy decisions from among designated alternatives. In this case, because the convention had been called by the people themselves through the initiative, and because the legislature had been lukewarm at best to the idea of statehood, no staff work had been done and the newly elected delegates faced the prospect of developing their constitution, quite literally, from scratch. On the morning after election day, the easy part was over, and the business of developing roles and structures, and ultimately of writing the law of the land, lay imminently ahead.

TABLE II: Voter Participation by Ward in the 1981 Election of Convention Delegates

	Ward 1	Ward 2	Ward 3	Ward 4	Ward 5	Ward 6	Ward 7	Ward 8	At-large
TOTAL POPULATION	78,700	81,400	77,800	81,900	82,600	75,700	82,400	77,000	638,400
REGISTERED VOTERS									
raw numbers	32,900	32,484	47,529	39,990	35,733	30,042	33,398	21,617	273,183
percentage of total population	41%	40%	61%	49%	43%	40%	41%	28%	43%
ACTUAL VOTES CAST									
raw numbers	7,995	7,805	17,497	15,472	11,919	8,784	10,842	5,548	85,862
percentage of registered voters	25%	24%	37%	39%	33%	29%	32%	26%	31%
percentage of total population	10%	10%	22%	19%	14%	12%	13%	7%	13%
VOTES FOR DELEGATES									
total votes cast*	19,814	19,759	35,912	33,477	22,770	18,937	24,367	12,411	187,061
divided by 5	3,962	3,952	7,182	6,695	4,554	3,787	4,873	2,482	37,412
percentage of actual votes cast	50%	51%	41%	43%	38%	43%	45%	45%	44%
percentage of registered voters	12%	12%	15%	17%	13%	13%	15%	11%	14%
percentage of total population	5%	5%	9%	8%	6%	5%	6%	3%	6%

*Since 5 ward delegates and 5 at-large delegates were to represent each voter, each voter had the right to vote for up to 10 candidates, 5 in his or her own ward and 5 in the at-large category. For purposes of calculating voter participation, therefore, the total number of votes cast in each category is divided by 5. To the extent that voters cast fewer than 5 votes to which they were entitled, this chart may understate the percentage of individuals who participated in the delegate election. It is the author's personal observation, however, that most voters who voted at all cast their full allotment of votes.

Source: D.C. Board of Elections and Ethics, Official Records of November 4, 1981, General Election, p. 2.

1. Until 1984, § 602(a) of Pub. L. No. 93-198 authorized a legislative veto by Congress of all laws approved by the District's Council. In October 1984, after the U.S. Supreme Court's decision in Immigration and Nationalization Service v. Chadha, 103 S. Ct. 2764 (1983) threw doubt on the constitutionality of this arrangement, the law was amended to provide that the District's legislation could be vetoed by federal legislation, but that this veto would have to be presented, like other legislation, to the President for signature or counter-veto. The 1984 legislation made it somewhat harder for Congress to overturn local D.C. laws, but it retained the distinction between their status and the legislation enacted in the fifty states.

2. *Ibid.* Under the 1984 amendment, the District's criminal legislation is subject to federal veto for a longer time than are its other laws, but action by one house is no longer sufficient to effectuate a veto.

3. Pub. L. No. 93-198, § 601 (Congress can amend or repeal).

Because article I, section 8 of the United States Constitution gives Congress exclusive jurisdiction over the Capital district, all laws granting home rule powers can be repealed, as they have been in the past. Only a constitutional amendment or statehood could alter this constitutional arrangement.

4. Pub. L. No. 93-198, § 603(a) (expenditure of tax revenues); 28 U.S.C. § 541(a) (1976) (appointing prosecutor); Pub. L. No. 93-198, § 433(a) (appointing judges); Pub. L. No. 93-198, § 602(a)(6) (forbidding tall buildings).

5. Interview with Jason Newman, Director of Georgetown University's Harrison Institute for Public Law (June 9, 1982); *cf.* Kurtz & Isikoff, "D.C. Home Rule: Congress Still Rules the Roost," *Washington Post*, Oct. 25, 1981, at A16. Mr. Newman has long been involved with the organization of the government of the District. He helped to secure passage of the home rule legislation and organized a training institute for the initial members of the District's Advisory Neighborhood Commissions. He directed a program under which law students assisted members of the District's Council in legislative matters, and wrote a compendium of legal materials bearing on the powers and functions of the District's government under home rule. *See* The D.C. Project; Community Legal Assistance, The District of Columbia: Its History, Its Government, Its People.

6. Although District residents pay federal income tax, only people residing in states may vote for members of the House of Representatives and the Senate. U.S. Const. art. I, § 2 & amend. XVII.

7. S. Smith, *Captive Capital—Colonial Life in Modern Washington* (1974), p. 54.

8. W. Bryan, *A History of the Nation's Capital*, Vol. 1, (1914) pp. 41–43.

9. S. Smith, pp. 38-39; C. Green, *Washington: Village and Capital, 1800-1878*, (1962), p. 8.

10. *New Letters of Abigail Adams* 1788-1801, (S. Mitchell ed. 1973), p. 257.

11. *The Federalist No. 43*, p. 280 (James Madison) (Modern Library ed. 1937); W. Bryan, *Volume 1*, pp. 387-91 (expectation).

12. C. Green, *Village and Capital*, p. 31 (Presidentially-appointed Mayor, elected Council), p. 89 (popular election of Mayor), pp. 335-36 (1871 territorial form of government).

13. W. Bryan, *A History of the Nation's Capital*, Volume 2 (1916), p. 622 (Shepherd appointed); C. Green, *Washington: Capital City, 1879-1950* (1962), pp. 45-46 (inadequate physical plant); W. Bryan, *Volume 2*, pp. 501-502 (massive construction program); S. Smith, pp. 44-45, C. Green, *Capital City*, pp. 345-51 (sums expended).

14. W. Bryan, *Volume 2*, p. 633 (Shepherd fled); S. Smith, p. 46, C. Green, *Capital City*, p. 360 (abolition of territorial form of government); W. Bryan, *Volume 2*, p. 626 (power vested in three-member Board).

15. Interview with Jason Newman.

16. C. Green, *Capital City*, p. 394, S. Smith, p. 46 (50%); S. Smith, p. 46 (one-third, not since exceeded).

17. C. Green, *Capital City*, p. 21; S. Smith, p. 50.
This growth in population occurred despite a physical contraction resulting from Congress' 1846 retrocession to Virginia of the third of the District that had been ceded by that state. *See* An Act to Retrocede the County of Alexandria in the District of Columbia, to the State of Virginia, 9 Stat. 35, ch. 35 (1846).

18. W. Bryan, *Volume 1*, p. 548 n.1 (1800); C. Green, *Village and Capital*, pp. 21, 89; S. Smith, pp. 21, 56.

19. C. Green, *Capital City*, pp. 109 (local government jobs for blacks disappear), 113, 215 (associations discourage black membership), 101-14 (civil rights laws violated; segregation), 266 (riot), 402 (hiring of blacks), 397 (slums), 458 (quoting Rep. Collins).

20. Kurtz & Isikoff, "Power of Congress Over D.C. Pales in Comparison to McMillan's," *Washington Post*, Oct. 25, 1981, p. A17 (domination by Southern whites); Interview with Jason Newman (June 9, 1982).

21. Kurtz & Isikoff, "D.C. Home Rule: Congress Still Rules Roost," *Washington Post*, Oct. 25, 1981, p. A16 (taxis and airport); Interview with Jason Newman (June 9, 1982) (police and tickets).

22. Wicker, "Peace Overtures Get No Response," *N.Y. Times*, Jan. 13, 1966, p. 15 (1966 Johnson attempt); Franklin, "Johnson to Seek a New D.C. Setup," *N.Y. Times*, Feb. 28, 1967 (authority to reorganize federal agencies); "Negro to be Named Washington Mayor," *N.Y. Times*, Sept. 7, 1967, p. 1 (abolishing Commissioners, appointing Washington as Mayor); S. Smith, p. 245 (delegate restored, Board of Education elected).

23. "Negro to be Named Washington Mayor," *N.Y. Times*, Sept. 7, 1967.

24. Interview with Jason Newman (June 9, 1982).

25. Kurtz & Isikoff, "Power of Congress Over D.C. Pales in Comparison to McMillan's," *Washington Post*, Oct. 25, 1981, p. A17; Editorial, "Democracy for D.C.," *N.Y. Times*, Dec. 22, 1973, p. 24 (power of Rep. McMillan); *See* Transcript, May 8, 1982, pp. 106-07 (Fauntroy campaign); Editorial, "Democracy for D.C.," *N.Y. Times*, Dec. 22, 1973, p. 24 (McMillan defeated).

26. *See* Pub. L. No. 93-198, § 602(a)(5) (taxation of commuters), § 604(a)(4) (selection of judges, prosecutors, and structure of judiciary), § 602(a), (b) (height of buildings), § 602(a)(1) (Congressional veto).

27. H. Res. 308, Oct. 1, 1981.

28. Pub. L. No. 93-198, § 603(a) (justifying line items); Kurtz & Isikoff, "D.C. Home Rule: Congress Still Rules Roost," *Washington Post*, Oct. 25, 1981, p. A16 (use of riders).

29. Pub. L. No. 93-198, § 104. "The Council shall have no authority to pass any Act contrary to the provisions of this Act. . . ." *Ibid.* § 602.

30. *See* Bakshi & Silverman, "A Growing Force—ANCs Get Attention, If Not Always Action," *Washington Post*, June 14, 1979, p. D.C.7.

31. U.S. Dep't of Commerce, Statistical Abstracts of the United States 10 (1981) (loss of 200,000 residents); U.S. Dep't of Commerce, Bureau of the Census, Provisional Estimates of Social, Economic, and Housing Characteristics 36-37 (1982) (poverty level); 1 U.S. Dep't of Health and Human Services, Office of Health and Research, Statistics, and Technology, Vital Statistics of the United States, Nationality 1-58 & tables 1-36 (1981) (illegitimacy rate); U.S. Dep't of Commerce, Statistical Abstracts of the United States 175 (1981) (crime rate); Sherwood, "Area Unemployment Hits Record High," *Washington Post*, Apr. 7, 1982, p. C8 (unemployment); U.S. Dep't of Commerce, Statistical Abstracts of the United States 129 (1981) (food stamps); Feinberg, "White Enrollment in City's Public Schools Takes Sharp Drop," *Washington Post*, Jan. 6, 1982, p. C7 (school system); Eisen, "Washington Places Fifth on 'Most Expensive' List."

Washington Post, Apr. 17, 1982, p. B7 (cost of living); Advisory Commission on Intergovernmental Relations, Significant Features of Fiscal Federalism 1980-81 Edition 98-199 (1981) (tax rate).

32. Kurtz & Isikoff, "Congress Still Rules the Roost in District," *Washington Post*, Oct. 25, 1981, p. A1, (comments of Mayor Marion Barry); Rogers, "No, It's Getting Better," *Washington Post*, Oct. 25, 1981, p. C8 (comments of City Administrator Elijah Rogers).

33. Interview with Jason Newman (June 9, 1982).

34. S. Smith, pp. 257-88. Smith's portrait of Hobson goes into greater detail than can be summarized here, and is an elegant portrayal which captures the feeling of love that those who survived him still carry.

35. Interview with Charles Mason, Counsel to Statehood Party Council Member Hilda Mason (June 11, 1982).

36. S. Smith, pp. 260-62.

37. Pub. L. No. 93-198, § 401(a)(2).

38. Hobson's political career is detailed in S. Smith, pp. 257-88.

39. Coleman, "Statehood Party Loses Political Clout," *Washington Post*, Mar. 1, 1979, p. D.C.3.

40. The biographical information on the Masons which follows is based largely on personal contact with both of them during the constitutional convention and on an interview with Charles Mason on June 11, 1982.

41. Coleman, "Statehood Party Loses Political Clout," *Washington Post*, Mar. 1, 1979, p. D.C.3.

42. The profile of Guinan is based on an interview with Barbara Maguire on June 3, 1982, and confirmed with Guinan in an interview on July 5, 1983.

43. The profile of Maguire is based on an interview with Barbara Maguire on June 3, 1982.

44. D.C. Code Ann. § 1-282 (1981).

45. Initiative No. 3.

46. U.S. Const. art. IV, § 1.

47. Tennessee provided the earliest example of this approach to statehood. In 1795 the territorial legislature provided for a census and a referendum to determine whether the territory met either of the prerequisites to statehood set out in the Northwest Ordinance: a free population of 60,000 or a showing that admission was "consistent with the general interest" of the territory. The results were favorable on both counts, and immediate plans were made for a constitutional convention. The constitution was drafted in three weeks and the convention further authorized the governor to conduct an election for state officers-to-be. Senators and state legislators were chosen a full two months before Tennessee officially became the sixteenth state. This history is contained in R. Corlew, *Tennessee: A Short History* (1981), pp. 95-104.

Alaska is the most recent state to utilize the "Tennessee plan" of drafting a constitution and electing a delegation to go to Washington to plead for admission. The three delegates elected in 1956 were refused seating in Congress, but as lobbyists they eventually achieved success when Alaska became a state in 1959. W. Hunt, *Alaska, A Bicentennial History* (1976), pp. 129-30.

48. W. Hunt, pp. 124-31.

49. Initiative No. 3, § 2 (requirement to reassemble), § 3.2 (Statehood Commission), § 3.3 (Statehood Compact Commission), § 1 (exclusion of federal area), § 5 (funds).

50. Interviews with Deborah Hanrahan and Richard Bruning (June 5, 1982).

51. D.C. Code Ann. § 1-82(a) (1973 & 1979 Supp.) required signatures of at least five percent of the registered voters. In addition, the five percent requirement had to be met in each of at least five wards. The city had 250,510 registered voters at the time, according to District of Columbia Board of Elections and Ethics records of registered voters.

52. Interview with Barbara Maguire.

53. Eisen, "Petitions Filed for D.C. Statehood," *Washington Post*, Feb. 12, 1980, p. C5.

54. Transcript of Meeting of the District of Columbia Board of Elections and Ethics, April 30, 1980, annexed as Attachment A to Plaintiff's Reply Brief in Support of its Motion for Judgment on the Pleadings in Guinan v. Board of Elections and Ethics, Civ. Act. No. C-6350-80 (filed June 27, 1980, D.C. Sup. Ct.).

55. *Ibid.*

56. Guinan v. District of Columbia Board of Elections and Ethics, Civ. Act. No. C-6350-80 (D.C. Sup. Ct., June 30, 1980).

57. Editorial, "D.C. Statehood and Gambling," *Washington Star*, Aug. 10, 1980, p. F2.

58. *See* H.R.J. 544, 96th Cong., 1st Sess., 124 Cong. Rec. 5274 (1974).

59. U.S. Const. art. V.

60. 124 Cong. Rec. S27,260 (Aug. 22, 1978).

61. Eisen, "Petitions Filed for D.C. Statehood," *Washington Post*, Feb. 12, 1980, p. C5.

62. Letter to constituents from Walter E. Fauntroy, Sept. 1980.

63. Isikoff, "Statehood Initiative: Bold Experiment or Endless Nightmare?," *Washington Star*, Oct. 26, 1980, p. B1.

64. Election Day Leaflet of the Statehood Initiative Committee, Nov. 4, 1980.

65. Isikoff, "Statehood Initiative: Bold Experiment or Endless Nightmare?," *Washington Star*, Oct. 26, 1980, p. B1.

66. S. Smith, p. 13.

67. District of Columbia Board of Elections and Ethics records as of July 26, 1979, showed 21,185 Republican registered voters in the District, 10,336 of whom resided in Ward Three.

Although Democrats constituted about 71 percent of the registered voters in Ward Three as of July 26, 1979, the Democratic candidate for Mayor in 1982 received only 51 percent of the votes in the ward. D.C. Board of Elections and Ethics, Official Results of Nov. 2, 1982, General Election, Ward 3.

68. *See* D.C. Board of Elections and Ethics, Official Records of Nov. 3, 1981, General Election, at 001.000 (highest percentage of residents voting in Ward Three).

69. Interview with Barbara Maguire.

70. Robinson, "Fauntroy Says Voters Will Approve Statehood," *Washington Post*, Oct. 22, 1980, p. B1.

71. D.C. Board of Elections and Ethics, Official Results of Nov. 4, 1980, General Election, at 001.000 (130,231 votes for Carter; 23,313 for Reagan; 16,131 for Anderson), 003.000 (Table).

72. Interview with Barbara Maguire.

73. The restructuring was detailed in a press release by the 51st State Committee on Jan. 30, 1981.

74. Richburg, "Timing of Review Period for D.C. Bills Questioned," *Washington Post*, Feb. 13, 1981, p. A41.

75. H.R. Con. Res. 75, 97th Cong., 1st Sess. (1981).

76. Nouvreau, "Statehood Squeaks By," *Washington Tribune*, Mar. 13-26, 1981, p. 1.

77. Richburg, "Wording Flaw May Force New Statehood Vote," *Washington Post*, Apr. 15, 1981, p. C2.

The initiative stated that the Board of Elections was "directed to conduct at the next scheduled general, special or primary election held after the effective date of this initiative an election presenting to the registered qualified electors of the District of Columbia for their approval or disapproval the proposition of calling a statehood constitutional convention, as well as ballot, pursuant to which such electors may elect, contingent upon the ratification of such proposition by a majority of the electors voting thereon, delegates. . . ." Initiative No. 3, § 3.

78. Richburg, "Wording Flaw May Force New Statehood Vote," *Washington Post*, Apr. 15, 1981, p. C2.

79. Board of Education member Carol Schwartz had announced that she would not run for re-election.

80. D.C. Council Act 4-62, § 2(c)(1)(A), July 20, 1981 (D.C. Register July 31, 1981, pp. 3376-82) (no further vote), § 2(c)(1)(B) (90-day limit); District of Columbia Statehood Constitutional Convention Amendment Act of 1981, District of Columbia Statehood Constitutional Convention Emergency Act of 1981 (D.C. Register August 14, 1981, pp. 3576-84) (single redraft).

81. D.C. Statehood Constitutional Convention Initiative of 1979, §§ 5(g), 6(c), 7(c). Isikoff, "Request for $700,000 for D.C. Statehood Plans is Challenged," *Washington Star*, June 4, 1981, p. D1 (proposals); D.C. Council Act 4-250 (D.C. Register, Sept. 18, 1981, p. 4062) (approval).

82. D.C. Board of Elections and Ethics, Notice of Emergency Rulemaking, Chapter 23—Candidacies: Delegates to the Statehood Constitutional Convention (D.C. Register June 26, 1981, p. 2929, § 2300.1).

83. D.C. Board of Elections and Ethics, Official Records of General Election of Nov. 3, 1981, p. 3.

84. Cassell ran at large; the other three candidates ran for ward seats.

85. Sherwood, "D.C. Statehood: Liberals Could Scuttle Statehood Chances," *Washington Post*, Oct. 20, 1981, p. B1.

86. *Compare* Table II *with* U.S. Dep't of Commerce, Statistical Abstracts of the United States 175 (1980).

CHAPTER 2

The Campaign for Election

Spring, 1980. Hanging around the lobby of a restaurant in Washington's small Chinatown, waiting to get a table. Lacking other diversion to pass the time, I look over the bulletin board. Among the notices left by seekers of roommates and sellers of cars, there is a small printed card: "Statehood for D.C." And a telephone number for volunteers to call.

I show the notice to my wife and children. "What a terrific idea," I tell them. "A shortcut to getting some votes in Congress. All it would take is a majority in each House. The state legislatures wouldn't get a chance to say no."

We talk a little about the idea. I tell my boys what little I know about D.C. history. A table is ready for us. We eat. It never occurs to me to call the number. It has nothing to do with me.

* * *

Fall, 1980. An article in the paper says there are to be two initiatives on the ballot: Statehood and gambling. Statehood is obviously a good thing. Gambling isn't difficult either; if people want to bet, why should the government stop them? I vote yes on both initiatives. The next day, I see that my fellow Washingtonians have agreed with me.[1]

* * *

Spring, 1981. Ronald Reagan is President of the United States, and is tearing apart social programs that have been laboriously constructed over many years. In reaction, liberals are stirring after years of inactivity. Friends who work in organizations such as the American Civil Liberties Union and the Natural Resources Defense Council tell me that money and memberships are coming in so fast they can't open all the mail. I want to write my Senator about a dozen outrages that the administration is committing. But I don't have a Senator.

I remember my vote for statehood five months ago. I haven't heard or read any thing about it since. That's strange; surely something is going on in the aftermath of the passage of the initiative.

Curious, I call information and ask whether there is a telephone listing beginning with the word "statehood." The operator gives me the number of a "Statehood Initiative Committee." A voice at the other end of the phone tells me that the Committee is the organization that ran the initiative campaign, that the name is being changed to "51st State Committee," and that a conference to reach out to new members is scheduled for a Saturday in April. I am invited to attend.

I think hard about whether or not to go, because I know that I am a pushover for causes that are clearly desirable but incredibly difficult to achieve. D.C. statehood seems to qualify on both counts. This could become a major commitment.

The crowd at Hine Junior High School in southeast Washington is smaller than I had expected. The auditorium is only one-third full; there are perhaps fifty people present when the program begins, an hour late.

I sit anonymously in the back of the auditorium and try to figure out what is going on. Half of the speakers are black and half are white; the audience is equally mixed. I am encouraged; the project will have to be integrated to have any political credibility, and it's also a big argument in favor of getting involved personally. Washington is surprisingly segregated for a cosmopolitan city that is seventy percent black; except in a few neighborhoods, housing patterns divide on racial lines, and the organizations of the Washington "establishment" tend to be far more white than the city as a whole.[2]

I look to the people on the rostrum for clues about the leadership of this committee. The chair of the conference is Wesley Long, a white. He seems to know what he is doing, judging by the fact that the conference has the usual trappings—a registration table, printed handouts, a schedule, and the like. Hilda Mason, a black member of the District's Council, is the President of the organization. This is even more encouraging; the effort obviously has the support of major political figures. Then there's a white-haired man whom everyone seems to recognize as the real founder of the effort, Ed Guinan. Most of the speakers are, however, not organizers of the 51st State Committee, but outside experts.

Impressively, the speakers make the basic points about what has to be done. The initiative calls for a constitutional convention to be held next spring, with elections for delegate this fall. The convention process, they agree, is full of traps. Some of the speakers have lived through and studied constitutional conventions in other states and territories. One of them, Arnold Leibowitz, a lawyer on the staff of a House subcommittee, seems to be Mr. Constitutional Convention himself; he was counsel to the conventions in both Guam and the Virgin Islands. Leibowitz, particularly, spouts warnings. Both of his constitutions were rejected by the voters at the polls.

"The problems of ratification are very real," Leibowitz cautions. I scoff inwardly; we may have horrendous problems with Congress, but surely an electorate which just voted by a sixty to forty margin to start a statehood process is not likely to abort it because of details in the proposed state constitution. "Many states have tried to adopt new constitutions in the last twenty years, and ten of the last sixteen have been rejected by the voters," Leibowitz says.

Two academic experts offer a checklist of suggestions for the convention.[3] Preparation long before the convention starts is essential, they suggest. The Maryland Convention of 1968 was preceded by a preparatory commission which worked with a full-time staff for two years before the convention opened, and was able to present the convention with a draft constitution. In the District, however, there are as yet no plans for any kind of preparatory work.

Keep the constitution simple and uncontroversial, the experts advise. No one votes for good government, but many people vote against constitutions if they contain anything unpalatable. The key to ratification of a constitution is keeping it sufficiently basic so that coalitions of minorities who oppose particular clauses can not, in the aggregate, form a majority. A number of particular recommendations flow from this premise. First, keep controversial topics, such as abortion and capital punishment, out of the bill of rights; leave them to the political process so that whichever side loses does not oppose the final product on that ground alone. Second, get the city's political leaders involved in the process as soon as possible; for example, encourage the Mayor and most of the Council to run for delegate and help shape the product, so that they have a personal stake in the outcome of the process.

Leibowitz adds a structural suggestion, which strikes me as intuitively correct. Do not create a convention committee on a subject unless you are certain that you want an article on that subject, because you create vested interests that will insist on inclusion of that article.

There is a lunch break, and I introduce myself as a newcomer to someone who seems to belong there. She is Jan Eichhorn, a 51st Stater from the Capitol Hill area. She walks me over to Lou Aronica, the 51st State Committee's chair for my ward, Ward Three, and we exchange a few words. I am impressed that there is a ward-by-ward structure.

In the afternoon, I attend two workshops. The first is largely a repeat of the morning's topics, but the second concerns the nuts and bolts of running for delegate. The possibility of running for this office and helping to write a constitution for a new state has begun to appeal to me.

The procedure for becoming a delegate appears incredibly easy. Only fifty signatures are needed on a nominating petition to run in one's ward, one hundred signatures to be sure of beating back any challenge. I could get that many myself. Then it's just a matter of finishing among the top five of whoever runs in the ward.

*   *   *

I sign up as a member of the 51st State Committee. More than just sign up—one of the handouts says that there are "outreach" and "legal" subcommittees, and I seek out Guinan and volunteer for the legal group.

The phone rings within a few days. A crisis has arisen. The legal subcommittee is to meet.

We convene a few nights later in a Dupont Circle townhouse, the law office of the subcommittee's chair, Dan Schember. To my surprise, I discover that I am a third of the legal subcommittee. The problem, Schember explains, is that the Board of Elections is claiming that the initiative's wording requires the electorate to vote once again on whether to hold a statehood convention. Its argument is a strong one. The initiative says that the Board of Elections is

> directed to conduct at the next scheduled general, special or primary election held after the effective date of this initiative an election presenting to the registered qualified electors of the District of Columbia for their approval or disapproval the proposition of calling a

statehood constitutional convention, as well as a ballot, pursuant to which such electors may elect, contingent upon the ratification of such proposition by a majority of the electors voting thereon, delegates . . . .[4]

There is no question but that the "effective date of this initiative" refers to some date in the spring of 1981, months after the voters approved it, because the initiative could not have become effective until it lay before Congress for thirty working days. It would seem, then, that all the voters did last November was put on the ballot for the following year the question of whether to start the statehood process.

How could this have happened? Schember and I turn for an answer to the third member of our subcommittee, who knows more about the circumstances in which the initiative petitions were filed.

This third member is an older gentleman, in his seventies. Like ourselves, he is white. He speaks slowly, methodically, with a strong New England accent. He is quite tall. Blue eyes sparkle behind out-of-fashion glasses with rims of pink plastic. He wears a frayed blue dress shirt. The most striking thing about him is the much-stretched pocket of that shirt. In it, along with a dozen pens and pencils, are crammed dozens of leaflets— the route maps and timetables for every bus line in the District of Columbia, all of them essential to the mobility of this man, who has never wanted or possessed a driver's license. He is Charlie Mason, Hilda's husband.

Mason explains that years earlier, his wife had introduced in the Council a bill originally sponsored by Julius Hobson before his death, calling for a public referendum on whether to have a statehood convention. Under the Mason bill, the vote would have taken place at the next election after the bill became effective. On the day that Ed Guinan had filed the proposed initiative language, before the signature campaign started, the Board of Elections' counsel had been in the hospital. The next most senior person in his small office, who had just graduated from law school, was in charge. She read the proposed initiative and saw at once that it was not well drafted; after all, Guinan had done it himself, without any legal advice. So doing her best to comply with the procedures specified by District law,[5] she determined to rewrite Guinan's words in a more proper format.

She consulted her boyfriend, who was a clerk in the office of a Council member. The boyfriend recalled the old Mason bill and obtained a copy. The young lawyer assumed that the Mason bill must have contained correct wording to generate a public vote on calling a statehood convention, and by patching its language into the Guinan draft, she inadvertently added the requirement of a second vote. She did not realize that requiring a subsequent vote on calling a convention was appropriate for a Council bill, because the people had not yet had their chance to vote, but not for an initiative. Untutored, opposed even in principle to having to rely on lawyers for advice, Guinan had not known about or taken advantage of the clause in the law allowing him ten days in which to sue the Board of Elections to challenge its redrafting of his initiative,[6] and he collected signatures to put the reworded proposal on the ballot.

Now the Board regards itself as bound by the literal words of the initiative, requiring a second vote. The 51st State Committee fears that it might lose in a new vote; in any event, its treasury is drained and it lacks the resources to mount a new campaign. There are only two choices: Sue the Board, or ask the Council to amend the law.

We share our opinions; we do not think that a lawsuit could be won. The Board had erred in changing the language, but the law provided a specific remedy for correcting an error of this sort—a suit within ten days—and the 51st State Committee had not used it.

So it appears that we must ask the Council to bail us out, but the risks are substantial. In the light of the ambivalent attitude of most of its members the Council might refuse, viewing a second election as a means of putting off the whole statehood problem. On the other hand, the Council might approve, but Congress might veto the amendment in order to confound the statehood process. Perhaps most likely, the Council might approve, but take the occasion—since the initiative was before them anyway—to make other, less desirable changes in the law. Still, it appears that there is no choice.

A few days later, Schember and I appear before the Council to testify on behalf of the 51st State Committee. I am delighted to be of help to my new organization so soon. I read my prepared statement, in which I show that all of the *Washington Post*'s stories on the initiative said that an affirmative vote would lead to a convention a year later, not to another vote on whether to have one. The Council, I say, should give effect to the obvious intent of the voters.[7]

The questioning from Council members is much tougher than I expected.[8] Polly Shackleton, from my own ward, says that my indictment of the *Post*'s inaccurate reporting does not justify the Council in changing the words that the voters approved. She asks whether I also combed the pages of the *Washington Star*, and I concede that I did not. Betty Ann Kane engages me in a long philosophical excursion on the conditions, if any, under which it is proper for a legislature to change what the voters have done in an initiative. This area is particularly tricky because as a secondary matter, the 51st State Committee would also like the Council to make other changes in the initiative—to remove, for example, the prohibition that Guinan had inserted against Council members running for delegate. The more effectively I argue that the problem of the second vote is a unique case, the more I will satisfy Kane, but I will undercut the justification for the other changes.

The League of Women Voters testifies against changing the law. Informed voters, they argue, knew the precise wording of the initiative, even though the League admits that the language didn't appear on the ballot itself. Informed voters should not have the results of their vote changed simply because uninformed voters made a mistake.

A week later, I sit in the Council chamber and watch the members debate and vote. As we feared, the Council has seized the opportunity to put the whole law up for grabs. Shackleton suggests that the whole convention be limited to a reasonable time period—a point not mentioned in the hearings. She suggests sixty days. Mason looks around at her fellow

Council members and sees that she does not have the votes to keep the convention unlimited in duration. She tells Shackleton that she thinks ninety days would be more reasonable. Shackleton is delighted to get a limit without having to go to a vote that she might lose. A ninety-day limit passes by consensus.[9]

Shackleton is ready with other strictures. She offers an amendment to strike the clause under which Senators and Representatives-elect will be chosen to lobby the Congress for statehood. She loses by a single vote. But she is successful in her effort to impose a limit of two on the number of times that the convention can offer proposed constitutions for ratification.

There is a provision in the initiative for delegates to be paid thirty dollars per day during the convention. Kane's effort to delete this clause is defeated.

The main question is called at last. The members rehash the arguments made at the hearing. There is a show of hands. The requirement for a second vote by the electorate is deleted. The convention will be held.

* * *

During the next month, I mull over the question of making the really big commitment of running for delegate. First, there is the question of whether I would be horning in on someone else's project. The answer to that is clearly no. A public election is supposed to be open to everyone, and besides, the whole point of the 51st State Committee's April conference was to bring new people into the Committee and its activities.

There is still the question of whether I wholeheartedly support statehood. Here, too, the answer is obvious. Helping to get two Senators for the District of Columbia would accomplish more than I could hope to achieve by any other means, for a whole variety of causes ranging from maintaining social programs to ratifying arms control treaties, particularly in the Reagan era. The District's Senators most likely would be black, Democratic, liberal, and pro-city. Their addition would make the Senate an often critical two percent more liberal than it would otherwise be. With the D.C. Voting Rights Amendment to the Constitution politically dead, statehood is the only way to seat those Senators.

The conference in April has suggested additional reasons to support statehood, beyond national politics or even representation of D.C.'s electorate or blacks generally in the federal legislature. Several of the speakers talked about self-determination, about all the ways in which Congress interferes in or limits the self-governance of the District. The right to self-government, to control the structure of one's own judicial system, for example, seems like a civil right of the most traditional sort.

Finally, there is the question of whether I'd be any good at being a delegate. Immodestly, I tell myself that I would. I'm a lawyer; I've drafted several statutes; I teach a course in legislation. I don't have well-informed ideas about what kinds of provisions should be in a state constitution, or in this one in particular, but I do have drafting skills to offer.

One potential reservation has been resolved by the Council's action. The initiative originally set no time limit on the convention. I could not have made an open-ended commitment. But the ninety-day limit means that the convention will begin in January and end in April. In my heart I am ready to run.

* * *

But can I win? The political situation is rather special. Ward Three was the only ward to vote down the statehood initiative. Most of the ward is hostile to statehood, and even my friends point to a conservative President and Republican Senate, suggesting that statehood is an idea whose time will never come. I point out to them that once a statehood application is made, it need never die; eventually a Congress will see statehood for the civil rights issue that it is and vote the District into the Union, irreversibly.

No one buys it. For those who believe that statehood is a good thing, it is a pipe dream. But this phenomenon makes me think my chances of winning the election are substantial, for it is plain that in Ward Three, at least, the election is not going to be taken very seriously. The other candidates will not be big names, because although many nationally and locally famous people, even former Senators and Cabinet members, live in the ward, they will not give this kind of contest the merest glance. I am utterly unknown within the ward, and I can not call on my skeptical friends for much assistance. But my opponents will be equally unknown, and their friends will think their efforts folly too. Indeed, in this anti-statehood ward, perhaps fewer than five candidates will declare, and if that happens I can win the election just by filing.

I make the assumption, which seems reasonable. that the campaign will be nearly invisible: The candidates will be unknown, none of us will spend much money, publicity will be negligible. I begin to consider the question of how a political nobody can beat other political nobodies, without media attention, in an uncaring electorate or one that is hostile to the whole idea of the election.

* * *

Before my decision to run becomes final, I consult an experienced observer of District politics, who agrees to talk with me only on the condition that I withhold his identity in any publication about our conversation. This man, who will therefore be known as my Source, knows more about the District of Columbia and its politics than anyone I know. Late one afternoon, we talk quietly in the seclusion of his office.

"Don't do it," my Source says. "It could be a disaster for you."

I am surprised. "What do you mean? I think I would have a chance of winning."

"That's the problem," he says. "It doesn't matter if you lose. The headache is winning."

"If you go to that convention," my Source tells me, "the resentment against you will be terrible. You're white, you're male, and you live in Ward Three. That's three strikes against you for openers. But worse than that, you're articulate, you have speaking and writing skills that many of the others don't have. They'll depend on you to some extent, and they'll hate you for it."

"And to top it off, you teach at Georgetown. You'll be identified with it. There'll probably be gays at the convention, who will hate the University because of the Catholic Church's line on homosexuality."

"You didn't mention that I'm Jewish," I jest. Half-jest.

"That, too," he says. "I didn't want to say it, but they'll be more circumspect about that. It won't be as clear."

I find it hard to believe him. The blacks and whites at the April conference, and at the one or two meetings I'd since attended, seemed to work well together. Surely he is overgeneralizing from some other experience.

I recognize that my unwillingness to take his warnings seriously is a measure of how far I am already committed to this adventure.

*   *   *

On warm weekend afternoons in July, I carry a clipboard of pink petition forms from house to house. I stay within my neighborhood because it's the easiest to reach, but I avoid my own street, unwilling to expose to my immediate neighbors my association with an effort that most of them probably oppose.

It is slow work, because two-thirds of the houses produce no response. In Ward Three, a lot of people go away for summer weekends. And many of the houses have no voters registered in the District. In some cases, they vote by absentee ballots in other states, where they can vote for Members of Congress.

"I'm Philip Schrag, from over on Ingomar Street," I tell a middle-aged man who is holding open his screen door. His children squirt water pistols at each other in a side yard.

The nearby street registers. He invites me into a darkened living room.

"I'm running for delegate to next year's constitutional convention, and I'm collecting signatures to get on the ballot. Would you help me to get on the ballot?"

His smile becomes a scowl. "This is that statehood business?" he asks. "I'm against statehood. Look at the way this city runs now. The streets are full of potholes. We constantly get tax bills for the wrong amount. And taxes keep going up. They can't run a city. How are they going to run a state? You know what I mean?"

I think I know what he means. When he says "they," he probably means "the blacks."

My objective at this juncture is not to educate one individual, not to argue with him or alienate him. My purpose is to get 100 signatures on my petition in as few afternoons as possible. My feet hurt from the hot pavement.

"Signing this petition doesn't mean you support statehood," I say. "In fact, this fall's election isn't a vote on statehood at all. There's going to be a convention. That's already been decided. The only question is who the delegates are going to be."

He shifts his weight from one foot to the other. "If Congress weren't there to stop them, they'd double our taxes and spend all the money on welfare. And graft."

"Ward Three needs its share of representation at the convention," I say. "I think that I have something to contribute."

"I guess I'd rather have you than someone else, someone I don't know," he tells me. "I'll sign your petition."

Ten minutes later, an elderly woman talks to me in a low voice through her screen door, not inviting me in. "I'll sign just because you're from around here," she tells me. "But I can't see being a state. Did you hear about the woman who was robbed on the way home three weeks ago? Right over there, behind that street." I turn to look, out of politeness. "A big buck, he was. Came out from behind a hedge and grabbed her pocketbook. The doctor had to come, she was so scared."

My petition campaign becomes a shocking experience. I did not expect support for statehood, and indeed I find so little that I wonder where the third of the people who voted for the initiative in the ward are hiding—certainly not in my part of the ward. There is some talk of D.C. being too small to be a state, some talk of the risk that Congress would use the occasion of statehood to withdraw the nineteen percent of the District's budget that it currently supplies, and some talk of the unlikelihood that the other states' Senators would agree to dilute their own vote by admitting the District.

But what stuns me is the relatively overt racism that lies behind much of the opposition. In a surprising number of cases, my neighbors reveal their fear of being a racial and political minority, and their satisfaction that Congress is protecting their interests. I can discern distinctions. Some believe that the black majority would not competently govern. Some think that the blacks would exploit an increase in their political power to tax the whites to the breaking point, requiring them to sell their homes and move away. Some simply fear the black majority, equating blacks with crime; these tell me all kinds of violent stories, including murders of years past. Several use the word "nigger" when they talk about crime. Wanting to get my signatures, to get it over with, I try not to reveal my revulsion.

* * *

My theory for winning an obscure contest is to let it remain obscure. Let the deadline for filing petitions pass without much public notice, so that well-known names are not encouraged to compete. Keep the race quiet, so that my opponents don't bother to build any organizations. Because my acquaintances are all scoffers, organization is not my strong suit. In the final week, I will take out a fairly large advertisement in each of the two ward-wide biweekly newspapers. There is probably a fairly good overlap between those in the ward who read the political advertisements in those newspapers and those who vote in minor elections. They may remember my name, and if my ad is good enough, some of them might actually vote for me. I keep reminding myself that all I need to do is come in fifth, and that everybody else is going to have the same problem.

The list of people who are circulating nominating petitions in Ward Three begins to grow. Lou Aronica, the 51st State Committee chair in the ward, is among them. He claims to be delighted that I am running, and he may actually be sincere, because five delegates can be elected and we could both be among them.

Aronica calls a couple of meetings, inviting all those in the ward who are members of the 51st State Committee, and all those, whether or not members, who are candidates. At these meetings, the paradox in which we find ourselves is evident. Aronica talks of all the work that needs to be done before the convention; for example, research on other state constitutions and catalogues of issues and options. But those of us with the greatest incentive to do this work, those who may have to work in an inadequately prepared convention if the work is not done, have to reserve our efforts for our campaigns. More significantly, it is becoming increasingly clear that no one of any prominence is going to run in Ward Three. It would certainly improve the prestige and credibility of the convention if Ward Three were to send some well-known national or at least community leaders, but it is not in the interest of the present candidates to encourage them. The meetings are desultory. Projects, including the stimulation of new candidacies, are suggested. There are occasional volunteers, but little comes of these efforts.

In September and October local community groups hold a series of "Candidates' Nights." These are dreary affairs in community centers and church basements, so sparsely attended by the citizenry that the candidates occasionally outnumber the voters. The contest for delegates to the convention plays second fiddle to the School Board election. In some cases, School Board candidates are permitted to speak to the assembled voters for ten minutes each, and statehood candidates for two. At other meetings, the statehood candidates are not permitted to speak at all, but are simply "introduced." After the first of this latter type, at which my name is mispronounced and we are permitted to stand so that the voters can choose among us on the basis of our physical appearance, I attend only when I can speak.

The first candidates' nights give me the opportunity to assess my competition, and for all of us to gossip about each other. Thirteen candidates have qualified to run for the five slots. Half a dozen of them, including Aronica, are people I recognize from 51st State Committee meetings. These include Bob Roehr, a young, bearded gay rights activist who won the Republican Party designation to run for Delegate in Congress against Walter Fauntroy in 1980, only to be disowned by the Republicans after the conservative faction took over the D.C. Republican Party; Bibiana Mays, a local Democratic Party activist; and Joel Garner, a Democrat and Justice Department social scientist who ran unsuccessfully in 1980 to become an at-large member of the Council.

I also meet the candidates whom I don't know. There is Frank Kameny, an older man, nearly bald, who had been fired by the federal government in 1957 for homosexuality and had become an early leader of the gay rights movement in Washington. Kameny seems easily excitable. Whatever he begins to say ends up as a kind of scream. But he is a no-nonsense liberal, and I hope he is one of the winners. There is Courts Oulahan, a conservative, silver-haired Republican, who refuses to say that he supports statehood, but claims that he wants to work for the best possible constitution. I do not see a role for statehood opponents in a statehood convention, and although I realize that he probably represents the ward more accurately than the rest of us, I hope he loses.

And then there is a loud, heavy-set blond woman, whom all the other candidates seem to know and dislike. She is Gloria Corn, and she cannot be stilled. She has an opinion on every subject and she lets everyone know what it is, at the top of her voice. When her turn comes, she does not stay within the time limit, but complains about it instead. Alone among the

Ward Three candidates, she scrutinized the nominating petitions filed by her opponents. She challenged three of them, and succeeded in knocking off the ballot on a technicality a member of the 51st State Committee, a woman who might have taken votes from Corn. She and Oulahan are the only candidates who do not say that they support statehood. I join the list of those who are suspicious of her.

The first of the candidates' nights has been organized by the Democratic Women's Political Caucus. They are going to endorse five of us at this meeting. I don't know what this endorsement is worth, but it seems better to have it than not to have it. I can tell from the written questionnaire that we have been asked to complete that the group is looking for liberal answers to its questions, and I expect to do well on its scale. When we speak, I follow the lead of the other candidates, stressing my background and experience and talking about the convention only in general terms. They receive me with a lot of applause, and I expect to receive one of the five endorsements.

There are about fifty people in the room, but only members of the caucus are permitted to vote on endorsements. There are only twelve members present. They vote on a complicated scale of one to ten, weighing the candidates' records, their responses to the questionnaire, and their oral presentations. When the votes are counted, Bibiana Mays, a member of the caucus, wins first place, with a perfect 120. I am down in the dust, unendorsed. Roehr, another loser, sits with me in the back of the room and explains. "The people who won, people like Aronica and Kameny, have known all twelve of those women for years, and have worked with them in countless causes. They're part of the network. Your qualifications have nothing to do with it. You never had a chance because you're a new boy on the block." For the first time, it occurs to me that I may lose this election.

*   *   *

As election day approaches, and candidates' nights proliferate, the candidates get to know each other better. With the exception of the two who refuse to support statehood, we become somewhat friendly, exchanging stories of the campaign trail. My advertisement goes to the printer and is set in type; there is no indication that any of the other candidates will be more visible. The running joke is the wager on how badly Gloria Corn will trail the pack; she seems to alienate audiences at every turn, and her campaign seems to consist primarily of distributing leaflets to which are stapled cellophane envelopes containing three kernels of candy corn.

An idea occurs to me. Since my advertisement has been set in type and I have a good page proof, why not reprint a few thousand copies and try to distribute them door to door? I have written a good ad, I think. Its text is crisp, and it portrays me as having spent my entire professional life in the service of reformist causes—civil rights, consumer protection, arms control. It says that I am a teacher and author, which should sell well in Ward Three. In order to get it distributed, I ask my son David, who is fourteen, whether he and his friends would be willing to spend an afternoon walking it around, in various parts of northwest Washington. "At what price?" he asks.

We agree on $2.50 an hour. Soon my little army of junior high school students is tramping the side streets, stuffing mail slots with Schrag for Delegate folders. Could any other candidate be doing the same thing? I watch in vain for signs of competition.

Until now, my wife has been a skeptic. But with election day a week away, the spirit in the household becomes infectious. "I could take a day off and hand out your leaflets at our local poll," Emily offers.

I almost tell her not to bother. There are twenty-one polling places in the ward; what difference would it make if someone is stationed outside one of them? I have never thought that the hordes of campaign workers who accost voters as they enter the polls can make much difference. Still, this is an election in which the candidates are all unknown. Some of the voters may not even know that the delegate election is on the ballot, and they may never find out, because the Board of Elections has decided to print the delegates' names on the reverse side of the School Board ballot. "Sure, that's a good idea," I tell her.

In the last days, her suggestion gnaws at me. If it is a good idea to cover one polling place on election day, why isn't it twice as good to cover two? My children could each tend one, at least after school. Some of my friends have said that they would be willing to help out in some minimal way; perhaps they could at least cover a poll for two or three hours during the heavy evening hours. And while few voters were reached in all of the candidates' nights put together, at each of them I was approached, after I spoke, by one or two local activists who had liked what I said and had offered to help. One of them was the would-be candidate whom Gloria Corn had thrown off the ballot.

I count the names of people who have volunteered, and discover, to my surprise, that I can staff sixteen of the twenty-one polling places, at least for the evening rush. Quickly, I call these supporters and assign them to schools and churches. It may not help, but it certainly won't hurt.

It is election day. The polls close at eight. At five, before going to my own polling station, I drive to the corners where my children are aggressively pushing my literature on the voters. It is grueling work, particularly since they are competing with adult representatives of other candidates, both for delegate and for School Board. Zachary, my eleven-year-old, is up against Gloria Corn herself.

"You've won, Dad," they tell me. "Everyone who reads your leaflet says he'll vote for you." I watch the other candidates' hawkers and am not so sure. It becomes clear that Kameny, at least, is well organized; he has one of his supporters at every poll.

I stand in the cold, damp darkness outside of the Cleveland Park Branch of the public library. I begin to distinguish the various types of voters. Some saunter up slowly, take literature from each of the nine or ten hawkers, and enter into a brief conversation or two before voting. Some take the literature to be polite, but have made up their minds and will drop it in a trash can as soon as they go inside. There are also those of a different breed, recognizable at 100 yards, even in the darkness, who put their heads down and charge through the throng of leaflet distributors, not seeing the people who are trying so hard to communicate with them, treating the political literature as though it were contaminated. Most of my fellow leafleters, including Mays and Roehr who share this polling place with me, don't even try to press their messages on these unwilling voters. I try with everyone. I am committed to spending this time, and I have nothing to lose. Or so I think—pursuing one of the reluctant voters, I step into a gutter and twist an ankle.

The last voter passes by. I get into my car and collect my family from dark street corners. Someone named Barbara Maguire from the 51st State Committee—I think she is a candidate in one of the other wards—has organized a party at a Capitol Hill bar. We drive downtown. It is a moment I have dreaded, for I know that the results may already be known. At noon on election days, the Board of Elections collects the ballots that have been cast during the morning, and it counts them during the afternoon. The results are released as the polls close. The final results rarely vary from this early count.

My family, however, is confident. We walk into the crowded bar. The first person I see is Wesley Long, from the 51st State Committee. He hands me a sheet of paper. It is the early count. I quickly find the Ward Three results.

It's unbelievable! Gloria Corn is far ahead of everyone else, with 2281 votes. Oulahan, the only other candidate who didn't advocate statehood, is second, with 1551. Then come Garner, Roehr, and Kameny. I am seventh, one vote ahead of Bibiana Mays.

I have lost, in all probability. The gaps tend to widen as later counts are received. I learn from Roehr that at the last minute, the Republican Party sent a mailing to every Republican in the ward, urging them to vote for the three Republicans who were running—Corn, Oulahan, and Roehr. So it figures: The three Republicans won because of the mailing, Garner because he had run before and his name was known, and Kameny because his constituency worked like crazy for him. I should never have been so naive.

The party has already soured for me. If I stay I might get later returns. There is still the possibility that such returns will change the result. I tend to vote in the evening; perhaps people like me, people who would support my candidacy, are also evening voters. And except for Emily, none of my poll workers covered the pre-work morning rush. But I am grasping at straws; I should accept defeat better. Most people who run for office lose on the first try. Word arrives that there are snafus at the Board of Elections, and there will be no more returns until two in the morning. My kids need some sleep. We go home and go to bed.

*   *   *

Someone is banging on my door. "Dad, you won," David calls. "The final results are in the *Post*." I can't believe it. He must be teasing me. But there it is, in print. Corn is still way ahead. Garner and Oulahan are neck and neck for second and third. I am fourth. Roehr is fifth, a mere handful of votes ahead of Kameny, with easily enough absentee ballots still to be counted to make the difference between the two of them.

I have always wondered what it would be like to go to bed with an election up in the air, and to find out in the morning whether you won or lost. Now I know. But for me, these morning results have no greater credibility than those of the evening before. I take the *Post* to be only presumptive evidence, and I drive downtown to see the official posting at the Board of Elections.

The posting confirms the *Post*. Something happened during the evening of the election. From an elections clerk, I obtain a tally that is broken down by polling place.

The explanation becomes evident. With each voter casting five votes among thirteen candidates, eight percent of the total vote was sufficient for victory. At the five polling places where I had no campaign workers posted, I did miserably—four percent at two of them. But my overall vote where my volunteers were handing out literature during the evening was much larger—about nine-and-a-half percent at most of them. Where Emily worked the entire day, my vote was over sixteen percent.[10]

So the election day effort, hastily organized, almost an afterthought, had won the election. Why didn't I know that before I started? I am glad to have squeaked it out, but my naivete about the election process gives me pause. As I bask in the congratulations of friends and prepare to be a delegate, I wonder: What else don't I know about politics that in retrospect will seem so obvious?

Notes to Chapter 2

1. D.C. Board of Elections and Ethics, Official Records of General Election of Nov. 4, 1980, General Election, at 003.000.

2. S. Smith, p. 17.

3. John Wheeler, Professor of Political Science, Hollins College, and John Killian, Senior Legal Specialist, American Constitutional Law Division, Library of Congress.

4. Initiative No. 3, § 3.

5. D.C. Code Ann. § 1-1116(c)(3) (1981).

6. *Ibid.* § 1-1116(e) (1981).

7. Testimony of Philip G. Schrag before the Committee of the Whole, Council of the District of Columbia, June 11, 1981, citing *Washington Post* articles of Feb. 9, 1980; May 1, 1980; July 1, 1980; Oct. 6, 1980; and Oct. 24, 1980, and the *Post*'s "Ballot Questions" guide on Oct. 30, 1980, in which the newspaper advised its readers that "[a] vote 'For' . . . means that the voter wishes to see a constitutional convention draft a proposed constitution. . . . This is . . . a vote calling for a convention to draft a state constitution." *Washington Post*, Oct. 30, 1980, p. D.C.10.

8. Tapes of Council Meetings are kept by the Council. For the events which follow, see the tape made on June 11, 1981.

9. Initiative No. 3, as modified by the D.C. Council on June 11, 1981.

10. *Compare* D.C. Board of Elections and Ethics, Nov. 3, 1981, General Election Report for Precinct 32 *with* D.C. Board of Elections and Ethics, Nov. 3, 1981, General Election Report for Ward Three.

CHAPTER 3:

The Genesis of Structure

Ed Guinan's dream of helping to lead the District of Columbia Constitutional Convention toward the completion of its mission was shattered on election day. Guinan had chosen to run for delegate at large, rather than running in Ward Three, where he lived. He may have thought himself too radical for Ward Three, or he may have thought that whatever increased prestige would attach to having been elected by the whole city would help him to influence the course of the convention.

His miscalculation was serious. Five delegates were to be elected at large, and of the nine at-large candidates, two were present or former members of the School Board and three were present members of the Council. These names were at least somewhat familiar to voters. All five of them won, Hilda Mason receiving the highest count of all. Guinan finished last, and Lillian Huff, who had succeeded Guinan as Chairperson of the 51st State Committee, was also defeated.[1]

The three Council members who were elected were significant District of Columbia politicians, but it could be argued that they were not particularly representative of the Council. For one thing, they were the only members of the thirteen-member Council who had been willing to run. Hilda Mason and Jerry Moore were also unrepresentative in that they were the only two members of the Council who were not Democrats; like Mason, the Republican Moore held his at-large Council seat as a result of the election law that guaranteed two seats to minority party candidates. David Clarke, the third Council member elected to the convention, was a Democrat, but he was one of the Council's only two whites.

Barbara Lett Simmons was the other Democrat elected at-large to the convention. She was a School Board member and, during the convention, a candidate for election to the Council in the fall of 1982. The fifth at-large delegate was Charles Cassell, an architect and Statehood Party member who had once served on the School Board and had been slightly active in the 51st State Committee.

The forty delegates elected from wards exhibited great diversity but relatively little previous political experience. Only three of them had previously held elected public office other than as a member of an Advisory Neighborhood Commission (ANC). On the other hand, a substantial number of the ward delegates, about forty-two percent, were employees of the District of Columbia government. And a significant fraction of the delegates, about one-third, had current or prior service as an ANC member. Table III summarizes the occupational backgrounds of the forty-five delegates.[2]

TABLE III: Occupational Backgrounds of the 45 Convention Delegates

Status at Convention Time	*No. of Delegates*
Elected D.C. officials	4
Other D.C. employees *	17
Federal government employees	3
Educators not in D.C. public system	3
Students or retired or unemployed persons	10
Other persons (one each):	8
attorney, computer specialist, concert promoter, minister, political organizer, psychologist, taxi driver, waitress	

* Includes teachers in public schools and public university.

It should be noted that the percentage of delegates who were lawyers—less than ten percent—was smaller by far than at other modern state constitutional conventions.[3] Furthermore, of the four lawyers, Clarke and Charles Mason worked full-time in the public service, and Schrag was a full-time teacher. Thus, despite the significant role that lawyers play in the economy and public life of Washington, Oulahan was the only delegate who was a practicing attorney. The relative absence of lawyers, and the complete absence of business persons, may have made it much easier for the convention to propose sweeping legal changes in its constitution.

The racial and sexual composition of the convention paralleled that of the District of Columbia as well as American political bodies ever do. Whites and males were over-represented, but only by relatively small margins. Among the white delegates, however, males were significantly overrepresented. Nonetheless, this was the first state constitutional convention in the history of the United States in which a majority of the delegates was black. Table IV compares the delegates and the District's population by race and sex.[4]

TABLE IV: Convention Delegates Compared to D.C. Population by Race and Sex

	No. of Delegates	*Convention Percentage*	*Population Percentage* *
Black Total:	**28**	**62%**	**70%**
Female	13	29	38
Male	15	33	32
White Total:	*17*	*38%*	*27%*
Female	5	11	14
Male	12	29	13

*"Other" races account for 3% of the District of Columbia's population but only blacks and whites were elected as delegates to the Constitutional Convention.

A further breakdown of the delegates, however, by both race and ward, shows that the delegations from the various wards were not as racially integrated as was the Convention in the aggregate. This is not surprising in light of housing patterns in most parts of Washington. Table V shows this breakdown; four of the eight wards produced all-black or all-white delegations, and thirteen of the seventeen white delegates came from only three of the eight wards.

TABLE V: Racial Composition of Convention Delegations by Ward

Delegation	Black Percentage	White Percentage
Ward 1	40%	60%
Ward 2	0	100
Ward 3	0	100
Ward 4	80	20
Ward 5	80	20
Ward 6	80	20
Ward 7	100	0
Ward 8	100	0
At-large	80	20

Finally, it should be noted that the political party representation within the convention was probably unique among state constitutional conventions in America. Of forty-five delegates, only four were Republicans, and even those four had little in common, for they came from different parts of the GOP. Council Member Jerry Moore was the top Republican officeholder in the District and tended to stay above internal party battles. Courts Oulahan was loosely associated with the conservative wing of the party, which had recently seized control of the GOP's local machinery. Oulahan had tried in vain to persuade other Republicans that seats at the convention were worth contesting, so that the party would not be frozen out of its activities; in the end, he alone among the GOP leadership had run. Gloria Corn had supported John Anderson for President in 1980 and had been associated with the liberal Republicans who had lost control of the party machinery that year. And William Cooper, an unemployed black delegate from Ward Four, was a Republican only by registration; he had not been active in GOP affairs within either wing of the party.[5]

Five of the delegates were members of the Statehood Party.[6] Given the nature and purpose of the convention, it is not surprising that a substantial number of Statehood Party members ran for delegate, and given the ambivalence of the Democratic Party establishment, it is not surprising that several of them won. Thus, the Statehood Party activists had far more influence at the convention than the tiny registration of the party would suggest.

One delegate was a Communist. Maurice Jackson was elected from Ward One, a racially integrated area of the city known as Adams-Morgan which has long been a center for liberal and radical political activity.

Jackson was chair of the District of Columbia and Virginia chapter of the Communist Party, USA. He had run for office before, without success.[7]

The other thirty-five delegates were all Democrats. Several of them were active at the precinct level in the Democratic Party, and seven of them served on its State Committee.[8]

Table VI shows the party composition of the Convention, by ward. A complete list of the delegates, showing ward, party, race, sex, occupation, and prior elective office is set forth in Appendix A.

TABLE VI: Party Composition of the Convention Delegates by Ward

	Democrats	Republicans	Statehood	Communist
Ward 1	3	0	1	1
Ward 2	5	0	0	0
Ward 3	3	2	0	0
Ward 4	3	1	1	0
Ward 5	4	0	1	0
Ward 6	5	0	0	0
Ward 7	5	0	0	0
Ward 8	5	0	0	0
At-large	2	1	2	0

With campaigning behind them, the forty-five delegates-elect had a formidable problem. Under the law, the convention had to be opened by the Mayor within sixty days after certification of the election results.[9] The process of counting absentee ballots could postpone certification by as much as three weeks, but the Convention would begin on some date in January, and it would have to end ninety days thereafter.

The time constraint would have posed enough difficulties if the delegates had begun, on the day after the election, with leadership and committee structures for their internal governance, a set of rules of procedure under which the convention would operate, a headquarters, a staff, a budget, and a library of research material. The delegates had none of these when the clock began to run. It was obvious to each of them that valuable use could be made of the sixty-or-so days before the ultimate timer, the ninety-day calendar, came into play. But each delegate knew only a few of the others, and none had the legal authority or the personal prestige to impose structure unilaterally or even to convene the delegates-elect. The Mayor, of course, might have anticipated the problem and provided resources such as a headquarters for the delegates to use as soon as they were elected. But while everyone associated with the statehood effort had concentrated on individual candidacies, no one had prodded the Mayor or his bureaucracy to prepare for the forthcoming convention. Whatever his political attitude toward the event, the Mayor was not in a position to provide the impetus for a prompt beginning to the convention.

An entire month was lost before any movement took place; the only event in November was that absentee ballots gave Frank Kameny, a Democratic gay activist, the edge over Robert Roehr, a liberal Republican gay activist, as the fifth delegate from Ward Three. Then, on Saturday, December 5, an outside force pushed the convention into a hazy zone of pre-existence. Under the prodding of Jason Newman, Director of Georgetown University's Harrison Institute of Public Law, Georgetown University hosted a one-day seminar on state constitutional law for the delegates-elect.[10]

Newman wanted to be helpful to the convention, but he understood that there were risks to the University in sponsoring the convention's first convocation. The main agenda of the meeting would be educational, but it would be surprising if the event were devoid of politics, such as early bids for convention offices. It would be highly undesirable, Newman reasoned, if the University were perceived, however inaccurately, to be using its premises in order to manipulate the convention in any direction at all. Newman was aware that the kind of political structuring that the delegates most needed would present the greatest risks to the University's neutrality. Newman therefore decided to schedule an entire day of speakers, with no room on the program for the delegates-elect to get to know each other or exchange ideas. Of course, Newman recognized that a certain amount of informal discussion would take place, particularly during a stand-up lunch that was provided. But by allocating neither space nor time for political activities, Newman hoped to minimize the likelihood that his meeting would become the beginning of pre-convention maneuvering.

Thirty-five of the forty-five delegates-elect attended. Volunteer speakers were recruited from the University and the private bar. They covered a broad range of potential constitutional issues: The legislative, executive, and judicial branches; bills of rights; taxation and bonding authority; amendments; and the process of transition from District to state. In all cases, they listed what they saw as the principal issues with which the delegates would have to grapple, and some of the possible policy options that were available. Most of the speakers said that they would not reveal their personal preferences among these options, and a few held to their resolve. Delegates were permitted to ask questions, and Newman was impressed with the seriousness and sophistication of many of their inquiries.[11]

The Georgetown meeting highlighted how much the delegates had to do. Lillian Huff, who had inherited whatever was left of the 51st State Committee, became pivotal in resolving the problem of initiating a mechanism for getting underway. She persuaded Howard University and the University of the District of Columbia (UDC) to put together an entire series of Saturday seminars for delegates. Like the Georgetown seminar, they included formal presentations by academic and other experts, but unlike the Georgetown meeting, they also included time on their programs in which delegates could discuss issues of common concern. The topic scheduled for the very first seminar, a week after the Georgetown meeting, was the procedural requirements of the convention.

Even though delegates received only a few days' notice of this meeting, two-thirds of them attended. The only scheduled speaker was the ubiquitous Arnold Leibowitz, who drew upon his personal experience in Guam and the Virgin Islands to explain to the delegates what to expect.

He laid out a general model of how conventions begin. As Leibowitz described a hypothetical composite convention, the Mayor would preside for the first few minutes, during which the convention would elect its president and any other officers; the election of a temporary chair was unnecessary. Then, over the next few days, the president would appoint members to committees, taking into account their expressed preferences and established talents. The number and identities of these committees could be decided either by the convention's officers or by the convention itself. Rules would be necessary because, at the very least, some legitimate procedural mechanism would be needed to govern the introduction, referral, reporting, and adoption of constitutional text. Leibowitz advised, however, that the rules should make reconsideration very difficult, because reconsideration votes, attributable to shifting majorities of delegates present and voting, tend to tear conventions apart. Rules, Leibowitz suggested, could be developed either by the officers after their election, or by the committee chairs, sitting as an executive committee.

The convention's committees would also need rules, Leibowitz noted. Their members and other delegates would need to be assured of due notice of meetings, and some procedure would have to be devised for the development of articles of the constitution. The committee in question could work from a staff proposal, or it could build each article up from scratch. There would have to be some method for reconciling inconsistencies between the various committees' products, either by an executive committee of committee chairs, by joint meetings, or by the convention as a whole.

In Leibowitz' hypothetical convention, a first round of floor debate would occur at this point, including adoption of a tentative constitution. He strongly recommended public hearings on this tentative constitution, both to help ferret out flaws that the delegates had missed and to give the public the opportunity for input, which would help in the ratification process. The proposed constitution might be altered, based on this expression of public sentiment, before final adoption and submission for ratification.

After Leibowitz spoke, the sponsors of the seminar suggested that the delegates divide themselves into two workshop groups—one on committees, rules, and calendar, and the other on officers and staff. In stark contrast to the procedure at Georgetown, the delegates were explicitly encouraged by the sponsors to constitute themselves as planning committees. Each workshop was given an academic facilitator from one of the sponsoring schools, and each was invited to bring explicit recommendations to the full assembly later that day.

In both workshops, there were substantial disagreements about how to proceed. In the workshop on committees, for example, Wesley Long proposed that in view of the small number of delegates and limited duration of the convention, each delegate should serve on only one committee. He proposed that there be eight substantive committees and five officers who would not serve on substantive committees. This was immediately objected to by Gloria Corn, who said that five-member committees were too small to be representative. Frank Kameny argued that the convention should decide what articles it wanted (and therefore what committees to have) rather than starting with an abstract number of committees. Charles Mason suggested that each delegate serve on two committees, each with about ten people; Brian Moore said he needed to know when and how often committees would meet before he could know how many he would have time to serve on; and Talmadge Moore suggested that time would be saved if the convention met only in a committee of the whole. Faced with a six-sided dispute at the very outset, the workshop tried to discuss which substantive committees the convention should have, but consensus on this topic proved equally elusive, with some delegates saying, for example, that a committee on intergovernmental relations, which some previous conventions had created, was unnecessary, and other delegates claiming that such a committee would be essential.

Similarly, the workshops were unable to produce any real agreement on how rules should be developed, what officers should be chosen, how often the convention should meet, or any other structural subject. In addition, those in a minority on these and other issues noted that a third of the delegates were not present, and that the meeting had been billed as a seminar, not as a planning session. It was therefore decided by consensus to hold a further meeting of all delegates-elect on the evening of January 4, 1982, for the sole purpose of planning the convention.

The January 4 meeting proved to be a pivotal event in the life of the convention. At that time, after prolonged discussion, the delegates concluded that they could not successfully plan the convention as a plenary group of forty-five, and that some differentiation of roles was essential. They therefore decided to create five committees to serve for the month until the convention was officially opened. These five temporary committees were to consist of one member per ward, chosen by the ward's five delegates, with the at-large delegates treated as a ward delegation for the purpose of staffing the committees. The five areas of committee responsibility were rules and calendar, officers, committees, budget and physical space, and resources and public information.

These committees began their work on the day of the next Howard-UDC seminar, January 9 (at which time the Committee on Rules and Calendar was enlarged by the addition of four members elected at-large), and they achieved a great deal by January 30, when the convention opened. In general, the committees met in available space in the District Building (Washington's equivalent of city hall) during weekday evenings, and reported back to the assembly of delegates-elect during allotted time at the end of the Howard-UDC Saturday seminar meetings.

The Committee on Budget and Physical Space was the first to mobilize itself, its timetable forced by decisions in the Mayor's office. In the middle of December, the Mayor had created a small task force in his office to help plan convention arrangements. The staff had not undertaken any planning with respect to the Convention's legal preparations, such as proposed rules or agendas, but it had begun to make commitments for physical needs. In particular, it had selected a partially used public school as convention headquarters, and was offering the convention eight classrooms, storage space, and the use of an auditorium during non-school hours.[12]

But as soon as the delegates learned that this space would be available to them only from 9 a.m. to 8 p.m., objections were raised. Fortunately, the convention's Physical Space Committee had just been constituted, so the Mayor's office was not faced with a choice between dealing with the convention as a whole or refusing to include the convention in the planning. By January 11, the Committee had already toured the school and concluded that in addition to the limited hours it was open, the school lacked sufficient space. By January 23, it had successfully pressed the Mayor's office into locating alternative space. At that time the delegates voted to accept as their headquarters the top floor of the University of the District of Columbia's downtown classroom building, formerly the property of the Potomac Electric Power Company, and therefore known locally as the "old Pepco building." The building was in the process of being depopulated as the University moved to its new uptown campus. This setting, too, would not be ideal: it was unavailable on Sundays and lacked parking facilities, but the Physical Space Committee had at least avoided committing the convention to a building whose limitations would probably have prevented the convention from operating.[13]

Three of the other committees were about as active as the Physical Space Committee. The Committee on Officers debated the choice between a traditional list of officers—a president, vice-president, secretary, and treasurer—and a larger group, spreading directorial duties among a greater number of delegates and constituting the officer group as a whole as an executive committee of the convention. In the end, the Committee decided in favor of a larger group of officers. The convention was to be governed by a president, three vice-presidents, a secretary, an assistant secretary, a treasurer, and a historian. This decision was accepted first by the Committee on Rules (which embodied it in the rules under development) and later by the Convention.

The Committee on Resources and Public Information downplayed the public relations aspect of its work in favor of the more urgent task of identifying resources, particularly donated ones, that could be obtained from schools and local business concerns. Unfortunately, its level of success was minimal.

The Committee on Committees discussed at great length the number of committees on which each delegate should serve, and the types of committees that would be needed by the convention. It recommended to the convention that there be ten substantive committees. Although there was to be no formal distinction among them, it was generally understood that five of the committees would be major and five would be minor. Table VII outlines the proposed committees (*facing page*).

It may be seen from this list that the convention committees covered subjects that were not legally essential to a state constitution, and which could be dealt with through ordinary legislation. These included, for example, education, health, housing, human services, economic development, and even initiative, referendum, and recall, which were in fact the subjects of ordinary District legislation, not of the home rule charter. Similar subjects, however, had been treated by other recent constitutional conventions,[14] and they were of intense interest to many delegates. Recalling Arnold Leibowitz' warning that human nature would produce an article in the constitution for every subject over which a committee had jurisdiction, the members of the Committee on Committees explicitly told their fellow delegates that although each of these subjects should be investigated by a committee, they need not be included in the final constitutional text.[15]

TABLE VII: Substantive Committees of the Constitutional Convention

"MAJOR" COMMITTEES

Preamble and Bill of Rights	Judicial Branch
Legislative Branch	Finance and Taxation
Executive Branch	

"MINOR" COMMITTEES

Local Government, Intergovernmental Relations, and Transition	Economic Development
	Suffrage and Apportionment; Initiative, Referendum, and
Education	Recall; and Amendments
Health, Housing, and Human Services	

The Committee on Committees suggested that the ten substantive committees be staffed by wards, with each ward selecting one major and one minor committee assignment for each member of its delegation. This procedure would ensure that all committees would benefit from geographical diversity. In addition, two operating committees were recommended—one on rules and calendar and the other on style and drafting—and these would be open to all who volunteered, regardless of ward, with a limit of twenty members per committee.

Of the five preparatory committees, the one with the most arduous responsibility was the Committee on Rules and Calendar. All delegates recognized that the convention could not operate without rules of procedure, and that every day the convention spent on its rules after the ninety-day clock began to run was a day lost to substantive consideration of constitutional matters. The Committee on Rules and Calendar therefore accepted as its principal task the development of a comprehensive set of rules that could be presented to the convention when it opened and quickly approved with only minor changes, if any. Nor was this the only responsibility of the Committee, for the convention also expected it to resolve the questions of what days of the week and hours of the day would be devoted to convention meetings, and whether the convention should request the Council to amend the Shackleton amendment to the initiative in order to extend the ninety-day limit. Finally, Committee members knew that the press would be particularly attentive to the convention in its first hours and days, and it took upon itself responsibility for devising some kind of initial agenda so that the convention would not open in chaos.

The Committee held seven meetings, averaging five hours each, between January 9 and January 29. At an early meeting, it tackled the question of the ninety-day limit, and decided to recommend that no extension be sought, at least for the present.[16] Although there were several reasons for this, the principal rationale was that the lack of any definite deadline might cause delegates to work less efficiently. With respect to days and times for convention meetings, the Committee surveyed delegate availability and discovered that only on Saturday afternoons were all delegates available to meet, but that delegates would prefer meetings to be held during the evenings.

In planning the agenda for the opening meetings, the Committee determined that elections of officers could not take place before adoption of rules, because rules would be necessary to govern the election. The Committee anticipated, particularly after its proposed set of rules grew longer and more complex, that the convention's adoption of rules could become a prolonged process. It therefore recommended to the delegates-elect that Robert's Rules be used to govern the convention until the convention's own rules could be adopted, and that the convention elect a temporary chair to preside until permanent officers were elected. The Committee even had a candidate for this position: Lillian Huff, who had made it possible for the pre-convention committees to function by organizing the Howard-UDC seminars. On January 21, 1982, the Committee made these recommendations to the delegates-elect, who approved each of them.[17]

The main business of the Committee, however, was the drafting of proposed rules. It began by listing the areas with which rules would have to be concerned: Quorum requirements and seating, officers, committees, the flow of proposals from introduction to adoption, voting procedure, motions, the daily order of business, and rule amendment. Each of these subjects was assigned to a member of the Committee for purposes of study and presentation.[18]

At subsequent meetings, each subject was taken up in turn and appropriate text was developed and agreed to by the Committee. Two of the subjects overlapped with areas being studied by other pre-convention committees, and these were handled specially. With respect to officers, the Committee on Rules and Calendar accepted the substantive proposals developed by the Committee on Officers, and incorporated them into proposed text.[19] The Committee on Committees, however, requested that it be allowed to report directly to the convention, and the Committee on Rules and Calendar therefore left an article of the proposed rules open so that provisions relating to committees could be inserted.[20]

The rules proposed by the Committee on Rules and Calendar required twenty typewritten pages. But the key provisions can be summarized as follows:

Officers. The convention's officers would be elected by roll-call vote.

Executive Committee. The Executive Committee, consisting of all of the officers, would establish general policy, to be approved by the convention, regarding schedules and budget.

Drafting procedure. Any delegate would be entitled to introduce "proposals" (the constitutional equivalent of "bills" in a legislature) on any subject. The president would decide to what committee or committees proposals would be referred. Committees would study these proposals and then would draft their own proposals, in the form of complete articles. An article proposed by a committee, with its report and any minority views, would be circulated and then, after a brief period during which the committee chair would respond to questions, considered formally on the floor of the convention. On this "first reading" it could be amended by simple majority vote. The amended proposal would then be edited stylistically by the Committee on Style and Drafting. After being edited into virtually final form, the proposal would come again before the convention for "second reading," but at this stage it could be amended only by a two-thirds vote. A proposed amendment could not be considered at so late a date unless it had been introduced, in substance, for the substantive committee's consideration before that committee had originally reported its proposals. Finally, the Committee on Style and Drafting would edit all of the articles to ensure consistency, and report the entire proposed constitution for "third reading." At this last stage, an amendment would require a three-fourths vote. These rules were intended to make reconsideration very difficult, as Arnold Leibowitz had suggested, and to force delegates to formulate their ideas early enough for them to be considered thoroughly, rather than at final floor consideration of a measure. It was recognized, however, that these rules might make it virtually impossible to make necessary corrections, particularly of inconsistencies between different articles. An exception was therefore incorporated: If the Committee on Style and Drafting called to the attention of the convention an inconsistency in the text, an ordinary majority could correct the inconsistency at any stage, in any way it wished.

Voting procedure. All votes were to be decided by show of hands unless a delegate requested a roll call vote and was supported by at least four other delegates. Proxy voting would be prohibited.

Order of business. An agenda was set forth that would apply to each meeting of the convention. Business was to begin with the call to order, followed by prayer, approval of minutes, presidential announcements, approval of the calendar, unfinished business, and, finally, the main business, such as consideration of proposals reported by committees. As under Robert's Rules, however, the convention could always change its agenda. The rules provided that a "special order" could be taken up at a particular hour on a particular day, regardless of whatever else was pending. A two-thirds vote would be required to make a matter a special order.

Quorum. Twenty-three delegates would constitute a quorum for the transaction of business.

Amendments. Amendments to the rules would require the support of at least twenty-three delegates for approval. In addition, no amendment could be considered unless it had been recommended by the convention's Committee on Rules, or alternatively, the delegate proposing it had given that Committee four days notice, so that the Committee on Rules would at least have had the opportunity to comment.[21]

*   *   *

When the delegates arrived at their swearing-in ceremony on January 30, 1982, they found on their chairs both the complete packet of proposed rules that the Committee on Rules and Calendar had developed and a six-page single-spaced insert, prepared by the Committee on Committees, of proposed rules for the creation and operation of committees. Both of these committees had met their reporting deadlines, as had the Committee on Officers, whose recommendations had already been incorporated into the proposed rules. Working with the Mayor's task force, the Committee on Physical Space and Budget had made the necessary arrangements for use of the old Pepco building, and had prepared preliminary estimates of how to subdivide the $150,000 budget. The fifth committee, on resources, was continuing its surveys of delegates' needs and had prepared a list of institutions which might be solicited for financial or other support.[22]

Perhaps best of all, the delegates had received a partial reprieve from the ninety-day limit. On December 23, the District's Corporation Counsel had written to the Mayor's task force that the ninety-day limit of the Shackleton amendment was apparently intended to apply to "the function of writing a constitution as opposed to . . . the constitutional convention itself." Therefore, a brief period at the outset, during which the convention adopted its rules and budget and elected its officers would not count within this limit. However, "anything above 10 days for a general organizational period might raise questions as to whether the constitutional convention was attempting to circumvent the 90 day requirement for writing a constitution." The Mayor's task force, apparently seeking to assist the convention by squeezing out every possible extra day, responded to the Corporation Counsel by asking whether a suggestion by the Mayor for a two-week organizational period would violate the law. The Corporation Counsel replied (albeit without any further rationale) that "it is our view that a two week period for organization of the convention would not infringe upon the ninety day period."[23]

At the end of January 1982, then, the pieces were all in place for a smooth transition, lasting two weeks at the very most, from pre-convention planning to the writing of constitutional text. Few if any of the delegates could have predicted that controversy over the proposed rules would be so intense that the beginning of substantive work would have to be deferred until March.

Notes to Chapter 3

1. D.C. Board of Elections and Ethics, Nov. 3, 1981, General Election Summary Report No. 6 (Nov. 4, 1981).

2. Interview with James Baldwin, delegate and member of the Democratic State Committee, and Delegates Janice Eichhorn and Brian Moore, Feb. 27, 1983, and from personal knowledge acquired during the convention.

3. The percentages of lawyers at the conventions in New York (1967), Rhode Island (1964-69), New Mexico (1969), Arkansas (1969-70), Hawaii (1968), Illinois (1969-70), and Maryland (1967-68) were, respectively, 69%, 40%, 23%, 46%, 31%, 40%, and 50%. Elmer Cornwell, Jay Goodman, and Wayne Swanson, *Constitutional Conventions: The Politics of Revision* (New York: Praeger Press, 1974). The percentage in New Jersey in 1947 was 66%. Richard Connors, *The Process of Constitutional Revision in New Jersey 1940-47* (New York: National Municipal League, 1970), p. 29.

4. *See* Appendix A.

5. Another liberal Republican, Robert Roehr, was originally declared a winner, but he lost to Democrat Frank Kameny when the absentee ballots were counted.

6. Sherwood, "45 to Draft Charter for Statehood," *Washington Post*, Nov. 8, 1981, p. B1.

7. Wheeler, "Maurice Jackson's Imprint on D.C.'s New Constitution," *Daily World*, Aug. 12, 1982, p. 10.

8. Interview with Delegate James Baldwin.

9. Initiative No. 3, § 4(a).

10. This brief history is reconstructed from conversations with Jason Newman, October and November 1981.

11. Conversation with Jason Newman, December 1981.

12. Information supplied by statement of Robert Young, Office of the Mayor, to the delegates-elect, at Howard University Law School, Jan. 9, 1982.

13. Report of the Committee on Physical Space, and vote taken to accept the old Pepco building, Jan. 23, 1982.

14. *See, e.g.*, Alaska Const. arts. VII (Health Education and Welfare) and VIII (Natural Resources) (1956).

15. *See* Transcript, Feb. 8, 1982 (Delegate Simmons). The transcript for Feb. 8, 1982, can no longer be located, either at the convention's archives or elsewhere.

16. Decision of the Committee on Rules and Calendar, Jan. 17, 1982.

17. *See* Planning Committee Reports and Delegate Decisions (Jan. 23, 1982) (incorporating decisions reached on Jan. 21, 1982).

18. Decision of the Committee on Rules and Calendar, Jan. 17, 1982.

19. Meeting of Jan. 27, 1982.

20. *See* Proposed Rules (Jan. 29, 1982) (Chapter 2).

21. Proposed Rules (Jan. 29, 1982), Rule 1.1 (officers), Rule 2.1 (Executive Committee), Rules 3.1-3.4 (drafting procedure), Rules 4.1 & 4.2 (voting procedure), Rules 6.1, 6.2 & 6.3 (order of business), Rule 8.1 (quorum), Rule 7.1 (amendments).

22. "Addendum B" to Report to Delegates from the Committee on Resources and Public Relations, Feb. 2, 1982.

23. Memorandum to Eric Grant, Staff Assistant, Office of the Mayor, from Inez Smith Reid, Chief, Legislation and Opinions Section, Legal Counsel Division, Office of the Corporation Counsel (Dec. 23, 1981) and Memorandum to Robert Young, Staff Assistant, Office of the Mayor, from Inez Smith Reid, Chief, Legislation and Opinions Section, Legal Counsel Division, Office of the Corporation Counsel (Jan. 20, 1982).

CHAPTER 4:

The Genesis of Procedure

The telephone rings while I am washing dishes. It is Wesley Long, whom I have met at a few meetings of the 51st State Committee. I congratulate him on his election as delegate. He congratulates me. We chat for a few minutes about our hopes for the convention. He asks me to support his bid for the presidency. Two weeks have passed since the election. Convention politics have begun.

I am astounded by his candidacy, and I tell him so. Isn't Hilda Mason the only possible president, I ask him. In the first place, doesn't the president of a mostly black convention, in a mostly black city, have to be black? And in the second place, isn't Mason "Ms. Statehood," in view of her long association with the movement, her having succeeded Julius Hobson on the Council, her presidency of the 51st State Committee, and the fact that she received more votes for delegate than any other candidate?

He concedes as much, but points out that Mason does not chair meetings very well, and that the 51st State Committee had worked as well as it had only because the leadership functions had been divided between Mason and Guinan, who had chaired meetings of its Executive Committee.

I point out that the president of the convention will have many functions in addition to chairing the meetings, such as representing the convention to the public and uniting it when it becomes deeply divided. I tell him that it seems to me that the president must be black, and that while I don't know most of the black delegates, Mason seems the obvious choice. To my surprise, he accepts this argument, at least tentatively. He says that he will think about the concept of a Mason presidency in which several vice-presidents, including himself, actually chair the meetings in some kind of rotation. We talk about the model of the United States Senate, where the official presiding officer, the Vice-President of the United States, in fact rarely presides. A few days later, he calls back and says that he has decided not to be a candidate for president. He tells me that he has asked Mason whether she would be interested in the presidency, and that she said that she would not turn it down, but she did not want to campaign actively for the position.

I have no contact with any other delegates until the delegates' seminar that Jason Newman convenes at Georgetown a few weeks later. I sit impatiently through the eight hours of speeches. They are excellent, but I wait in vain for a delegate to say what I suspect all of us are thinking—that our greatest need is not for lectures on the law but rather a discussion of ways to get organized so that we do not waste the time before we are officially called together at the end of January. Newman may have a good reason for scheduling time for political organization into the program, but I hope that someone will disrupt the agenda so that we can talk about a temporary structure. No one does.

In the evening, a few hours after the seminar ends, there is a second event. A few days earlier, we had all received invitations from Charles Cassell, one of our fellow delegates-elect, to attend a jazz concert that he was producing. He also invited us to meet with him to discuss the convention for an hour before the concert. The invitation, coming on the heels of Long's phone call, makes me wonder if this, too, is a part of an early bid for the presidency. Along with half a dozen other delegates, I wait for Cassell in an anteroom at the Ethical Society Hall, where the concert is being held. The musicians are rehearsing on the other side of the door, so that bits of saxophone and trumpet music punctuate the meeting. Those of us who are there are surprised at how few of us have come; we assume that most delegates are equally eager to talk with each other, but that everyone is exhausted from the marathon session at Georgetown. Concert engagements delay Cassell and he arrives half an hour late. The meeting, of necessity, will be very brief.

Tall, with a beautiful white beard and a sonorous, booming voice, Cassell dominates the room. He has been busy with his concert and unable to attend the Georgetown seminar. He asks us to fill him in. We have only half an hour to discuss my predominant concern, organization, and I do not feel like summarizing the day's lectures.

Neither do the others, it seems. David Clarke gets to the heart of a procedural issue that is of central importance for him. He thinks it is impossible for the convention to write a constitution in ninety days. He wants us to tell him whether he should introduce a bill in the Council to repeal the ninety-day limit. He says this should be done now, if it is to be done at all, because to do it toward the end of the convention would appear an admission of failure.

Cassell opposes such a move. The legislature gave us ninety days, he notes, and we all ran for office aware of the limit. We should therefore try to meet the deadline. Thinking about the need for a short deadline to get everyone working, and about my own time limitations, I support Cassell. The introduction of such a bill by Clarke might encourage the delegates to relax, and if the bill then failed, we would be worse off than we were before it was introduced. Long adds that the money that has been budgeted will barely sustain a minimum staff for ninety days, and that the prospects for getting additional funds are very slim. He suggests legislation to delay the opening of the convention for several weeks, during which the delegates-elect could work together, informally, without staff.

Corn makes a new point in favor of delay: The work will go more slowly than we suspect, because it will take some weeks for the delegates just to get to know each other and to work out clashes of personality. Kameny lashes out at her with surprising vehemence: "I'm not trying to arrange a series of marriages—I'm trying to write a constitution."

The concert is about to begin, and the meeting ends inconclusively. Clarke is still eager for support from delegates for eliminating the deadline. I wonder whether he has reasons he is not divulging. He is running for President of the Council in the fall. Does he want the main work of the convention postponed so that in this election year he will not be forced to split his time between the convention and his Council seat, and thereby be compelled to do only a mediocre job at one or the other? Does he perhaps fear that the constitution will be so poor or so controversial that he wouldn't want to be identified with it while he is running for office? Does he want to put the vote on ratification and the concurrent vote for United States Senators and Representative-elect off until 1983 so that he can be seated as President of the Council and then run for the office of Senator-elect? Or am I ascribing to Clarke a covert agenda that he does not really have?

Cassell says nothing at all about wanting to be elected to a convention office. Either I was wrong and he isn't interested, or his strategy is a lot cooler than Long's.

* * *

At last there is an opportunity to begin to get organized. After the first seminar at Howard Law School, we can divide into workshops to begin planning together. The choices are officers and staff, or committees, rules, and calendar. It's a difficult choice, but I select the workshop that includes rules, because rules are something I can be particularly helpful with. In the workshop I notice something quite odd. Although the delegates-elect as a whole are sixty-two percent black, nine of the fourteen delegates who've selected this workshop are white. Most of the blacks have gone to the other workshop. The significance of this is not clear to me.

The dialogue in the workshop is confusing. On every issue there are as many different proposals as there are delegates. The principal issue on everyone's mind seems to be whether it is possible and desirable to extend the ninety-day limit. Amid objections to any action based on lack of notice, the meeting ends in a decision to hold another unoffical plenary meeting on the fourth of January. By then, two months will have passed since election day, and the opening of the convention will be less than thirty days away.

* * *

All of the other delegates from Ward Three have urged that the five of us get together to talk. I have resisted, fearing that too much "ward identity" in the convention could make consensus difficult. But it's hard to argue against meeting just to see whether we have something to say to each other, and I don't want to be a spoiler.

We get together late one afternoon in Oulahan's law office. There is a thin crust of snow on the ground, and Oulahan's conference room is warm and cozy. He supplies beer and cokes.

Oulahan is terribly nervous about the impending organizational meeting in January. He envisions a scenario in which a small group of people he doesn't know will draw up the convention's rules and present them as a *fait accompli* to the convention. A caucus acting before the formal swearing-in, even a caucus open to all delegates-elect, bothers him, because he fears it may set a precedent for the convention itself. Corn shares his concern and thinks no action should be taken until we are sworn in at the end of January. Oulahan and Corn are Republicans; they are a small political minority at this Convention, and formal, regularized procedures are one of their few protections.

The three of us who are Democrats try to reassure them. We tell them that there is no reason to suspect that they will be railroaded. Anything approved before the convention opens would have to be ratified by the convention, under its formal rules, after it began. We argue that we can't afford to waste the month of January, and that organizational activity is likely to happen anyway. It's better for it to be open and inclusive than for it to be driven underground. Oulahan's concerns are somewhat tempered.

We decide to explore the kinds of substantive committee assignments each of us would prefer, to see if there will be competition within the ward as well as with delegates from other wards. Garner, who plans to seek his party's nomination for election to the Council in the fall, wants the Committee on the Legislative Branch, a useful credential. Corn, who has her eye on the Republican nomination for the same seat, wants that committee as well. Kameny, who is not only a gay rights leader but a strong civil libertarian in general, wants to serve on the committee working on the bill of rights. Oulahan, who is trying to be nominated for a judgeship, wants the Committee on the Judiciary. It is my turn. I would like to be on any of the committees that the others have mentioned, and I see a way to lay the foundation for some future horse trading. I tell them, truthfully, that I would like to serve on the very committees that they have mentioned, but I have special skill and experience in legislative drafting. If it comes to a choice, I would rather be on the Committee on Style and Drafting, which the convention will surely need, rather than on any particular substantive committee. It is apparent that they understand the potential for negotiation, should the right circumstances ever arise. But I continue to feel like a political babe. I fear I may have revealed too much about what I want, too soon.

*   *   *

My impatience grows greater with each day of inaction. But there is something I can do that might eventually help get the convention going. The delegates, however they organize themselves, eventually will need rules of procedure. They will have to get a first draft from somewhere. The process of putting together a first draft could take a long time, because the only adequate models are the rules of other states' conventions, and these are both unfamiliar and peculiarly tailored to the jurisdictions in which they were used. Unlike most delegates, I have copies of all of them, because they were reprinted in a volume that I purchased from the National Municipal League in New York.[1] I could at least put together a set of proposed rules, and at some point save the convention a lot of time.

But I recall the warning from my source about resentment against those with special expertise, particularly whites. I could do this work, but I have no idea how to present it to the delegates in a way that does not lead to its rejection for reasons wholly unrelated to its quality. I do, however, have two contacts who know their way around politically and might be able to advise me—the Masons. Perhaps if they like the draft, they could present it as their own. It might be more easily accepted from them than from me.

With painstaking care, I develop a complete draft, borrowing words and phrases from other conventions' rules and, where appropriate, from Robert's Rules of Order. The work teaches me how difficult this task is. In some states, the rules of the most recent convention are overly general; the words alone resolve few conflicts. These rules could only work if constantly interpreted by a convention president whom everyone knew and trusted.[2] Other states' rules appear unnecessarily detailed. I feel that a relatively brief set of rules, rather than an encyclopedia, would have a much greater chance of being grasped immediately and accepted by the delegates. The procedural rules of the District's Council are of very little help, for they fail to cover many of the subjects, such as motions, that the convention's rules will have to regulate.

I recognize, of course, that it is impossible to write a full set of rules of procedure without making policy choices that will be the subject of substantial convention debate. Attempts to prejudge the outcome will surely create a backlash, and I am more interested in bringing about some set of rules than in resolving any particular policy questions. As I work, therefore, I leave blanks where words might raise potential policy conflicts. I provide, for example, that each substantive committee "shall have—members," and I leave the list of such committees to be developed by whomever will be working with this draft. After finishing the draft, I mail it off to the Masons, noting that I have not shown it to anyone else. I ask both for their reactions to the substance of the draft and their advice on "what, if anything, should be done with it."[3]

I receive no reply from the Masons.

*   *   *

The plenary meeting on the evening of January 4 is held in the somewhat cavernous moot court auditorium at Howard Law School. It is a room seven or eight times larger than the delegates need, emphasizing isolation rather than togetherness, but it is all that is available. The seats, all fixed, face forward, and tend to force the delegates to speak to each other through a moderator.

But there is no moderator, and people mill about long after the meeting was scheduled to begin. Lillian Huff, who was expected to open the meeting, is nowhere to be seen. I look for the Masons to ask for their reactions to my letter, but discover they are not present either.

The delay becomes embarrassing. Michael Marcus, a white delegate who is a vice-president of the 51st State Committee, goes to the front of the room. His reluctance to appear to be bidding for leadership is evident. Within seconds, he asks Arnold Leibowitz, who had come to observe the meeting, to serve as "facilitator," and then sits down. Leibowitz assumes a new role in the group.

Joel Garner makes the first proposal, which he has previously sent to each delegate by mail.[4] I know before he makes it that it will not be accepted. This first business meeting has an undefinably tense quality, and although we have seen each other at two seminars, most of us do not yet know each other's names. Despite the advance circulation, a proposal from a Ward Three white is not going to be well received, at least not at the very outset of this meeting.

Garner suggests that an unofficial "Preparations Committee" be created, to consist of one delegate from each ward, chosen by that ward's delegation. The committee would "develop materials and make advance preparations for the adoption of rules, the election of officers, and the creation of convention committees." The committee's goal would be to develop alternatives for the convention's consideration, and all recommendations would have to be approved by the convention after the swearing-in.

"I'm opposed to that!" a voice calls. They are the very next words spoken, and they come from Victoria Street, a black delegate. "It's too exclusive. Forty-five of us were elected, and thirty-six of us shouldn't be excluded from making the ground rules."

"This proposal would divide us," complains Charlotte Holmes, another black delegate. "Who wants it? What would it do?" Because Garner has just said that he wants it and has described what he thinks it will do, I hear her questions as, "Why does he really want it? What would it really do?"

Marcus steps in and tries to defend the proposal, explaining that it would only create a temporary body to prepare options, and could not bind anyone.

He, too, is swept aside. "If you don't utilize all the people here, it would be a disservice to our constituents. They elected all of us to work on this," Talmadge Moore, a black delegate, complains. Cassell agrees; anything we do has to be participated in by everyone, or there will be a lot of controversy.

Kameny expresses his puzzlement. All that Garner has proposed is an efficient mechanism, a committee, for developing proposals that all delegates will eventually consider, he says.

But something is wrong already. White delegates are defending Garner's proposal, and are trying to persuade the group to accept it. This is only increasing the suspicion of black delegates, none of whom are eager to explore it. I recall Oulahan's fear that this meeting would lead to a railroad, excluding him from participation. It sounds as if the black delegates have precisely the same concern.

In the best tradition of facilitators, Leibowitz depolarizes the situation. He hauls a blackboard from a corner of the room and makes a list of all the tasks that delegates have suggested need to be done: Rules, space, budget, committees, calendar, research, officers. As he does so, a new strain enters the dialogue. No action should be taken at this meeting, say four of the delegates, because notice of the meeting was not sent to each delegate. The only thing that should be achieved is agreement on a new meeting date.

A delegate counters that everyone did receive notice. To be sure, the notice that everyone expected to get from the 51st State Committee wasn't received by anyone, but everyone got Joel Garner's letter which included the time and place of the meeting. Leibowitz calls for a ward-by-ward survey, and it turns out that thirty-five delegates are present and each of the other ten knew about the meeting but was unable to attend.

It is clear, though, that the delegates need a regular mechanism for communicating with each other in the pre-convention period. The mailing list that Garner used was not entirely up-to-date; a yellow pad is passed around on which delegates can list their current addresses for a roster. David Clarke offers to mail, at Council expense, any information that the delegates want circulated.

There is, again, a chorus of protests, led by Cassell and delegate David Barnes. "Sending out notices is a *job* for someone," Barnes says. His meaning is not lost on anyone. This looks like a power play by Clarke: first he becomes the de facto corresponding secretary, and in a flash he'll be a leader of the convention.

Maurice Jackson, our Communist delegate, speaks out for the first time in the convention. He is appalled by the trivial nature of the debate. "Let's move on and make history," he complains, "and not spend an hour deciding who can send out a mailing."

But the need for mailings is a practical problem that has not gone away. The 51st State Committee is proposed as the logical center for mailings, but it is protested that the committee is incompetent and nearly defunct. Delegates begin to ask why the 51st State Committee's notice for this very meeting was not sent out as promised.

Lillian Huff enters the room as if on cue, just as delegates are venting all their anger on her. A mistake was made, she explains. She had been told that the mailing had gone out. Someone had taken the day off and it was not sent. She says, however, that the 51st State Committee can be trusted to send out mailings in the future. All this time, a pantomime is being played out between Leibowitz and Huff, as he tries to hand her the gavel that symbolizes chairmanship of the meeting, and she, sensing the crowd's hostility, pushes it away, forcing him to continue to moderate.

More than two hours have passed. The debate turns back to the original question of how the delegates will get themselves organized, and Eichhorn says what many must be thinking but no one has had the courage to say. "As a practical matter, we're going to have to narrow down to committees. We're all so suspicious that an offer to help is just an expression of ambition, that we refuse all assistance. We're afraid to create committees and we don't even trust anyone to do a mailing. If someone sends out a Christmas card we think he's running for president of the convention."

Her speech has a sobering effect, reinforced a few minutes later when Jerry Moore takes the floor. Moore, a minister as well as a Council member, has a slow and beautiful style of speech, and he is the only delegate who commands absolute silence from the other delegates. He speaks the common sense of a professional legislator: Forty-five people in a general assembly can't accomplish very much; they have to break down into working units which report back to the full body.

It is Leibowitz' chance to intervene with a resolution. There seems to be a consensus on having several committees rather than one, he announces, and there seem to be more than enough tasks for several committees. He points to the blackboard and looks at Garner. "Is that acceptable, Joel?"

Garner turns to Street, the first delegate who had attacked his plan, and hands the question over. Is a multiplicity of committees acceptable to her?

She says it is, but she would like to have five committees created. She doesn't have to explain the magic of five; it enables each ward to have one member on each committee.

Leibowitz returns to his blackboard, eliminates the trivial tasks such as development of a mailing roster, and rearranges the rest of them into five groupings: Rules and calendar, officers, committees, physical space and budget, and resources. I think quickly about the conflict the emerging plan might create among the delegates in my ward. The first four committees have substantive duties, but the fifth may be something of a throw-away because it has services to perform, but will involve few policy decisions. We might all be thrown into a fight to be on the first four committees. I suggest that public information be added to the fifth committee to equalize its importance, and this suggestion is accepted by the group.

There is some discussion of whether each ward should be required to select only one of its delegates per committee, or whether wards could put two members on one committee and none on another. The delegates are wearying of the discussion, now in its fourth hour, and recoiling a bit from the shock of discovering how hard it is to accomplish anything quickly in this diverse group. Again Leibowitz asserts himself, suggesting that the simple system, a required single representative from each ward on each committee, will avoid dispute. The group recognizes the truth of this observation, and accepts the suggestion.

Again a delegate voices the concern about power within the convention that has been lurking beneath the surface all evening. "There are people in here right now," warns Teresa Jones, "who are thinking that despite the fact that these committees are 'temporary,' they'll chair one of these committees in order to chair something permanent at the convention."

But the meeting ends, and there is a quick Ward Three caucus to select our representatives to the five committees. Oulahan has had to leave early, and he misses the caucus. Among the other four of us, there is a quick agreement that I will go to rules and calendar, Corn to space and budget, Kameny to committees, and Garner to officers. That leaves the least interesting committee, the Committee on Resources, to our absent member. But Corn assures us that Oulahan will be busy with legal work during January, and would prefer the assignment involving the least amount of work. Garner appears only slightly miffed by the rejection of his plan; at least he has catalyzed some organizational decision by the body. We part on a happy note.

*   *   *

Oulahan calls me the next afternoon, furious with Corn's suggestion that he would happily accept what he calls "the dead end committee." I offer to meet with the others in the ward to work it out. But he resists that, too;

Garner has already offered to trade, and Oulahan has refused. He will accept his assignment, but he wants us to know that he is angry. Even peace within the ward delegation is not going to be easy to maintain.

*   *   *

I call Charles Mason and ask for his comments on my draft rules. He thinks that they are fine in substance and is as baffled as I am about how to have them considered. But he and I are both to be on the Rules Committee, so we will together watch for an opportunity.

*   *   *

The following weekend the next delegates' seminar convenes, and at the end of the seminar the five committees are scheduled to hold their initial meetings. For several hours we hear lectures on the types of provisions that a state constitution might include with respect to the three branches of government. All the standard issues are touched upon: Whether to have one house or two in the legislature, which executive branch officials should be elected, how judges should be selected. Once again, the quality of the presentations is high, but I am eager to get to work.

After the lectures, there is a question and answer period. As on past occasions, Corn jumps in with the first and most frequent questions, and tends to make speeches, so that the moderator is forced to tell her to come to the point. The other delegates are becoming visibly annoyed, and I worry that her behavior will affect their image of the entire Ward Three delegation. The expressions of the others from my ward betray a similar concern.

After the question and answer period, a member of the Mayor's task force makes a brief presentation about the developing arrangements for the convention. He talks about the swearing-in ceremony and reception that will be held on the 30th of January, and about the school building that is being readied for convention use. When he reveals that the building will be open only until 8 p.m., he is attacked so ferociously by the delegates that the Howard professor who is moderating has to remind us that the speaker is only conveying a message and is not responsible for the decision. Members of the Committee on Physical Space assure us that they will look into the matter.

My mind flashes to a logistical problem. If on the first day the Mayor merely swears us in and holds a reception, we may have trouble convening for business, because we will not yet have a leader of our own with formal authority for bringing us together. As Arnold Leibowitz has outlined a convention's prototypical first day, the Mayor would preside over the actual first business of the convention, election of its own officers. It occurs to me that we are going to need at least a brief business meeting while the Mayor or his representative is still on hand, and I ask the Mayor's task force member whether any plans have been made to set a room aside for a business meeting on the day of the swearing-in.

He has not thought about it, he says, and makes a note. Almost immediately, Talmadge Moore, a black delegate to whom I have never spoken, rises and points his finger at me. "When I work, I work, and when I party, I party," he says, loudly and, it seems to me, with a trace of anger in his voice. "I don't know why this delegate is so uptight about having a meeting the day we're sworn in."

There is a little chorus of guffaws, and I redden. If Moore wanted to know more about the rationale for my suggestion, he could have asked me. Instead, he has pointed to me as the delegate who is "uptight," who doesn't know enough not to mix business with pleasure, and who doesn't know how to have a good time. I also hear in his second sentence a hint of suspicion that I have a hidden agenda, that I must have some personal reason for wanting an early meeting.

The Mayor's man leaves, and I expect us to break for lunch and then to go to our committee meetings. At this point, however, a delegate I have not seen before steps up to the front of the room and says that she would like to speak to all of us. She is a tall, rather heavy black woman with a deep, hoarse voice, and she introduces herself as Janette Harris from Ward Four.

Janette Harris

She missed the January 4 meeting in the auditorium, she tells us, and thinks we have made an error in deciding on the structure of the committees. We have made each committee the same size, one member from each ward and one from the at-large group of delegates. But the Committee on Rules is the most important committee, Harris says, and it should have a larger membership, so that it is more representative. We should therefore elect four additional members to the Committee on Rules and Calendar, right now. These four would serve on their other committees as well.

Several delegates groan. We spent hours on this structure just a few nights ago. Is nothing ever settled? Wesley Long passes me the list which he has compiled of the members of the Rules Committee, including himself. There are five blacks and four whites. Charles Mason is the member who was chosen by the delegates from Harris' ward.

Several delegates protest that we have been over this ground at length, that the decision to have only one member from each ward on any one committee was deliberate, and that while we are sorry that Harris wasn't at the meeting to make her point, we can not reopen all our decisions. Barbara Lett Simmons supports Harris, though, saying that it would be "myopic" not to reconsider when a delegate brings up a serious point. Jan Eichhorn objects that there was no notice that this decision was to be reopened, and the group, convened today as a seminar, has no power to do it. Kameny takes issue with Harris' premise, arguing that all five committees are of equal importance. Corn supports him, but Cassell agrees with Harris that the Committee on Rules is the most important group. Almost exclusively, blacks support Harris' suggestion, and whites oppose it.

A motion is made to adopt Harris' proposal. The delegates are tired of arguing, and it is impossible to tell from what has been said which side will prevail. The Howard professor who has been officiating at the seminar asks whether the group is ready to vote. Eichhorn's objection to deciding is not repeated. There is a show of hands, and the motion to enlarge the Committee is carried twenty-one to seventeen.

Nominations are made for additional members. Blacks nominate blacks, including Harris, and whites nominate whites. In all, five blacks and three whites are nominated.

The moderator suggests that delegates write down the names of up to four candidates whom they favor, and pass the papers to the front. Hilda Mason objects to the use of non-standardized ballot forms, which could enable some delegates to vote twice. The level of distrust in the room is mounting rapidly. When the ballots are counted, the winners are all blacks, including Harris. The Committee on Rules and Calendar is now nine blacks and four whites.[5]

* * *

The Committee on Rules and Calendar holds its first meeting after lunch. Anita Shelton, a black delegate whom I do not know, suggests that we need to elect officers. I am surprised by the constant attention to election issues. Several of us offer the view that we should try to work collegially, without officers, and the subject is dropped.

Samuel Robinson, a black delegate with whom I have had no previous contact, suggests that we list the various subjects with which rules might be concerned, and parcel them out to the members of the Committee to prepare first drafts. Several heads nod approvingly. It seems too early for me to make a move, but if I don't do something, his suggestion will be adopted and we will have to work on the basis of thirteen uncoordinated packets rather than a comprehensive draft. I look to Charlie Mason for a signal, but he offers no help.

I don't dare reveal that I have already worked on a draft, for jumping the gun on the Committee will certainly be resented. Heart in hand, I mention that I have copies of the rules of some previous conventions, and I offer to prepare for the Committee a streamlined composite, leaving blanks where policy judgments are to be made.

As I feared, even this suggestion begins to bring down the roof. Robinson is visibly angry. "I'm opposed to that, sir!" he says. The "sir" startles me. "That procedure would give you a monopoly on knowledge and would minimize the education of all the rest of us!"

I don't respond, for it is clear that I will only make matters worse for myself. But David Clarke, who had been jumped on earlier in the week for offering to send out a mailing, rises to my defense. "We've got to stop being so distrustful of anyone who offers to help us," he argues. "We don't have to accept what Schrag suggests, but let him bring in anything he wants, and we can look at it. The same goes for everybody here. Anybody should be able to bring in an idea for us to look at."

His speech defuses the tension. It is agreed that, in addition to anyone's proposals, copies of the Council's rules will be copied and circulated and we will all look at Robert's Rules. The discussion then evolves into yet another debate on whether to ask the Council for an extension of the ninety-day limit. Clarke presses for the Committee to endorse an attempt to get an extension. We agree only to discuss this question again at our next meeting, and we adjourn.

I realize that I have made Robinson distrust me, and that this is a poor way to begin. On the other hand, at least my draft of the rules will have an airing, and it may help to move the process along. On balance, I'm happy that I made my offer.

But something still bothers me. In order for my offer to have any chance of being accepted, I had to withhold from the Committee the fact that the draft was already finished and could have been immediately distributed for study. What is there about our situation that is inhibiting us from making full use of each delegate's work? And was my withholding of this information an immoral deceit, sophisticated politics, or both?

* * *

The Committee on Rules and Calendar meets again on Sunday, January 17, and in Washington it is the coldest day since 1934. All over the city, water pipes are bursting and cars are rebelling against attempts to start them. Our meeting place is a kind of quonset hut behind a public school near the eastern corner of the District. My toes are numb from walking the half block from my car, and they are to remain numb for the four-hour meeting, because the small heater in the room is no match for the day's below-zero temperature.

The first person I encounter is Charlotte Holmes, who had missed the previous meeting. She is a black delegate from Ward Six, which includes the area southeast of Capitol Hill. Her wide, thick glasses peer from between a woolen coat collar and a large hat.

I don't know her very well, and I try to strike up a conversation. "I know why you are wearing your hat in here today," I offer, shivering.

She looks at me as though I'd made an indecent remark, and strikes like a snake. "You do *not* know why I'm wearing my hat today!" she tells me, glaring. This effectively ends the conversation. I mutter something about how cold it is, wondering whether perhaps I have accidentally touched upon a sensitive subject, and back off to move chairs.

We are seated, and copies are distributed of a memorandum in which the District's Corporation Counsel says that a ten-day organization period need not count against our ninety-day limit. This provokes an immediate discussion on an old topic, whether to seek a legislative extension of the ninety-day period. Clarke is still eager to be asked to try to get one through the Council. I am still opposed.

Gwendolyn Paramore suggests that we solve the problem by counting only days on which the convention actually meets, and not the intervening days, toward the ninety-day limit. I tell her that this is not a permissible reading of the legislation's wording or intent. Clarke agrees. Already the lawyers are telling their lay colleagues what they cannot do. I resolve to try to avoid that particular stereotype.

The delegates begin to take sides, and at once it becomes clear that, as usual, there are more than two points of view. Clarke favors an indefinite extension, or at least one that will not require the convention to finish before the Council elections in the fall. Long agrees with him that ninety days are not enough, but he favors only a thirty-day extension. Clarke would rather have no extension at all than use up bargaining chips to get a mere thirty days. The debate becomes prolonged, and several committee members who favor an extension point out that at this stage they have no idea how much extra time might be necessary. Others counter that if we wait until we know how much more time we need, we will be too late to obtain the necessary legislative action. Once again, the District's legal status becomes ironic. Because ordinary Council legislation extending the convention's ninety-day limit could not take effect until it sat before Congress for a thirty-day review period, the Council could not honor a last-minute request for an extension unless it passed "emergency" legislation. Emergency legislation would require a two-thirds vote rather than a simple majority.[6] The very strictures that prove the need for statehood again become a barrier to the process of achieving it.

After two hours of debate, I sense that the committee has tired of this issue, and a count of those who have spoken suggests that most of the members either favor sticking with the ninety-day limit or do not know what kind of extension they prefer. I make a motion that we recommend to the convention that no extension be sought at this time. To my surprise, it carries by a huge margin, ten to two.

We spend the next hour studying the results of a survey of times that delegates would prefer to meet. The results are both partial and inconclusive, and we agree that we need more information from delegates who have not responded. Dusk is already falling, along with the temperature, as we turn to the subject of rules.

I hand out my draft to the delegates, and take a low profile for the discussion. The other members barely look at the draft before quickly concluding that there are too many subjects for any one person to deal with initially. They divide the various aspects of the rules among nine of the members. Each of the nine is to make a presentation at a subsequent meeting about his or her topic. I volunteer to take the issue of drafting procedure, of how paper will flow through the convention, one of the longest sections of my draft. It is not clear what the people making presentations are supposed to do—discuss the subject generally, offer suggested changes in my draft, or write a new draft covering the subject. I decide that this is the wrong moment to point up the ambiguity, because it will appear to be insistence that everyone work from my draft, which no one has yet read.

Three evenings over the next nine days are reserved for additional meetings. During discussion of these meeting times, Long suggests that we "circulate our resumes to each other, so that we can get to know who we are." Holmes squints at him through her thick glasses and, in the same tone she used on me, asks him, "Why do you need to know who I am?" What is she worried about, I wonder. What is the source of her deep suspicion?

Long replies that he thinks it would be good to know more about each other so that we can work together more easily and take advantage of each other's expertise. Several delegates chime in to say that they have no intention of exchanging resumes. Once again Clarke becomes the peacemaker, noting that no one can force anyone to divulge information, and that there is no cause for jumping on Long for encouraging those who want to exchange information to do so.

As we complete our scheduling of the next meetings, Jeannette Feely points out that in snowy weather we need to designate one person to cancel or reschedule meetings, if necessary. There is general agreement with this thought. "I therefore move," says Feely, "that Charlotte Holmes be elected chair of this committee."

For a moment there is utter silence. I am amazed at this development for two reasons. Feely has justified the need for a convener, and we have agreed, but it is a long move from that point to the conclusion that we need a chair. Indeed, we have functioned rather well for four hours without one. Also, by naming one individual, rather than suggesting that we elect a chair through an open nominating process, Feely has personalized the issue. Speaking against having a chair (or, for that matter, in favor of having additional nominees) would likely be interpreted, at least by some, probably including Holmes, as antipathy to Holmes. Although I do feel uneasy about Holmes, I don't want to be forced to reveal this, particularly because I may already be on thin ice with Robinson.

Charlotte Holmes

I am speechless, but Clarke breaks the ice. "Jeannette, do you really mean as 'chair,' with all the duties of a chair, or only as a contact point in case of bad weather?" He is subtly calling her on his ploy, I think, and giving her a chance to back down.

She looks him straight in the eye and will not be cowed. "I mean as chair, with all the duties," she tells him.

Holmes is about to be elected. The process by which she is being forced on us, with no alternatives, makes me uncomfortable, but I see no way out. I could nominate Clarke or Long, but they would probably decline rather than lose on a racial vote. I could nominate one of the other blacks, but I don't know any of them well enough to have any idea of their relationship with Feely or Holmes, and none of them are stepping forward to support each other, a sign that Holmes has it in the bag. Stalling for time, I ask whether we are all sure that we need a chair rather than a convener, but Harris says that the "question has been called" and it is time to vote on the motion.

"I smell a steamroller," Long complains, but no one else takes up the cry.

I debate with myself over how to vote on Feely's motion. If I don't vote for Holmes, it will alienate the chair of my committee, and perhaps other members as well. But I can't bring myself to vote for her. Her only contributions to this meeting were the remarks directed at Long and myself, and I have no reason to think that she will be any good as a chair. On the other hand, I have no reason to doubt that she'll be a good chair, and my real quarrel is with Feely for the manner of this nomination, not with Holmes.

Charlotte Holmes is unanimously elected chair of the Committee on Rules and Calendar, delegates Schrag and Long abstaining.

*   *   *

The next meeting of the committee is in a conference room at the District Building; at least we have some warmth. For some reason, Cassell, who is not on the committee, is present as an observer. As we assemble, Holmes passes out an agenda listing the issues to be taken up and the members making presentations on those issues. My topic, the drafting procedure, which was supposed to have been on today's agenda, does not appear. Could it be that Holmes is retaliating for my abstention? But there is no need to say anything; the topic can't be skipped.

We begin with a two- or three-hour discussion of how to get the convention off the ground. Anita Shelton has thought through the logisitical problems of starting up without officers or rules. We will either need to elect officers right away or to elect a temporary chair. Feely favors a temporary, honorary chair, "because there is likely to be someone we'd like to honor." She does not say who she has in mind, and no one asks.

Robinson agrees, and suggests that there be two honorary vice-chairs as well. The temporary officers will be "equal to what has been talked about in our process, as in our convention, one chair and two vice-chairs." This is the first that I have heard of such a plan, and I wonder whether I have missed a meeting. Perhaps he had been talking with members of the Committee on Officers and has followed their suggestions.

As usual, new concepts emerge: Honorary co-chairs, honorary Fellows who would not do any chairing, first-day ceremonies to honor those non-delegates such as Julius Hobson who have brought us this far. Clarke points out that the press will attend the convention more heavily on its first and last days than on any others, so the first day should be entirely ceremonial. He suggests that no business should be transacted unless it is completely prearranged to avoid controversy. This thought—concealing our usual bickering from the press—becomes the first basis for consensus. We agree that the meeting the Mayor convenes on Saturday should take no action beyond adjourning to Sunday, when the real work of the convention will commence.

Now Feely reveals what she has in mind. Just as she suggested Holmes for chair of our committee, she proposes that Lillian Huff be the temporary chair of the convention.

I dislike the way that Feely jumps in suddenly with candidates, but her suggestion strikes me as an excellent one. Huff was defeated in her effort to become a delegate, so she cannot be a candidate for permanent president of the convention. She has performed a major service by getting the delegates together before the formal opening of the convention. By honoring her, we honor all who worked in the 51st State Committee and are not delegates. And although I do not know what kind of chair she will be, she will only serve for a day or two until we have adopted our rules and elected our permanent officers; how much could she do in that time? We vote unanimously to recommend to the delegates that Huff be the temporary chair.

We need not only a temporary chair, but temporary rules to govern us while we adopt our permanent rules. I propose that we use Robert's Rules temporarily. I am worried about Robert's because they are hundreds of pages long, full of thousands of details that can become the basis for hours of argument among the delegates. But there is no realistic alternative, and my motion carries unanimously.

The next issue is convention seating. Geraldine Warren distributes a sheet of paper with options: "(1) We could seat by Wards with At-Large Members first. (2) We could have every other Ward seated. (3) We could have half on one side and half of the delegates on the other. (4) Have all officers or the executive committee on the first row."[7]

One problem with these alternatives strikes me. All of these options are likely to have the effect of isolating the members of the two all-white delegations, from Wards Two and Three, from the rest of the convention. Ward seating, however the wards are arranged, will require ten of the seventeen white delegates to sit together where they will be less able to engage in political trades with the black majority. In addition, any news photographs or television pictures will tend to make the convention appear racially divided. My hope is that the convention will build bridges, and these seating plans threaten to dig chasms.

I try to be as diplomatic as possible. No motion is before the committee yet, so I move that we be seated alphabetically. This, I argue, will encourage racial integration in the convention. I do not expect anyone to argue with this reasoning, and no one does. But my motion is defeated, three to five. The three who favor it are white.

Now the proponents of ward-by-ward seating begin to speak, Robinson and Harris arguing that we should not lose the "unity of our wards" or create a false semblance of integration. I fear that one of the plans for ward seating will carry, but Charlie Mason saves the day, suggesting that we make no rule on the subject, but simply have forty-five seats and let everyone sit wherever he or she wishes. This proves to be acceptable.

The next topic on Holmes' agenda is the quorum requirement. Warren, the delegate making a presentation on this subject, has not written any actual text; she simply suggests that twenty-eight to thirty delegates be required for a quorum. But a quorum rule needs to be somewhat more detailed than this. It must, for example, authorize a smaller number of delegates to adjourn the meeting to a particular day so that the absence of a quorum does not cause a total lapse in the proceedings.

Fortunately, the very first paragraph of my proposed text is a quorum rule. It requires only a majority of all delegates, rather than twenty-eight or thirty, but after some debate, the committee accepts my argument that, given our conflicting schedules, requiring more than an absolute majority may make obtaining a quorum too difficult. With only a minor change in wording, my motion to use my first paragraph is carried. At last we are working on an actual text of rules, and there has been no revolt in principle to using my draft.

Charlie Mason catches the momentum and moves we adopt the next paragraph of my draft, which would require that all meetings be open to the public. Harris proposes an amendment to permit a closed executive session to be held pursuant to a two-thirds vote. There is extended and heated debate on this suggestion, several members believing that as a matter of principle it would be wrong for the convention ever to close its doors to the public. Harris' motion wins, seven to four. I am on the losing side, but we are really moving through the draft.

Though it is getting late, there is time for one more issue, the procedure for electing officers. The next paragraph of my draft describes a procedure including an alternative choice between open and secret balloting. Cassell hands Harris a copy of my draft with penciled markings on it.

A delegate moves that my paragraph be adopted, and Harris proposes that roll-call voting rather than secret voting be required. Though she has just argued for the possibility of secret meetings of the convention, she now urges maximum openness. Harris and I always seem to be on opposite sides of an issue. Although this troubles me, I cannot agree with her. Like her, I now flip-flop and argue for the secret ballot, because it seems to me that whoever votes for the losing presidential candidate may be punished with poor committee assignments or whatever other measures the president has the power to influence. Expected patronage is, I argue, not the basis on which we want our fellow delegates to cast their votes for our officers.

Up to this point, Holmes has been a reserved and neutral chair, but she suddenly becomes more animated. "All right, those in favor of having roll-call voting for officers," she says, raising her own hand high. There are four votes for, five opposed, two not voting, and two absent. "I didn't get everybody," she announces. "Let's do that again so I can get a good count. All those in favor of the roll call!" And again she raises her hand high. Three other hands go up, as before. She waits. Another hand is raised, then another. The remaining delegates, including all of the whites, are opposed; the motion carries six to five. Clarke chuckles at Holmes, both admiringly and sarcastically: "You really massaged that one, Charlotte!"

The convention is not shaping up in the way I expected. Meetings are marked by distrust and hostility, not closeness and cooperation. This meeting has seen two procedural votes along racial lines, and no one has remarked that if anything will doom our work, it is racial division. I am deeply disturbed by the black support for ward-by-ward seating; what can it portend?

Packing up my papers after the Committee meeting, it occurs to me that perhaps I should be less aloof about the question of leadership. I have thought very little about it since my conversations with Wes Long, expecting Hilda Mason to emerge as the obvious leader of the convention and to be elected its president by acclamation. But that scenario seems increasingly doubtful, for Mason has been extremely quiet while others, particularly Harris and Feely, have emerged as the only delegates who seem to know what they want. I am afraid that Harris and Feely will be much more likely to polarize the convention than to bring it together. Hilda Mason, a peacemaker with deep roots in both the black and white communities of Washington, could probably best put an end to the increasing factionalization. Perhaps it will not do for her to sit back and wait for a draft.

Her office is in the District Building, so on my way out of the meeting I walk by, hoping she might be there. It is 10:30 at night, and she is still at work behind her desk, a wiry woman of sixty-five going on fifty. I tell her about the disturbing aspects of the meeting I have just attended, and that I would like to see her President of the Convention. She has obviously given the matter some thought and is willing to serve, but she knows that her election is not a foregone conclusion. "And I can't run for it openly," she explains. "I'm up for reelection as a member of the Council this year. I can't take the chance of running for this office and losing on the eve of that election." I understand her problem, and ask whether she would mind if her supporters take some soundings for her. She agrees to that. I tell her that I don't yet know many of the black delegates, and I don't know anything about their political allegiances. She replies that she will have one or two of the black delegates do her soundings among the blacks.

*   *   *

Because snow forced the cancellation of the Howard University seminar the previous Saturday, the delegates reassemble in the auditorium for a make-up session on Thursday night. Lillian Huff is serving as moderator. Again the evening is billed as an academic session, but by now I know that any time this group is convened, there is likely to be a political element.

This occasion is no exception. There are lectures on how state constitutions treat taxing and borrowing authority, on local government units and special districts, and on state bills of rights. As usual there is a question period, with Corn asking the first and longest questions. The other Ward Three delegates avoid sitting with her, fearing guilt by association.

Committees are called upon and asked whether they have anything to report. Charlotte Holmes rises and announces that our committee has decided that the first day of the convention should be purely ceremonial, largely to recognize and honor others who have taken us this far. She adds that we determined that the real business should begin the next day, with the chair of the 51st State Committee, Lillian Huff, in the chair of the convention until we elect our own officers.

A voice calls out of the audience: "I move the Report."

This is unexpected. Holmes' report was accurate, but we never discussed when the group would be asked to act on it. Also, attendance on this cold evening is lighter than usual, with only twenty-seven delegates in the hall.

Corn is on her feet. She makes a substitute motion that Hilda Mason chair the convention until a permanent chair is elected. Oulahan supports her.

This is the kiss of death: Mason as the candidate of the two white Republicans who appear not to support statehood. Don't they have any common sense? Besides, it would hurt Mason's candidacy for president if she were elected temporary president; that could be a way of honoring her and being done with it.

Barbara Maguire is obviously agitated. She says she is very uncomfortable discussing a temporary chair with so many delegates absent, particularly without notice. To my surprise, Harris reinforces Maguire's point. She mentions that she is a member of the committee and says that her understanding was that we only would discuss whether or not to have a temporary chair, deferring the question of who should serve in that position. Holmes seems to retreat, saying that what needs to be decided is whether the first day should be ceremonial, and whether people who are not delegates should be honored.

But the issues of honoring non-delegates, having a temporary chair, and permitting a non-delegate to serve in that position become hopelessly jumbled. Amid motions and counter-motions, an enormous confusion descends on the body, with points of order and inquiry following quickly upon each other, and many demands for restatement of the question. Huff is not up to navigating the parliamentary thicket that is constructed, and being an interested party anyway, she turns the gavel over to one of the Howard professors. Finally, Oulahan gets the floor again and obtains a clarification of the main motion on the floor. It pertains only to honoring people, Holmes agrees, not to making anyone temporary chair. He and Corn withdraw the substitute.

Courts Oulahan

Several delegates are still unclear about which isssue is before us, and Holmes is asked to restate once again what we are voting on. "We recommend that January 30 be set aside as a ceremonial day to recognize several chairs and vice-chairs," she says, reintroducing the confusion and even adding to it by mentioning the issue of officers which was raised but not acted upon in the rules committee meeting. And she adds: "That's number one." Barbara Lett Simmons asks whether this resolution contemplates requesting the Mayor to issue a proclamation; the discussion veers off on the proclamation point, and the question of "recognizing several chairs and vice-chairs" is not returned to. I keep my peace, aware that I might be able to help separate the strands, but also believing that the number of times I can intervene is limited. In any event, I support the drift of the committee's recommendations, although I don't like the way that Holmes has expressed them.

Homes' motion is easily approved, and she is on her feet again. "And number two, that Lillian Huff chair the convention until a permanent chair is elected." She beams at Huff.

This is precisely the issue that Oulahan thought he had been assured was off the table; now he and others are on their feet objecting. Maguire is so visibly upset that her hand keeps darting up and down. Several delegates speak against the motion. All of them are white. None criticize Huff, though they are clearly leery that something is being put over on them, and that Huff is part of it. They talk of waiting until the next gathering, in two days, when more delegates are present and better notice has been given. Maguire's hand is still popping up and down, but she is not recognized.

Several speakers support the motion to put Huff in the chair, and all of them are black. They see no need to wait; Huff is the obvious candidate for temporary chair.

This is as bad a development as we could possibly have, I think. There is about to be a vote on an important issue, and the convention will split along racial lines. The whites will lose and will feel that they are being railroaded. I raise my hand. When I am recognized, I speak as strongly as I can in support of the motion to put Huff in the chair. It is a good temporary solution, and although I don't say it, it is going to happen anyway. I am speaking primarily to my fellow whites, not mentioning race but trying to get them to make Huff's election a biracial one. I succeed in part; there is a scattering of white votes for Huff, along with solid black support. But in the middle of the voting, Barbara Maguire erupts, accusing all of us of trampling on her right to speak, for she has never had the chance to speak to the second part of Holmes' motion. She storms from the hall on the verge of tears. No one tries to stop her; no one leaves to comfort her.

*   *   *

The convention is becoming ugly and I don't know why. Surely the blacks can see that the whites are being offended and alienated; why don't they make some effort to work with us, rather than taking us by surprise with their sudden proposals and nominations? I ask Hilda Mason what is going on.

"We have to keep our cool," she tells me. "This only appears to be a racial issue. But it isn't. It's a group of people who have worked together for years, in many kinds of meetings and organizations. This is how they operate. They do the same thing to control meetings that are all black. It just happens that whites are on the other side of it this time. But it's not directed against the whites." Now I am more confident than before that Feely's nomination of Holmes was not spontaneous.

* * *

The next night's meeting of the Rules Committee is businesslike and routine. We have not yet received any recommendations from the committees dealing with officers of committees, so I recommend that we defer those issues until our next meeting, at the beginning of the week. That brings up the section that is mine to present—the flow of proposals through the convention. This time it is on Holmes' agenda. We work through my proposed text, paragraph by paragraph. The debate is serious and the issues technical. Amendments are made, and several pages of proposed rules are completed. When we leave the District Building at eleven o'clock, a heavy snow is falling.

* * *

The snow falls all night; on Saturday morning, local streets are impassable, but our final seminar—and, more importantly, our final opportunity for preconvention organization—is scheduled for nine a.m. I manage to get to the University of the District of Columbia's uptown campus by ten a.m., hoping that I will not be too late. I am one of the first to arrive, and the building in which we were to meet has been closed because of the snow. As more delegates appear, the University finds a classroom for us. But it is very small, and as still more delegates arrive, we are being packed closer and closer together.

As people are arriving there is an opportunity for gossip. The big news is that Charles Cassell is running for President of the Convention. Does this have anything to do with the way that organizational matters have been handled? No one is certain. I remember him handing Harris the proposed changes to my draft rule on balloting for officers, but I am not certain that he personally advocated her successful proposal requiring an open roll-call vote. It would not have been odd for him to have taken a position anyway; by that time he had been elected the chair of the Committee on Officers.

We have our final seminar lectures—on past constitutional treatment of education, the amendment process, and the relationship between the D.C. statehood movement and similar movements in Puerto Rico, the Marianas, and other territories. The committee reports begin. The Resource Committee is seeking help for the convention from schools and businesses; it is in the process of compiling lists of organizations to be solicited. The Officers Committee is still mulling over the options on which officers the convention should have. The Space Committee recommends that we vote to make the old Pepco building our headquarters, rather than the school building that the Mayor originally offered. We unanimously accept this suggestion.

Next, Holmes speaks for the Committee on Rules and Calendar. She reports that we have determined to ask the group, at this meeting, who should be honored in the program that the Mayor is having printed for the swearing-in ceremony. Some names have already been suggested, such as Julius Hobson, Ed Guinan, Lillian Huff, and Lou Aronica. Who else should be added?

David Clarke suggests naming only Julius Hobson. Hilda Mason supports this idea, because in making a list of those who have contributed to statehood, we would inevitably overlook some people who should have been listed, or who will think that they should have been. Hobson is preeminent, and is deceased—an easy case for special attention. Clarke puts his view in the form of a motion.

But Cassell opposes it, and he makes a rather eloquent speech. Hobson provided the impetus for statehood, he says, but he couldn't have done it without others. He begins to list the honor roll, and describes what each man and woman has done. As I listen, I begin to believe that Cassell has just found a way to hold a kind of test vote against Mason, one that he is likely to win. Cassell is far more eloquent than Mason, and he is appealing to the delegates to honor people with whom they have worked for years, while she is concerned about hypothetical slights that will only come about if the delegates who compile the list make inadvertent omissions. His victory on this vote will demonstrate graphically, to any who do not already know it, that he and his contingent know how to lead this convention where it wants to go, while Mason is a cautious nay-sayer. "Julius Hobson was my mentor," he booms, "and I loved that man. He was our guiding genius. But it would not be right to honor only him, and he would not have wanted us to do so. I don't care how long the list of honorees is. This historic convention should recognize that it is only here because of the efforts of a great many others!"

The seating of delegates at this meeting is not exactly segregated, but people are grouped by race more than at any other previous meeting. The two back rows are almost exclusively black, while the whites are in front. When Cassell completes his oration, the back rows burst into applause. Mason sees that she is licked, and suggests a compromise: Hobson's name could be printed on the program, while the others appear on an insert. Cassell has made his point and accepts this suggestion. Clark's motion is defeated, twenty to four. Cassell quickly follows with Mason's compromise; he puts it into a motion before she steps forward to do so, and it passes, twenty-six to two. Cassell is, at least for now, effectively the leader of this convention.

* * *

There is other business for the meeting, such as setting a time and place for the first real business meeting, and establishing that we will adopt rules before electing officers, employing Robert's Rules temporarily. Mason remains silent through the remaining hours.

The meeting has shown Cassell to be forceful, with a flair for the dramatic, while Mason is quiet and thoughtful, and essentially pragmatic. I am less and less comfortable with the drift. Cassell and Mason are the only apparent candidates for the presidency. Can some energy be injected into her?

After the meeting, four white delegates ask to see me to learn the details behind the rumors they have been hearing of disturbing developments in the Committee on Rules and Calendar. These four are part of a substantial group who consider themselves socialists, and who were endorsed for election by the Democratic Socialist Organizing Committee. We find an empty classroom, and I fill them in on the Committee's decisions. They are deeply distressed by the prospect of an open roll-call vote for president, because they do not expect to vote for Cassell, and they fear that a vote against him will cost them membership on desirable committees if he wins. They are equally troubled that a procedure has been inserted for closing meetings to the press and public. And they feel a sense of doom about the election that is shaping up. Mason, they say, is too gentle to control the crowd that is currently in charge; she could not be an effective president. Some of them doubt she could win, for although they say that virtually all of the whites are beginning to identify Cassell with the sources of white unease, the number of whites is six short of a majority, and the meetings of the convention have not revealed any group of blacks, even a small one, associated with Mason. Furthermore, they ask, what would a Mason victory be worth if it were based on seventeen whites and a small minority of the convention's blacks? Would such an election not wreck the convention? And there is an important philosophical question as well. The whole point of the convention is that a black city is captive to colonial white rule, and is seeking self-determination. Shouldn't the whites stand aside and let the representatives of the black majority elect the president of their choice?

Bob Love, a young, bearded psychologist, has a plan. He would prefer Mason to Cassell as president of the convention, but he gives her, at the present, no chance at all of winning the office, an assessment more pessimistic than any of the rest of us venture. Love advises us to work on the assumption that Cassell will win the election. Our objective, then, should be to knock out the open ballot and to reduce the powers of the presidency, thereby reducing the opportunities for retaliation. Besides, avoiding strong-man control over the convention would be consistent with democratic socialist theory.

We should remember, he tells us, that the Committee on Rules is more tilted toward Cassell's bloc than are any of the other temporary committees, a result of Harris' *putsch*. The effort, then, should be to reduce the influence of the Committee on Rules and to strengthen the other committees with respect to decisions on how the convention is organized. He is a member of the Committee on Committees, and he has an idea about how that Committee, composed largely of moderates, can help.

He follows up the next day, and calls me with the results of the meeting of the Committee on Committees. It has resolved to assign jurisdiction to substantive committees in such a way that all of them are of equal importance and none can become a graveyard for the leadership's political opponents. It will also recommend that there be ten committees, two for each delegate, and that committee memberships be assigned by ward delegations, just as was done with the temporary committees, so that the convention leadership will be entirely removed from the assignment process. Finally, it will suggest that committees elect their own chairs so that this decision, too, is not conferred upon the president or the Executive Committee. As a first step toward making these decisions stick, the Committee on Committees is writing a letter to the Committee on Rules, requesting that the Committee on Rules draft no rules on the subject of committees—that a blank section be left in the proposed rules to be filled by the Committee on Committees. Since the Committee is united, with none of the bickering that has at times characterized the Committee on Rules, the letter will come from none other than the Committee's chair, Barbara Lett Simmons, who is capable of asserting a certain degree of influence.

* * *

Hilda Mason replies evasively to my questions about the degree of her support among the convention's blacks. She says that although the majority of blacks will support Cassell, enough blacks will back her to elect her president if she is also supported by nearly all of the whites. She won't name names, however, and I wonder if she really has the pledges. I don't know her well enough to really press her.

"You know I really don't want to be president," she tells me. "I'm chairman of the Council's Education Committee and I'm running for re-election, and I don't have the time. But I have to run because I can't let Cassell just walk away with it."

I am puzzled about her desire that Cassell be opposed, even though she is so reluctant to seek the office for herself. I ask around, seeking explanations. A delegate familiar with Statehood Party history speculates that an old conflict may be responsible, a conflict dating from the last meeting of the Statehood Party that Julius Hobson attended. According to the delegate, Cassell had become a relatively inactive member of the party, but when Hobson was about to die, Cassell attended a meeting that had been called to elect new leadership. He arrived with a large number of newly registered members, including students and teachers from the University where he worked. Cassell was nominated for party chairman, and in his speech, he complained that the party's leadership was too tied to whites. This hurt Hobson, who wheeled his chair up to Cassell and with tears in his eyes pleaded with him not to destroy the party. Cassell lost that election, but many of those who were present are still members of opposing factions, and some of them are deeply offended by Cassell's invocation of Hobson's memory, and by his frequent references to Hobson as his mentor.

* * *

It is the Tuesday before the opening of the convention. I have been at so many meetings over the past two weeks that they all begin to blur. I am grateful that the arrival of the opening day will bring an end, at last, to the seemingly endless chain of pre-convention meetings. Tonight the Rules Committee is scheduled to consider several major areas—officers, motion procedure, and perhaps the order of daily business—which will move us a lot closer to completing our work.

Harris, however, has other plans. She arrives at the meeting with a series of what she calls "inconsistencies" she says she had noticed in the work that we have done to date. Her items are, in reality, proposals to reconsider or to amend the work that we have already done. All of the items that she wants changed are proposed rules that I drafted or supported.

We had, for example, adopted a proposed rule that says, "Any delegate may make a proposal that a subject be incorporated into the Constitution."[8] She claims that this "sounds too definite, as though we were letting one delegate, rather than the convention, dictate what goes into the constitution." She is a professor of history, and I am surprised that she can read that meaning into the word "proposal." She wants to change "incorporated" to "considered for incorporation." The point is trivial and not worth a fight. Although I very much dislike letting her change the agenda and go back over old ground, I agree to the alteration. But she has many others.

A message arrives from the Committee on Committees–a letter from Barbara Lett Simmons. She requests that the section of proposed rules that would deal with committees "be referenced only and the substances of same be appropriated from the Committee on Committees which has organized its work in a manner to acquaint, analyze, and compare the structure of committees utilized by other Constitutional Conventions in the past three to five decades." Simmons also tells us what her committee suggests: "The composition of these committees is recommended to be nine in number with the respective wards determining their representative and the body of nine, in turn, determining the chairperson."[9]

Our committee lays aside its pending business to consider this request. Several members speak against acceding to it. We are the Committee on Rules; therefore all rules, whatever their subjects, should be written by this committee. The committees on officers and committees should be required to make their recommendations to the convention through us, in order to ensure consistency among the rules.

I argue that with only a few days remaining, the ideal of formal consistency is a luxury we can't afford. We should be grateful that one of the other committees is willing to draft a portion of the rules.

But a motion is made to insist that we write all the rules, rather than deferring to other committees. This motion is carried overwhelmingly, only Long and I opposing it. I notice that Feely has prepared a draft on the subject of committees, which we had deferred until we heard from the Committee on Committees. It calls for the convention's permanent Rules Committee to propose to the convention a slate determining all committee memberships and it is silent on how the Rules Committee itself is initially to be selected.[10]

We return to Harris' list of "inconsistencies." She objects to the routine provision we adopted two meetings ago under which, if a quorum is not present, those who are present can set the time of the next meeting. She argues that when a quorum is not present, those who are present should have no power at all. Several of us ask how the time of the next meeting is to be determined, and she replies that the president should make that decision. Her proposal is narrowly defeated, four to five.

She has other proposals as well. There is, for example, a suggestion to permit delegates to edit their remarks before the transcript is circulated. This suggestion is dropped in the face of massive opposition to any tampering with the historical record.

The hour is getting late, and although none of Harris' suggestions have been adopted, other than the editorial change about introducing proposals, we have not yet begun to work on the evening's agenda. But Harris asks that we take up a question that was debated at great length two meetings earlier; she continues to believe that a mere majority of the convention should not be permitted to act, and that thirty delegates should be required for a quorum. My patience exhausted, I point out that this is a reconsideration, and that we cannot discuss it without first voting to reconsider it. We don't really have rules of procedure for our committee, so this objection, based on standard parliamentary practice, could be overruled, but somewhat to my surprise, Holmes says that I am correct. So a preliminary vote on whether to reconsider is taken. We divide along racial lines, and Harris prevails, five to four, Holmes breaking the tie.

This debate is prolonged, and it becomes apparent that we will not transact any other business this evening. The familiar arguments are trotted out: Fears of takeover by an unrepresentative bare majority versus fears of paralysis because not enough delegates are in attendance. At last it is time to vote, and I expect the vote on the merits to be the same as the vote on reconsideration–just enough to overturn the quorum rule that we had approved the previous week.

But there is a surprise. There are four votes for Harris, and four opposed. Everyone has voted as they did on the motion to reconsider, except that Charlotte Holmes has not raised her hand for either side. "Aren't you voting, Charlotte?" Harris asks.

"Do you see me voting?" Holmes shoots back. Harris glares at her, speechless.

*　　*　　*

Still another meeting, the following night. As we are assembling, Holmes reminds us of Simmons' request that we defer to her committee in its sphere, and says that we will do so unless there is an objection. None is made, but several members have not yet arrived. I wonder whether we are really through this storm. Harris is absent, and we go forward rather than backwards. Cassell is in attendance to present the recommendations of the Committee on Officers. We are to have a president, two vice-presidents, a secretary, an assistant secretary, a treasurer, and an historian. Collectively they will comprise an Executive Committee, the duties of which are defined only vaguely. I would like some additional time to think about the description of these duties, and perhaps to consult with other delegates, but my motion to postpone drafting this section for a day, until our final meeting, is trounced, six to three. Expeditiously, we draft Cassell's recommendations in the form of rules, and move on to other aspects of the rules.

There is one amusing incident. Cassell's committee has recommended that one of the president's duties be to refer proposals to appropriate committees, but in contemplation of receiving proposals from the public, Cassell's committee has not restricted the initial introduction of such proposals to delegates. I point out that every legislature that I know of requires its work product to be funnelled to it through its members, and that if a public proposal has any merit at all, or perhaps even if it does not, it will receive the support of at least one delegate. Feely agrees with me, and tells Cassell that this is no substantial barrier. "So when we get a proposal from the public, we can introduce it and pass it on to you for referral to committee." She has already elected him president.

*   *   *

Charlotte Holmes phones me at work the next afternoon. She asks me to run through with her what items remain for the final meeting, and I do so. At the end of the conversation, she asks me to draft a statement from her, to be attached to the package of proposed rules, thanking all the members of the committee for their help. "But," she adds, nearly causing me to drop the telephone, "the only ones that the statement is really for are you, Wesley, Charlie Mason, Robinson, and Harry Thomas. I don't owe it to anyone else. Harris had made it impossible to get anything done." I begin to wonder whether Holmes is more complex than I had first believed.

A few hours later, a white delegate calls to tell me what he has learned from a black delegate on the Rules Committee: a secret "black caucus" within the Committee has been meeting regularly. The source, whose name I never learn, has been meeting with the caucus, but is nevertheless disturbed. The purpose of the caucus, my informant was told, is to ensure that the black members of the Committee control the Committee's decisions.

The final meeting of the Temporary Committee on Rules and Calendar begins at five p.m. My secretary has typed up what we have done so far, but we need to finish by nine so that final changes and additions can be added and the entire package duplicated for distribution to the delegates at the swearing-in. They will need to have it then if they are to begin debating it on Sunday, for the package will run twenty pages.

The meeting runs smoothly, and we complete the agenda. Nothing has been said about the missing section on committees. I make a motion to adopt the rules as we have drafted them. The members begin to move back their chairs, and to stand, the vote being uncontroversial and pro-forma, and it looks as though our committee will end on a quiet note.

But Wesley Long is compelled by his conscience to make a statement. He will vote for the rules, he says, but he doesn't agree with every one of them, and he reserves his right to object to a few of them on the floor.

"Oh, I agree with that and I reserve the same right," Feely says with some heat.

Other members ask her what is bothering her, and she points out that we never considered her presentation on the rules governing committees.

Confusion breaks out. Some members say they didn't realize we had overlooked it, and that we should turn to it immediately. Others say that we had voted to defer to Simmons' committee. Still others recall the vote not to defer. I recall Holmes' statement at the previous meeting that we would defer if no objection was made. But those who are most vocally supporting Feely were not there when Holmes spoke.

One of the delegates moves to adopt Feely's presentation as a section of the rules. This would be a disaster, because at this hour there is no time to debate it carefully, and it would probably be approved without the kind of complete and careful study that we have given the other sections. Quite apart from the fact that her proposal to have the Rules Committee nominate the members of all other committees is entirely at odds with the Simmons-Love plan to decentralize committee appointments, it is likely to have all kinds of kinks that need to be worked out. I counter by pointing out that there is already a motion on the floor to adopt our proposed rules as a committee recommendation to the convention.

Holmes agrees with me, and the committee must take its final vote. The tally is five to four in favor of adopting the proposed rules as a committee recommendation. For some reason, Feely abstains; had she voted against the rules, our entire product would have failed. Too close for comfort.

The temperature in the room has risen appreciably, and Clarke tries to cool things down. He asks Feely whether she wants the committee to work on her section on committees, declaring himself ready to go to work. But she says that she has an appointment and cannot work any longer this evening.

She leaves, but discussion of working on her section continues. Several delegates propose meeting again after the opening of the convention.

I am eager to keep this committee's gloves off the Simmons recommendations and seek a principled ground on which to do so. I think I find one, based on my consistent position that we should respect a sister committee's request for deferral. I announce that because I hold this view, I would not be able to attend a meeting called to replace Simmons' recommendations with our own.

It is a colossal blunder, and the roof collapses at once. Harry Thomas, an elderly black member who has always voted against my position but who has never been obstructive or hostile, is deeply offended. "You're getting yourself in deep trouble on that," he warns me, wagging a finger. "By saying that, you have just polarized this convention, and I deeply regret it. I am going to have to fight you on that, on the floor and in every way I know how." Other members also attack me, and even Charlie Mason says that I am "way off base."

I keep my mouth shut to avoid deeper insertion of the foot. The group agrees that, if Feely so desires, it will meet with her on Saturday night to work over the ideas on committees. I know that if the meeting takes place, I will have to be there.

*   *   *

I arrive early Saturday afternoon at the Dunbar Senior High School, all the existing copies of the proposed rules in my fat briefcase. The auditorium is beginning to fill with the relatives and other guests of the delegates. On the stage are rows of wooden chairs for those who are to be sworn in.

I am tired. The Council's Xerox machine kept breaking down, and its collator failed altogether, compounding the problems of an unexpectedly late start. Charlie Mason and I didn't finish copying, collating, and stapling the proposed rules until two in the morning. But I see the brass band and the colorful flags that have been provided by the Mayor's office, and I have to chuckle at how much toil and conflict is concealed behind the bunting and oratory of political celebrations.

I mount the stage and place a copy of the proposed rules on each chair; against all odds, our committee has met its deadline. Someone else, from the Committee on Committees, has brought a proposed insert, so the package is complete. Indeed, a member of the Rules Committee tells me that Feely is no longer asking for another meeting, although the resentment she harbors may still be considerable.

A *New York Times* photographer asks if I will pose for a picture. It is not particularly easy to say no to having one's picture in the *Sunday Times*, but it is not hard to picture the explosion if I am the delegate whose picture appears. In the back of my mind, my source warns me away. Besides, there is better use to be made of the space. Hilda Mason is the delegate whose picture you should take, I tell him. The *Times* should have the leader of Washington's statehood movement. He agrees to wait for her arrival, and hers is the image that appears.

The hall is nearly full, and the last delegates to arrive are finding their places on the stage. From somewhere above, bright lights go on, and television cameras begin to whirr. The District of Columbia Statehood Constitutional Convention is about to begin.

Hilda Mason

Notes to Chapter 4

1. *National Municipal League, Constitutional Convention Rules* (1970).

2. See, for example, the three-page Rules of the New Hampshire Constitutional Convention in *National Municipal League, Constitutional Convention Rules* (1970).

3. Letter to Hilda and Charles Mason from the author, Dec. 17, 1981.

4. Letter to delegates-elect from Joel Garner, Dec. 28, 1981.

5. The original members were Delegates Shelton, Long, Schrag, C. Mason, Robinson, Holmes, Johnson, Paramore, and Clarke. The members added by vote of the delegates-elect were Harris, Feely, Thomas, and Warren.

6. Pub. L. No. 93-198, § 412.

7. *DC Statehood Convention Delegates*, distributed at the meeting of the Temporary Committee on Rules and Calendar (Jan. 20, 1982).

8. Proposed Rule 9, adopted in committee, Jan. 22, 1982.

9. Letter to Charlotte Holmes from Barbara Lett Simmons, Jan. 26, 1982.

10. "Temporary Rules and Schedules," distributed by Jeannette Feely in the Temporary Committee on Rules and Calendar (Jan. 22, 1982).

CHAPTER 5

The Struggle over Rules

THE OPENING DAY

The convention's opening ceremonies marked an important moment in the history of the statehood movement. A Mayor of the District of Columbia was committing himself, by his personal presence and by his statements, to the objective of statehood.

The installation ceremony was held in the auditorium of Dunbar Senior High School, a mile north of the Capitol. The delegates were seated on the stage, alphabetically, in four horizontal rows. In front of them, where the television cameras could easily pick them out, sat the leaders of the government: the Mayor, the President of the Council, the court of appeals judge who would administer the oath of office, and even the Delegate in Congress who had been the most vocal opponent of the statehood initiative, Walter Fauntroy.

At the request of the delegates-elect, Mayor Marion Barry had issued a proclamation terming the day "Statehood Convention Day." In his proclamation, the Mayor officially recognized that the citizenry had elected delegates and given them a "mandate to write a constitution for statehood." He called upon all D.C. residents to join him in honoring the delegates on the "historic occasion" of their inauguration.[1]

The program for the ceremonies had been carefully arranged by the Mayor's task force to alternate speech-making with entertainment, much like a Fourth-of-July political program.[2] The invocation was given by Rev. David Eaton, a political ally of the Mayor who had recently been elected a member of the School Board. The invocation was followed by a flag ceremony, the presentation of colors by the D.C. Public Schools Corps of Cadets, and the National Anthem. The Proclamation was then read aloud, and Hilda Mason, the only delegate to speak, paid homage to the friends of statehood who were not delegates, many of whom were among the 700 people in the audience.

Council President Arrington Dixon gave a brief address, followed by a local soloist and a spiritual, Rodgers' "Climb Every Mountain"; the latter was undoubtedly a musical allusion to the uphill battle for statehood that was still continuing. Then Delegate Fauntroy rose to speak, and the political reporters present became more attentive, because the day's only news, apart from the set-piece of the ceremony, might lie in the degree of commitment to statehood that the once-hostile Fauntroy might now make. Fauntroy chose not to make headlines, however, delivering instead a warm but not effusive speech in which he called the convention a "new chapter in our continuing struggle for self-determination." In a reference to his support for a constitutional amendment to give voting representation in Congress to the District as an alternative to statehood, he noted that "[s]ome say full voting rights is incompatible with" statehood. But he left his own position somewhat ambiguous, neither backing away from his support of the amendment nor proclaiming the two efforts compatible and worthy of simultaneous support. "Well, what we're saying," he continued, "is pass the buck [sic]—full self-determination for the citizens of the District of Columbia."[3]

After another musical interlude the delegates were sworn in, and Mayor Barry gave his address. He, too, obliquely referred to the cool support he and most other city leaders had given the statehood effort, and to the fact that the voters had settled the issue, at least for the moment. "Some of us came over on a ship called home rule," he said. "Some of us came over on a ship called constitutional amendment. And some of us came over on a ship called statehood. Well, whatever ship we came over on, we're in the same boat now."[4]

The delegates were called to the front of the stage where the Mayor shook their hands and hung red and white ribboned commemorative medallions around their necks, talismans that some of them were to wear to convention meetings for days to come.

A reception was held for the delegates and their guests, but as prearranged, the delegates slipped away after an hour and a half, and returned to the auditorium for a pro-forma business meeting. The principal purpose of the meeting was to set formally a time and place for the first real session, but the delegates also adopted Robert's Rules as their temporary rules of procedure and elected a temporary chair and secretary. These temporary officers were, respectively, Lillian Huff, from the 51st State Committee, and William Cooper, a delegate from Ward Four.[5]

THE CONVENTION'S FIRST WORKING SESSIONS

The first real meeting of the convention took place the next day. It was held in the Council chamber, one of the few public buildings in the city available for use on a Sunday. The delegates had previously agreed, informally, that the first order of business would be to consider the rules that had been proposed by the temporary Committee on Rules and Calendar, but the session "became bogged down almost immediately in wrangling over procedure and the day's agenda."[6]

The parliamentary tangles that the delegates created for themselves during their first meetings are worth describing in some detail, for they characterize the manner in which the convention operated during its entire existence. In general, the delegates agreed that proper procedure should be followed, but despite the existence of written rules, delegates often lacked consensus about what the rules required. This was due in part to the delegates' unfamiliarity with parliamentary rules and in part to the fact that no rule system can either cover all cases or avoid giving clever advocates the opportunity to argue that each of several mutually inconsistent rules apply to a particular case.[7] The account of the first two meetings which follows, however replete with the mundane detail of motion and counter-motion, is actually a simplified, streamlined summary of what actually occurred. The minutes showed that at the first and second meetings, respectively, no fewer than thirty and twenty-seven motions and amendments were made and voted upon. In fact, the number was nearly twice as high, because the minutes do not include the making or passage of motions to move the previous question. By the third meeting, this number jumped to seventy-two, again exclusive of motions to close debate.[8]

This first meeting was derailed at the very outset because although the meeting started forty minutes late, the minutes of the previous day's pro-forma meeting were still being duplicated.[9] Marie Nahikian, who had served as chair of the temporary Committee on Resources, asked permission to make a report from her committee while the delegates were waiting for the minutes to arrive. But temporary chair Huff, in the first of a long series of rulings revealing that she, as much as any delegate, believed in adhering strictly to rules of order, regardless of the practicality of their application or the informally sensed mood of the body, determined that the report would be out of order because it was not on the agenda. In fact, no agenda had been formally adopted, but there had been an informal agreement that consideration of the proposed rules would be the first order of business.[10]

One of the delegates appealed the ruling of the chair, but the chair was sustained. The minutes arrived and were approved, and to avoid another dispute about the agenda, a delegate moved that the next order of business be the adoption of rules. Another delegate offered a substitute motion, however, to proceed with the rules after first allowing fifteen minutes in which final reports of the pre-convention committees would be presented.

This proposed substitute created considerable confusion. One delegate claimed that the substitute was improper because the "maker of the motion is attempting to adopt a motion and also suspend the rules. They should be separate items." After some debate, however, the substitute motion carried. Despite the fact that this action explicitly provided for fifteen minutes of committee reporting, a new motion was made to permit such reporting. It was passed, but even this double action did not end the matter; the Chair suggested that "to be more comfortable, let us 'reaffirm' the Agenda at this time." The motion carried for a third time.

The outcome of this series of motions resulted in still another problem. A delegate claimed that the committees that were scheduled to report as a result of passage of these motions had gone out of existence at the time of the inauguration; more motions would therefore be needed to reconstitute the temporary committees for fifteen minutes so that they could report. In response, a motion was made to permit the temporary committees to "remain in effect until their reports have been disposed of"; this motion was countered by a substitute under which the committees would be "reconstituted for the sole purpose of giving the reports at this meeting and . . . dissolved at the conclusion of their reports." After several minutes of debate, memories had faded with respect to the wording of the substitute, so the Secretary was asked to restate it. His restatement was incorrect and was rejected by the chair; the movant restated the substitute motion correctly, an oral vote was inconclusive, and the chair asked for a roll-call vote, which, despite the close division on the oral vote, produced a thirty-eight to five vote in favor of the substitute. By this point, the delegates had already produced forty-six pages of transcript.

But the problems were only beginning. Four pre-convention committees indicated a desire to report. The delegate who gave the first of the reports used her time to point out that the work of her temporary Committee on Resources had not been completed, and that it might be desirable to do a mailing to survey available resources. Another delegate responded with a motion to establish a temporary committee to undertake this task, but the chair ruled that any motions would be out of order, because the agenda contemplated only the receipt of reports, not consideration of recommended action. In the midst of requests for clarification of this ruling, a delegate made the point of order that the fifteen minutes allotted for all four reports had expired, to which the chair responded, "let's not get pickie" [sic], and then permitted additional reporting.

When the time came for consideration of the proposed rules of the convention, delegate Clarke noted the need for someone to make a presentation to the body. In proposing that Charlotte Holmes, the chair of the pre-convention Committee on Rules and Calendar, make the presentation, Clarke made an inartfully drafted motion that generated fresh difficulties. He moved that Holmes "chair the preconvention rules committee when [the rules] are presented to us." Other delegates, fresh from the battle over reconstituting committees, were quick to notice that Clarke had proposed that Holmes chair a committee no longer in existence. One delegate, believing she had a procedurally better way to accomplish the same result, offered a substitute "that first of all we establish a temporary rules committee."

Another delegate suggested that all five committees still had work to do, and proposed an amendment to the substitute that would reconstitute all five of the temporary committees. Still another delegate objected, claiming that both motions would require a suspension of the rules (pursuant to a two-thirds vote), because the agenda required moving directly to consideration of the proposed rules. The chair overruled the objection, and another delegate offered an amendment to the substitute motion to provide that the temporary Rules Committee would dissolve when the rules were adopted. This motion failed for lack of a second, although several delegates attempted to second it when the chair announced the result.

A delegate next moved that Holmes "proceed to give us some information about rules," a motion that the chair allowed despite the pendency of another motion. An effort to offer a motion to require Holmes to deal with calendar issues before rules issues was turned aside because of the pending motion, but an amendment to permit Holmes to call upon other delegates to help her present her report was allowed and carried.

This amended motion to have Holmes report the proposed rules was at last adopted.

Almost immediately, however, the delegates began to disagree about what they had just done; that is, whether Holmes' "report" on the rules could include motions to adopt rules as they came up in the report. A motion was made to confine Holmes to reporting and to defer section-by-section consideratIon until the following meeting. The delegates were by time wearying from several hours of procedural debate. The motion carried, and finally, to the accompaniment of "vigorous applause in unison," Charlotte Holmes rose to report.

Within moments, Holmes' report was interrupted by a barrage of questions about the justifications for her committee's recommendations. After perhaps half an hour of questioning which never got beyond the first few sentences of the lengthy package of draft rules, the delegates realized that they were not going to get far. A delegate moved to adjourn the meeting until two days later, and other delegates grafted to this motion various amendments as to time and place, and various procedural motions such as a motion to divide, so that by the time adjournment was agreed to, about an hour later, the delegates had produced another forty-seven pages of debate just on the question of adjournment.

The convention's first meeting thus came to an end without a start having been made on actual consideration of the proposed rules, and with four-and-a-half hours having been taken up with parliamentary squabbles over the most trivial matters. The day's efforts did not augur well for the future of the convention, which, after all, would eventually be considering matters of political principle on which members would have very strong feelings. Some of the delegates undoubtedly believed that the first few meetings, in which delegates still did not feel they knew each other, could be expected to be uncharacteristically difficult, but many were alarmed by how little had been achieved in the session. "If this is what we're going to be doing, I'm greatly disappointed," one of the delegates told the press.[11]

The second meeting showed little improvement in the convention's ability to conduct its business. Although the delegates began to debate and adopt their permanent rules, in five hours they were able to complete work on only the first four-sentence subsection of the first proposed rule. This constituted only half of the first page of the thirty-page amalgam of rules proposed by the temporary committees on rules and committees. Again, parliamentary tangles contributed to the slow pace, but policy disagreements about the procedure and organization of the convention also played a major role.

The meeting began with a motion to adopt the first subsection of the proposed rules, the titles of officers and procedures for electing them. Immediately, a point of order was interposed, noting that the convention had previously agreed to hear a report on the proposed rules before taking action on them.[12] The validity of this objection was unclear. The minutes of the previous meeting, which had just been approved, showed that *after* the convention "received" the rules "report," it had then agreed, rather inconsistently, to "receive" the "report" on rules, adjourn, and reconvene two days later.[13] There was nothing to indicate whether the act of receiving the report was an instantaneous one that would be achieved prior to adjournment, or a continuing matter that could consume hours of the following meeting until the Rules Committee deemed its report to be complete. In any event, the temporary chair of the convention sustained the point of order on the ground that the report of the Rules Committee had not yet been completed, and a motion to suspend the rules to permit the body to begin to act was defeated. Thus, members of the committee began to answer questions about the proposed rules.[14]

As the process of question and answer continued, several delegates' frustration with the pace of the process appeared to increase. A motion to limit further reporting on the proposed rules to thirty minutes was carried by the necessary two-thirds vote. But the questions raised in the next half hour stimulated still further questions, and when the time limit expired, many delegates still had questions that had not been asked or answered. Motions were made to extend the reporting period, one of them by a delegate who originally had advocated bypassing the report altogether in favor of beginning the voting process, but these were defeated.[15]

More than two hours had passed. Evidently trying to establish a definite and orderly timetable, a delegate moved to have the convention establish "special orders" for itself—a device in Robert's Rules whereby a body can force itself to take up questions at a particular date and time.[16] His proposal was to vote at 8:30 p.m. (about half an hour from the time the motion was made) on the first subsection and, the titles of officers having been identified by adoption of those sentences, to elect permanent officers of the convention one hour later.

The presiding officer ruled this motion out of order, again citing the fact that, under the previously adopted agenda, the only business in order was to continue to hear the report on rules, time for which had not quite expired. The movant appealed, claiming that a motion to establish special orders took precedence, and this time the chair was overruled. The effect of the vote was, of course, not to approve the motion, but only to put it on the floor.

In the debate that followed, those who took the floor to speak opposed the motion. They argued that it was pointless to elect officers when only the titles of those officers, and not their duties (which were described in subsequent subsections of the rules), would be known.[17]

A motion to divide the proposal was made and carried, requiring separate votes on setting specific times during the meeting for voting on the first subsection and on electing officers. Both portions of the divided motion required two-thirds vote to be carried.[18] The first portion received the necessary margin, with one vote to spare, but although a majority of the convention favored proceeding that very evening with the election of permanent officers, this second part of the motion failed to receive the necessary special majority.

With this digression disposed of, the first real issue reached the floor. Jerry Moore, a Council member, moved to amend the first subsection of the proposed rules to provide that officers be elected by secret ballot, rather than by an open roll-call vote. The issue was debated at some length, proponents of the amendment stating that post-election relationships among delegates would probably be more harmonious if the voting for officers were secret, and opponents arguing that delegates owed it to their constituents to let them know who they had voted for to lead the convention. The secret ballot amendment was defeated on a roll-call vote, twenty-six to seventeen. One odd feature of this roll call, remarked upon by a delegate later in the meeting, was the high degree of correlation between the race of the voter and his or her position on this relatively minor procedural issue. Although a black delegate had sought the amendment, all but two of its supporters were white, and all but one of its opponents were black.

The final issue for the evening was the list of officers to be created by the convention. The Rules Committee had proposed that, among other officers, there be two vice-presidents. A third was added during the floor debate, and the convention authorized itself, in its discretion, to elect a delegate as "honorary chair." This latter proposal generated some confusion, because this duties of the officer were to be specified in some later section of the rules, and some delegates declared that they could not vote on an honorary chair until after the duties of the office were specified. Though the first subsection of the first rule was finally approved, Delegate James Baldwin probably summed up the feeling of many others when, at the close of the meeting, he expressed his continuing dissatisfaction with the delegates' method of working: "I am sure that many of us see nothing wrong with spending five hours in adopting one motion, but I do, and I am going to continue to say it . . . [U]ntil we do something about this, we will be forever writing this Constitution."[19]

*   *   *

By the end of the second meeting, the pattern for sessions of the convention had emerged. The delegates placed consistent reliance on formal parliamentary procedure, with half or more of the actual debate time devoted to the making and determination of procedural motions, or to debate about the propriety of the procedures being followed. As a result, the adoption of the convention's own rules of procedure required a total of nine convention sessions (in addition to the weeks of work on these rules in committee) and was not completed until the eighteenth of February.[20] By contrast, the Alaska Statehood Constitutional Convention had appointed its rule-drafting committee on its first day, and the committee's proposals, presented to the convention on the third day, were approved a mere two days later.[21]

The long debate on rules was necessitated by the delegates' simultaneous adherence to two somewhat conflicting principles. On the one hand, delegates thought that their ability to be heard by the convention, and to represent effectively the interests of their constituents, required a set of rules ensuring widespread participation by all delegates, untrammeled debate, and many opportunities for the assertion of minority interests. Simultaneously, the delegates also recognized that to complete the work in ninety days, it would be necessary to create mechanisms that would delegate authority to the president and to committees, end debates, and permit the majority on an issue to have its way. The principal issues that were contested after the first two days emerged from these conflicting needs. The recurrent themes in these debates over convention procedure were the proper scope of presidential authority, protection of the rights of political minorities, protection of majorities from the possibility that a minority might gain momentary control, and the degree of control that the convention would retain over the actions of its committees.

THE CONVENTION PRESIDENT'S AUTHORITY

A major issue underlying much of the debate was the question of how much authority the convention was willing to vest in its president, and how much it would reserve to itself or assign to other centers of power, such as committees. The contest between those who believed that the convention required a strong executive and those who favored greater decentralization of power was played out with respect to several different issues.

Two of these issues involved the question of the president's appointive authority. The Committee on Committees (to which the Committee on Rules had deferred) had proposed to permit substantive committees to elect their own chairs. On the floor, a motion was made to permit the president to appoint these chairs. Proponents of presidential appointment argued that it was necessary to have a "strong person" as president, that the delegates should not "tie his hands," that the leadership of the convention had to be in "one place," and that the convention had to have "faith" in its president. Advocates of election of chairs by committee narrowly prevailed, however, after arguing that the convention's process should be "open, democratic [and] inclusionary," with a "maximum amount of participation" and that the members of a committee would be in a better position than the convention president to know who would be most capable. Similarly, the convention debated whether the president's authority to appoint "ad hoc committees" should be circumscribed by a limitation that these committees be "non-substantive." Those favoring the restriction feared that without it, this "carte blanche" power of appointment could enable the president to infringe on the authority or circumvent the privileges of other convention institutions. On this issue, the advocates of presidential power were successful.[22]

Several issues involved the degree to which the rules would explicitly constrain the president to observe the standard rules of fairness in managing debate. The Committee on Rules had proposed, for example, that the president "shall recognize all those who desire to speak unless debate is closed," and that the president would be barred from recognizing delegates during roll-call votes. It had also proposed that delegates be required to stand up to seek recognition, so that the president could not overlook an effort to gain the floor or be charged with such an oversight.[23] All of these provisions came under attack on the floor, with delegates who supported presidential power and discretion asserting that the language was unnecessary because "the President [already] knows what his role is," and because the proposed language "sounds like low trust level of the Chair's competence."[24] Two of the provisions were in fact deleted, but the requirement for recognition of delegates remained.[25]

The two most important issues of presidential authority involved the margin necessary to overturn his or her procedural rulings and the question of his or her tenure in office. Under Robert's Rules of Order, a simple majority of the members of a body is sufficient to sustain an appeal from a procedural ruling, and the Committee on Rules had proposed to adopt this same device for the Convention.[26] The proposal was strongly attacked; it was argued that "nowhere do you find a majority of the people being allowed to appeal the ruling of the chair. You appoint a chair because you have faith in him and he knows the parliamentary procedures. If and when you appeal a ruling of the chair, usually, for the most part, you require two-thirds [so that appeals are not lightly taken]." The committee defended its position on the ground that in theory, the chair was merely the servant of the body, which normally expressed itself by majority vote. A motion to change the required percentage to two-thirds carried easily, however, and probably contributed significantly to deterring later efforts to alter presidential rulings.[27]

With respect to tenure in office, the proposed rules were silent. Delegate David Clarke proposed that officers' terms be limited to one year (a proposal which would have required new elections only if the proposed constitution were defeated at the polls and the delegates were reconvened to revise it) and that the officers be subject to removal by a two-thirds vote. He and others argued that recall of officers was a traditional and fundamental right of public bodies. Again, the principal argument on the other side was the need to create a presidency that was powerful both in fact and in semblance. The motion failed, first on a tie vote by show of hands, and then by a one-vote margin on a call of the roll.[28]

THE RIGHTS OF POLITICAL MINORITIES AND MAJORITIES

The second prominent theme in the long struggle over the rules concerned the rights of political minorities. Without substantial disagreement, numerous procedural protections were embodied in the rules. These included assurance that any individual delegate could introduce a proposal, a requirement that a committee would have to invite that delegate to its meeting when it discussed the proposal, a guarantee that any member of a committee could file a minority report, and that the majority report would be held up for a day so that the minority report could accompany it thereafter, and a provision under which minority proposals from committee members could be moved as substitutes for majority proposals on the floor.[29]

Two other protections for minorities, however, were argued at some length. The first protection dealt with the procedure for terminating debate. Robert's Rules includes a privileged, undebatable motion for the previous question; it requires a two-thirds majority, which if attained, immediately closes debate on the question to which it applies.[30] The rule is problematic in practice because the motion is undebatable, and members of a body must vote on it without knowing anything of the content of the debate that they are cutting off (which might even include amendments that have not been proffered because their sponsors are waiting for recognition). Voters are forced either to take the chance that they will not hear something that they would have wanted said, if only to get other views into the open, or to take the chance that, if debate remains open, it will add nothing new. The rule is often harsh because it is surprisingly easy to obtain the two-thirds majority when a body is in a rush and does not comtemplate what it might be missing. Recognizing this, the convention adopted a temporary rule at one of its early meetings, which required the presiding officer to rule out of order a motion to close debate unless at least two proponents and two opponents of the pending question had been afforded an opportunity to speak. This rule was eventually made permanent, despite some objection that it would be "cumbersome" and would deny the motion for the previous question its traditional privileged character.[31]

The other controversial protection of minority interests involved a proposal that delegates be permitted, within ten days after the convention's close, to file dissenting or other comments in the official record. This suggestion was defended not only as a political right of a minority (akin to the right of a judge or member of a legislative committee to file an official dissent from a decision), but also as a tactic that could improve chances of ratification by enabling delegates to demonstrate to skeptical constituents that although they had gone on record in opposition to some aspects of the proposed constitution, they were supporting it as a whole. The proposal was suspect, however, because it was moved by Delegate Courts Oulahan, who had not been willing to support statehood publicly. The proposal was denounced as a way to give dissenters a "way to disrespect the vote" and "get on a TV program or in the *Washington Post*, and was defeated.[32]

The delegates also believed that the convention would require protection from majorities, because the majority present on any particular day might not faithfully reflect the sentiment of the majority of all delegates. This concern first found expression in the convention's determination that the motion for reconsideration, which under Robert's Rules may apply to any decision of a body, would, for the convention, apply only to "main motions other than those approving Constitutional provisions."[33] The effect of this rule was to protect a majority decision from being unravelled by a subsequent and different majority. An escape clause, should the convention make a grave error, was included by virtue of the provision requiring that all provisions of the constitution be open for amendment at a "second reading," although in fact the opportunity to amend on second reading was limited by many restrictions including a requirement for a two-thirds vote. The issue of protection for the majority next arose in the context of the size of the majority necessary for amendment of the rules themselves. The pre-convention Committee on Rules had recommended that the rules be subject to change (after special notice to all delegates and an opportunity for the permanent Committee on Rules to comment) by a majority of all delegates. While the recommendation required an extraordinary majority compared with the usual requirement that a mere majority of those present and voting approve a decision, the possibility of rule change was limited even more severely when an amendment was offered and approved requiring the votes of two-thirds of all delegates to change the convention's rules.[34]

These decisions paved the way for suggestions that even in the routine handling of the convention's business, temporary majorities needed to be checked. Although in most parliamentary bodies the quorum requirement is a majority or fewer of the membership,[35] and the Committee on Rules had recommended that a majority of delegates constitute a quorum, it was suggested that a larger proportion should be required. As the challenger to the majority requirement put it, "since 30 has been agreed upon by this body in an action to amend the rules, I would think that we would want at least that number to transact business. The business of this body is more important than the rules, I submit." The proposal was withdrawn after it was argued that this restriction would impose on the convention an "undue hardship,"[394] but its essence was reintroduced in a similar effort to ensure that only genuine majority sentiment could be expressed by the convention.

An effort was mounted to require an absolute majority—twenty-three votes—to pass any motion whatever. The delegate who made this proposal pointed out that with simple majorities required both to make a quorum and to carry a vote, it could happen that a mere twelve delegates (outvoting eleven others) could adopt an article of the constitution on first reading. Others pointed out, however, that under the proposed rule, a minority of one or two could block action by an overwhelming majority (of twenty-two), even on such privileged procedural questions as adjournment. The argument that eventually led to the defeat of the proposal was that if the constitution were ratified by the voters with low participation and a close vote, Congress might use the absolute majority rule as an excuse for rejecting the District's statehood application. If the delegates themselves were unwilling to accept a majority of those present and voting to conduct convention business, Congress could raise a strong argument that a bare majority of those present and voting should not be able to impose statehood on all the District's residents.[36]

THE ISSUE OF COMMITTEE CONTROL

In debating its rules, the convention expressed concern not only about its officers and its permanent and temporary majorities, but also about its committees. In adopting its rules, the convention took several actions to reduce the likelihood that an unrepresentative minority that happened to control a committee could either embarrass or steamroll the convention. A provision was included in the rules authorizing the convention to discharge any committee of any proposal before it. This provision was a "way of saying . . . that the committee could not control what was going on."[37] Committees were also required to report their work to the convention in the form of complete articles, rather than sections, so that the committees could not hold back part of their work and require the convention to vote on a portion of the whole without knowing what was coming next.[38]

The right of committees to hold public hearings was also a matter of concern. Recognizing that some control over the power of committees to attract press attention through public hearings might be desirable, the Committee on Committees had recommended that notice of proposed hearings be filed in advance with the president.[39] The convention regarded this as insufficient protection, rebuffing the view of one of the proposal's authors that "we sort of thought the committees would probably be responsible."[40] The convention required that all proposed hearings be approved in advance either by the convention or its Executive Committee, and that the approval of the convention itself be obtained before any committee be permitted to meet outside of convention headquarters, as for example, in the neighborhoods. Finally, two relatively minor aspects of the rules were also designed to prevent committees from dictating policy to the convention. To discourage committees from holding back their recommendations until the last moment, and thus giving other delegates insufficient time to study them and to prepare proposed amendments, the convention imposed a three-day waiting period between receipt of committee proposals and the onset of floor debate. Finally, as a more or less symbolic demonstration of the convention's supremacy over its constituent parts, the committees were prohibited from meeting without convention permission while the convention was in plenary session.[41]

ELECTION OF THE CONVENTION'S OFFICERS

The long debate over the rules was suspended during a portion of the session on February 11 for the election of the Convention's officers. Two leaders of the statehood movement were nominated for president, Charles Cassell and Hilda Mason. Mason was nominated by Chestie M. Graham of Ward Six, who cited Mason's long record of service to the community in education, housing, and "all aspects ... of human beings living together."[42]

Like Mason, Cassell was an at-large delegate.[43] The son of a prominent architect who had founded Howard University's School of Architecture, Cassell had himself studied architecture and practiced his profession as a federal civil servant. In the 1960's, he had met Julius Hobson and had become an ardent supporter of statehood and an activist who opposed freeways and other congressional initiatives that appeared to be harmful to the interest of Washington's residents. At the time of the convention, Cassell was a member of the staff of the University of the District of Columbia. His passion, however, was jazz, and most of his outside energies were devoted to promoting jazz concerts through his organization, the Charlin Jazz Society.

Cassell had held public office once before, the result of a two-vote victory for School Board in 1968. He had run unsuccessfully in three elections after that.

Cassell was nominated by Samuel Robinson, who called him "a man whose history is rooted in statehood." After several secondary speeches on behalf of each candidate, Cassell was elected on the first roll-call ballot, by a vote of twenty-three to twenty-one.[44]

The election of the other officers followed immediately. A few of the positions were contested, but most of the other officers were elected by acclamation.[45]

Cassell delivered a short inaugural address at the following meeting, in which he declared his confidence that the convention's work would in fact lead to statehood. "I look forward to what we are going to do as the production of a document which will be accepted by the citizens," he said. "I also feel that there is no reason for us at this point to be doubtful about the possibility of the United States Congress accepting this."[46]

THE ISSUE OF THE BUDGET

When the convention completed development of the rules, it turned briefly to the budget, and in particular to the question of whether limits should be imposed on the number of days per week on which the delegates could collect the thirty dollars per diem stipends to which the initiative entitled them. The problem was that if all the delegates accepted their stipends, and if the stipends were payable for the entire ninety days of the convention, the stipends would amount to $121,500, leaving only about $30,000 (plus whatever the Mayor was willing to transfer from his own budget lines) to cover all the rest of the expenses of the convention. The convention's treasurer recommended capping the stipend expenditures by permitting delegates to receive the funds only with respect to days on which they attended plenary or committee meetings, and only up to five days a week, even if more meetings were actually attended. This motion was accepted, increasing the amount of funds available for other purposes to about $63,000.[47] Virtually all delegates continued to regard the budget as hopelessly inadequate in relation to the task, particularly because of the limits that it would place on the availability of staff assistance. Several went on the record to protest that adoption of a $150,000 budget should not be regarded as acquiescence in the Council's judgment that the task could be accomplished for that sum.[48]

Charles Cassell

THE FINAL TASK: FORMATION OF THE CONVENTION COMMITTEES

The final organizational task before the convention could begin to draft a constitution was the organization of its committees. Committee assignments were reported to the Convention by the various ward delegations at the convention meeting on February 20, the first meeting after the rules were adopted. At that time, President Cassell began the process of staffing the two operating committees (Rules and Calendar, and Style and Drafting) by announcing that a sheet was available for signature by volunteers.[49] Committees elected their officers at their initial meetings during the following week, and reported their elections at the next plenary meeting, on February 27. The organization process had taken a full month, twice as long as the "two-week" extension of the ninety-day limit that had been allowed by the Corporation Counsel's opinion. Nevertheless, President Cassell declared that the ninety-day clock would only begin to run on March 1, and he was never challenged on his implicit ruling that the law permitted greater latitude, even by a press that tended to be skeptical about the convention and statehood in general.[50] During the first week of March, he presided at a press conference at which he declared that the process of writing a Constitution was underway; the long countdown to May 29 had begun.

1. Proclamation of Mayor Marion Barry, Jr. (Jan. 30, 1982).
2. *See* Program, Installation and Opening Session, Jan. 30, 1982.
3. Valentine, "Close Ranks, Statehood Conventioneers are Urged," *Washington Post*, Jan. 31, 1982, p. D1.
4. *Ibid.*
5. Minutes, Jan. 30, 1982.
6. Valentine, "Disputes Snarl D.C. Statehood Convention Meeting," *Washington Post*, Feb. 1, 1982, p. D5.
7. The convention had a temporary parliamentarian, Associate Dean Warner Lawson of Howard University Law School, but Lawson, a volunteer, was not able to attend all sessions and was often not consulted by the presiding officer during those sessions he did attend.
8. *See* Minutes, Jan. 30, Feb. 2, and Feb. 4, 1982.
9. The events of this first meeting are found in the Transcript, Jan. 31, 1982, pp. 7-166.
10. *See* Minutes, Jan. 30, 1982, and Jan. 31, 1982.
11. Valentine, "Disputes Snarl D.C. Statehood Convention Meeting," *Washington Post*, Feb. 1, 1982, p. D5 (quoting Delegate Talmadge Moore).
12. Transcript, Feb. 2, 1982, pp. 16-18.
13. Minutes, Jan. 31, 1982.
14. Transcript, Feb. 2, 1982, p. 23.
15. *Compare ibid.* p. 19 *with ibid.* p. 75 (demonstrating change of position by Delegate Kameny); *ibid.* pp. 42-78.
16. Robert's, p. 309.
17. Transcript, Feb. 2, 1982, pp. 79-89.
18. Robert's, p. 157.
19. Transcript, Feb. 2, 1982, pp. 96-151.
20. Rules were debated at the meetings of Jan. 31, Feb. 2, Feb. 4, Feb. 8, Feb. 9, Feb. 11, Feb. 13, Feb. 16, and Feb. 18, 1982.
21. Victor Fischer, *Alaska's Constitutional Convention* (Fairbanks: University of Alaska Press, 1975), pp. 28, 32, 35.
22. Transcript, Feb. 4, 1982, pp. 67-71; Transcript, Feb. 9, 1982, pp. 26-34.
23. Proposed Rules (Jan. 29, 1982), § 8.4 (recognize all); 4.3 (barred during roll-call); § 5.1 (stand for recognition); Transcript, Feb. 13, 1982, pp. 79, 83 (purpose for standing).
24. Transcript, Feb. 16, 1982, p. 106 (president knows); Transcript, Feb. 13, 1982, p. 72 (low trust).
25. Rules, § 8.4; Revised Rules, § 5.2(B)(1).
26. Robert's, p. 220; Proposed Rules, § 5.2 (Jan. 29, 1982).
27. Transcript, Feb. 13, 1982, pp. 111-23.
It is possible that the outcome was influenced by the fact that an appeal from a ruling of the chair (to the effect that a previous resolution of the body to permit two speakers on every side of an issue, regardless of cloture, had been meant to apply only to the particular session at which it was approved) took place during the very debate on the appeal procedure, that the appellant (Delegate Long) was a member of the Committee on Rules and a principal defender of the committee's majority-rule proposal, and that his appeal was defeated only by a slender margin (14-16). Some delegates may have taken this event as evidence that a simple majority requirement would in fact open the floodgates.
28. Transcript, Feb. 4, 1982, pp. 165-78.
29. Rules, § 3.1, Revised Rules, § 2.7(A) (introduction of proposal); Rules, § 2.6, Revised Rules, § 2.7(H) (delegate at discussion) (as a practical matter, this forced committees to discuss all formal proposals sooner or later); Rules, § 2.9,

Revised Rules, § 3.2(A), (C) (minority report); Rules, § 2.9, Revised Rules, § 3.2(D) (minority proposal moved as substitute).

30. Robert's, pp. 168-69.

31. Rules, § 5.2, Revised Rules, § 4.2(G); Transcript, Feb. 13, 1982, pp. 100-01.

32. Transcript, Feb. 11, 1982, pp. 50-59.

33. Robert's, p. 268; Rules, § 5.2, Revised Rules, § 4.2(O).

34. Rules, § § 3.2, 3.3, Revised Rules, § 3.3(D)(3), (4) (second reading); Proposed Rules § 7.1 (Jan. 29, 1982) (pre-convention committee recommendation); Transcript, Feb. 16, 1982, pp. 50-57, Rules, § 7.1, Revised Rules, § 6.1 (adopted two-thirds rule).

35. Robert's, p. 294 (majority).
The quorum requirement in the Committee of the Whole, in which the U.S. House of Representatives does most of its plenary business, is 100 of the 435 members. W. Brown, *Rules of the House of Representatives*, Rule XXIII (2)(a), (1979), p. 553; Lewis Deschler, *Deschler's Procedures* (Englewood Cliffs: Prentice Hall, 3d ed. 1979), p. 543.

36. Transcript, Feb. 16, 1982, pp. 60-80.

37. Rules, § 2.8, Revised Rules, § 2.8; Transcript, Feb. 9, 1982, p. 73.

38. Rules, § § 2.7, 3.2, Revised Rules, § 3.1(A); Transcript, Feb. 11, 1982, pp. 15-16.

39. Report of the Committee on Committees, § 9 (Jan. 29, 1982).

40. Transcript, Feb. 9, 1982, p. 78.

41. Rules, § 2.10, Revised Rules, § 2.10 (hearing approval); Rules, § 2.10, Revised Rules, § 2.9(B) (approval to meet outside headquarters); Rules, § 3.2, Revised Rules, § 3.3 (three-day wait); Rules, § 2.5(F), Revised Rules, § 2.6(G) (no committee meetings during plenary session).

42. Transcript, Feb. 11, 1982, pp. 69-71.

43. The following biographical sketch was derived from Bonner, "Charles I. Cassell: A Study in Contrasts and Controversy," *Washington Post District Weekly*, Mar. 11, 1982, p. 1.

44. Transcript, Feb. 11, 1982, pp. 71-83.

45. The officers who were elected were Charles I. Cassell as president, James W. Baldwin as first vice-president, Janette Harris as second vice-president, Alexa Freeman as third vice-president, William Cooper as secretary, Richard Bruning as assistant secretary, Theresa Howe Jones as treasurer, and Victoria Street as historian.

46. Transcript, Feb. 13, 1982, pp. 10-11.

47. Transcript, Feb. 18, 1982, pp. 82-99; Statehood Convention Budget, Feb. 18, 1982, p. 1.

48. Transcript, Feb. 20, 1982, pp. 98, 107, 109.

49. Transcript, Feb. 20, 1982, pp. 57-72 (under the convention's rules, the ward delegations were to determine membership in the 10 substantive committees. Rules, § 2.3(A)(1)), 13 (staffing operating committees).

50. Transcript, Feb. 27, 1982, pp. 123-30.

CHAPTER 6:

The Struggle over Roles

I try to imagine what the audience sees—neat rows of officials and delegates listening intently to the opening day speeches, the Mayor shaking the hand of each founding mother and father and placing ribbons around their necks. But I can't see it myself. I am both short and alphabetically disadvantaged, and the bright television lights glare into my eyes. I stare resolutely into the back of the head of the delegate in front of me.

It is easier to look along the row that I am sitting in than to catch a glimpse of the ceremony at the front of the stage. Delegates in my row are seeing the proposed rules for the first time, having taken them from their chairs. They are holding the rules on their laps and, hidden from public scrutiny by the bodies of those in front of them, madly crossing out phrases and writing in new ones.

* * *

The reception is cheerful, an expectant prelude to the creation of a state constitution. Delegates walk their friends and relatives around the room to meet their new colleagues. After a while, we filter out of the crowd and return to the auditorium. We have agreed to meet for some housekeeping chores, but no preparations have been made, and we assemble in the back of the darkened room, in seats underneath the balcony. There is much milling about. No one knows what to do next, for Lillian Huff cannot call us to order until she is elected as temporary president.

It is a perfect moment for Hilda Mason to show some leadership, to stand and convene the group, and to preside during the election of Huff. Her taking charge would remind everyone that she is the symbol of statehood, the logical person to speak for the convention. But she remains in her seat, and it appears that in another minute or two Cassell will march to the front and get us started.

I walk over to Mason and whisper a few words in her ear. She steps to the front and convenes the meeting, but I begin to wonder whether she cares enough about being president to put together an election victory.

We have all previously agreed on the agenda and the outcome on each point, so it should take only two minutes to elect Huff, approve Robert's Rules as our temporary rules, and agree to adjourn until our first real meeting, tomorrow. In fact, the meeting takes forty-five minutes, for something unexpected happens. Departing from the script, Wesley Long moves to appoint Irene Morris, a non-delegate who has worked closely with Huff on the 51st State Committee, as temporary secretary, an office

Wesley Long

that has never been discussed. Barbara Lett Simmons puts another name in nomination—that of William Cooper, a young delegate whom I don't know at all. Cooper is asked whether he even wants to serve as temporary secretary, since having to take minutes may make it more difficult for him to operate on the convention floor. Cooper says that he would very much like to serve, and Morris' chance of being chosen immediately becomes zero, since no delegate is going to vote for a non-delegate over a delegate who desires an office.

There is a long, confused discussion, with several themes: Do we need a temporary secretary? Should a delegate be elected? Was Long's motion out of order because he put a name before the body (just like he had seen Feely do with Holmes) before we had agreed to create the office? Huff eventually rules the motion out of order. Long tries again, with a motion to open nominations to elect a temporary secretary. He is shouted down; nominations cannot be opened, either, until we have voted to establish the office. Once more, Long is recognized. He moves to elect a temporary secretary, and the motion carries unanimously. I am beginning to get an idea of what this convention is going to be like.

This time, Cooper is the only candidate nominated. It seems to me that everyone knows but no one is saying what is really happening—that although Cooper is being elected as temporary secretary, it is unlikely that anyone will challenge him for the permanent job once we get to voting on it. Unless he makes some terrible blunder in the next few days, he will be the Secretary of the constitutional convention. Nominations are closed and he is elected by acclamation.[1]

*   *   *

The first real business session, in the Council chamber, confirms my worst fears—and apparently those of everyone else—about becoming prisoners of parliamentary procedure. We seem to spend the entire afternoon arguing about whether or not motions are in order, whether some proposed action has already been disposed of by a previous motion, whether people will or will not be permitted to speak. All of us seem to want to move on and adopt the rules, but collectively we seem unable to get from here to there.

At the very beginning of the meeting, Huff refuses to permit Nahikian to make a report while we are waiting for the minutes to arrive, because it is not on the agenda.[2] Long appeals her ruling. He is correct but the convention trounces his appeal and upholds her. He does not lose because people think he is wrong; the point is a technical one, and it would take longer study than we give it for most of the delegates even to have a considered opinion. And he does not lose because the delegates do not want to hear from Nahikian while they have nothing else to do. Instead, it seems to me that Long's appeal is defeated because he is a white delegate challenging the parliamentary skill of a black chair, and in the opening moments of the convention, at that. Can the black majority perceive his motion as anything but an effort to embarrass Huff and thereby reduce her authority? The very taking of the appeal, regardless of its outcome, is one of a thousand small steps that is dividing this convention racially.

Late in the meeting, when delegates are asking members of the Rules Committee about the meaning of their proposals, I hear an interesting question from Rev. James Coates, a black delegate who has not been active in the pre-convention planning. He asks why the committee has proposed an open roll-call vote during the election of officers, rather than a secret ballot.[3] This is the single feature of our Temporary Committee on Rules and Calendar proposal that I am most uncomfortable with, and in view of the racial division on the subject within the Committee, it is good to hear that blacks who were not on the Committee are also concerned. It suggests that the provision can be reversed on the floor. I make a mental note that when the time comes, I should ask Coates to make the motion to reverse this decision; it will stand a far better chance if it originates with a black delegate.

* * *

Michael Marcus calls me after the session ends, overflowing with concern. A black delegate revealed to him during the meeting that sixteen black delegates had met the previous evening to work out a slate of officers to be supported and elected by the convention. Is this, I wonder, why Feely abandoned any request that the Rules Committee reconvene that evening to work on the rules for committees? The next day, Bob Love calls with another message. Five of the whites have now also met to discuss slate-making. Their plan is to develop their own slate and to negotiate the final outcome with the blacks. Their tentative position, on which they seek my opinion, is to support Mason for President, let the blacks pick their own first vice-president, and insist upon a white for second vice-president. I suggest that there are a lot of risks in negotiating between slates, rather than holding an open election. In particular, identifying Hilda Mason as the candidate of the whites could severely hurt her chances of winning the election.

* * *

The convention's headquarters are not ready for us by February 2, so we are back at the Howard Law School auditorium. The temporary parliamentarian, an associate dean, has to take time out from his official duties to ask delegates to avoid spilling coffee on the carpet. The meeting itself is a horror.

The convention's mood, which I share fully, is one of extreme impatience. We are anxious to begin voting on the rules, but Huff continues to rule that the agenda at this point contemplates only a report. Once more, Wesley Long jumps the gun, this time with a motion to suspend the rules so that we can begin to work. It is not as direct a challenge to Huff's authority as an appeal from her ruling, but Long has not learned: he still appears to be a white trying to instruct a black, in public, on how the agenda should be organized. For whatever reason, his motion is defeated.[4]

Charlotte Holmes is at the front of the room answering questions. When an inquiry concerns a section of the rules that some other member of the committee initially suggested, she calls on that member to respond. A curious dialogue takes place when Holmes calls on Gwendolyn Paramore to report on the proposed procedure for electing officers. "You had not finished your report [from the last meeting], so you have to come up and read your report," Holmes says.

Gwendolyn Paramore

"It has been read," Paramore replies, still seated.

"It has not been read," Holmes insists.

"The people can read the report for themselves," Paramore says. She makes no move to step forward.

Holmes seems annoyed that Paramore is leaving her to defend and explain the committee's work by herself. "Are you saying that you are not coming up to give or finish your report?" she asks.

Paramore smiles. "I am giving my time to you, as the chair, to use." Holmes has no choice but to speak for the committee herself.

There is a lot of discussion about how long the reporting will continue before we begin actual debate on the rules. I see that Rev. Coates is sitting by himself, and this is a good opportunity to ask him to make the motion for secret ballot election of officers. I decide to begin circumspectly.

"Jim, do you have a minute?"

"Sure, Phil," he replies in a smooth, drawn-out Southern accent. "What's on your mind?"

"I listened carefully to your question on Sunday," I tell him. "You wanted to know why the committee had recommended a roll call rather than a secret ballot."

"Yes, I did."

"I just wanted to tell you that I agree with you. I was on the committee that wrote the rules, and we were very closely divided on that one. But I agree with you. Whoever wins those elections, we'll probably all be able to work together somewhat better if we haven't . . . "

He stops me. "When I asked that question, I hadn't really made up my mind on the issue, Phil. And since then, I've thought a whole lot more about it. A whole lot more."

I know what's coming.

"And I've come to the conclusion that there ought to be an open roll call. That everything we do in this convention ought to be open and public. So I'm comfortable with what your committee did. I'm going to support the committee on that one."

"Well, thanks anyway," I tell him, and return to my seat. Someone has talked to him, I suspect. Someone has heard his doubts when he asked that question. Some person or faction is going to make sure that we have an open vote, so that black delegates won't dare vote against Cassell.

A tall delegate with black-rimmed glasses makes his way to the front. He has lost much of his hair, and this makes him seem older at first glance than he appears on closer inspection. Someone whispers to me that this is James Baldwin, formerly the director of the District's Office of Human Rights, a job now held by another delegate, Anita Shelton.

Baldwin makes a motion for a special order; if it's carried, we are to elect our permanent officers tonight, in an hour. A buzzing erupts among the white delegates, most of whom are sitting near each other. We are outraged by this sudden surprise. Obviously the black group has put their act together, while Mason and her supporters have not, and they want to win in a sudden coup.

Huff rules him out of order, surprising everyone. Baldwin appeals. Instantly I am faced with a dilemma. Baldwin is technically correct; his motion is privileged and he has a right to offer it. But the effect of Huff's ruling, if it is upheld, would be to stave off the immediate vote on officers; it would not even come to a vote. My sense of what is parliamentarily correct conflicts head-on with what I want to avoid.

I cannot bring myself to support a ruling that I know is wrong, and I vote for Baldwin's appeal. So do nearly all the black delegates and a handful of other white delegates. The appeal is successful; we are to vote on whether to elect officers tonight. Fortunately, Baldwin's motion will require a two-thirds special majority, and although the appeal succeeded by this margin, it did so just barely. If all the other votes stay the same, my switch will alone suffice to defeat Baldwin's motion.

The mood among the white delegates is one of increasing alarm, but we do not dare to say in public what we are feeling. A transcript is being made, and a *Washington Post* reporter is present. How can we say out loud that Baldwin's surprise motion makes us feel surrounded and attacked, and that in the context of Harris' surprise motion to enlarge the Rules Committee and rumors of black slate-making, it gives us the sense of being shoved around? How can we make them understand without embarrassing the convention in public and jeopardizing the chances of achieving statehood?

There is one white delegate, though, who is rarely inhibited from speaking her mind. She is recognized by Huff.

"Gloria Corn, Ward Three," Corn says for the record. The others of us from Ward Three shudder each time she reminds everyone of her association with us. "I get the distinct feeling that I am being railroaded and so do a number of other people. I would like to say this very clearly for the record, and I do not care if the press is listening or not."

Several delegates interrupt her, claiming that her remarks are not directed to Baldwin's motion and are therefore out of order. They are trying to prevent her from producing the next morning's newspaper story.

"Yes," Corn continues, "the motion is a railroad operation, and if a sizeable minority of us dissent from it and officers are elected and rules are pushed through we are going to be unhappy throughout this entire convention."

Corn is gavelled out of order and forced to sit down.

Two other white delegates make short speeches against the motion, arguing that it is pointless to elect officers before adopting the rules that define their duties. But the speeches only harden the delegates' positions. Huff asks us to stand to be counted. A massive number of black delegates stand to support Baldwin's motion. What seems by comparison like a handful of white delegates, plus Hilda Mason and perhaps two or three other blacks, oppose it. To my surprise, Charlotte Holmes is one of those dissenting black delegates.

The move to elect officers right away easily gets a majority, but it fails by a slim margin to achieve two-thirds.[5] Baldwin appears disgusted. A white delegate tells me, "That's all the power we have in this convention, the power to stop whatever takes a two-third vote. Like closing debate. You better start learning how to filibuster."

There is a recess. In the lobby, Hilda Mason whispers to me, "I'll bet a thousand dollars that nothing comes out of this convention."

* * *

The recess has done little to cool the angry atmosphere in the meeting hall, and the very first item of business is debate on the secret ballot issue. Mason has persuaded her colleague, Council member Jerry Moore, to make the motion to keep the ballot secret.[6] Perhaps that will persuade some of the blacks that this is not an issue on which the races have different interests. The debate is not encouraging. All the speakers favoring Moore's motion are white. All those opposing it are black. Coates speaks, and although he acknowledges that a "lingering bitterness" may follow the election, he says that there is an overriding "principle of openness."

A "lingering bitterness" pervades even this debate. At one point Long reports that this was an issue on which the Rules Committee was closely divided, six to five. Janette Harris rises to dispute his claim and says that the committee was unanimous in its support of an open vote. I become more angry about this history professor's distortion of history—of *my* vote in committee—than I am about the main dispute.

I hope for a surprise, but I don't expect one. Nor do I receive one when the roll is called. Every white but one votes for a secret ballot. Every black but Hilda Mason and Jerry Moore vote for an open roll call. Within the space of three days, the convention has become a gloomy affair.

The meeting continues with the question of what officers are to be created. The convention quickly approves the list recommended by the committee. At the suggestion of Chestie Graham, a black delegate, it also adds a third vice-president. Neither I nor those around me understand why this office is being suggested, but we see no reason to oppose it.

Then Jan Eichhorn proposes that we also authorize ourselves, at our discretion, to elect an "honorary" chair. I understand the purpose of this motion as soon as she makes it. She may have given up on electing Mason as President of the convention, and is opening the door for the convention to save Mason's face when it rejects her leadership. I am opposed to it at once, for the unthinkability of turning down the District's most prominent statehood advocate as leader of the convention is still one of Mason's strongest assets; Eichhorn's motion will undercut Mason's candidacy as well as save her face. I ask Mason whether Eichhorn has consulted with her before making the motion. She has not.

Everyone knows the purpose of this motion, but the rules of politics won't permit anyone to say it out loud. To the contrary, delegates ask what the purpose is, and even make it clear that they believe that some covert objective underlies the concept. "Believe me, we all know that something is going on," Michael Marcus says. "I think that we would all like to get to the bottom of that." Several delegates call for the duties to be spelled out before the position is created, but the matter is never clarified. A voice vote is held. I don't know what to do, and so I do nothing. The motion carries.

At the end of the meeting, Brian Moore rises to speak to the delegates. Moore, a young Irishman with a long background in neighborhood organizations, is serious and independent; what he has said, both in the pre-convention meetings and at these early sessions, suggests that he tries to think through every issue on its own merits. He seems curiously aloof from the hidden political agendas that the rest of us perceive swirling through the convention. Red hair glinting, he speaks the unspeakable.

"This has been quite a learning experience for me," he says. "More than I expected. What has been frightening to me is that the vote breakdown from a lot of these votes has been along racial lines." I am dismayed that a delegate would say such a thing on the record, from which it can be quoted in the press. He is hanging us with our laundry. A chorus of denials—"Oh, no," rises from the black side of the auditorium. But Moore perseveres, and it becomes apparent that his purpose is not to threaten the blacks with public exposure but to make a personal offering of peace and to ask other whites to follow him. "I think all of us have been supportive of ideas with regard to racial harmony. . . . I would encourage all of us to perceive the agenda and to perceive the way we go about things maybe differently, and possibly when we see something which we think goes against our conscience it may be more destructive from a harmonious standpoint in the long run. I know that I will reconsider my vote on a lot of issues because of the issue of harmony more so than my conscience or what's right or what's wrong."

Nevertheless, Moore's motivations may have little to do with the news value of his observations about the convention's voting patterns. Huff therefore hastens to correct—or perhaps to muddy—the record. "Mr. Moore, I don't think your observation is totally correct. . . . There will be times when you get to the substantive issues that the vote will be totally different. It depends on the issue and how strong people feel about it. It will also depend on where people live in this City, on a given issue. . . . I really hope that you do not feel like the votes are along racial lines. . . . I think you do not need to raise that perception."

Huff's speech blurs Moore's candid account of what is happening in the convention. But it is in the long-term interests of statehood not to contradict her, and I don't. Or is it just that unlike Brian Moore, I don't have the courage to say in public the things that everyone knows are true?

*   *   *

In the morning, the phone won't stop ringing. I hear the same gossip from half a dozen of the white delegates. The story is that during the meeting, Eichhorn learned from a black delegate that the convention's "black caucus" had decided on its slate of officers and had determined that only one white would be included—the token white would be Richard Bruning as assistant Secretary. She had quickly told several of the blacks that whites were furious about how the convention was going.

During the meeting's recess, the black caucus had met in a classroom, and it had summoned Eichhorn and Nahikian to meet with its leader, James Baldwin. As they had arrived to meet with Baldwin, the other blacks had filed out of the room, and it appeared that every black delegate except Mason and Moore had been part of the meeting, although it was possible that one or two others might not have been there.

The two whites had told Baldwin that continued racial division of the convention was unacceptable; in response, he'd asked what, specifically, the whites wanted. They had replied that they could speak only for themselves, but they thought that two conditions were essential. First, there would have to be two whites, not one, among the seven officers. Second, they knew that several whites were nervous about the potential power of Cassell, as president, to deny them assignments to committees on which they could make contributions. It was essential, therefore, to approve the recommendation of Simmons' committee that the membership of committees be elected by wards rather than appointed by the president.

Baldwin had said that those two demands seemed reasonable, but he had insisted that they speak with the other whites, so that the black caucus did not have to negotiate individually with each white delegate and be subjected to conflicting desires. The women had agreed to do so.

Then, in the meeting, Graham had moved, with black support, to create a third vice-presidency. To Eichhorn, this had seemed like a betrayal; instead of giving whites two out of seven officers, they now planned to give them two out of eight. In the morning, she had called Baldwin to complain, and to remind him that some of the blacks supported Mason for president. Baldwin had replied that creating a third vice-presidency was a course independently urged by Chestie Graham from which the caucus could not dissuade her, and that the blacks had decided reluctantly to go along with her rather than fight her in public. As for Mason, she had been nominated for president within the caucus but had lost to Cassell; caucus members were now bound to support the winner of that contest. Baldwin had reiterated his request that Eichhorn speak with the other whites. He had suggested that the whites appoint one or two negotiators to make a deal with black caucus leaders, on officers and rules, before tomorrow night's meeting.

For this reason, a meeting had been called for this evening, in Oulahan's law office. Mason and Jerry Moore had been invited, along with all the whites except Corn who, it was felt, might monopolize and disrupt the meeting. Mason and Moore had genuine commitments elsewhere, but it appeared that all of the whites who were invited would come. Would I?

This is easier for me to decide than it should be. I should object to the way this is happening and refuse to participate. Decisions of a constitutional convention should be made in its meetings, not in caucuses hidden from public view and particularly not in racial caucuses. By meeting, we whites are just adding to the racial bifurcation of the convention. But if we don't meet, we will have no way of knowing what we think collectively, or how to respond to Baldwin. And I would hate to be the only one who doesn't know what is going on. After thinking about it for an hour or two, I agree to go to the meeting.

*　　*　　*

Another phone call, just as surprising. Charlotte Holmes wants to know if I can give her an extra copy of the rules committee's proposals, but she lingers on the telephone to tell me what's been happening to her. "Did you see that, where Paramore refused to come up and answer questions last night? Did you see that? Do you know what that was for?"

"No. Why?"

"That's 'cause they won't have anything to do with me. Not at all. They don't socialize with me, and they won't talk with me."

"Who won't?"

"You know, the caucus."

"Aren't you a member of the caucus?"

"I was, but I'm not any more. I am in the doghouse with them. They're pissed off with me because I abstained in the committee on that vote on reconsidering. On the number for a quorum. They say I have no integrity. And last night I voted against them on going ahead and having elections for officers right away. So I'm in the doghouse twice now."

"If you're voting for what you think is right, then you're the only one who does have integrity," I tell her.

"Well I know that," she tells me. "I can't have people plucking my toenails off because I don't do what they tell me to."

I feel sorry for Holmes, and am surprised at how quickly I can feel sorry for someone that I regarded, only a week or so ago, as the embodiment of all the iciness that characterizes this convention. What courage it must have taken for her to break from the other blacks that night. Well, maybe it wasn't just courage. Holmes was the chair, trying to get something done, and maybe Harris had gone too far with her string of motions to reconsider, pushing Holmes over the edge. But it certainly took courage to break with the caucus a second time, and to open up a dialogue with me. I am encouraged; maybe there is some hope for this project yet; maybe this call marks a turning point, the first step in the disintegration of the racially-drawn lines of the convention.

*   *   *

I can't believe I am here. In the 1960's, I had a black college roommate, took a job with a primarily black civil rights organization, shared an office with a black colleague. Twenty years later I find myself a member of a white caucus. This can't be happening to me. I look at the thirteen other white faces around Courts Oulahan's conference table, and although I like every one of these people, I feel slightly ill. From what they say, I gather that most of them do too.

The irony of this situation is apparent to all of us. In most cities and states, blacks have often felt themselves politically disadvantaged because of their political minority and because of the tendency of some white politicians to organize their informal political groupings along racial lines, depriving the blacks of even their proportionate share of power. For years, many of us in this room have participated in voter registration campaigns, lobbying, litigation, and other political action designed to redistribute political influence in favor of those who have relatively less of it, and we have decried whites' use of race as a basis for political organization. But here we sit, united politically by the fact that we are white, experiencing the very sense of powerlessness that our black counterparts might feel at a constitutional convention in any of the fifty states.

We recognize, nevertheless, that although we hate being defined by the color of our skin, the only chance we have to make any changes in the way this convention is going is to have this meeting, to talk about it. It is not easy, however, because most of us seem ill at ease in our new roles as members of a powerless racial minority, and because there are many different definitions of the problem.

"The problem is the election of officers," one delegate says. "They've picked their slate now, and in addition to Cassell, it's Baldwin for the first vice-president and Harris for second vice-president. They want us to agree to a quick vote, and they'll let us pick two officers, the third vice-president and the assistant secretary."

"The fact that they want to negotiate means that they're not certain that they can hold their coalition together," responds another. "They want us to help them nail it down for Cassell by abandoning Hilda Mason."

"No, they haven't asked us to support Cassell. I don't think they expect us to back away from Mason. But they want the rest of it to go smoothly. And they want to put Cassell in quickly, too. It could be because there are strains within the caucus, but it also might be that Huff is calling the shots as she sees them, and they don't have the control over her that they thought they'd have. Remember, she ruled Baldwin's motion out of order."

"Mason told me today that if we all stay with her, she has the votes to win," someone says. "But I don't know. The pressure for loyalty to the caucus is pretty intense. Her black votes may just slip away."

Cokes are passed around the table and a different tune is struck. "The issue isn't this damn election at all. If we lose an election, that's just life. Just politics. It doesn't matter so much. The issue is whether racial division is going to permeate this convention. Whether the black caucus is going to pick the committee members, appoint all the chairs, and decide what provisions go into the constitution. The question is whether we're going to get cut out of this process. Whether we're just window dressing."

A delegate who has not yet spoken now takes his turn, and none of us has ever seen him so angry. His hand trembles, his fists are clenched. "The problem is, very simply, that they have no regard for us. No regard at all. The Baldwin motion to ram through the elections without telling us in advance, contrary to all the prior understandings about completing work on the rules first, is an outrage. A complete outrage. They have no sensitivity to the fact that we're human beings. That we have feelings. And that we don't like being kept in the dark, and excluded, and shoved around.

"I don't think we should negotiate with them," he says. "That's just playing their game, and it means a perpetuation of racial politics in this convention. By making demands on them, as they want us to do, we make it legitimate for them to continue to think about the process in terms of 'us' and 'them.' I think we've had enough of that."

"So what do you suggest?"

"I'll vote for Hilda because I'd like her to be president, and because I could never vote for Cassell after this," he replies. "But for the rest of it, I think we should just give it to them. We should tell them that they have all the power. They can have any officers they want and run the convention any way they want. But the choice is theirs as to whether we have a constitution or whether the whole thing goes down the drain."

"That's like telling Santa Claus, 'bring me what I want but I won't tell you what it is,'" a woman objects. But I am already sold on the idea of not negotiating and so are most of the others. Not the least of its attractions is that negotiating tends to imply that this de facto white caucus will continue to have to meet, an abhorrent thought. Taking what now gets tagged the "position of principle" holds out the possibility, at least, that the white caucus will never meet again.

I point out that, in addition, negotiations can't possibly produce most of the safeguards that we'd want, because the presidency is not negotiable, and the president will have enormous personal power. Either alone or with the Executive Committee, which the caucus will control, the president will be the point of contact with the press, the person who hires all the staff, the person who decides which committee considers each proposal, the one who sets the agenda of meetings and the person who either does or does not fairly recognize all those who want to speak. And by listing "demands" with respect to the rules—for example, by insisting on support for the recommendation that committees elect their own chairs—we would be telling the caucus exactly how to reduce our influence if the negotiations break down.

There are some who are unconvinced. "Giving up isn't how the game of politics is played," they tell us. "They've given us an opening to play a role, within the structure of negotiations. We shouldn't throw it away. In fact, it would be disrespectful to the caucus, and an insult to the blacks, to refuse to respond to their request that we negotiate."

This argument moves us a little, not to the point of listing demands and negotiating, but to the point of responding to the caucus. We decide not to insist on particular officers or rules, and we take no position as a bloc, either for or against the caucus slate of officers. But we draw up a list headed "Delegate Concerns," and Alexa Freeman is appointed to hand it out to all delegates as they enter the next meeting. To demonstrate respect for the leadership of the caucus, which had asked us to present demands and appoint negotiators, Freeman will also telephone Baldwin to tell him that the list is coming, and she will offer to meet with him, if necessary, to explain it. Not to negotiate, but only to explain.

We work over the list. When it has been completed, I realize that the tactic we have adopted is not so unfamiliar a response to overwhelming power. It is the bureaucratic equivalent of nonviolent resistance, of going limp in the hands of brutal cops. "A demonstration of goodwill," says our list. "Open communication. Fairness, democracy, harmony and justice. Openness, fairness and maximum participation." The final item on the list is our suggestion that we have a party for all delegates. We are throwbacks to the sixties, stuffing flowers into the barrels of guns.

Toward the end of the meeting, Oulahan has to leave for another engagement. As he is about to depart, his hand on the door of his conference room, this conservative Republican turns and casts a some-what sheepish smile to the assembled group of leftist Democrats, socialists and gay rights leaders. "The room is yours as long as you want it," he says. "I want you to know that I think this is a really terrific group. I trust you a lot. Whatever you agree to do, you'll have my support."

*   *   *

The call to Baldwin is made, and he shows no interest in meeting. The list of concerns is distributed at the beginning of the meeting, and it seems to sink without a trace in the sea of procedural minutiae constituting the business of this session. The meeting starts out badly, with Corn enraged when she learns about the meeting of the white delegates from which she was excluded, and with yet another procedural surprise. Jackson, the Communist delegate, complains that debate over the rules is taking too long; he moves to restrict debate on each proposed amendment to three speakers per side and five minutes per section of the rules. Kameny seeks to speak on Jackson's proposal, and when Jackson claims it is undebatable, Kameny explodes, warning that the convention will be "seething with resentment" if debate is so restricted that people are routinely prevented from speaking. We descend again into the whirlpool of Robert's Rules. There are amendments to Jackson's motion, substitutes for it, and motions to divide it. Huff has to resort to a blackboard diagram to explain the many pending motions. Forty-five minutes later, the convention votes to abandon the whole effort and return to the business of debating the rules.

The tone of the meeting improves gradually, and we make better progress. The pace picks up another notch as delegates tacitly agree that no one will second the frequent spur-of-the-moment amendments that Corn is in the habit of offering. There is, nevertheless, an undercurrent of distrust which surfaces whenever a proposed rule touches the distribution of power within the convention or the rights of political minorities to be heard. The working assumption is that Cassell will be president and that the caucus will be in control. There are a few efforts by whites to whittle down presidential authority, such as Love's proposal to permit the president to appoint ad hoc committees only if they are "non-substantive," and Oulahan's motion to authorize the president to speak for the convention only "in accordance with policies approved by the convention." The blacks usually make each of these into an issue of trust, a vote of confidence in Cassell, and whenever they do, the whites' efforts are not successful.[7]

*   *   *

The next few meetings feel like slogging through slush. We have finally agreed on a particular date and time for the election of officers, in one week, so that no one will be taken by surprise. The politicking seems subdued, because the whites have no choice but to vote for Mason and little ability to persuade blacks to do so. Mason continues to claim that she has the votes and is protecting her supporters from pressure by not revealing their identities. I hope she really has the votes, but most of the whites don't believe she does. Holmes calls me to say that she is thinking of running against Harris for second vice-president. She asks for my vote and I gladly promise it to her.

In our consideration of the rules, we finally reach the section that has been reserved for the report of the Committee on Committees. The first big issue is which committees to create. Three of the committees that have been proposed deal with subjects that could be controversial and that don't have to be covered in a constitution at all: education, economic development, and health, housing, and human services. We all remember Arnold Leibowitz warning that the decision to create a committee is really a decision to have an article on that committee's subject, and several delegates suggest deleting those three committees on the ground that their areas of concern should be regulated by the legislature, not by the constitution. Regardless, I know that the arguments against having these committees have little chance of causing them to be deleted. Many of the delegates work in these areas, as teachers, for example, and they want to be able to contribute their particular expertise to the constitution. Moreover, some of us will support the creation of these committees just so that there are ten substantive committees in all. If one or more were deleted, there would no longer be any logic to selecting members by ward elections, and Cassell would be in a position to argue for presidential appointment. He would be able to play favorites. The ten committees survive the challenge, propped up by the power politics of this convention. We adopt the fiction that we are only giving "respectful consideration" to the subjects in the three areas, and that we may decide eventually to leave these subjects out of the constitution.[8]

Surprisingly, one of the most likely controversies never erupts. The proposal for each ward to divide up the committee memberships among its delegates, rather than permit the convention leadership to appoint delegates to committees, is quietly moved and quietly approved; there is not even a motion to alter it. Perhaps the list of "delegate concerns" has made an impact, although I doubt it. Perhaps the caucus is hedging against the possibility that Mason has the votes after all. Most likely, Cassell realizes that if he obtains the power to make committee assignments, there will be no end of squabbling, even among caucus members, and he would just as soon not have to deal with the matter.

But almost immediately, there is a serious fight over the related issue of how committee chairs are to be selected. The Committee on Committees has recommended that each committee elect its chair, but Harris moves to let the president make these determinations. There is a chance that Harris will lose. Although several members of the black caucus support her vocally, Barbara Lett Simmons defends her committee's product, and perhaps Simmons will be able to peel off enough members of the caucus to prevail. On the other hand, three white delegates have not yet arrived and their votes will be lost.

A standing vote is held on Harris' amendment. Not one white is among those on their feet to support it. The opponents stand, and they include a scattering of blacks. Harris' motion is defeated, twenty-one to nineteen. It is not the end of racial politics, for the whites voted as a bloc. But it may be a sign that the caucus will not permanently control the decisions of this convention.[9]

* * *

Election night.[10] Mason has told me during the day that she would be nominated by a black delegate, and that several others had predicted to her that she would be victorious. She wasn't claiming victory, and she knew that the election was very close, but she thought she could do it. Holmes called, too, and her contest likewise seemed to turn on one or two votes.

We have agreed that the vote will not be held until 8 p.m. to give everyone a chance to attend the meeting. Meanwhile, we continue to plow through the proposed rules. We are meeting at our permanent head-quarters in the old Pepco building now, and we are fairly cramped together. The enforced closeness is greater than ever tonight because as people drift in, attendance reaches a new record of forty-three. We have also picked up an audience of members of the public. The room becomes warm, and as the clock passes seven, the excitement of the impending ballot can be felt.

The two missing delegates are both supporters of Mason: her two fellow Council members, Jerry Moore and David Clarke. Clarke has sent her his regrets, having flown out of town for an unavoidable previous engagement. Moore had promised to come, but he has not arrived. More time passes, and there is a flurry of whispers among the white delegates. Someone goes out to try to call him. Rev. Moore is in a prayer meeting and cannot be disturbed.

The hour for elections arrives and Moore still has not come. Nominations are opened, and Chestie Graham nominates Mason. Sam Robinson nominates Cassell. As we get ready to ballot, the door opens and Jerry Moore strides slowly into the room. Had it been Jesus, the effect could hardly have been more electric. The convention utters a collective gasp.

Now there are forty-four delegates; Mason will need twenty-three votes to win, or twenty-two to deny Cassell a first-ballot victory and then pick off one more caucus member. She should have sixteen whites, plus her own vote, Jerry Moore, and Chestie Graham, her nominator. I have a hunch, based on the disaffection she has revealed to me, that Charlotte Holmes will vote for Mason. Can two more votes be found?

A few delegates offer speeches for one candidate or the other. There are no surprises, but Corn's speech for Mason is more insistent than most. "If you are in fact representing your constituents," she instructs us, "you must vote for one who came in with a higher vote count in every precinct in your ward." I try to imagine how I would feel if someone from another ward told me what I had to do to represent Ward Three. I can't imagine that she has won votes for Mason, and I hope she hasn't lost any.

The call of the roll is begun. Holmes does vote for Mason. There are no further surprises until the roll comes around to Norman Nixon, at nineteen, the convention's youngest delegate. Nixon passes until others have voted!

Anita Shelton votes for Mason, a surprise I hadn't anticipated, for she had been part of Harris' bloc through all the Rules Committee votes. And Harry Thomas, Nixon's political mentor and fellow delegate from Ward Five, also passes. I am counting rapidly. Each candidate has twenty-one votes; Nixon and Thomas will be the kingmakers, either way. Cooper, calling the roll as temporary secretary, calls Nixon's name again. Nixon looks at Thomas. There is a suspenseful pause.

"Cassell," Nixon says.

Thomas, too, is called a second time.

"Cassell," Thomas calls out.

The hall erupts in a hubbub. Cassell has squeezed out the twenty-third vote and will be president of the convention.

He asks Huff to continue to chair the election meeting and nominations are opened for first vice-president. Only Baldwin is nominated, and he is elected by acclamation, for there would have been no point in contesting his election.

Harris and Holmes are nominated for second vice-president. Most of the whites have had little contact with Holmes and have heard moderately negative stories about her stewardship over the Rules Committee, with all its racially divided votes. But Harris seems to symbolize, for most of them, all that has gone wrong in the convention, starting with what they regard as her "power play" to pack the Rules Committee. There will be a large bloc for Holmes; again the voting will be close.

The roll is called again. As in the Mason-Cassell contest, most of the votes are predictable, with whites and a few blacks—primarily her personal friends—voting for Holmes. Like the other delegates, I keep a running tally. The candidates are neck and neck throughout the call, but when it is over, Harris has won, twenty-two to twenty-one. Cooper announces a tie, however, with each candidate having twenty-one votes, leading to protests from several delegates who, like myself, have unofficial records showing a Harris victory. Delegates argue that Cooper must be wrong; there are forty-four delegates in the hall, and only Eichhorn abstained. Apparently Cooper mistook the word "Harris" for the word "pass" when Delegate Talmadge Moore cast his vote, but although Cooper supports Harris, he declines to correct himself. Huff is still in the chair, and rather than calling for the court reporter to read back the transcript of the vote, she calls for another roll call.

It occurs to me that the new roll call vote does not have to reflect what would have happened if Cooper had not erred. Harris' near victory was made possible because one white delegate, Janice Eichhorn, had abstained while all of the others voted for Holmes, and everybody now knows this. The pressure on Eichhorn is enormous. Will she abstain again, or will she deadlock the election and prevent Harris from winning?

When Cooper reaches her name, she pauses, and instead of abstaining, passes on the first call. When he comes to her name again, she passes a second time. And when he gives her one last chance to vote, she votes for Holmes, tying the election at twenty-two each.

The tension in the room is enormous. The bloc that had supported Mason is deliriously happy to see the caucus tie itself in a knot. The caucus group is furious at Cooper for counting incorrectly, and at itself for losing control of the convention just as it had seemed to have taken charge. A Cassell-and-Harris supporter makes a motion for a recess, which is carried.

Out in the corridor, the politicking is fierce. Cassell and Baldwin are trying to find one white or one dissident black to bring into the Harris fold.

William Cooper

Gloria Corn

A few of the whites are trying to find a black who will be willing to break with the caucus and run for second vice-president as a non-caucus compromise candidate. To judge from the intensity of the conversations, no one is budging. And then a remark is heard, which echoes around the crowd: Gloria Corn is nowhere to be seen.

The meeting reconvenes. No new candidates are nominated; we are to have a third Harris and Holmes ballot in an attempt to break the deadlock. There is a rumor, though, that if the balloting again ends in a tie, one or more of the less devoted caucus members will break with Harris and run on their own, ending Harris' chances of winning the position.

Cooper starts down his alphabetical list once again. Gloria Corn's name appears early in the order, and she passes, setting off suspicions that she alone among the white delegates may not vote for Holmes. Eichhorn, who had abstained on the first ballot and voted for Holmes on the second, also passes.

When the roll has been called, Cooper returns for the votes of those who have passed. Corn again passes, but Eichhorn votes for Holmes. Cooper calls Corn's name for the third and last time.

Corn is frantically examining her tally sheet, checking and counting. "Am I the last one?" she asks. Cooper indicates that she is. The count, without Corn's vote, is Harris twenty-two, Holmes twenty-one.

Corn completes her tallying and looks at Cooper. "Abstain," she says, and Harris is elected to the second vice-presidency.

The next position is that of third vice-president. There have been no negotiations with the black caucus, but they know that the convention will never survive the criticism of the press if no white is included among the three vice-presidents. Alexa Freeman wants the office, and to the best of anyone's knowledge no other white does; the caucus knows of her interest, and the expectation has been that the caucus would nominate her as the only candidate for the position.

Cassell is on his feet, signaling to Huff. "Madam Chairman, Madam Chair." She recognizes him to make the first nomination. He nominates Gloria Corn.

There is obvious consternation among the black delegates; they have had a hard time putting up with Corn's diatribes and repeated, time-consuming motions for the past several weeks. They want to follow their new leader, but they clearly have sudden doubts about his judgment. None of them calls him on it, but a white delegate does. "Oh, Charlie, how could you?" Richard Bruning says quietly, the slightest smile crossing his face.

I am sitting across the table from Cassell, and I take him to task more privately. "You know that Freeman would be a much better vice-president," I tell him. "This is a pretty smelly deal."

He looks at me severely, upbraidingly. "You had your chance to vote for a perfectly suitable candidate whom the caucus nominated for second vice-president," he says. "You had your chance, and you blew it. We had to do what we could to win without you. And I think that Corn will make a fine vice-president."

His face relaxes a little, and a little grin escapes. "Besides," he adds. "Just watch what happens now."

Hilda Mason is recognized, and she nominates me for third vice-president. I hastily decline, both because the job ought to go to Freeman if it goes to any white, and because even if I could win, it would be unpleasant beyond belief to have to assume the role of perennial dissenter in the Executive Committee that is taking shape. In turning it down, I counter-nominate Hilda Mason, who also declines. I am in no way surprised.

Marie Nahikian nominates Freeman, an apparently futile gesture. There is nothing to be done.

Baldwin rises to give a seconding speech. He takes my breath away; the person whose nomination he seconds is Freeman, not Corn. Slowly, I begin to understand what Cassell said to me. He must have promised Corn that he would nominate her, not that he could or would instruct the caucus to vote for her; she must have trusted him to make his nomination stick. Baldwin's seconding speech may be the signal to the caucus that it is all right to vote for Freeman.

A handful of other caucus members follow Baldwin's lead in seconding Freeman. Other caucus members, including Janette Harris, second Corn, though this maneuver by our second vice-president moves the delegates to laughter. Following this pattern, the caucus splits its votes between the candidates. With no votes from the white delegates but her own, Corn cannot put together a majority, and Freeman wins the election.[11] Red-faced, Corn glares at Cassell through the remainder of the meeting.

The other elections are unsurprising. When the final vote is taken, the Executive Committee looks exactly the way that the caucus had proposed it should look when Baldwin had talked to Eichhorn more than a week earlier. The two whites will serve in the token positions allotted them: Third vice-president and assistant secretary. There is at least one good thing about this convention. We whites are learning, and not in any shallowly intellectual way, what it means to be a racial minority.

* * *

Corn has no car, and I frequently drop her off on my way home after convention meetings. One evening I ask why she was willing to let Harris win the election. Was the third vice-presidency worth it, particularly in view of the distrust of her, from both whites and blacks, that she knew the deal would exacerbate?

"I thought that Harris was a better candidate than Holmes," she says. "She's a professor, after all." She pauses, lights a cigarette. "But I'll tell you. My main motive was revenge, revenge against all of you for not inviting me to your meeting. But in addition it wouldn't be bad to be an officer of a constitutional convention."

"What went wrong?" I ask.

"It all happened too fast," she answers. "Cassell just didn't have time to tell everyone to get in line and vote for me. He came up to me afterwards and apologized for not being able to deliver because there was so little time. He told me that he'd take care of me later on in the convention. You know what I said to him? I said, 'You're damn straight you will, because you owe me now, Charlie, and are you going to pay!'"

* * *

The debate over rules continues for three more sessions but is anti-climactic. One of the longest and most heated arguments, which I carefully stay out of, is the battle over whether the rules will require that each session begin with "prayer," "voluntary silent meditation," a "moment of silence," a "moment of silent prayer," a "voluntary moment of silence" or nothing at all. The convention includes both militant atheists and those who say that it is "beyond me that we, living in the United States of America, a God-fearing country, would delete prayer and ask that the Almighty be excluded from our deliberations." After much parliamentary maneuvering, beginning each meeting with "silent prayer" is approved.[12]

Compared to the struggle over prayer, the merely secular debates are easily settled. The final issue affecting the power of the caucus is the question of how the convention's rules may be amended. After the election, the white delegates have become jumpy: if the caucus could double-cross Corn, might it also double-cross the white minority by amending the rule that we have already passed which provides for wards to assign committee members and committees to elect their chairs? So long as the rules can be amended by a majority of the convention, the caucus can do anything it wants. A two-thirds rule would protect what we have gained, but how can we get it?

Surprisingly, Harris herself raises the issue. The rule proposed by the Rules Committee would permit amendments to be made by "the vote of a majority of all delegates." Harris misreads this, saying that the proposal "is that these rules may be amended by a majority vote of our delegates. This means that if a quorum is twenty-three and there are twelve people there, they can amend rules." She moves to replace "majority" with two-thirds.[13]

The proposed solution involves some overkill. A requirement of two-thirds of those present and voting is sufficient protection for the minority, and to require two-thirds of all delegates may demand such a high proportion—even exceeding 100% of those present at any particular session—as to make amendment impossible. But some of us see Harris' fear that twelve of us will be able to change the rules as our only hope of securing permanently the committee appointment system that we have embedded in the rules. We make no fuss. Her motion is carried easily. But other delegates also realize that Harris has misread the proposed rule. Considerable debate ensues over whether the number of delegates needed to amend the rules should be thirty or some smaller number. After two attempts to pass a number lower than thirty are rejected, the two-thirds figure is carried easily.[14]

* * *

Ward Three has a crisis. We have to apportion our five members among two groups of five committees. The second group may be relatively easy, but in the first group, Oulahan wants the Judicial Branch Committee; Corn, the Legislative Branch; Kameny, the Bill of Rights; Garner, Taxation and Finance; and I—I will take anything but Tax and Finance, which doesn't interest me as much as the others, or the remaining choice,

Executive Branch, whose work is more likely to be straightforward and uninteresting. The convention allows each ward to decide for itself the method by which it will assign its five members to the five committees. Garner, Oulahan and Kameny want to get it over with by having an election within the delegation: they will elect me to the Legislative Branch Committee and consign Corn, with whom they are now barely on speaking terms, to the Executive Branch. Corn argues, to deaf ears, that because she got a higher vote count in the ward than any of the rest of us, she should get first choice of committee assignments. If not, she says, assignments should be made by lot.

Further conflict in this convention, and a continuing feud within our own ward delegation, is not, I think, what we need. I push for a meeting of the ward so that we can all come to some agreement on committee assignments, but some of my colleagues are so angry at Corn for making a deal with Cassell that they refuse to meet with her.

One night, driving home from a meeting, Corn confides that she has attempted to solve the problem on her own. "Charlie gets to appoint the chairs of the two operating committees," she tells me. "He owes me, as you well know. He's offered me the chair of the Style and Drafting Committee.

"What I really want, though, is to be a member of the Legislative Branch Committee. I have a lot of ideas about how the legislature should be structured, and I want to run for a seat in it, when we're a state. With the kind of vote I got, I could win. Particularly if we make the districts small enough, so you don't have to be a millionaire to run a campaign."

"Statehood is still a long way off, Gloria."

"Sure. But even if Congress doesn't make us a state for a long time, maybe they'll amend our Home Rule Act along the lines of the constitution, with the kind of legislative districts we recommend."

"Maybe."

"Anyway, I'd much rather be a member of the Legislative Branch Committee than chair of Style and Drafting. But that's the one thing Charlie can't give me, because the wards control the committee memberships."

I see what's coming, and I feel a clot in my stomach.

"So I went to Charlie, and I told him to make you the chair of Style and Drafting if you would let me be on the Legislative Committee. I told him Style and Drafting was what you really wanted."

I hold it in, and keep on driving. I want to scream at her, "Sure I'd like to chair that committee. But don't you know it's out of reach now, after the election we've just been through? Who asked you to go negotiating with Cassell on my behalf? The last thing in the world that I want to do is give him the satisfaction of saying no to something I want! And how is he to know that you took this package to him on your own, without consulting me?"

But I don't say that. I don't say anything. I think about our first Ward Three caucus meeting, and how foolish I was to be open about what committee I was interested in. I'd been thinking since the night of electing officers that we'd made a terrible mistake to exclude Corn from the caucus meeting in Oulahan's office, but maybe it was better that way, after all. Who knows what damage she might have done?

Corn has not finished. She has the punch line yet to deliver. "Unfortunately, Charlie wouldn't buy it. 'Schrag voted against us at every turn,' he told me. 'Schrag gets nothing from me.'" She turns the phrase over in her mouth, with perhaps a little pleasure. "Schrag gets nothing."

So she let him have the satisfaction.

"But I did everything I could for you, Phil. Now wouldn't you step aside and let me have the Legislative Committee?"

*   *   *

The rules of the convention are finally adopted. Editorially, they are a jumble, a result both of committee drafting and of the adoption of dozens of amendments that were hastily drafted on the floor. The first task assigned to the Style and Drafting Committee is to revise them so that the form is internally consistent and the grammar sound. This will be, for Style and Drafting, a kind of shake-down exercise before pieces of the constitutional text arrive from the floor for similar editing.

I am somewhat reluctant to join the Style and Drafting Committee, now that Corn will be chairing it. But I try not to lose sight of ultimate goals amid the web of racial schism and personal quarrels. I can help to make this constitution into a document that people won't have to be lawyers to understand, while still producing an effective legal document. That is why I wanted to join Style and Drafting in the first place. It is still a powerful and valid justification for joining, even though, with Corn as chair, the committee is likely to be fractious. I put down my name for service on Corn's committee.

Meanwhile, Corn has contented herself with being a chair and has agreed to permit Ward Three to put her on the Executive Branch Committee. My committees will be Legislative Branch and a sort of catch-all committee called "Local Government, Intergovernmental Relations, and Transition." I'd sought the second committee from our ward caucus because it had seemed to me that most of the people who got themselves onto that committee would be interested in the first two of its subjects, and that the complex legal problems of transition from District to statehood status might tend to get overlooked.

At a meeting of the convention, Cassell asks each ward to report its committee assignments. A hitch occurs when Harris reports from Ward Four that Charles Mason has been assigned to the Health and Housing Committee and is dissatisfied. Mason says that there was no meeting or other give-and-take within the ward delegation; he was simply told what his assignments were. Diplomatically, he says nothing about race, but all of the delegates listening to his complaint know that he is the only white delegate from Ward Four.

Harris explains that "each person was called on the phone. Feely was called first, and Street and Cooper, and Mason, who was in a meeting, and Harris," and members of the delegation were given the right to pick committees in the order in which they were reached. Mason wasn't located until all the other slots were full." She had called Mason's office and left her name, but her call was never returned.

Hilda Mason is indignant and demands the floor. She reports that her office staff keeps a carbon record of every call that the office receives. "There was nothing on record showing that you had called," she tells Harris. "I have good staff people."

Harris will not let the matter rest. "I think your staff might have been slipping, Council Member Mason," she responds.

Cassell separates the contestants and asks Ward Four to work its problem out. But he doesn't get much further before another contest breaks into the open. Holmes reports on Ward Six, which includes the assignment of Chestie Graham to the Legislative Committee and Jeri Warren to the Executive Branch Committee. "I have a preference given to me by . . . Jeri Warren which is different from that," Cassell says.

Three people wanted the Legislative Committee, Holmes replies. The ward held a meeting to take a vote. Warren was invited to the meeting. She'd said that she was coming, but had sent her regrets at the last minute. She had been nominated, along with others, but Graham had won the election.

Cassell asks Ward Six, too, to resolve its selections.[15]

Holmes fills me in on what has been going on beneath the surface of this public record. Warren, she says, voted for Cassell for president of the convention because he had promised that caucus members of the Committee on the Legislative Branch would make her its chair. The cement that had held the caucus together, in fact, had been the promise of convention offices and committee chairmanships to those who observed its discipline; there had even been a meeting at which the caucus had agreed on the committee chairmanships. But Warren hadn't anticipated that the caucus might not control the Ward Six delegation. As a white delegate, Eichhorn was never a member of the caucus, and Holmes was evicted from it early in the convention. Graham left it after she nominated Mason and supported Holmes over Harris for second vice-president, a vote on which only Warren, of the Ward Six members, had supported Harris. In the Ward Six election, the vote had been four to nothing to put Graham rather than Warren on the Legislative Committee. Because Warren wasn't on the committee, she couldn't be elected its chair, no matter how tightly the caucus controlled the committee.

Now, Holmes reports, the caucus has a double problem. With Graham on the Legislative Committee instead of Warren, Warren can't be repaid for past services. Not only that, but the caucus has a four-person minority on that committee, and a nonmember, even Graham, could become the chair.

* * *

Three days later, we assemble for our first committee meetings, those of "major" committees. There is confusion in the hall; no one knows what room to go to, and all the delegates assemble in the plenary meeting room to sort it out. Warren complains that although Ward Six has now voted again, and she has received her first choice among the "minor" committees, she still has not gotten the "major" committee that she desires, the Legislative Committee. Cassell asks Ward Six to caucus again, right away, to make one last effort to satisfy everyone.

While Ward Six is meeting, the rest of us go to our first committee meetings. Harris is in our Legislative Committee meeting room. She says that in her capacity as the vice- president in charge of "coordinating" our committee, she has asked Jeannette Feely, our Ward Four member, to serve as our convener until we elect a chair.

Hilda Mason, our at-large member, seems astounded. "I've participated in meetings high and low, all around the world," she tells Harris angrily. "I'm sixty-five years old and I have been going to meetings all my life. I have never, ever been in one that needed a 'convener.'" Mason heads for the door. "I used to teach the third grade. My third graders were able to meet in a group and pick their own leader without a convener," she says. And she is gone. At that moment, the Ward Six member of our committee enters. It is Jeri Warren.

I follow Mason to bring her back. We are probably going to elect a chair. I hope to persuade her to run, but she should at least vote. Before I find her, I run into Chestie Graham, who appears despondent. At the Ward Six caucus, Eichhorn had suggested reopening the entire process to achieve a result that everyone agreed was fair. She had persuaded the others to assign the Legislative Committee by lot, and Graham had agreed and lost, though she now regrets having consented to the procedure. She leaves the convention headquarters, too upset to go to the meeting of her new committee, the Executive Branch.

I find Hilda Mason and persuade her to return to the committee. There is still a possibility, I point out, that the caucus plan to impose Warren as chair could be upset. The committee has three whites, plus herself, whom the caucus can't control. It has at least four dedicated caucus supporters. But there is a slim possibility that the ninth member, Jim Terrell, may be a swing voter, though so far he has consistently voted for caucus candidates. I know from a brief conversation that he has had some small contact with Mason in the past, and feels badly that she's been deprived of convention office. Perhaps he would vote for her, if she ran. She doubts it but is willing to seek the chair.

Warren and Mason are both candidates, and the next few minutes confirm my suspicion that it's not locked up. Terrell moves for a postponement of the election until the next meeting, so that he can think about the candidates. No one opposes his suggestion, perhaps for fear of alienating the one member who now makes a difference. I shudder to think of the pressure that will be brought to bear on him in the next few days.

* * *

Given our method of selecting committees and their chairs, it was mathematically impossible for a caucus with a bare majority of the convention to control more than a bare majority of the committees. It was even statistically probable that the randomness inherent in ward selections of committee assignments would produce one committee with a majority of white members, a committee that might well elect a white delegate as chair. The Local Government Committee turns out to be that committee. At its first meeting, Talmadge Moore declares himself for the position of chair. Marie Nahikian, a white delegate who has deep roots in the Advisory Neighborhood Commission system, is also a candidate. A black delegate nominates Moore. A white delegate nominates Nahikian. Clarke, who is white, abstains, but William Blount, a black, is absent. The four white delegates who are present and voting vote for Nahikian. The three black delegates vote for Moore. Nahikian becomes the chair, and Moore is made vice-chair by acclamation.

* * *

I see Terrell in the hallway before the Legislative Committee is due to meet. "Have you made up your mind whom you are going to vote for?" I ask.

"I've thought about it hard," he tells me. "I've really given it a lot of thought. I'm going to vote for Warren."

"Well, thanks a lot for considering Mrs. Mason," I tell him. And I run off and advise Mason to withdraw rather than lose an election. A few minutes later, I see her in an animated discussion with Terrell.

The committee convenes for its election. Theresa Jones, the convention's treasurer, nominates Warren. Hilda Mason asks to speak . . . and she nominates Terrell. Terrell does not decline; he says that if he is elected, he will do the best job he can to facilitate the work of the committee.

The roll of the committee is called. There are four caucus votes for Warren. I don't know Terrell at all. I have no idea about what kind of chair he'd be, and I don't like his bucking the caucus to elect himself when he refused to do so to support Mason. But I've been battered by the caucus and feel like fighting back, and the more that can be done to confound the caucus and bring about its internal disintegration, the better. I'm using him, I realize, for the ulterior purpose of getting at the caucus. But then, he's also using me. I vote for Terrell. So do Mason and the two other whites. So does Terrell. Moments later, after the meeting ends, Harris can be observed chewing Terrell out in a back corner. But I know from his brief speeches to the committee that our new chair is not about to back down.

* * *

Ever since election night, Charlotte Holmes has been bringing home-baked cake for me to snack on during plenary meetings. In her characteristically pithy way, she sums up the state in which the delegates find themselves as the ninety-day time limit finally starts to run. "They're supposed to be writing a constitution," she tells me. "But how can they write a constitution? They've been so busy fighting about power, and who controls what, that they haven't got so much as a pencil to write with. Or a piece of paper. Lined or unlined."

Notes to Chapter 6

1. The actions of this meeting are recorded in Minutes, Jan. 30, 1982.

2. Transcript, Jan. 31, 1982, pp. 8-10.

3. *Ibid*. pp. 100-01.

4. The following actions of this meeting are recorded in the Transcript, Feb. 2, 1982, pp. 23-87.

5. Transcript, Feb. 2, 1982, pp. 83-84. The vote was 25-16; three switches would have changed the result.

6. The following actions are recorded in the Transcript, Feb. 2, pp. 101-150.

7. Transcript, Feb. 4, 1982, p. 14 (Jackson motion), 22 ("seething with resentment"), 53 (abandoning Jackson motion), 63 ("non-substantive"), 84 (Oulahan motion).

8. Transcript, Feb. 8, 1982.

9. Transcript, Feb. 9, 1982, pp. 20-34.

10. The actions of this meeting are recorded in the Transcript, Feb. 11, 1982, pp. 70-136.

11. Transcript, Feb. 11, 1982, p. 136. The vote was Freeman 24, Corn 13, Holmes 6.

12. *See* Transcript, Feb. 16, 1982, pp. 10-30.

13. Proposed Rule 7.1 (Jan. 29, 1982); Transcript, Feb. 16, 1982, pp. 47-48.

14. Transcript, Feb. 16, 1982, pp. 48-57.

15. Transcript, Feb. 20, 1982, pp. 63-69.

CHAPTER 7

Committees: An Overview

IMPACT OF THE COMMITTEES

In constitutional conventions, as in legislatures, most of the making of public policy is accomplished in committees; although in principle any committee proposal can be amended in all respects on the floor of a convention, most delegates tend to defer to the greater attention that committee members have paid to the subject matter on which they have reported.[1] Floor amendments usually focus on a few sensitive or symbolic aspects of committee recommendations, rather than rewriting the committees' efforts from scratch. In the District of Columbia Constitutional Convention, as in its predecessors in other jurisdictions, committee proposals set the agenda for the floor debate, and in many cases, they virtually determined the action that the convention later took.

The ten substantive committees began their work on March 1, 1982, and most of them completed their tasks shortly after April 26, when floor debate began. The five committees that were considered "major" met every Monday and Wednesday evening, usually from six o'clock to nine or ten o'clock, and the other five committees met Tuesdays and Thursdays. The convention met in plenary session each Saturday afternoon, from noon until 5 p.m., during the period of committee deliberations, and the two operating committees—Rules and Calendar, and Style and Drafting—met on Fridays. Each delegate, then, was obligated to attend at least five long meetings per week, and members of the operating committees could count only Sundays as their own. The punishing nature of this schedule is all the more striking when one considers the fact that thirty-five of the forty-five delegates were employed in other capacities throughout the convention, almost all of them in full-time jobs.[2]

Committee work was similar in some respects to the work of committees in other constitutional conventions, but in some ways the uniquely populist composition of this convention made the task and procedures of the committees strikingly different. In particular, the fact that relatively few delegates also held legislative or other major public office, and that half of the four who did were rarely in attendance, meant that this Convention, unlike others, was not divided primarily between officeholders seeking to preserve the status quo and reformers trying to overturn it.[3] Because few delegates held major public offices, the convention's delegates had significantly less than the normal degree of experience with the detailed practices of government. The Education Committee included several members who were employed in the school system, but the other committees were not so fortunate.[4] The Judiciary Committee had no judicial members, because no judges or former judges had run for delegate. Further, the relative paucity of legislators or former legislators among the delegates meant that the committees had very few members with experience in the process of considering and passing legislation. This may have accounted for the fact that despite rules of procedure modeled on those of legislative bodies, which followed the standard pattern for the introduction of proposals (bills), hearings, committee adoption, and minority reports, most committees improvised their procedure for making proposals to the floor, within the limits imposed by the rules.

WORKING CONDITIONS

Of the convention's $150,000 budget, $83,850 was consumed by per diem payments to the delegates, leaving less than $66,000 to pay for whatever staff, supplies, and services the convention needed and could not secure from the Mayor's office.[5] This amount proved to be inadequate, and committee work, in particular, suffered from the lack of sufficient staffing. What staff there was could not be focussed on a single body, but had to be divided among ten substantive and two operating committees. Complaints from delegates were common, particularly during the plenary sessions held on Saturdays. Early in the ninety days, President Cassell identified "getting clerical people to assist the . . . committees" as a "major problem," and conceded that, more than five weeks after the delegates had been sworn in, the Convention still lacked designated space for committee meetings, file cabinets for their records, and "somebody to keep the minutes of their meetings." In addition, the convention's Xerox machine was, in President Cassell's words, "breaking down fairly regularly [and had] a rather low capacity."[6] Although the support problems were identified early in the life of the convention, most were never corrected, and, given the convention's meager budget, could not have been. The decrepit copying machine, for example, was never replaced.

PHASES OF COMMITTEE WORK

The rules of the convention called for the committees to receive and consider typewritten proposals that had been formally signed by a delegate and submitted to the president, and then referred by him to the appropriate committee. Early in its life, the convention had expressed concern that delegates' proposals, even though formally submitted, might be ignored by the committees to which they were referred, and had required its committees to give twenty-four hours notice, and a right to testify, to the authors of proposals before they could consider the subject matter to which the proposals related.[7]

Similar provisions had governed the work of other constitutional conventions, at which formal proposals from delegates had been the characteristic mechanism for the origination of committee work. In the Illinois Constitutional Convention of 1969-1970, for example, 582 proposals were introduced; in the Missouri Constitutional Convention of 1943–1944, 375 proposals were put forward.[8] Despite these precedents and the convention's own rules, almost none of the work of the D.C. Constitutional Convention originated as formal delegate proposals; only twelve such proposals were ever made.[9] Instead of working with formal suggestions from delegates and amending them as needed, the committees received informal suggestions from their own membership and built committee proposals from the ground up.

Although each committee adopted a slightly different procedure, the work tended to proceed in four phases. For the first several weeks of committee meetings, the committees tended to hold informal discussions, or "round tables," with local experts on the subjects within their jurisdiction, and studied relevant portions of constitutions of states and other countries. During the second phase, which lasted from late in March until the middle of April, the committee members debated substantive concepts among themselves and organized public hearings. The third phase consisted of the hearings themselves, at which committee members took testimony from the public for use in their final consideration of proposals under development. In the final phase, the period between the end of public hearings in mid-April and the beginning of daily plenary mark-up of committee proposals at the end of the month, the committees wrote their own formal proposals and approved them for floor consideration.

It should be noted that the order of these phases differs significantly from the order normally followed in a legislature. While legislative bodies generally hold hearings on specific proposals, public hearings by the convention's committees preceded the development of detailed proposals of constitutional text. The principal reason for this change in the usual routine is that the convention's ninety-day timetable and the paucity of professional staff did not give the committees sufficient time to write detailed proposals in advance of the hearings. This effectively denied the public an opportunity to comment on specific proposals before they were presented on the convention floor.

It is arguable, however, that it would have made little difference if more detailed text had been available. First, the public received only a few days' notice of the hearings, which made testimony difficult both because of schedule conflicts and because most organizations require a longer period of time in which to study proposals, determine their own positions, and clear those positions through their internal bureaucratic processes. Second, most of the political, business, and social leadership of the District did not testify, through some combination of unawareness of the hearings, insufficient time to prepare or aloofness or hostility to statehood or to the convention. Finally, the *Washington Post* virtually ignored the work of the convention's committees, including the public hearings.

The work of all of the individual committees proceeded simultaneously; it is summarized here in the order in which committee reports reached the floor of the convention.

THE COMMITTEE ON THE JUDICIAL BRANCH

The Committee on the Judicial Branch began its work by identifying the principal issues on which it would be called to make policy choices: the procedure for selection and removal of judges and whether the court structure would have two or three tiers.[10] The first of these issues was closely related to grievances about the District's lack of self-determination. By act of Congress, all judges of the D.C. courts are nominated by the President of the United States from a list supplied by a Nomination Commission consisting of one member appointed by the President, two appointed by the Board of Governors of the Bar, two appointed by the Mayor, one appointed by the D.C. Council and one, a federal judge, appointed by the Chief Judge of the United States District Court for the District of Columbia. A presidential judicial nominee must then be confirmed by the United States Senate. District residents, therefore, are able to select, even indirectly, only a minority of the panel that nominates judges. Residents have no real influence over the selection of a judge from the names proposed, or over the confirming body.[11]

Clearly, this had to be changed in the constitution of the new state, but in what direction? The two principal methods for selecting judges are appointment and election. Many states use some combination of both methods. As of 1980, judges were elected directly by the people in thirty states and appointed, by the Governor, the legislature, or the judiciary, in the twenty others. In about two-thirds of the states that use "appointment" for some judicial offices, a nominating commission aided the appointing authority. Although a majority of the states had adopted the apparently more "democratic" method for judicial selection, election of judges would represent a very radical change for the District, with its history of commission-aided executive appointment. Furthermore, the national trend was swinging sharply in favor of using nominating commissions for judicial selection. The trend was arguably a result of criticism that the direct election system favored those who had name recognition, a substantial bankroll, or partisan political capital, rather than those who had legal talent or a sense of justice; that low voter turnout in judicial elections favored incumbents and made it impossible to remove judges who performed poorly; and that campaigning for election or re-election required judicial candidates to take public stands on controversial social issues likely to come before them on the bench.[12]

The other principal issue before the Committee, court structure, was also one on which a significant split of opinion could be expected. Most states, as of 1982, had three levels of courts, giving litigants at least one appeal as of right while freeing the state's highest court to hear a second appeal on a discretionary basis, limiting such review to the most significant cases.[13] But the District had only two levels, although most members of the court of appeals were known to favor the creation of an intermediate court that would review the routine cases. This measure would obviously reduce pressure on the highest court, at a relatively small cost in tax dollars, but it could significantly increase the expense to which litigants could be put, as well as the time required for final disposition, affording some advantage to whichever party to a lawsuit was best able to bear the expenses of litigation.

The Committee began its work by meeting with Thomas Duckenfield, the Chief Clerk of the D.C. Superior Court, who described the existing judicial system, and with O'Neil Smalls, an instructor at American University, who discussed that system's history.[14] After three weeks of study, the Committee met to consider whether to propose a tentative draft article on the judiciary to which the public could react in open hearings. Delegate Janette Harris, a member of the Committee, persuaded the Committee that it should not attempt to do so, both because it lacked sufficient time in the month before hearings were scheduled and because the public could provide views that would assist the Committee to write its initial draft. The Committee then spent the following several weeks in more general discussions of issues, in meetings with visitors to the Committee, and in preparation for its public hearings.[15]

The hearings presented a special problem. Although Chief Judge H. Carl Moultrie I of the Superior Court was invited at an early date in the convention to meet informally with the Committee and was invited to testify at the hearings, neither he nor any other District of Columbia judge participated in the work of the convention. Similarly, the D.C. Bar, the organization to which all lawyers in the District are required to belong, did not testify or otherwise participate. Two days before the three-day hearing was scheduled to begin, the chair of the Committee issued an "appeal to all of the delegates to assist us in trying to get witnesses [because] I'm not sure we are going to have anybody at our public hearing."[16]

The hearings took place, although the duration was shortened to two sessions. Fourteen witnesses testified, but of these, eight were delegates, citizens, and the convention's research assistant. The witnesses associated with constituency groups were the counsel of the D.C. Republican Party, a member of the Democratic State Committee, two members of the Board of the Washington Bar Association (the District's minority bar association), and an official of the National Lawyers Guild. The chair summarized the testimony in the aggregate, reporting to the convention that "eleven witness[es] favored complete appointment of judges by the Governor from a list provided to the Governor by a judicial nominating commission. . . . Ninety percent supported tenure of 10 or 15 years. . . . Many favored the present system as is. . . . The majority favored a two-tier system with a supreme court and a superior court."[17]

In the five days following the hearings, the Committee drafted its proposed article.[18] The major issues were decided along the lines recommended by a majority of the witnesses. The draft article provided for a two-tier system of courts and any inferior courts established by the legislature. The judges of the major courts would be nominated by the Governor from a list of three names submitted by a nominating commission, and confirmed by the legislature. The nominating commission was to be composed of five members elected by the public, two appointed by the Governor, one appointed by the bar, and one appointed by the legislature.[19]

As the Committee's draft was circulated among delegates, it became clear that some of them were dissatisfied with what appeared to them to be insufficient popular control over the judiciary, and although they accepted the framework of appointed judges, they began to prepare a number of proposals to give the citizenry a greater influence over the courts.

THE COMMITTEE ON THE EXECUTIVE BRANCH

The Committee on the Executive Branch used its first meetings to plan its work. For purposes of study, it divided the executive branch provisions of all fifty state constitutions among the members of the Committee. It sent letters to state governors, particularly of the East Coast states, asking them for "their best judgment and their best thinking . . . [as to] what has been most profitable, most efficient, and most beneficial from their perception of having an effective and good government." The Committee also asked any of these governors who happened to be in the District during the convention to visit with the Committee, and it planned to tape such meetings for Committee members who could not attend. The Committee also decided to seek the participation of both governors and scholars in its formal public hearings. To increase efficiency, the Committee determined that the information that was gathered would be collected in a standard format: "We've done an outline," the Committee's chair told the convention, "so that as you do the states, as each person is assigned, there's very specific nuggets of information and so it can be done on a chart basis. . . ." Finally, this Committee, alone among the ten substantive committees, accepted the standing offer of help that had been tendered at the Georgetown seminar by the Washington office of Sidley and Austin, a large national law firm.[20]

In the second phase of its work, the Committee discussed general concepts. Like the Judiciary Committee, it determined that it would not begin a draft or make any decisions until after it held public hearings.[21]

The Committee's hearing—the first to be held by the Convention— was somewhat disappointing. No state governors had met with the Committee informally, and none testified at the hearing. Mayor Marion Barry was the first witness, and he was followed by the Chief of Police, several other D.C. officials, the chair of the D.C. Republican Party, and four junior high school students and their teacher.[22] The Chief of Police testified that "the executive should be strong . . . and that the Chief of Police should be appointed by the Governor and that the staff should be elected at the local subdivisions by the people." The Superintendent of Schools testified that when the Superintendent is selected by an elected School Board "you get advocates for education," and that she had not experienced that when she worked for the State of Maryland where the members are appointed by the Governor.[23]

The principal policy debate in the Executive Branch Committee involved whether to adopt the standard model of a Governor who would have the power to appoint the heads of the executive departments, or whether those chief operating officers should be directly elected by the people in an effort to make them more accountable to the constituents that they would serve. The witnesses at the hearing, and particularly the Mayor, favored a strong Governor, which would require giving him or her the power to appoint and remove lesser officials. Eventually the Committee resolved this issue by adopting the traditional model.

The Committee's proposal to the convention also provided for three other elected officers, a Lieutenant Governor, a Secretary of State, and an Attorney General. It limited the number of executive departments to twenty. Despite some disagreement within the Committee, the principal executive officers were given terms of four rather than two years.[24]

THE COMMITTEE ON SUFFRAGE

The Committee on Suffrage was required to deal with much more than enfranchising the population; it had jurisdiction not only over suffrage but also over apportionment, the initiative, referenda, recall, and constitutional amendment and periodic revision. It divided up the tasks of research and drafting on these subjects among four subcommittees, and it subsequently produced proposals on each of these topics.[25]

In general, the work of this Committee raised the questions of who comprised the citizenry and how much the drafters of the constitution wanted that citizenry to be able to govern their affairs directly, as opposed to through elected representatives. With respect to both questions, the Committee's populist bent led it to consider seriously, and in several instances to adopt, innovative concepts, but it stopped short of endorsing the most unusual ideas that it analyzed. For example, the Committee guaranteed convicted felons the right to vote, without requiring them to petition for restoration of their civil rights, but it barred them from voting while actually incarcerated. It permitted, but did not require, the legislature to authorize residents to register on the very date of an election.[26] It rejected, however, proposals to permit resident aliens to vote, to permit public high school graduates to vote regardless of their age, and to impose criminal penalties on those who did not vote.[27] The Committee also permitted only a three percent deviation from the average in the populations of legislative districts. The tension between innovation and conformity to precedent was recognized by the Committee itself, which debated the strategic choice between "creativity in drafting the articles versus a more moderate approach that may have more appeal to the electors and the Congress."[28]

It was inconceivable that a convention called by use of the initiative would not draft constitutional provisions to guarantee that residents of the new state would be able to use this device and its companion measures, referendum and recall, and the Committee followed the predictable course. One of the Committee members, Charles Mason, was familiar with the initiative and referendum procedures of the Commonwealth of Massachusetts, his native state, and those procedures became the model for the Committee's work, although other states' provisions were also studied and, in some instances, used.[29]

The major division within the Committee on the subject of initiative and referendum concerned what, if any, requirement should be imposed on sponsors of such measures to obtain petition signatures throughout the state, rather than in only one or two areas. Geographical distribution requirements make it difficult for one region of a state, reflecting a parochial interest, to force a statewide vote on an initiative or referendum. Given the small size of the state being created, it may seem surprising that this was an issue in the Committee. It was argued forcefully, however, that neighborhoods of Washington, like parts of states, might indeed have parochial interests, and that District law already included a distribution requirement that a percentage test be met in five of the eight wards. Some Committee members even favored requiring that some (perhaps reduced) burden of signature gathering be met in every legislative district. Ultimately, the Committee recommended a percentage requirement applicable to two-thirds of the state legislative districts.

The direct and personal experience of delegates influenced the Committee on Suffrage not only by making initiative provisions inevitable, but also by restricting the adoption of amendments to laws passed by initiative. Delegates felt the pressure of the ninety-day deadline and the $150,000 appropriation, and were keenly aware that these limitations had come about as a result of Council amendment of the statehood initiative. In reaction to what seemed to most delegates a political interference with the expressed will of the electorate, the Committee proposed that the state legislature be barred from repealing initiatives, and that amendment of initiatives could be accomplished only by a three-fourths vote of the legislature.[30]

THE COMMITTEE ON THE LEGISLATIVE BRANCH

Like most of the substantive committees, the Committee on the Legislative Branch spent several weeks studying relevant provisions of state constitutions and meeting informally with knowledgeable persons from the Greater Washington area. It was clear from the beginning of the Committee's work that the two issues that would spark the greatest interest were the questions of the size of the legislature and whether it would have one house (as in Nebraska) or two (as in the forty-nine other states).[31]

Both of these questions related to the more general underlying issue of professionalism. In most states, the legislature consists primarily of part-time citizen lawmakers, who spend most of their work year at other tasks and occupations. In California, New York, Illinois, Michigan, and the District of Columbia itself, professional politicians, whose primary work tasks are lawmaking and constituent service, make up the legislature.

Because full-time, year-round legislators must be paid a far larger salary and provided with more substantial staff than part-time members, a decision to have a large number of legislators would make the system more costly, and thus make it more difficult to adopt the full-time model. Moreover, a decision to have a bicameral legislature would, for the same reason, push the convention in the direction of a part-time legislature. Arguments could be made in favor of either the citizen-legislator, who might be more closely in tune with constituents' interests or less likely to set himself or herself apart as a member of a remote elite, or the professional, who might be better able to engage in such ongoing tasks as overseeing executive branch agencies, drafting bills with precision, and studying problems of public policy with deliberation and care.[32]

Other arguments also influenced the Committee's consideration of the question of bicameralism. The historical precedent for a two-house legislature in most of the states was cited in favor of that model, as was the desirability of having two houses to check errors that each would make if it acted on its own.[33]

Eventually the Committee settled on a unicameral legislative body called the Senate, although the issue was destined to provoke one of the hottest floor fights of the convention.[34] The reasons given by the Committee for its decision were the fact that the District already had a one-house legislature which was familiar to its residents, the desirability of pinpointing in a single body responsibility for passing or failing to pass legislation, and the lower cost of not having to duplicate either advocacy or enactment of bills.[35] To provide a check on errors, the Committee's proposal did require most legislation to be passed by the legislature twice, in identical form, at least two weeks apart.

With respect to the size of the Senate, the Committee recommended a body of twenty-four members. This represented nearly a 100% increase from the size of the thirteen-member Council of the District of Columbia, but the Committee's minority, which was disappointed by the prospect of an elite, full-time legislature, would have preferred a still larger body. Two minority reports, representing the views of four of the Committee's nine members, dissented from the Committee's recommendation on this point; the two reports proposed that the legislature be comprised of thirty-three and forty-eight members. This issue, too, would become a major source of contention on the floor.[36]

The other recommendations of the Committee on the Legislature were more routine. It proposed relatively conventional provisions governing qualifications and disqualifications for legislative office, a four-year term for legislators, annual sessions of undetermined length, an "anti-rider" ban against bills dealing with more than one subject, a gubernatorial veto with a procedure for overriding it, and procedures for the impeachment and removal of executive branch officers.[37]

THE COMMITTEE ON ECONOMIC DEVELOPMENT

A state constitution does not need to have provisions on economic development; it would be legally sufficient for a constitution to establish a structure of government and leave all matters of economic regulation to the state legislature. But many of the delegates to the District's Statehood Constitutional Convention believed strongly that at least the general direction of the state's economic policy should be spelled out in the constitution. Further, given the composition of the convention as a whole and the fact that economic activists from the various wards were likely to seek their ward's seat on this Committee, it was not surprising that the Committee's work would cover many aspects of economic regulation, or that the product would have a leftward bent.

The Committee moved quickly to manage a large potential agenda. In its first week, it established three subcommittees: Business, Industry and Labor; Utilities, Transportation and Energy; and Resources and Land Use. The Committee lined up volunteers from local organizations of activists to review the proposals it would develop. In the area of conservation, a consultant came from the Energy Conservation Coalition; in public utilities, consultants came from the Environmental Action Foundation, from Citizens for Constitutional Concerns, and from the National Public Power Institute; in energy, a consultant came from the Institute for Local Self-Reliance; and in business matters, from the Center for Community Change.[38]

Within the Committee, a division developed between those who wanted to present to the convention proposals for "some innovative . . . and very controversial things"[39] and those who preferred as conventional an approach as possible, leaving political controversy to the state legislature after statehood had been achieved. The Committee itself acknowledged that "the extent of detail depends a great deal on our expectations about congressional acceptance of statehood. If we believe Congress will accept, then write a bland document. If we expect they will automatically reject, then write a detailed constitution with the aim of influencing future legislation concerning the District."[40]

The combination of significant political disagreement and insufficient resources occasionally caused tempers to flare. The Committee's minutes of March 9, 1982, for example, reflect that "too much irritated discussion ensued concerning the staff's capabilities . . . the clerical staff on loan from the city government, the responsibilities of the Convention President and the Executive Committee. . . . [The] Committee adjourned at 8:42 p.m. and stamped out."[41]

The Committee eventually reported six separate draft articles for the convention's consideration. Several of them reflected the efforts of the innovators to go beyond what other states had done in their constitutions. The articles on land use and the environment were relatively traditional. They permitted takings of property by eminent domain if just compensation was paid; required the Governor to propose, and the legislature to adopt, a comprehensive land use plan every ten years; and authorized the state to acquire interests in real property to control future growth and development, to prevent pollution, and to preserve and develop open space. The most innovative provision of these articles was a section declaring that "each person has the right to a clean and healthful environment [which he] may enforce . . . against any party, public or private, through appropriate legal proceedings, subject to reasonable limitations and regulation as provided by law." The Committee stated that this provision "does not attach constitutional implications to littering," but it did not attempt to draw more precise lines to define which activities could result in lawsuits in the absence of limiting legislation.[42]

Similarly, the draft articles on banking and corporations and on water resources were unlikely to raise eyebrows. The articles on banking and corporations directed the legislature to establish a state banking commission to regulate state-chartered financial institutions and a depositors' insurance fund. It also authorized the state to charter corporations and to regulate business entities of various kinds. The article on water resources directed the state to control the use of its water and marine resources for the benefit of its people.[43]

The least traditional feature of these articles was a section directing the legislature to establish a State Economic Development Bank, the "primary responsibility" of which would be to "provide loans to those individuals [and businesses] that are unable to obtain loans from any private bank [or other commercial lender] within the state." The purpose of this provision was to provide credit to high-risk borrowers, but since, by definition, lending to these borrowers was an economically unsound market decision, the provision could be viewed as a direction to the legislature to commit the state to probable losses in its dealings with them. How large a projected loss the framers desired the state to incur was not discussed by the Committee in its report.

The most unusual proposals of the Economic Development Committee were contained in its draft articles on utilities and labor. A proposed clause provided that utility rates "shall not be so excessive for the service rendered as to take rate-payer's [sic] property." The idea, the Committee explained, was to give consumers a "property right" in "cost efficient utility service". The use of the word "right" and the concept of a "taking" embodied in the constitutional provision implied that consumers could go to court to challenge excessive rates on the ground that they were confiscatory. How the clause was intended to apply in actual practice was left unexplained. Any utility charge is a fee for service rendered and its payment "takes" some property (money) from the purchaser. The drafters could not have meant that utility services were to be provided for free. At the same time, although their report spoke of "cost efficient" service, the drafters did not stop at requiring the state to regulate utilities in the interests of insisting on efficiency, or even at giving consumers a private right of action to backstop the official state organs that would be charged with this responsibility. The use of the takings idea was a novel addition to a constitution, and the Committee did not explain why it had chosen that particular concept.

With respect to labor relations, the draft article guaranteed workers the right to organize and bargain collectively, and assured them the right to strike. On the volatile issue of strikes by public employees, the Committee negotiated a hard fought compromise between members who preferred an unlimited right to strike and those who would have preferred to leave such a controversial issue to the legislature on the ground that it could make congressional approval of statehood much more problematic. Public employees were given the right to strike, subject to "narrowly drawn" regulation that "serves a compelling governmental interest" when "no alternative form of regulation is possible." Although the compromise was accepted by the Committee because the qualified right to strike was "more politically acceptable than language making that right absolute," delegates on both sides of the issue remained dissatisfied and the clause was destined to provoke one of the major floor fights of the Convention.[44]

THE COMMITTEE ON FINANCE AND TAXATION

In its early meetings, the Committee on Finance and Taxation assigned each of its members to study five or six state constitutions to help the Committee decide which issues it should consider.[45] After a period of study, it became clear that the controversial issues would be those involving deficit spending and borrowing authority. The Committee would have to decide whether the constitution would deal with the issues of requiring a balanced budget and whether to impose substantive or procedural limitations on indebtedness.

The most significant ideological contest in the Committee concerned the balanced budget issue. Some members of the Committee found a constitutional requirement for a balanced budget attractive in view of "sound fiscal management" and the negative effect of unbalanced budgets on bond ratings. The Committee was fully aware that as the convention was meeting, the District was unable to get any bond rating at all because it had a large current deficit. On the other hand, other members of the Committee believed that a balanced budget requirement would "not allow the flexibility needed in times of economic crises," and at least some members of the Committee argued that a balanced budget requirement would "prevent redistribution of wealth." The Committee's attempted solution was to propose that the Governor submit a balanced budget for each fiscal period, but to permit the legislature to authorize deficit spending with a recapture of the deficit in the succeeding fiscal period. Through what may have been a drafting error, however, the actual text of the proposal forwarded to the convention did not mention either the escape clause for deficit spending or the recapture provision; it merely required the legislature to adopt a "balanced budget for the state."[46]

The Committee further considered the issue of debt. It considered establishing a debt ceiling in the constitution itself, but rejected this approach in light of the impossibility of projecting future needs, the fact that the bond market would itself cap the state's borrowing capacity, and the recognition that debt limits in other jurisdictions were often evaded through legislative creation of special revenue districts. The Committee then turned to procedural mechanisms, rather than substantive limits, for limiting public indebtedness. It considered requiring referenda to approve the issuance of debt, either in all cases or in instances in which the legislature had approved a capital project with less than a specified supermajority. The requirement of a referendum in all cases of debt was rejected because of the experience of some states that were unable to build essential public works or even keep schools open when procedural snarls occurred. The latter, more limited requirement was rejected because of antipathy to specially empowering a minority of the legislature to block legislation. Ultimately, the Committee decided to authorize the legislature to engage in debt financing as it wished, subject to the public's right to reverse the decision through a referendum launched by petition, and to a requirement that debt service never account for more than fourteen percent of the revenue in any fiscal period.[47]

The Committee took an unusual position with respect to exemptions from real estate taxes. Most states exempt from property tax all land held by nonprofit institutions that are exempt from federal taxation, at least to the extent that such land is used for the public purpose for which the federal tax exemption is granted. The Committee found, however, that almost fifty percent of the land of the District of Columbia was held by governments or by nonprofit institutions such as universities, churches, and research centers. As a means of increasing the revenue of the new state, it wrote into its draft a provision prohibiting the legislature from granting real estate tax exemptions to educational or charitable organizations. Concomitantly, it proposed to bar the legislature from making any payments, such as grants, to any educational institution (including a college) controlled by a religious organization.[48]

THE COMMITTEE ON EDUCATION

The Committee on Education determined, at its first meeting, to focus initially on "educational concepts"; for example, as one delegate put it, "the use of computers and a big emphasis on educational finances. Also the broadness of education." After some division of state constitutions for purposes of research and some meetings with experts, the Committee decided to focus its efforts on the provision of public education, equal educational opportunity, authority for school administration, school finance, aid to church-operated schools, higher education, and special features of the D.C. educational program.

The key policy decisions of the Committee were reached at the end of its first month of operation. The first of these was to make school attendance compulsory up to the age of eighteen (or high school graduation, if that occurred earlier), as opposed to the age of sixteen, the age required by the law of the District at the time.[49] This decision was made despite one member's warning against decisions that could "create practical impossibilities or expenditures."[50]

The second key decision was to continue to have an elected school board, with eight members elected, each from one of eight separate districts. The Committee did add a ninth board member—a student elected by the public senior high school student population. In its report, the Committee stated that the "reason for keeping the eight electoral districts [despite the fact that the advent of statehood would bring an end to the District's eight political wards] was also based on maintaining a system with which the voters were familiar." If maintaining the political support of the eight incumbent School Board members (including the husband of the chair of the Committee on Education)[51] was also a motive, it was not mentioned by the Committee.[52]

THE COMMITTEE ON LOCAL GOVERNMENT, INTERGOVERNMENTAL RELATIONS, AND TRANSITION (CLGIRT)

Most state constitutions require provisions dealing with local governmental authority, because much state authority is delegated to the numerous counties, cities, towns, and other subdivisions. The District's compact size and density of population may have made it less necessary to provide for local governmental units within the state that was being created, but many delegates thought that their neighborhoods or political wards should have some separate political authority. Several of the delegates had also had positive personal experience with neighborhood organization as members of Advisory Neighborhood Commissions.[53] Delegates who had special interests in local government or community authority tended to seek positions on the CLGIRT, which seriously explored the possibilities for some form of neighborhood self-rule. The Committee began its work by agreeing on certain basic principles: Maximizing citizen participation in government, strengthening the "power and authority of local units in the areas of public policy and planning," and "insuring greater accountability of elected officials in regard to neighborhood service delivery as well as the equalization of services and resources."[54] After study and a series of briefings by experts, the Committee decided to give the new state eight counties, and a week later, it circulated to the delegates and to the public an elaborate proposal for a system of local governments.[55]

Under this proposal, the state would have been divided into eight wards, each of which would have had three or four Neighborhood Districts; each such District would have been congruent with a state legislative district. Each Neighborhood District would, in turn, have been divided into four or five Neighborhood Council Districts. Each Neighborhood District would have had a Neighborhood Council consisting of one elected member from each of the Neighborhood Council Districts and the state legislator representing the Neighborhood District. The Neighborhood Councils would have been empowered to advise the state government on all matters of public policy affecting their Districts and would have been authorized to expend public funds for public purposes.

In addition, each of the eight wards would have had Ward Councils, composed of all of the members of Neighborhood Councils within the ward. These Ward Councils would have been given the authority, under the constitution, to negotiate with all government agencies regarding the delivery of state services within the ward, and to "oversee" the delivery of services and the implementation of policies affecting the ward. The state, in turn, would have been bound to negotiate in good faith with the Ward Councils.[56]

A few weeks later, however, the Committee decided that it was not wise to recommend so detailed a structure, and instead recommended to the convention a draft article that permitted local areas to petition the state government for a charter, under which they could exercise such local authority as the legislature might by law provide. The legislature was directed to pass enabling legislation to implement the chartering process within two years of the convening of the first state legislature, and such chartering legislation (but not the granting of charters themselves) was required to be brought before the voters in a referendum. If the chartering law was defeated, a revised law was required to be passed and submitted for voter approval every other year for sixteen years unless it was approved.[57]

In addition to its pathbreaking work in developing a conception for local governmental power in an urban state, the Committee prepared for the convention more routine proposals for defining the boundaries of the new state and for governance of the new state during the period before its first governor and legislature were installed.[58]

THE COMMITTEE ON HEALTH, HOUSING AND HUMAN SERVICES (CHHHS)

The Committee on Health, Housing and Human Services approached its task even more ambitiously than the other committees, studying the constitutions not only of several other states, but also of Canada, the Scandinavian countries, African nations, and Eastern European countries. The Communist delegate, Maurice Jackson, had visited many of the socialist countries and he was assigned to report on the health and welfare provisions of the constitutions of the U.S.S.R., Poland, East Germany, Bulgaria, Czechoslovakia, and Cuba.[59] Like other committees, the CHHHS also met with experts and local officials. After three weeks, the Committee was able to identify the central strategic question that it would have to address: Whether to guarantee health and welfare benefits in the constitution itself, thereby entitling residents to sue to obtain benefits not authorized by the legislature, or merely to permit the legislature to enact health and welfare legislation.

Nearly the entire life of the Committee was devoted to the study of other constitutions, meetings with experts, and preparation for public hearings. It was not until the Committee's second-to-last meeting that it began to look at draft textual language, in the form of ten proposed provisions suggested by Committee member Janette Harris. Delegate Harris' draft was apparently approved in principle at this meeting and approved formally, with minor amendments, at the Committee's last session.[60]

In its proposal, the Committee resolved the conflict between granting rights directly to the people and authorizing the legislature, in its discretion, to grant those rights, by doing some of each. It mandated that the state "shall provide for the protection and promotion of public health and guarantee assistance to its residents unable to maintain standards of living compatible with decency and good health care." It said that each person "has the right" to a clean and healthful environment and that the state shall provide treatment, care, education, and training for the mentally ill. But with respect to unemployment compensation, worker's compensation, day care, prisons, and low-income housing, the CHHHS recommended only that the State "have the power to provide" these services. The Committee's report did not explain the basis on which it decided to distinguish between entitlements and authorizations. On the contrary, explaining its use of the phrase "shall have the power to" in connection with public housing, the Committee "noted that most state constitutions which included a section on Housing did use the stronger language (shall)."[61]

THE COMMITTEE ON PREAMBLE AND THE BILL OF RIGHTS

At the first meeting of the Committee on Preamble and the Bill of Rights, its chair asked for volunteers to work on "word concepts" for these two portions of the constitution and to "bring back something in draft form."[62] Four volunteers, Delegates Jackson, Kameny, Marcus, and Rothschild, became a drafting subcommittee, under Marcus as chair, and the first three of these delegates became the primary drafters of the constitution's bill of rights.[63]

The first month of the Committee's work was devoted to development of a relatively uncontroversial draft preamble. A month before daily plenary meetings were scheduled to begin for the purpose of approving text, the Marcus subcommittee presented the full Committee with a list of possible concepts that might be covered in a bill of rights, and the Committee began to select those concepts to be used. The subcommittee had no lawyers among its members; a member of the full Committee suggested that the Committee needed legal advice, but she was informed that the Convention's counsel had resigned and that the Convention was seeking a new attorney.[64]

A list of concepts, but no actual text, was approved by the Committee and made available to witnesses at the Committee's public hearing. Some of the ideas presented in this paper represented efforts to pin down with greater specificity the content of particular liberties that had long been recognized but were always subject to constriction by narrow court interpretations. For example, the Committee proposed to prohibit unreasonable searches and seizures and to draft "a definition of 'unreasonable'," to guarantee a speedy trial and to "define 'speedy'," to ensure fair trials and to "define 'fair'." In a few cases, the Committee appeared to narrow existing rights. For example, it proposed to limit the freedom of the press by providing that "the press shall be required to report all sides of an issue" and to restrict freedom of speech by prohibiting "public advocacy promoting the extermination of any group of people based on race, religion, national origin, sexual preference, etc."

In several cases, the Committee's concept paper suggested new rights not found in other states' constitutions. Its nondiscrimination idea, for example, proposed to guarantee equal protection of the laws not only to those who might be discriminated against on the basis of race or gender, but also such factors as "sexual orientation, age, marital status, personal appearance, disability, family responsibilities, matriculation, political affiliation, source of income [or] place of residence or business." It suggested that the "people have at all times an unchallenged right to change their form of government in such manner as they deemed expedient." It proposed Constitutional abolition of litigant-paid court fees. And in the seed of what would become the most controversial feature of the constitution, it proposed that "[e]very citizen shall have the right to a job."[65]

In the draft bill of rights that was eventually presented to the convention, the Committee drew back from some of its more ambitious efforts. It did not attempt to define the broad terms by which the rights of criminal defendants were protected, nor did it try to limit the right to speak or to publish. In fact, the draft not only guaranteed freedom of press, speech, and other forms of expression, but it included a reporter's privilege to be free from searches, seizures, or compulsory testimony for the purpose of discovering information from confidential sources. The list of characteristics forming the basis of prohibited discrimination was narrowed to "factors such as race, color, creed, citizenship, national origin, sex, sexual orientation, poverty or out-of-wedlock birth," though the types of discrimination that were banned were expanded to those both "public or private." Individuals were given the "inviolable" right "to decide whether to procreate or to bear a child," an elliptical reference to abortion. The language regarding the right to change one's form of government was toned down by deletion of any reference to expedient means. Finally, the list of economic rights was expanded to include not only "a job or an income sufficient to meet basic human needs" but also "safe and decent housing, health care and protection, . . . adequate child care, and leisure, recreation and culture." All of these rights were qualified, however, by an additional phrase: "within the state's ability to provide." Because the judgment of the state's ability to provide these benefits would, at least presumably, be primarily legislative, the addition of the qualifying phrase appeared to reduce the clause from a judicially enforceable guarantee to a statement of goals for social welfare programs.[66]

THE OPERATING COMMITTEES OF THE CONVENTION

While the convention's ten substantive committees debated concepts for the constitution of the new state, the two operating committees—the Committee on Rules and Calendar and the Committee on Style and Drafting—met periodically to improve the convention's machinery for consideration of committee proposals once they reached the convention floor. Because the convention's rules had been debated at great length and were being polished editorially in the Committee on Style and Drafting, the Committee on Rules and Calendar concerned itself primarily with the convention's timetable. The Committee noted that by the time the substantial committees reported at the end of April, only about thirty days of plenary time would be available for floor debate before the ninety-day limit would be reached. It therefore suggested, in mid-March, that the convention plan to meet all afternoon on Mondays, Wednesdays, and Fridays during May and all evening on Tuesdays and Thursdays of that month in order to allocate sufficient time for deliberation. The President of the Convention, however, resisted the proposal for daytime meetings during the week, because it seemed unrealistic to expect that delegates, even those on the District's payroll, could obtain paid leave from their regular jobs for the better part of a month. He proposed, instead, that the convention meet from 5:30 to 11 p.m. each weekday night in May. The matter came to a head in the middle of April when the Committee on Rules and Calendar not only restated its proposal, including a noon to 5 p.m. meeting on Saturdays, but noted that it, rather than the president, had responsibility for the convention's calendar, claiming that its proposal should take precedence over that of the president. Eventually the competing proposals were put to a vote of the convention, which supported the president.[67] As it turned out, even the calendar that the convention adopted was unrealistic; during plenary deliberations on the constitution, a quorum was rarely assembled before about 6:30 p.m. or even later, significantly reducing the time available for markup.[68]

The Committee on Style and Drafting met frequently during March and April. During those months it could not proceed with its primary task of editing constitutional text that had been approved on the floor, for none had yet been reported by substantive committees, much less by the convention. But the Committee had been asked by the president to edit the convention's rules of procedure, which had emerged from the lengthy procedural debate and amending process in a somewhat confusing form. That debate had sensitized the delegates to the relationship between rules of procedure and the balance of power within the convention, so stylistic amendments were debated as vigorously, and at as great a length, in the committee revision process as the rules themselves had been on the floor.

The Committee's consideration was not helped by the repeated difficulties it had in obtaining a quorum at its meetings. Delegate Gloria Corn, who chaired the Committee, repeatedly called for its absentee members to appear for the meetings or to resign their seats. They did neither, but the convention eventually reduced the quorum requirement for operating committees from half of their membership to one-third. Even so, the Committee was unable to report its proposal for a revised edition of the rules until April 24, just forty-eight hours before debate began on the text of the Constitution.[69]

THE PLENARY MEETINGS
DURING THE COMMITTEE PHASE

The Saturday afternoon meetings of the convention during March and April had three purposes. First, they were an attempt to increase the convention's sense of unity and its public visibility during months in which most of the business was being done in small groups. The effort to make the convention visible involved inviting leading political figures to speak to the delegates during these afternoon sessions. The convention was addressed by the Mayor, the President of the Council, the District's Delegate in Congress and a leading member (Representative John Conyers) of the Congressional Black Caucus, among others, all of whom gave their endorsement to the effort for statehood.[70]

The second function of the plenary meetings was to hear weekly reports from the committees. The committees were required to make such reports to the convention's Executive Committee in writing, but because they were never able to command the clerical resources to have reports typed, written reports were not prepared. The only way for anyone to learn in a systematic manner what was happening in the committees was to observe the weekly hour or two of oral reporting.[71]

The most important aspect of the plenary sessions was the convention's housekeeping. For example, the convention used some of its plenary time to establish a calendar for debate on the constitutional text, to reduce the quorum requirement for its operating committees, and to approve a revised edition of its rules. In addition, this time was used to survey the ever-pressing problems of resource shortages, to coordinate the committees' hearing schedules, and to recommend to the Council of the District of Columbia that the scheduled election for United States Senators and a Representative be moved back a year, so that the public vote on ratification of the constitution would not be muddied by a simultaneous contest involving personalities. None of the housekeeping tasks proved easy; like the early conflicts over convention rules, decisions even on minor issues were characterized by numerous motions and extensive argument about the application of procedural rules of order.[72]

LOCAL PRESS COVERAGE DURING THE COMMITTEE PHASE

Although the major decisions about the shape of the new state were being shaped in the convention's ten substantive committees, press coverage of this activity was extremely limited. The *Washington Post* was the District's only widely circulated newspaper during the period in which the committees did their work, and a *Post* reporter, Paul Valentine, was often present at committee meetings. On each day, however, five substantive committees met simultaneously and Valentine could do little more than sample the process. Furthermore, the *Post*'s editors did not treat the convention as though it really involved the creation of a new state and a new method for governing most of the newspaper's readership. Valentine's stories appeared only rarely prior to the final month of the convention, and when the *Post* did run a story on the convention, it almost always appeared in the "Metro" or "D.C." sections of the paper, rather than in the general news sections.

Furthermore, the stories that the *Post* did run tended to emphasize the politics of the convention, or the most outlandish ideas that were offered by individual delegates, rather than the more routine decisionmaking on issues of governmental structure that were being made in the committees. The *Post* published eleven stories during the committee phase of the convention. Of these, three described political conflict, such as a debate over whether former Secretary of Housing and Urban Development Patricia Roberts Harris, who was then running for Mayor, would be permitted to address a convention committee; two covered formal speeches to plenary sessions of the convention by political notables; two described highly controversial proposals put forward by individual delegates, such as a proposal to prohibit the new state from adopting any gun control legislation; one discussed the possible failure of the Convention as it neared its deadline; and only three articles in the course of two months, one of them only seven sentences long, described the substance of committee debate, or proposals, or testimony at any of the ten sets of public hearings. As the convention entered its final phase in which committee proposals would be debated and made final on the floor, the general public was almost entirely in the dark about what its delegates had been doing.[73]

Notes to Chapter 7

1. *See* Elmer Cornwell & Jay Goodman, *The Politics of the Rhode Island Constitutional Convention* (New York: National Municipal League, 1969), p. 35.

2. *See* Appendix A (listing occupation of delegates).

3. *See, e.g.*, Elmer Cornwell, Jay Goodman & Wayne Swanson, *Constitutional Conventions: The Politics of Revision* (New York: Praeger Press, 1974), pp. 32-34; Elmer Cornwell & Jay Goodman, *The Politics of the Rhode Island Constitutional Convention* (New York: National Municipal League, 1969), pp. 37-38.

4. The Education Committee's nine members included a School Board member and two teachers, as well as the spouse of another School Board member.

5. Forty-three of the 45 delegates accepted the statutory $30 per diem allotments, but the convention passed a motion limiting the per diem to five days per week even for delegates who attended meetings six days in a week. Therefore, only a maximum of 65 days of per diems were required to be paid to each of the 43 delegates.

6. Transcript, Mar. 6, 1982, pp. 24-25.

7. Rules, § 3.1, Revised Rules, § 2.7 (reception of proposals and referral); Rules, § 2.6, Revised Rules, § 2.7(H) (notice and right to testify).

8. Samuel Gove & Thomas Kitsos, *Revision Success: The Sixth Illinois Constitutional Convention* (New York: National Municipal League, 1974), p. 69; Martin Faust, *Constitution Making in Missouri; The Convention of 1943-44*, (New York: National Municipal League, 1971), p. 27.

9. *See* Transcript, Apr. 28, 1983, p. 146. April 28 was the final plenary session before the convention took up substantive consideration of committee drafts on a daily basis.

10. Transcript, Mar. 6, 1982, p. 48.

11. Pub. L. No. 93-198, § § 433, 434 (appointment), § 433 (confirmation).

12. Berkson, *Judicial Selection in the United States: A Special Report, Judicature* (1980), Volume 64, p.178.

Between 1970 and 1980, 28 states adopted or extended a commission plan. *Ibid.*

13. Henry Glick & Kenneth Vines, *State Court Systems* (Englewood Cliffs, N.J.: Prentice Hall, 1973), p. 28.

14. Transcript, Mar. 3, 1982, p. 48; Transcript, Mar. 10, 1982, p. 132.

15. Judicial Branch Committee Minutes, Mar. 22, Mar. 29, and Apr. 7, 1982. The Committee heard informally from Dr. Mary Berry, Professor of History at Howard University, and from Patrick McGuigan, an official of the Free Press Foundation.

16. Transcript, Mar. 13, 1982, p. 133 (Chief Judge Moultrie I invited); Transcript, Apr. 10, 1982, p. 65 (committee appeal).

17. Judicial Branch Committee, Summary of Week's Activities, Public Hearings, Apr. 12 and 14, 1982, p. 2; Transcript, Apr. 17, 1982, p. 33.

18. The hearings ended on April 14, 1982, and the article submitted by the Committee is dated April 19, 1982.

19. Judicial Branch Committee, Proposed Article (Apr. 19, 1982), § 1 (two tiers); § 3.10 (nominated by Governor); § 3.14 (nominating Commission).

20. Transcript, Mar. 6, 1982, pp. 63-66; Transcript, Mar. 13, 1982, pp. 74-75.

21. Transcript, Mar. 27, 1982, p. 31.

22. The list of witnesses was compiled by Dr. Bobby Austin, the convention's research coordinator.

23. Transcript, Apr. 10, 1982, pp. 61-63 (Report of Committee Chair Barbara Lett Simmons).

24. Report of the Executive Branch Committee (undated), pp. 3-4; Executive Branch Committee Proposal, SC1-3A-0003, Apr. 24, 1982, § § I-IV, VIII.

25. Transcript, Mar. 13, 1982, p. 158; Committee on Suffrage Proposals, SC1-10A-0009, Apr. 28, 1982 (Suffrage); SC1-10-0008, Apr. 28, 1982 (Apportionment); SC1-10A-0005, Apr. 28, 1982 (Initiative and Referendum); SC1-10A-0007, Apr. 28, 1982 (Recall); SC1-10A-0006, Apr. 28, 1982 (Constitutional Amendments and Revisions).

26. Committee on Suffrage Proposal, SC1-10A-0009, Apr. 28, 1982, § 1(D) (felon vote), § 1(E) (election-day registration).

27. Report of the Committee on Suffrage, Apr. 27, 1982 (no alien vote); Delegate Proposal 1-0006, Apr. 16, 1982 (high school graduates); Delegate Proposal 1-0008, Apr. 18, 1982 (penalties for not voting).

28. Committee on Suffrage Proposal, SC1-10A-0008, Apr. 28, 1982, § 2 (three-percent deviation); Committee on Suffrage Minutes, Mar. 16, 1982 (tension recognized).

29. *See* Transcript, May 6, 1982, p. 68; Report of the Committee on Suffrage on Initiative and Referendum (undated).

30. Committee on Suffrage Proposal, SC1-10A-0005, Apr. 28, 1982, § 2(f) (two-thirds of districts), § 4(f) (amendment and repeal of initiatives); Report of the Committee on Suffrage on Inititiative and Referendum (undated).

31. Transcript, Mar. 6, 1982, p. 69; Transcript, Mar. 13, 1982, pp. 79-80; Transcript, Mar. 20, 1982, p. 84. As early as March 20, word spread that the Committee was considering the question of the number of houses in the legislature, and a delegate took the floor to request assurances that the Committee would not close the issue quickly. Transcript, Mar. 20, 1982, p. 85.

32. *See* Linde & Frohmayer, *Prescription for the Citizen Legislature: Cutting the Gordian Knot, Oregon Law Review* (1977), Volume 56, pp. 1-11. Members of Congress are also full-time legislators.

33. *See* Committee on the Legislative Branch Minutes, Mar. 15, 1982. One delegate suggested in the Committee that a one-house legislature would prompt Congress to think of the potential new state as a city, and to reject its statehood application.

34. Committee on the Legislative Branch Proposal, SC1-2A-0017, May 1, 1982, § 1.

35. Report of the Committee on the Legislative Branch, Apr. 29, 1982, p. 14.

36. Committee on the Legislative Branch Proposal, SC1-2A-0017, May 1, 1982, § 16 (pass legislation twice); § 2 (body of 24); Minority Report of Delegates Feely, Jones, and Warren, May 3, 1982 (33 members); Minority Report of Delegate Love, undated (48 members).

37. Committee on the Legislative Branch Proposal, SC1-2A-0017, May 1, 1982.

38. Committee on Economic Development Minutes, Feb. 25, 1982; Committee on Economic Development Minutes, Mar. 2, 1982.

39. Transcript, Mar. 27, 1982, pp. 27-28.

40. Committee on Economic Development Minutes, Mar. 2, 1982.

41. Committee on Economic Development Minutes, Mar. 9, 1982.

42. Committee on Economic Development Proposals, SC1-9A-0010 and SC1-9A-0011, Apr. 29, 1982 (land and environment proposals); SC-9A-0011, Apr. 29, 1982, § 3 (right to clean, healthful environment); Report of the Committee on Economic Development, Apr. 30, 1982 (committee statement on littering).

43. Committee on Economic Development Proposal, SC1-9A-0014, Apr. 29, 1982, § § 1, 2, 4 (banking); Committee on Economic Development Proposal, SC1-9A-0015, Apr. 29, 1982, § 1 (water).

44. Committee on Economic Development Proposal, SC1-9A-0014, Apr. 29, 1982, § 3 (state loans), SC1-9A-0012, Apr. 29, 1982, § 2(a) (no excessive

rates), SC1-9A-0013, Apr. 29, 1982, § 1 (right to strike); Report of the Committee on Economic Development, Apr. 30, 1982.

45. Committee on Finance and Taxation Minutes, Mar. 8, 1982.

46. Committee on Finance and Taxation Proposal, SC1-5A-0004, May 7, 1982; Report of the Committee on Finance and Taxation (undated). This provision survived and became article VII, section 3 of the constitution. The Committee rejected a balanced budget requirement by a vote of six to two. Committee on Finance and Taxation Minutes, Apr. 5, 1982.

47. Committee on Finance and Taxation Minutes, Mar. 13, 1982; Report of the Committee on Finance and Taxation (undated); Committee on Finance and Taxation Proposal, SCI-5A-0004, May 7, 1982.

48. Report of the Committee on Finance and Taxation (undated); *see* Committee on Finance and Taxation Proposal, SCI-5A-0004, May 7, 1982.

49. D.C. Code Ann. § 31-401 (1981).

50. Committee on Education Minutes, Feb. 25, 1982, p. 3 (concepts), Mar. 2 and 4, 1982 (experts), Mar. 9, 1982, p. 3 (focus), Mar. 23 and 30, and Apr. 6, 1982 (key policy decisions), Mar. 23, 1982, p. 4 ("practical impossibilities"); Committee on Education Proposal, SCI-7A-0018, May 12, 1982, § 2(A) (school until 18).

51. John Lockridge, a member of District of Columbia Board of Education, was married to Mildred J. Lockridge, Chair of the Committee on Education.

52. Committee on Education Proposal, SCI-7A-0018, May 12, 1982, § 2(B); Report of the Committee on Education, May 17, 1982.

53. *See* Appendix A (listing delegates with Advisory Neighborhood Commission experience).

54. Report on Local Government of the Committee on Local Government, Intergovernmental Relations and Transition (hereinafter referred to as CLGIRT) (undated).

55. Transcript, Apr. 3, 1982, p. 85; Transcript, Apr. 10, 1983, p. 76.

56. CLGIRT, Committee Draft on Local Government, Apr. 8, 1982, § § 1, 5, 6, 7, in Memorandum to Delegates from Marie Nahikian, CLGIRT Chair, Apr. 10, 1982.

57. Report of the CLGIRT (undated); CLGIRT Proposal, SCI-6A-0019, May 14, 1982, § § 1, 2.

58. CLGIRT Proposal, un-numbered, debated, amended, and approved as amended by the convention on May 21, 1982.

59. Report of Delegate Maurice Jackson, appended to the Report of the CHHHS, May 12, 1982.

60. CHHHS Minutes, Mar. 4, 18 and 23, 25 and 30, and Apr. 1, 6, 8, 15, 20, and 22, 1982.
See CHHHS Minutes, May 18, 1982: "The proposal already adopted on April 22, 1982 along with attachments and acknowledgments was accepted by the Committee in its entirety." The convention's records reflect the Committee's discharge of its draft article on April 24, 1982. *See* the secretary's notation on CHHHS proposal, SCI-8A-0020, May 21, 1982.

61. CHHHS Proposal, SCI-8A-0020, May 21, 1982, § § 8.1, 8.2, 8.3. 8.6, 8.7, 8.8, 8.10.

62. Committee on Preamble and the Bill of Rights Minutes, Mar. 1, 1982.

63. *See* Transcript, Apr. 26, 1982, pp. 141-70. Rothschild became less active after he dissented strongly from the proposed preamble.

64. *See* Committee on Preamble and the Bill of Rights Minutes, Mar. 3, 6, 8, 10, 15, 29, and Apr. 5, 1982.

65. Committee on Preamble and the Bill of Rights, "Conceptual Framework for a Proposed Bill of Rights for the State Constitution," Apr. 9, 1982, § 4(a) ("unreasonable"), § 6(e) ("speedy"), § 6(g) ("fair"), § 6(b) (press report all sides), § 16 (not advocate extermination), § 21 (discrimination of factors), § 1(e) (challenge government), § 26(d) (court fees), § 25(f) (right to job).

66. Committee on Bill of Rights and Preamble Proposal, SCI-1A-0021, May 21, 1982, § 2 (reporter's privilege), § 17 (discrimination factors), § 18

(procreate, bear children), § 22 (change government), § 20 (economic rights).

67. Transcript, Mar. 13, 1982, pp. 159-60, 163; Transcript, Apr. 10, 1982, pp. 15-19, Transcript, Apr. 17, 1982, p. 177-205 (the president's proposal had been amended to include Saturday meetings).

68. *See, e.g.*, Transcript, Apr. 27, 1982, p. 7 (call to order at 6:56 p.m.); Transcript, Apr. 28, p. 1 (6:50 p.m.); Transcript, Apr. 29, 1982, p. 1 (6:53 p.m.).

69. *See, e.g.*, Transcript, Mar. 13, 1982, pp. 106-07, Transcript, Mar. 20, 1982, p. 149, Transcript, Mar. 27, 1982, p. 90 (Delegate Corn's call); Transcript, Mar. 27, 1982, p. 110 (reduce quorum); Transcript, Apr. 24, 1982, p. 79.

70. Transcript, Apr. 17, 1982, p. 40 (Mayor); Transcript, Apr. 24, 1982, p. 136 (Council President); Transcript, May 8, 1982, p. 99 (Delegate in Congress); Transcript, Apr. 17, 1982, p. 164 (Rep. Conyers).

71. Transcript, Apr. 3, 1982, pp. 89-91.

72. Transcript, Mar. 6, 1982, pp. 27-34, Transcript, Mar. 13, 1982, p. 17, Transcript, Mar. 20, 1982, pp. 11-13 (resource shortages); Transcript, Mar. 27, 1982, p. 60 *et seq.* (hearings); Transcript, Apr. 24, 1982, p. 14 *et seq.* (elections). See, *e.g.,* Transcript, Mar. 13, 1982, pp. 82-93 (procedural battles over permitting one of the committees to interview a Howard University professor at his office rather than at convention headquarters); Transcript, Mar. 20, 1982, pp. 110–113 (conflict over the procedure for closing a debate).

73. *See* Valentine, "Some Delegates Upset by Mayoral Politics' at Statehood Meeting," *Washington Post*, Mar. 18, 1982, p. D.C.5, Valentine, "Sarcastic Newsletter Stirs Debate Among Statehood Delegates," *Washington Post*, Mar. 21, 1982, p. B2, (reporting that anonymous newsletter delivered to delegates' mailboxes triggered debate whether to restrict mail to delegates), Valentine, "Dixon Asks Delay of Elections Linked to Statehood," *Washington Post*, Apr. 15, 1982, p. A22 (reporting that D.C. Council Chairman proposed Council legislation to delay congressional elections under the statehood initiative); Valentine, "Barry Backs Strong State Executive," *Washington Post*, Apr. 6, 1982, p. B2, Valentine, "Fauntroy Advises Convention on D.C. Statehood," *Washington Post*, Apr. 18, 1982, p. C1, (formal speeches); Valentine, "D.C. Convention Fight Looms on Abortion, Guns," *Washington Post*, Apr. 17, 1982, p. Bl, Valentine, "Rugged Constitution Needed to Digest All the Ideas," *Washington Post*, Apr. 12, 1982, p. B2 ("Reference materials for delegates to study at Convention headquarters include womb-to-tomb welfare provisions of the Soviet Union Constitution submitted by Ward 1 delegate and Communist organizer Maurice Jackson"); Valentine, "Some Delegates Fear D.C. Constitution May Miss Deadline," *Washington Post*, Mar. 31, 1982, p. D.C.5; Valentine, "Statehood Preamble Stresses D.C. Diversity," *Washington Post*, Mar. 19, 1982, p. B1, "Unicameral Legislature Eyed for District," *Washington Post*, Mar. 23, 1982, p. B3, Valentine, "Public Hearings Set on D.C. Constitution," *Washington Post*, Apr. 1, 1982, p. C30, "Unicameral Legislature Eyed for District," *Washington Post*, Mar. 23, 1982, p. B3.

CHAPTER 8:

Committees: The Underside

THE COMMITTEE ON THE LEGISLATIVE BRANCH

It is a night late in winter, and nine of us occupy a dingy room in the Old Pepco building. We must design the legislature of the fifty-first state. Everyone wants to know the right way to get started, but we have no handbook, no instructions. We are on our own.

We look to Terrell, our chair, for guidance, some eagerly, others resentfully. Terrell is a mild-mannered, patient man, who appears to be in his thirties. He has a quiet voice, and a small moustache. He is being peppered with questions. What staff is the Committee going to have? Is someone taking minutes for this meeting? Will a lawyer be assigned to work with us? Can we get volunteers? If a member is sick and misses a meeting, can he make up the per diem allowance? What is our deadline? Terrell himself would like to know the answers.

Two of the members seem to have some sense of direction. Theresa Jones, the convention's treasurer, is a member of this Committee who had been a solid caucus supporter and was rewarded with an officership. She seems to be doing a conscientious job of getting the per diems paid on time. She is able, by virtue of her seat on the Executive Committee, to keep our Committee posted on what resources we can expect to command and why they are so slow in coming. She acknowledges the poor working conditions, urging us to be patient.

The other key member is white, a young psychologist named Bob Love. Love has ideas for potential Committee resources: We could seek out volunteers from political science departments of local universities, hold an early hearing before developing a draft, and send a questionnaire to the Advisory Neighborhood Commissions to get their views on how a legislature should be structured. Love becomes a fountain of ideas. He suggests that we have someone cut and paste together the legislative portions of the fifty state constitutions, that we meet with experts, and that we make a list of topics and divide them among ourselves for study and reporting.

Despite Love's creativity and additional ideas from others, the meeting ends without any direction—neither assignments, nor a calendar, nor a common focus. When the second substantive meeting gets under way, there is little sign of improvement. We have no assigned room, no secretary, no tape recorder for the meeting, not even a drawer in which the Committee can keep any files it collects. Not that it is likely to collect

Robert Love

many files, for the convention's only copying machine is kept locked when the convention's secretary, Delegate Cooper, is not in his office.

Terrell senses the drift, and he asks that we focus on setting a calendar for our work. It seems to me that we should aim to finish our draft article a couple of weeks before the absolute deadline, so that if the convention doesn't like what we have done, it can refer the text back to us for another try. Jones and Love together pounce on my naivete. We should delay submission of our draft article until the other articles have been circulated, Jones says, "so we're not chewed and edited to death."

We agree on a calendar—a week of self-education, a few roundtable discussions with experts, and ten days or so of drafting, so that by the first of April we will have a draft article to share with the public at hearings during the second week of that month. We will spend the last two weeks of April redrafting the article in light of the hearing testimony, and we will finish by April 28.

Hilda Mason questions the schedule, pointing out that we have already had many briefings and that we need to get started with pencil and paper. But Love points out the psychological dimensions of our task, the reason why we have to slow down. He did more homework than anyone else on his pre-Convention committee, he tells us. Instead of being regarded as a resource for others to draw on, he says he was accused of knowing more than the others, of having a head start, and he encountered a lot of hostility. We have to begin slowly enough for all of us to start with a common base, he advises, so that none of us is accused of having special information.

I understand what Love is saying, but my sentiments are with Mason. The legislative article is likely to be the longest and most complex piece of the constitution; it certainly holds that honor in the United States Constitution. There will inevitably be policy debates on perhaps dozens of issues. If we are to issue a draft for public consideration in four weeks, we have to start at once. I avoid taking an early position on issues, but to move things along, I distribute to the Committee a list I have made of thirty issues that we will have to deal with, issues such as qualifications of legislators, the size of the legislature, procedures for passing laws and overriding vetoes, and officers of the legislature. The members take my list, but nothing is said about it, as the meeting ends.

The Committee staggers through its next session.[1] Delegate Fauntroy's Legislative Assistant has been scheduled to speak to us, but he is detained. In his absence, the Committee resumes its efforts to organize the task before it. Someone suggests writing to the public schools and asking that seniors in government classes be permitted to participate in the Committee's work for credit. Others suggest calling on university graduate students, but it is objected that supervising students properly is more work than doing research oneself. Another delegate proposes that we ask Fauntroy to direct the Library of Congress to write position papers for the Committee. There is an effort to divide up my list of issues for study, but one delegate has "left it home on the dining room table," and the only person with a key to the copier has left for the day. I am frustrated with the way we are wasting the entire meeting. I am not alone in this feeling.

Talmadge Moore, an older black delegate and a retired Army colonel, gives voice to my impatience. "I don't think we are making much progress," he says. "We [are] sitting here talking and just talking and nothing [happens]."

I see an opening to get the Committee focused on something substantive, and, agreeing with Moore, I offer to make a five-minute speech advocating a unicameral legislature, just to get a debate going.

Jones objects. Schrag is a teacher, she points out, and she is not; Schrag is "prepared to give a five-hour speech, the rest of us don't do that. . . . I am not prepared to do a five-minute speech on it. I have to prepare myself to do that." It is just as Love has predicted; for that matter, it is just as my Source predicted so many months before. I am going to have to learn more patience, but it is so much at odds with my personality and background to sit back and wait, rather than to move a cause along as fast as it will go.

* * *

The next several meetings bring us together with outside speakers: a Howard University professor, a member of the Maryland legislature, a Congressman who once served in Nebraska's unicameral legislature, and Delegate Fauntroy's Legislative Assistant. These authorities understand their role in sitting down with us, and for the most part, they lay out alternative models and do not try to instruct us on what to do. Their relative neutrality is a mixed blessing: Their deference to the Committee as a political body is welcomed, but they do not resolve any of the policy arguments that will eventually have to be addressed. As I listen to them, however, my views on some of the issues begin to change. I came into the Committee with the idea that I had few, if any, firm notions on substantive policy decisions. I thought that my role would be primarily one of helping the Committee to draft whatever it wanted and helping to keep its decisions within the bounds of what the public and the Congress would think reasonable. But as I am exposed to the questions and answers in these sessions with our experts, the idea of continuing to have a small, relatively expert legislature, as opposed to a large, part-time body, seems to make more and more sense. In part, my reaction against a part-time legislature is a reaction against making laws the way we are going about writing a constitution—hurried, unstaffed, and without the time or resources to become thoroughly versed in the complex policy issues.

Slowly, without quite realizing it, I am preparing to become an advocate against drastic change in the structure of the District's governing body. The discussion with some of our guests reveals that others, too, are beginning to take sides. Love advocates a large legislature so that a citizen can run an effective campaign without substantial funding, simply by walking the streets of his or her neighborhood. Fauntroy's assistant replies that the argument for a smaller, more elite legislature may be "a premium kind of thing," and Jones objects that the rich are "not always premium people."[2]

Terrell's responsibility for producing a product compels him to ask for action. By the middle of March, one quarter of the way to the Committee's deadline, he asks the Committee to begin making at least some "tentative, reversible" decisions on issues of policy, so that the drafting can begin.

Love opposes the process of beginning to vote; he hopes that the Committee will be able to reach its decisions by consensus rather than by voting, and would prefer that the outcome be unanimous, "like a jury." He acknowledges that voting may be necessary, but doesn't want the Committee to vote unless it's "unavoidable." Without resolving this question of Committee procedure, we enter into a substantive discussion of the threshold issue, whether the legislature will have one or two houses. After perhaps an hour of debate, Terrell returns to the procedural point: "We have a commitment," he says, "to begin to make decisions. Is the Committee ready to make a tentative decision on the question?" He asks for a show of hands on this point, but his proposal to hold a vote on the merits of unicameralism is defeated on a tie vote, four to four.

The blocs in this first vote, though it is only on a point of procedure, seem roughly to reflect the major divisions developing in the Committee. Those in favor of deciding are those who have made favorable statements about a small, one-house legislature: Terrell, Hilda Mason, Talmadge Moore, and I. I think of those who voted with me as the Committee's conservatives, and although I have never before thought of myself as a conservative, odd groupings in this convention are driving me into unaccustomed roles. Those opposing the motion are Love, Jones, Jeannette Feely, and—a surprise—Wesley Long, who probably favors unicameralism but may be siding with Jones and Love because he wants more debate or for some tactical reason. He later tells me that he had invited an expert on this subject to meet with the Committee, and he had not wanted to pre-empt his guest by participating in a Committee vote before the expert spoke. Geraldine Warren, who lost the chair to Terrell, would, I think, vote with Jones. If this vote is any indication of what will happen on the merits, the conservatives will win or lose on a five to four vote, depending on which side Wesley Long eventually chooses.

* * *

It seems at times that we may never begin to draft our article. The members of the Committee have divided up my list of thirty issues, and we report on how other states have handled issues such as how many constituents each legislator represents in the various states and how much legislators are paid. Terrell interjects periodically to ask whether the Committee is ready to begin to make tentative decisions. But Feely suggests that more study is necessary before the Committee can decide the structure of the legislature; she suggests that the Committee prepare a questionnaire on this subject and administer it to the members of the Council, the Mayor, and the former Mayor. Jones and Warren support her, though Talmadge Moore asks, "When we get results from the survey, are there going to be more delaying tactics?" Secretly, I share Moore's impatience, but I do not speak, being intensely aware that the sponsors of the questionnaire are all black delegates.

Despite my restraint, I find it increasingly difficult to work with Feely, Warren, who edged Chestie Graham off the Committee on the Legislative Branch, and now Jones. Jones represents Ward Eight, the southern portion of Anacostia, one of the poorest areas of the city, and she apparently views herself as the spokesperson for the lowest income citizens of the District, for she uses every opportunity to needle me about the affluence of my constituents. Making the point that a larger number of legislators, representing smaller districts, would better be able to demand and obtain state services for those who elected them, she says that in Ward Three trash cans are picked up from garages, whereas in her ward people have to roll them out to the street.

I rise to the bait and say that I've never heard of trash being picked up from garages in Ward Three. But she corrects me from what she claims is personal experience: "To obtain my education, I worked as a housekeeper and you sometimes got invited into the kitchen if you were liked. And I've seen this."[3]

The issue of the number of state legislators gradually assumes more and more prominence, and becomes as important to the Committee as the decision on the number of legislative houses. No Committee member believes that the number of legislative districts should be as small as eight, the number of wards in the District, or thirteen, the number of members of the Council. There is a wide gap, however, between those, like Love, who want citizen-legislators in close contact with the majority of their constituents, and therefore favor as many as sixty-five legislators, and those like Long, who favor a legislature of about twenty members.[4] These different numbers represent, to their sponsors, different abstractions about the nature of the legislators. Long makes it clear that his state legislature would be essentially an expansion of the Council; the members' salaries would be similar to those of present Council members ($41,000), and each member would have staff. Under this model, a very large legislature probably would be prohibitively expensive. Love, however, would pay his members only a few thousand dollars each, and would expect them to spend most of their time at other occupations. Jones supports Love on the ground that if the salaries are too high, candidates will be willing to spend a lot of money to campaign, and poor people, unable to raise these sums, will be squeezed out of the legislature. I wonder how many of my fellow Committee members favoring small districts and low campaign costs see a future for themselves in the state legislature. There is no way of knowing.

* * *

Three of our eight weeks have passed. We are supposed to hold a public hearing in two weeks, but we have yet to put pen to paper. Terrell continues to press for action. At our March 22 meeting, he gets his break; Feely and Warren are absent. We continue to debate the now-intertwined issues of the size and structure of the legislature. The debate makes it clear that while the size issue is still fluid and may be difficult to resolve, a bare majority of the Committee, and a much larger majority of those present at this meeting, favor a unicameral body. Love can count the votes, too, and he tries to salvage as much as he can by saying that he will support a unicameral legislature on the assumption that this body will be large, and that he will reverse his position if the Committee ends up with too small a legislature. Terrell finally prods the Committee to make its first real decision, and unicameralism wins by six to one. The vote suggests that

James Terrell

Terrell may have a slim working majority of the Committee—Long, Moore, Mason, myself, and himself. Love has joined us this time, Jones has dissented, and Warren and Feely have missed the vote.[5] With some pleasure, I note that although two blocs are emerging in the Committee, both are biracial, and both include supporters of both Cassell and Mason for president.

In the desultory discussion of size that follows, I venture a position for the first time. I suggest a twenty-three-member legislature on the theory that if this proves too small a number, it can always be increased, whereas it is likely to be impossible, as a political matter, to reduce the size of a legislature, unseating numerous incumbents in the process. Also, moving from a thirteen-person legislature to one as large as forty or more could seem like a drastic, expensive step to the voters, reducing the likelihood that the constitution will be ratified and impairing the prospects for statehood. No one supports me, but perhaps I have turned Long's proposal of thirty-two legislators from an extreme position into the middle ground.

Before the next meeting, Terrell telephones me and asks for suggestions on how to get the Committee moving. I offer him an idea: The Committee might undertake its drafting effort by working from the Model State Constitution, a concise model that has been developed over many years by political scientists and published by the National Municipal League. I note that the Committee might be more receptive to this plan if it comes from him rather than from me, even if everyone actually knows that it was my suggestion. He agrees and floats the idea at the next meeting.

Love is adamantly opposed; he claims that the National Municipal League has a view of government different from his, and that working from the Model State Constitution will tend to push us in the League's direction. He does not elaborate on these philosophical differences, and I am unable to spot the bias in the League's model, which, for example, includes both unicameral and bicameral alternatives and leaves a blank for the number of legislators.[6] Talmadge Moore suggests a satisfactory compromise, with which the Committee agrees: We will work on subjects in the order in which they appear in the Model and will look at the Model with respect to each subject, but any member will be free to suggest alternative drafts. At last, I think, we are on our way towards writing a constitution.

* * *

Home becomes a rundown nine-story office building on E Street. I pass through its lobby six days a week—on Monday and Wednesday evenings for the Legislative Branch Committee, on Tuesdays and Thursdays for the Local Government Committee, on Fridays for Style and Drafting, and on Saturday afternoons for plenary meetings of the convention. The building is the downtown campus of the University of the District of Columbia. On the ground floor, the campus bookstore's windows advertise "Gifts! T-shirts! Souvenirs!" and are filled with every kind of Snoopy doll, plastic and stuffed. The entrance to the building includes a sequence of swinging and revolving doors; they are so close together that people who are unable to open the swinging door quickly enough are often hit by the revolving door through which they have just come. Four dim chandeliers afford just

*Flaking paint and a
white-tailed deer
March–April 1982*

page 163

enough light to examine the marble lobby. The walls are covered with student posters: "Pan-African Cultural Extravaganza," "Fund-raiser for Caribbean Students Association," "The Macho Show with Male GoGo Dancers, Male Models, Karate Experts and Hair Designers." In the center of the lobby, an insignia built into the floor spells out "PEPCO," the Potomac Electric Power Company, which has long-since moved to quarters it deems more suitable.

Four elevators creak upwards to the top floor where a state constitution is being written. Each elevator operator wears a brown glove for protection against callouses that would be raised by constant handling of the large metal door.

Upstairs, many of the fluorescent bulbs are gone; those that remain flicker. The motif is green. The top two-thirds of the corridor is light green, the bottom third a solid bright green. The floor begins as linoleum squares of light and dark green but stops abruptly where the Committee on the Legislative Branch meets, becoming red and black specks with a border of brown and white specks. The ceiling is white, broken frequently by hanging sheets of flaking paint.

A large bulletin board in the corridor features two American Revolution posters and a large photograph of Charles Cassell, with the *Washington Post*'s biography of him.

Water runs in the drinking fountain, but a large, hand-lettered sign above it reads, "DO NOT USE. BY ORDER OF THE DEPT. OF ENVIRONMENTAL SERVICE." A few feet away, a sign on an empty glass case reads, "FOR FIRE ONLY."

The Committee on the Legislative Branch meets in Room 903. In this room I spend what seems like years. The walls are light green, smudged with years of scuff marks, revealing plaster where the paint has peeled. In the center of the room are a metal desk and two scratched work tables, pushed together to form an impromptu conference table. The delegates sit in black molded plastic chairs; Terrell, like the other delegates, has a molded chair, but his is yellow with arms that have become brown from use by many elbows. Visitors to the Committee, such as the press, sit on metal folding chairs along the walls.

In a corner of the room stands a brown filing cabinet onto which delegates pile their coats. A brown trench coat with a plaid lining remains perpetually on top of this cabinet, forgotten or abandoned. The drawers of the cabinet are labeled "Committee on Economic Development" and "Committee on Education." They are empty.

A stack of looseleaf pages from a desk calendar, liberated from their binder, lies on Terrell's table. The walls bear colored prints of butterflies, a mountain goat, and a white-tailed deer.

Under each of the three windows is a radiator. On one of them an arrow-pierced heart proclaims the love of BAA and WBT. On the floor behind this radiator lie piles of used metro tickets, empty Pepsi cans, cigarette butts, and candy wrappers. The view from the windows looks east onto the backs of old office buildings. Looking down, one can see the alley, filled with green dumpsters overflowing with garbage.

Here in Room 903 we design the legislature of the fifty-first state. Bob Love brings us mountains of written material: provisions from state constitutions, statistical tables displaying data on the legislatures of the states, articles from books of political science, and large numbers of his own drafts to counter the language proposed by the Model State Constitution.[7] As a checklist of issues, that Model keeps us moving forward, but it is really Love who sets the agenda, for it is he who determines which issues will be contested, and at what length. He proposes, among other things, to make explicit the scope of the legislature's investigative power, to eliminate lame ducks by having legislators take office the day after election, to open legislative sessions to television, to limit the legislature to ninety days of session a year, and to limit legislators to eight successive years in office. Some of his proposals are creative and some not; some are well-conceived and some not; some are approved and some not. Working through them is time-consuming, but Love's challenges to the Model State constitution do give us some sort of framework for debate. His proposals force discussion on each of fifty or so policy issues that might otherwise go unexamined.

We repeatedly postpone the issue of the size of our unicameral legislature, for it is clear that this issue will be the most volatile.[8] But we make steady progress on many other issues, even those as technical as whether the constitution should provide a procedure for discharging legislative committees, whether the four-year terms we have agreed upon should all run simultaneously or should be staggered, and whether we should insist that the legislature hold public hearings before it passes a bill. The five-member working majority that emerged early in the Committee's life tends to stay together on most issues, and is occasionally joined by other members. As a result, we continue to make progress through the Model State Constitution, and although the language is changed or replaced in many instances, the basic structure of the Model becomes engrained in our constitution. This troubles Jones increasingly, and she finally complains. "I don't understand why we are resolving all this with Model Constitution language," she says. "I have got a funny feeling that there is somebody outside of this convention that is controlling it from a satellite." But Terrell rolls on. Many debates on minor points take more than an hour, and, consequently, we have to postpone our hearings and schedule extra meetings. But our chair can push only so hard, because members are saying, with some justification, that they have too little time to study the many issues on which they are being pressed to vote. We are paying now for the slow pace with which we started. And we are working against a firm deadline, for the convention has mailed out notice of our forthcoming hearing.

* * *

We make our way through all the small issues, and the question of the size of the legislature is all that remains. The public hearing is scheduled for tomorrow; the calendar will force us to make up our minds at this, our final meeting before we make a proposal to which the public can react. There is nothing to do but to face the issue. I am fairly confident that the advocates of a large legislature will not prevail. Not only has their number on the committee never seemed to be more than four, but Warren, one of the four, is absent tonight.

Love makes the first move, proposing that the legislature itself be authorized to set its own size, within a range of thirty-two to forty-eight. I do not jump in right away; I am more convinced than ever that the increase in the size of the legislature should be modest, but it would be counterproductive for me to lead the charge. Talmadge Moore speaks against both the idea of a range and Love's particular numbers. We should be specific, he says, and he has "received several messages and input from people in my ward" saying that they would regard a large increase in the legislature as "money wasted." He recalls that both Delegate Fauntroy and Professor Walters, one of the Committee's experts, had recommended a legislature of twenty-four, and he echoes my argument that it is easier to increase the size of a legislature than to reduce it. Love's motion dies on a show of hands, and we are back to picking a single number.

Moore makes a motion for twenty-four legislators. Love makes a final speech against a small legislature, noting that the average state senate has thirty-nine members and that the average house has 140. But weeks of debate have solidified positions in the Committee. Love asks for a roll call, and the result is no surprise. Our five-member bloc of "conservatives" supports Moore, and his motion is carried, five to three.[9]

*   *   *

All this work has been building up to our public hearing. We have spent some time during each of our meetings drafting the language of fliers that will notify the public and the press of the hearings. We have also spent time making lengthy lists of community organizations to which the fliers will be sent.

For the first time in the convention, I sit on the dais of our meeting room, as if I bore some authority. But I feel silly, for the room is nearly empty. The only Committee members with me at the table are Terrell and Moore; in the audience are two of my students and our only witness for this first of two hearings, Bob Roehr, the Ward Three candidate who lost to Frank Kameny in a recount and is now testifying on behalf of the Republican Party. Roehr reads a prepared statement that quibbles only with minor details of our proposed article. He would prefer that legislators be required to meet only a one-year rather than a three-year residency requirement, and would like the constitution to require adequate notice of legislative hearings.[10] Love arrives and takes his seat at the table; he complains to the witness that we've proposed a "carbon copy of our highly paid Council." Roehr declines to join Love in attacking the basic thrust of the document. It is all over in a few minutes. There will be a second hearing a few hours later, at which the Committee will hear from Warren's husband from the chair of the Statehood Party, from Common Cause, from Delegate Rothschild, and from three citizens. But this hearing has been set for the same time as the hearing of the Committee on Local Government, on which I also serve, and I cannot attend.

Despite our having advertised our hearing widely, including sending out personal notices to numerous VIPs, no members of the present D.C. Council have asked to testify. Nor have any District of Columbia government officials. Nor have any people in business, law, or the other professions. Nor have any labor leaders. Not even academicians have

Theresa Jones

asked to testify. Any hope we had of using the hearings to help build a significant, District-wide consensus on the shape of the future legislature must be abandoned. We delegates are taking ourselves very seriously. But does anyone else know or care about what we are doing?

* * *

There is time for only one more meeting, for cleaning up the wording and the final vote on the article. The rules of the convention require that the draft article be accompanied by a Committee Report. With time running very short, I tell Terrell that if he wishes, I could draft the blandest possible section-by-section analysis for the Committee to review at its final meeting. He accepts this offer eagerly, but he naively introduces the document at the Committee meeting as "the section-by-section analysis . . . that Delegate Schrag has prepared for us to get us thinking."[11]

Jones is horrified. She turns to Terrell. "Then are you saying that I can sit down and analyze each section by section and bring it in and this committee will give it equal weight with Delegate Schrag's section-by-section analysis?"

Terrell replies, "I hope you will do it tonight because we don't have time . . . ." Cassell is putting pressure on him to turn in his article and report, and he cannot afford any more delay.

Jones turns from Terrell to me. "How is it that you did this? I mean, what provoked you to do it?"

Terrell steps in to reply that he had asked me to write a draft report, but Jones is by no means satisfied. "Nowhere did [the convention rules] say that one delegate would write the analysis without the agreement of everybody on the Committee . . . . I don't want to react to somebody else's document. We've been reacting to Phil Schrag ever since the first day we got here; it was the first day I laid eyes on him."

I explain that I prepared the draft, and marked it as that, to "help the Committee move along under very great time constraints," and that we can tear it up and start over if the Committee would prefer. But there is no way to undo the damage; the cumulative anger of the Committee's minority, dating all the way back to Terrell's election, must find an outlet at this, its last meeting.

During a tedious debate over small working changes, Terrell loses his patience with the minority. "You know we can sit here and rant and rave all night long over these sections," he explodes, "We have a deadline to meet . . . ."

"I didn't know we were ranting and raving," Jones replies.

"We are," Terrell insists, his voice turning staccato. "And we are getting away from what is before us, and that is to act on this."

"I have heard people rant and rave in mental institutions," Jones says. "And that is not going on in this room . . . . I resent the fact that you said that we are in here ranting and raving."

A few minutes later, Feely points out that at our only post-hearing meeting, "we ought to be going through what people had to say at the hearing." She has a point; the whole purpose of public participation is to give those who have something to say about what we are doing some real input into our drafting. I do not even know what most of the witnesses said, because I had two hearings scheduled at the same hour. And there are other members who missed one or both of our public hearing sessions. But Terrell points out the unrelenting clock. "We don't have the transcripts yet," he advises us. "The only thing that we can act upon as far as the hearing is concerned is what various members have in our notebooks."

At the end of the meeting, after all the editorial changes have been made, Terrell again notes the need for a report. He asks Committee members to come to one more meeting, at 8 a.m. Saturday morning, a time that will not conflict with other convention business, if they have any changes to make in my draft report. But the pressure is on: It is 10 p.m. and the elevator operator is calling for us to vacate the building. We have not yet voted to approve the article, and it seems clear that many, perhaps most, members are not willing or able to attend an early meeting on a Saturday. Terrell adds, "if you elect not to come to this meeting on Saturday and we have a quorum, it is too late after that fact to talk about what you want to have . . . ."

Feely jumps in, angered. "You know that it is not necessary for you to have to make that statement," she tells him. "There are those of us who have done assignments for this Committee and you have totally ignored the work that we have done. So you don't even need to say that."

Even as she is saying this, members of the minority are beginning to leave; any possibility of consensus at the end of the process is literally disappearing. The elevator operator is yelling at us from down the hall. When Terrell asks for a vote on the article as a whole, only six delegates remain in the room. The vote is five in favor, one opposed, with three not voting. We have written and approved an article on the legislative branch. But those of us who are satisfied with the result have no illusions that the others will accept it. We are well aware that on the major issues, such as the size of the legislature, a heated floor fight lies just ahead.

THE COMMITTEE ON LOCAL GOVERNMENT

The principal problem for the Local Government Committee is revealed in its first meetings: Should the new state have divisions of government below that of the state itself, and, if so, what powers should these other governments have? In the speech that she makes preceding her election as our chair, Marie Nahikian sounds the call to arms: "If I have a strong bias it's trying to figure out how you give local neighborhoods and local communities control over as many things as possible. . . . Why couldn't neighborhoods, for example, be involved in their own trash collection?"[12]

I am willing to listen, but I am intuitively skeptical. If there is a case to be made for giving power to neighborhoods, shouldn't it first be tried in a city whose other political institutions are well established, rather than in one that is undergoing a massive institutional reconstruction at the same time? Furthermore, creating neighborhood governments in Washington would be one of the most controversial, unusual things that this convention could do; in a sense we would be breaking free not only of federal control but of central city control as well. I am inclined to make the constitution as conventional as possible in order to avoid giving Congress excuses for rejecting our statehood bid. Once we become a state, if we want to amend our constitution to experiment with novel structures, so be it.

Nahikian, who has been fighting for years to strengthen the powers of the District's Advisory Neighborhood Commissions (ANCs), sees the convention as a unique opportunity to make a fundamental change in the structure of the city. It also appears that several other members of the Committee agree with her. Because the country has no other city-states, other state constitutions have little to offer us by way of precedent. Instead of looking to existing legal models, the Committee devotes its first meetings to roundtable discussions with people who have thought about the issue of local power. In the dialogue with these experts, some Committee members reveal the direction of their own thinking, and others, including myself, are exposed for the first time to the arguments in favor of decentralizing municipal services.

The most important of these sessions is an afternoon with Milton Kotler and Nelson Rosenbaum of the Center for Responsive Governance, a Washington-based consulting office. Kotler has written numerous articles advocating neighborhood government, and he urges us not merely to permit the legislature to empower neighborhoods, but to delineate neighborhood power in the constitution itself "so that the politicians can't abolish it." He concedes to me that no other cities the size of Washington have ceded more than advisory power to their neighborhoods, but he advocates leading the way.

Jan Eichhorn, like Nahikian a long-time veteran of ANC battles, agrees with Kotler that District agencies don't take seriously local bodies whose powers are merely advisory. Talmadge Moore, who serves with me on this Committee as well as the Legislative Branch Committee, is also an ANC Commissioner, and he explains the bind that local officials are in if they lack real power. "I'm frustrated because I can't get a sewer fixed," he says. "But my constituents expect that [because I'm a Commissioner I can] get things done." And Absalom Jordan, from Anacostia, where voter turnout is particularly low, explains to Kotler and to the Committee the relationship between empowerment and political participation: that people will not take part in politics if they do not see any way in which elected government improves their lives.

Kotler takes the point a step further. If the ANCs had real power, he says, vast numbers of citizens would participate in ANC elections. The issue, he says, is getting ever larger numbers of people involved in the life of the city. That's a more important purpose, he claims, than better delivery of municipal services. I ask him why he wants people to participate for the sake of participation, and he says that we need a new American Dream in the political life of a people. "We have to break through the fear, so people can find a new kind of humanity." It's good rhetoric, and it kind of hooks me, but I keep thinking about the pragmatic issue of statehood.

The discussion moves from general philosophy to particular legal devices. Kotler distinguishes between the concepts of negotiated service budgets and neighborhood delivery of services. Under the former, neighborhoods would be given the authority to negotiate with the central government about how money was going to be spent in their areas. For example, a neighborhood might demand more frequent pickup of residential garbage and fewer alley sweeps, or more recreation and less sanitation. Under the latter concept, neighborhoods would be given a share of state revenues and would be responsible for actually administering the services, through a local civil service system, or by contract, or through some other method. Kotler suggests that the new state could give its neighborhoods the power to deliver some services themselves, such as sanitation, police, parks, and road maintenance, while negotiating with the state government for others.

Interwoven with these concepts are two related concerns—those of the appropriate size of "neighborhoods" and of economic and racial equality. As we think about these new ideas, none of us on the Committee is clear on whether we are using the word "neighborhood" to mean something like an ANC area, with about 15,000 residents, or a ward, with about 75,000. If the "neighborhood" is too small, it will be extremely inefficient; it is hard to imagine, for example, forty neighborhoods independently maintaining snow removal or road surfacing equipment; most of the appeal of "neighborhood government" seems to be the allure of service delivery by a real community, by people who are one's neighbors, to whom one can talk about how things are going. And when we think about creating "neighborhoods" along the ward model, we all see the spectre of the two wards that are basically white and relatively affluent being able to manage quite well, while the other wards struggle along at best. At least a central government can concentrate services where they are most needed, even if this system provides fewer resources to more affluent regions. In principle, a neighborhood government system that relies exclusively on centrally levied taxes could still subsidize the poorer areas. The discrimination in favor of poorer areas, however, would be more obvious if dollars rather than services were being allocated differentially to neighborhoods. The pressures for political readjustment might be much greater in such a situation.

The issues are intellectually challenging, and I am happy that I landed on this Committee. Here, as in the Committee on the Legislative Branch, the racial divisions in the convention seem muted, as though we can't afford wasting time on racial conflict in light of the enormity of our immediate assignment. To the extent that interpersonal conflict lingers, its focus has shifted; it is increasingly becoming a case of everybody against the convention's leadership, which is getting the blame for the lack of professional or clerical staff, library resources, and equipment.

* * *

I play hooky from the Committee for one evening, and it turns out to be a bad mistake. While I am at the symphony, the Committee decides to "brainstorm" some ideas on local government. The plan is to write down anything that any member wants to have listed, without evaluation. This procedure conforms with the usual rules for brainstorming, but after the Committee makes up its unedited list, it decides to "work with experts in drafting something from the Committee's brainstorm."[13] The list includes the most far-reaching ideas that have been discussed, including "assumption of need for a form of local government to be mandated in the constitution," "mandate a relationship between local gov't unit & executive branch re: defining local service budget priorities, i.e., negotiated service contracts," and "city services should be divided by geopolitical units." The Committee's "shopping list" includes a disclaimer that it does not reflect any final decision, but it does establish an agenda, and, perhaps more important, it reflects the aims of my fellow Committee members in drafting our article.

* * *

The Committee asks Eichhorn, Moore, and me to meet with Ann Witt, Director of the District Government's Solid Waste Management program, who reportedly has given a lot of thought to program management in Washington. Just as I am beginning to warm, however slightly, to the idea of neighborhood power, Witt's remarks quench the fire. We sit across from her at a long conference table in the District Building.[14]

The District government is moving as quickly as possible away from geographically-based service delivery, Witt explains. The new concept is management by technology; the administrative bureaus are increasingly organized by function (e.g., truck-hoisted garbage can emptying) rather than by region. This is much less expensive, she tells us, because it avoids the need for numerous area managers and permits the government to put a single manager in charge of several different technologies.

Nor is the concept of negotiated service budgets any better than neighborhood-delivered services, Witt says. In practice, budget reviews and determinations that are made a year in advance are not very meaningful, because programs constantly change as a result of budget cuts, union contracts, and new technology. A neighborhood could not meaningfully participate in budget planning merely by having input into an annual contract. Instead, the neighborhood would have to appoint someone to monitor constantly each program affecting the neighborhood, and make regular amendments to the plan as necessary.

Then Witt delivers the final blow. It is possible that neighborhoods could deliver services to their residents more cheaply than the central government now does. But the reason for this is that, in a new constitutional order, the neighborhoods might be able to escape from contracts that the District has signed with its unions and to contract with private enterprises to deliver services at below-union wage scales. Our radical ideas for neighborhood government turn out to depend for their economic viability on their union-busting potential.

* * *

Jan Eichhorn circulates to the Committee a draft article on local government. It is labeled "a 1:00 to 3:00 a.m. draft—an option." She proposes to divide the state into eight counties, each containing several Neighborhood Councils, which are to succeed the present ANCs. Counties are to be governed by County Councils consisting of state legislators elected from the county and seven to nine members elected from the Neighborhood Councils. The County Councils are to "assist

agencies that deliver services with the county in the preparation of service statements for the county and review such statements." To make the work easier, State agency heads are required to organize their service delivery districts along county lines for housing code enforcement, street repair, refuse collection, parks and recreation, police patrols, sewer maintenance, health, public housing, social services, elementary and secondary school education, and several other programs.[15]

It seems likely that the Committee will pass some sort of article empowering local governments, so rather than trying to defeat all proposals like Eichhorn's, I draft a less ambitious alternative. Instead of creating two sublevels of local government (counties and Neighborhood Councils), which strike me as holdovers from the District's current ward and ANCs system, I propose to have sixteen Community Council areas. Each would be governed by an elected Community Council, which would have the power to advise the state government on matters of policy (like the ANCs), consult with state government with regard to planning for service delivery, and exercise any other powers that the legislature provides. The state would be obligated to "give great weight" to the views expressed by a Council "with respect to the types of services to be provided . . . and consult . . . on an ongoing basis with respect to evolving changes in operations and programs . . . ."[16]

The Committee convenes on March 25 and spends most of its time discussing witness lists for its upcoming public hearings.[17] After two hours, nothing has been said about the substance of the work, and there are only four meetings left before we must hear public reaction not only to our ideas about local government, but also to two other articles which are ours to draft, one on intergovernmental relations and one p oviding transition arrangements between the time that Congress admits us to statehoood and the election of the first legislature. I plead with the Committee—a bare quorum of five is present—to turn to the policy issues before us, and I move the Committee to work from my draft.

Will I ever learn not to stick my neck out in front? Have my Source's warnings and my subsequent experience taught me nothing? This Committee seems entirely free of racial tension, lulling me into the belief that my work would not automatically be viewed with suspicion. But there is not even a second to my motion. To the contrary, Barbara Maguire, Victoria Street, and Nahikian all say that Eichhorn's draft is preferable to mine because it contains more of the items from the Committee's shopping list. Nahikian knows which way the Committee on the Legislative Branch is going; she adds that since a unicameral state legislature affords citizens so few chances for political input, there should be multiple levels of local government.

Eichhorn is absent from the meeting, and I wonder if the members are defending her draft more strenuously than she would. She wrote her draft before we met with Ann Witt; I wonder if that meeting has changed her views at all. In her absence, it is impossible to know. It doesn't matter very much, for the meeting ends abruptly when Cassell summons Street, who is also a convention officer, to a meeting of the Executive Committee, breaking our quorum.

Janice Eichhorn

* * *

The debate over the basic structure of local government focuses on whether we are going to create one or two levels. It would be equally sound to determine the functions of local government before determining its structure, but structure appears first in both drafts and is easier to grasp. Eichhorn makes a motion in favor of two levels, with eight counties as the top level. The debate is lively. Moore and William Blount, a relatively taciturn member of the Committee, support having only a single layer, on the ground that the public does not generally approve of more bureaucracy than is necessary. Nahikian, Eichhorn, and Jordan want a two-level system so that people can have some unit of government close to them, and to maximize citizen participation. The Committee takes its first substantive vote. The two-level system passes, five to two. The surprise is that Blount, who spoke for a single level of local government, votes for the two-level system.

Outside, in the corridor, I ask him why. "I was tired of all this talking," he tells me. "All we do is talk. I just wanted to vote on something and get done with it."

A reporter comes up to me after the meeting and asks for a quotation about why I voted against the motion. I decline to talk with him. The last thing I need is for the others on the Committee to read about my disagreement with the Committee majority in the press. I can imagine rekindling all the fear about Ward Three's access to the media, and I want no part of it.

* * *

The room in which the Committee on Local Government meets is the only aesthetically pleasing site in the building. It is a small room, with the standard uncomfortable furniture and two windows facing the glass and cinder block J. Edgar Hoover FBI Building across the street. The walls are light green, the ceiling white, and the floor is, amazingly, carpeted—a dirty gray-green.

What makes this room pleasant to work in is that Nahikian has plastered the walls with maps, all kinds of maps, of the District of Columbia. We have an historical district map, a map of jurisdictional areas, and maps of each ward, in ten colors. These maps are entitled "Generalized Existing Land Use—Presente Uso del Suelo en General-1980." The residential areas are yellow, commercial offices are red, federal buildings are blue, parks are green, and so on through the spectrum. When the meeting gets tense, one can always find new patterns in these colored maps.

This wall display is further embellished in an all-day meeting at which the Committee does most of its drafting. I have lost the initial battle for simplicity, and my choice now is to sit back and watch, or to contribute to a draft article with which I will probably disagree. The latter strategy seems both more honorable (I recall how everyone, including myself, felt about my threat to boycott the final meeting of the pre-convention Committee on Rules and Calendar if that Committee would not defer to the judgment of the temporary Committee on Committees) and more likely to result in a draft that will not reduce the chances for statehood. The process, it turns out, is great fun. Nahikian has purchased a big pad of large pages of newsprint, and as each of Eichhorn's concepts is discussed, I quickly draft some legally suitable language and enter it onto a page of newsprint with purple magic marker. Then we tape the paragraph to the wall and edit it with a brown magic marker. Soon the room's maps are surrounded by paragraphs of text: purple paragraphs, green arrows, brown interlineations. It may succeed better as a work of modern art than as constitutional law, but the result is an entirely novel approach to neighborhood government. Although it has two levels rather than one, the draft merges Eichhorn's proposal with my own.

In the plan we have worked out, the two levels of local government are composed of the same individuals, wearing different hats at different times. This reduces the total number of elected officials. As members of Neighborhood Councils, these officials have authority to advise the state government on policy and on decisions affecting their neighborhoods. The state must give "great weight" to their views and also must put in writing its reasons for not accepting a recommendation made by a Neighborhood Council. All of the Neighborhood Council members within a ward (we have renamed the counties as wards) would sit at a second level as the Ward Council, which would have greater powers. These Ward Councils would "negotiate regularly" with each state agency that affected the ward and "oversee" the delivery of services and the implementation of policies in the ward.[18] Much of the power of the Ward Councils turns, of course, on the interpretation of the words "negotiate" and "oversee."

There is little agreement in the Committee on the meaning of these terms. Indeed, we have gone around in circles trying to find more suitable words, such as "direct," "consult," enforce," and "monitor." The words we have used were the only ones that commanded a consensus, though none of us really has a good idea about how a local government agency without independent political power will be able to make effective demands on the state. In the end, we have pinned our hopes on giving the Ward Councils some real clout with the state government by including in their membership the three or four state legislators representing the ward.[19]

I have mixed feelings about the product. I would still rather keep the constitution short and unremarkable to reduce to a minimum the controversies surrounding statehood. But considering the underlying preference of many, perhaps most, members of this Committee to give neighborhoods the power to direct the flow of state services and to deliver their own local services, this draft is relatively moderate. Still, the most ardent supporters of neighborhood control probably worked within their ward delegations to be placed on this Committee; the convention as a whole might want to accept a much more modest proposal. Should I dissent and offer a draft that merely gives the legislature the power to create and empower local governments if it so desires? Or would this be viewed by Nahikian, Eichhorn and the others as an act of betrayal that would ruin my ability to work with them on other issues, and perhaps provoke them to amend the draft on the floor and make it still more radical? I have a little time to decide, because the Committee votes to distribute its draft to delegates at the next plenary meeting, but it will not take a final vote on the article until after the public hearing.

* * *

Howard Hallman, a writer on neighborhood government who is active at an organization called the Civic Action Institute, leads off the hearing on our article.[20] He blasts it from the left. What we call local government is merely advisory. It doesn't go far enough; we should be directing our neighborhoods to deliver services themselves. Patterning myself on the role of a skeptical legislator, I ask him whether he has any figures to show that any services could be delivered more cheaply in the District if the neighborhoods were in charge. He does not. Have I scored a point with my fellow Committee members or do they resent my cross-examination of this witness, one of the few who have bothered to give us their time?

Haywood Sanders of the Brookings Institution cannot understand why we have created a two-level system of local government; the two levels seem to have similar functions. He balks at the word "oversight." It is unrealistic, he believes, to establish oversight without giving the neighborhoods any real muscle. He would have us give neighborhoods a veto power over zoning, street closings, and planning unless overridden by an extraordinary majority of the legislature. As for our Ward Councils, they may become just another device for collecting complaints which are then ignored.

Nelson Rosenbaum, one of our first roundtable experts, delivers what seems to me to be the final blow. Our draft is totally inadequate as a charter for local government, he says. It offers no realistic promise of improvement. "Why exchange what we have for a bird-in-the-bush if it doesn't promise something better?" he asks us. He would have us move to a service delivery model, but he tells us that if we are not going to go that far, we might just as well leave the whole matter to the state legislature.

I can hardly believe what I am hearing. Our witnesses are hardly representative of the District; they are a self-selected few who are advocates of neighborhood government. They are the most vocal constituency that exists for the direction in which the Committee has moved. But they are dumping all over our work. If we haven't satisfied even them, why are we doing this?

Hearings are not thought to be very important in the calculus of what actually influences legislators, but I wonder whether this hearing has not changed the views of some of my fellow members. Perhaps now they also think that we have built a house of cards, that we were all along beyond our depth, trying to do much too much with too little understanding and too little time. As we clean up the papers on the Committee table, I ask Nahikian and Moore whether they now think that we should leave these issues to the legislature rather than report our draft formally to the convention. To my surprise, they tell me that they are persuaded; we should recommend a less detailed proposal, leaving matters to the legislature.

So we have come full circle. We may end up with the kind of product that I would have preferred on the first day, but such a result was politically impossible until we had gone through the laborious process of trying to do something more ambitious.

* * *

I draft a one-paragraph substitute article which permits the legislature to create and empower local units of government, and I distribute it to Committee members. A meeting is scheduled for 4 p.m. to take final action on the local government article, but an important meeting of the Committee on Style and Drafting is scheduled for the same hour. I arrange with Nahikian that I will go to the Style and Drafting meeting, and she will have the Committee work on its other articles until 6:30. At that time, I will present my substitute proposal.

I arrive at 6:30 p.m. Maguire, grinning impishly, tells me that my substitute has been considered and rejected, and that the Committee's pre-hearing draft has been given final approval, with the wards once again called counties.

The five other members who are present laugh at my shock. Nahikian is not present. She had realized after we had made our arrangement that she had an engagement to speak, in connection with her campaign for member of the Council, at five o'clock. When she had left the meeting, she had asked the remaining members to defer consideration of the local government article until she and I were present, but bowing to Maguire's objection, they had refused, and in our absence, voted in favor of the Committee draft.

Marie Nahikian

Maguire had voted with the majority, despite having told me on the telephone after the hearing that the hearing had changed her mind, too. Why, I ask her. "In thinking about it, I just got mad at all those witnesses," she tells me. "Who are they to tell me what to say about local government? I know local government as well as they do."

* * *

There is one last chance. Our article is overdue, and floor debate on committee proposals has already begun. But Nahikian schedules a final meeting of the Committee to consider other aspects of our work, and she allows me to ask a member of the Committee who voted with the majority to make a motion for reconsideration. I prepare for this meeting with some care. I compile a list of nine separate arguments against the draft that the Committee has approved: Its complexity, the risk it poses to ratification, the diffusion of accountability inherent in the extra layer of government, the additional cost, and so forth. Then I work these arguments into a speech which praises the Committee for the excellent work that it did under intense time pressure. I weave the hearing witnesses' testimony into my speech, using their words, rather than my own, to criticize our work.

In the Committee, I make it clear that I am going to make a long speech.[21] The members are patient because they know I did not have an opportunity to speak at the previous meeting. I give the talk, and when I finish I can see at once that people are having some second thoughts. I complete my talk by handing out a new, even simpler substitute, and instead of taking issue with my attempt to reverse the Committee's decision, the members start to bicker with the language of the substitute.

As debate proceeds, it is clear that the Committee is moving away from its commitment to its product. I don't try to push it; I let the clock do that. Jan Eichhorn is among those who are convinced that we have to change our position, and she begins to construct modifications to my draft. When other convention business presses us to end our meeting, Eichhorn makes the motion for reconsideration. It passes unanimously. At one more special meeting, we pin down the wording of what becomes the final Committee product, an article that leaves the issue for future legislative work, but requires the state's first legislature to propose a local government law within two years and to hold a referendum on approving it every other year for sixteen years, until it is endorsed by the people.

Why has the Committee reversed itself? My speech was merely a device to make the group take itself seriously and stop to think, so I cannot believe that my words were even primarily responsible. I believe several factors turned the Committee around: The criticism by the witnesses; the presence of a group in the room that was slightly different in composition from the group that voted for the Committee draft; Nahikian's growing doubts about what we had done; and most importantly, the fact that in the days before the reversal, floor debate had begun, and members had watched how the Judiciary Committee had been forced to defend every sentence of its proposed article during a three-night barrage of questions and doubts. The experience of legislating is apparently turning us into legislators.

THE COMMITTEE ON STYLE AND DRAFTING

Until language for the text of the constitution is approved in preliminary form on the floor, the task of the Committee on Style and Drafting is to edit the convention's rules and propose a more readable version to the delegates. It is a dry run for the Committee, and the work is more tedious than anyone could have imagined. Meetings often take all day on Fridays; in nine hours of debate over vocabulary, grammar, and punctuation, we sometimes get through only a few pages of the rules. A debate over whether a colon should follow the words "as follows," for example, takes more than half an hour to resolve. Delegate Corn does her best to insist that the Committee's product remain consistent with the Government Style Manual, but a majority of those present often prevail in choosing a different wording.

Fourteen people have signed up for the Committee, and obtaining or maintaining a quorum of eight proves to be very difficult. At times, those who are present constitute themselves as a "work group" which asks for ratification of its product when a quorum assembles. The legitimacy of this procedure troubles everyone, but there is no choice.

Gradually, the members lose patience with the editing process; they do not like spending their Fridays arguing over punctuation marks. But the most active members worry that if they don't show up, other members will make substantive rule changes in the guise of stylistic editing. Corn continues to proceed deliberately, forcing the Committee to consider several plausible alternatives for each phrase. The Committee becomes frustrated with the pace. The manner in which she was appointed as chair contributes to the unease. There is talk of recalling her, or of asking her to assume a titular leadership while some other member actually presides over disposition of the rules. Corn is aware of the growing discontent, but she sees the text of the rules, and eventually the constitution, as her product, and wants them to be grammatically perfect.

One of the final sessions for editing the rules is scheduled immediately after a routine Saturday plenary meeting. We work in our Committee room from 4 to 5, but the building closes before we finish and we have to adjourn to a local bar. There, under a Pabst-on-tap mirror and in the midst of a full house of patrons, we get some beers and spread our papers onto a cocktail table. The usual committee process breaks out. Astonished customers watch as Corn yells at Kameny: "No. Goddammit, that should be a colon, not a semi-colon," and Kameny returns, "Shut up, Gloria, I know punctuation better than you do." After about half an hour, the bar's other patrons tell Corn to keep the noise down, and she explains to them the duties of the constitutional convention and its drafting committee.

Jeannette Feely

*   *   *

After nearly two months of working on the rules, the Committee is nearly finished with its work, which still has to be approved on the floor. We honor a request to give an advance copy to Samuel Robinson, the chair of the Rules Committee. But in two months, the revised rules have come to look very different from the rules as passed on the floor, and Robinson seems quite upset. There could be a big floor fight over changes in the rules, and if Style and Drafting's package is rejected on the floor after two months' effort, there may be massive resignations from the Committee, making it impossible to edit the actual constitutional text.

Now that the Committee's work is under attack, the members become more united than ever before, and they develop a strategy for floor approval of the revised rules. The Committee will impress the convention with the seriousness of its effort by presenting a slide show at a plenary session. With an overhead projector, a member of the Committee will show the delegates a sample page of the original rules and the corresponding sections of the revised rules, demonstrating that while the words have been tightened up and the order made more logical, the meaning has not been changed. Wisely, Corn steps aside and this task is assigned to Feely, who is not only a black delegate and a teacher of English, but who also probably contributed more than any other Committee member to making the revised rules readable.

THE PLENARY MEETINGS

Most of the acrimony that I recall from the days before the election of officers seems not to affect the Committee meetings. The delegates do continue their battles, however, using procedural weapons in the Saturday plenary sessions. An early incident results from Corn's announcement that Chestie Graham has been elected vice-chair of Style and Drafting. William Cooper, the convention's secretary, challenges her right to be a member, much less an officer, of the Committee. He says that under the rules, a delegate could volunteer for this Committee by notifying the President of the Convention, and that although he was given notice, he did

Barbara Lett Simmons

not pass it on to Cassell, making Graham's service on the Committee improper. After substantial debate, Cassell pleads with the delegates not to eat up the afternoon with such trivia and requests that the convention accept his ruling that Graham be permitted membership on the Committee. But Cooper refuses to go along with what he considers an illegal appointment, and debate continues. I offer that the president *was* notified, because he had indicated to the convention that the secretary, Cooper, was his delegate for the purpose of giving him notice. To my surprise, Cassell rejects my reasoning, saying that he can rule that Graham is a member of the Committee "on the basis of . . . [his] prerogatives" and that Cooper is not his agent for receipt of notice.[22] Graham eventually wins this battle, but in the course of the debate a black delegate whispers to me why Cassell rejected my attempt to help him. Graham had bolted the caucus to nominate Mason. She had been edged off the Committee on the Legislative Branch and some delegates wanted to keep her from joining Style and Drafting as well. "He's saying to you, this is the business of black people," my colleague tells me. "We'll do it our way."

This incident, however, is thankfully one of only a very few reminders of the racial division that characterized the convention's first two months. Another develops from Barbara Lett Simmons' weekly circulation of photographs she has taken at the convention, which she sells to the other delegates at cost. Two such photographs show the black caucus at work, and one of them includes a blackboard on which are recorded the results of the caucus elections for chairs of all of the committees—a photograph taken before those committees, which were to select their own chairs, had any members. Two weeks later, an anonymously authored satiric newsletter appears in delegates' convention mailboxes. An entry reads: "Convention Photographer: Our thanks to BLS for the wonderful photos of convention activities including the candids of the Black Caucus' meeting to select committee chairs."[23] Simmons complains on the floor that "sovereign sanctity" ought to attach to a delegate's mailbox, and that "it should not be available for anyone's garbage." Her motion to secure the delegates' mailboxes opens a major debate on the issue of free speech, including a lengthy argument over whether a delegate can "call the question" without first being recognized by the chair.[24]

Lengthy battles over procedural points continue to characterize the plenary meetings. The president is compelled to ask the secretary to "stop obstructing," and delegates wonder whether the convention will really be able to approve constitutional text, where real policy issues will be at stake, in only four or five weeks of debate. But one expected battle never materializes. On the day before the convention is scheduled to begin debating committee proposals for constitutional text, the Committee on Style and Drafting presents its slide show on the revised rules. The presentation fits into the agenda late in the afternoon. None of us knows where the opposition is going to come from though we can all sense that it is there. But a few minutes pass before the room is darkened and the equipment focused. During this time someone announces that a vendor has arrived with food. Many delegates take advantage of the hiatus in the proceedings to obtain refreshment. The hall is nearly empty when Feely finishes discussing how old rule 3.4 has become new rule 3.3(g). The package is approved unanimously on a quick voice vote.[25]

With approval of the rules, the stage is set for debate and voting on the structure of state government. Will it be possible, I wonder, for debate on delegates' concerns to proceed as Cassell says he wants it to: with "that tension removed, and an open, democratic full discussion of all things done without bitterness"?[26]

PRESS COVERAGE

The *Washington Post* has been a big surprise, for it seems to have missed both of the real stories of this convention: The existence and role of the black caucus, and the fact that, despite the ideological passions of the delegates, their relative legal and legislative inexperience, and their lack of financial and other resources, a responsible constitution is emerging from the committees. Instead of reporting these events, the *Post* contents itself with articles about the wildest ideas that delegates put forward, even though most are not adopted by a committee, and with editorials arguing that "[b]y larding up their draft document with words about every delegate's favorite cause, pet peeve and/or recipe for instant nirvana, the convention members can assure a guaranteed negative reception in Congress . . . ."[27] At the end of a session, I corner the *Post*'s reporter, Paul Valentine, and ask him why the paper is focusing on the fairly radical ideas being proposed by individual delegates for the bill of rights rather than the less radical work being approved by the other committees. He tells me that he has been arguing with his editor about just this point, but she wants him to omit what he is writing about how conventional most of the convention's product is. "'Can't you just leave all that out?' she keeps asking. 'The people don't want to read that.'"

Mine, I suppose, is every elected official's complaint about the press. And his is the standard reply.

Notes to Chapter 8

1. The following events are recorded in CTR, Legislative Branch, Mar. 8, 1982, pp. 9-19.

2. The following events are recorded in CTR, Legislative Branch, Mar. 16, 1982, pp. 15-40, and Committee on the Legislative Branch Minutes, Mar. 15, 1982, p. 9 (vote).

3. *See* Committee on the Legislative Branch Minutes, Mar. 17, 1982, pp. 2-9.

4. *See* Committee on the Legislative Branch Minutes, Mar. 22, 1982, p. 7.

5. *Ibid.*

6. *National Municipal League, Model State Constitution* (6th ed. 1963, rev. 1968), § 4.02.

7. *See* Committee on the Legislative Branch Minutes, Mar. 29, 1982, p. 7 (Delegate Long says that Delegate Love has "come in with 25 documents").

8. *See* CTR, Legislative Branch, Apr. 5, 1982, pp. 10-14.

9. CTR, Legislative Branch, Apr. 14, 1982, pp. 11-23; Committee on the Legislative Branch Minutes, Apr. 14, 1982, p. 2 (vote).

10. *See* Statement of Robert Roehr, for the D.C. Republican Central Committee, before the Committee on the Legislative Branch of the District of Columbia Constitutional Convention, Apr. 15, 1982.

11. The following events are recorded in CTR, Legislative Branch, Apr. 21, 1982, Part 2, pp. 2-49.

12. CTR, CLGIRT, Feb. 25, 1982, p. 5.

13. CLGIRT Minutes, Mar. 11, 1982.

14. The following is a description of the Committee interview with Ann Witt, Mar. 22, 1982.

15. Eichhorn, Draft Article, Committee on Local Government, Mar. 17, 1982, § § I, V, VI, VII. The Eichhorn draft also provided for County Service Cabinets to coordinate state programs in each county, and required annual justification for any differing levels of state expenditure from one county to another. *Ibid.* § § VIII, IX.

16. Schrag, Draft Article, Committee on Local Government (undated).

17. CLGIRT Minutes, Mar. 25, 1982, pp. 1-2.

18. CLGIRT, Committee Draft on Local Government, Apr. 8, 1982, § § 1, 5, 6, 7.

19. CTR, CLGIRT, Apr. 6, 1982, part 3, pp. 26-35 ("the word negotiate isn't strong enough, because you and I could negotiate for days, but there is nothing in the Constitution saying that you had to do anything other than talk to me regularly"); CLGIRT, Committee Draft on Local Government, Apr. 8, 1982, § 1.

20. Hearings before the CLGIRT, Apr. 13, 15, 1982.

21. CTR, CLGIRT, Apr. 27, 1982, pp. 13-19.

22. Transcript, Mar. 13, 1982, pp. 113-22.

23. Alternative Caucus News, v. 1, no. 1, Mar. 20, 1982.

24. Transcript, Mar. 20, 1982, pp. 104-20.

25. Transcript, Apr. 24, 1982, pp. 79-86.

26. Transcript, Apr. 3, 1982, p. 128.

27. *See* Valentine, "D.C. Convention Fight Looms on Abortion, Guns," *Washington Post*, Apr. 17, 1982, p. B1; Valentine, "Rugged Constitution Needed to Digest All the Ideas," *Washington Post*, Apr. 12, 1982, p. B2; Editorial, "How to Kill Statehood—Fast," *Washington Post*, Apr. 24, 1982, p. A16.

CHAPTER 9:

The Floor: Policies in Conflict

Floor debate on proposals for constitutional text began on April 16, 1982, and ended on May 29. Under the convention's rules, each proposal was to be given three readings, with successively higher majorities required to make changes in content. An ordinary majority, however, would be sufficient to make any editorial changes that had been approved by the Style and Drafting Committee.[1] In fact, the time constraints under which the convention was operating, even more than the requirement of extraordinary majorities, served to discourage reexamination of anything that had been approved on the floor. With only three exceptions on the second reading,[2] and none on the third reading, the text that was hammered out on first consideration of a proposed article became the final text of the constitution.

During this period, the delegates met in plenary session five evenings each week and most of the day on Saturdays. A few of the committees, particularly the Committee on the Preamble and Bill of Rights, had not completed their work by the time that the marathon of plenary sessions began, and they had to schedule extra meetings on weekday afternoons to complete their proposals. The Committee on Style and Drafting also had to meet during the day to edit text that had been approved on the first reading. Because most delegates held full-time jobs in addition to their convention duties, the workload was very heavy.

The first portion of text considered on the floor was the preamble. Because the proposed language was symbolic, there were disagreements over the choice of symbols. Amendments were offered, for example, to insert a reference to God, and to delete a reference to "reach[ing] out to all peoples of the world." But the committee's proposed preamble was approved on the floor without any change whatever, in large measure because of an eloquent oration by the committee's chair, Reverend Jerry Moore. He urged delegates to reject floor amendments because when an individual "undertakes to become a committee and report to the convention . . . [h]owever eloquent, however well-meaning, however astute may be the intention . . . I do not believe that it reaches the apex of what a convention committee can do." This speech may have set the tone for the weeks that followed. Although many amendments to committee proposals were offered, very few made significant policy changes in what committees had proposed. Most of the amendments that were approved on the floor were perfecting amendments, often accepted by the sponsoring committee.[3]

THE JUDICIARY

The two principal contests with respect to the article on the judiciary involved the number of layers to the court system and the method for judicial selection. The Committee on the Judicial Branch proposed a judicial system consisting of two tiers of constitutionally established courts, plus such inferior courts as might be established by statute. Delegate Charles Mason noted that another proposed constitutional provision required the state's highest court to sit en banc rather than in panels, and that the District of Columbia Court of Appeals in fact almost always sits in panels because it could not otherwise handle the volume of appellate cases.[4] He suggested that a three-tier court system, including an intermediate appellate court, would be necessary if the highest court were to sit en banc. The Committee responded that "there was no demonstrated economic or judicial management need for an intermediate appellate court," and that "every one of the people who testified before our committee said there was no need for a three-tier system." A motion to add a third tier was defeated on a voice vote.[5]

Just before adoption of the article on the judiciary, however, Delegate Kenneth Rothschild reported on a telephone conversation he had had with a former clerk of the D.C. Court of Appeals. This clerk had said that the two-tier system which was about to be approved by the convention was "not workable," because it would not be able to handle the predictable appellate volume. This disclosure did not prevent adoption of the article on first reading, but it did raise questions in delegates' minds. On the second reading of the article several weeks later, Delegate Alexa Freeman, then a law student at American University, raised the issue again. Her research had revealed that even with the court of appeals sitting in panels, appeals were backlogged for more than a year. If the convention did not permit the legislature the option of creating an intermediate appellate court, she concluded that "you are going to have poor people sitting in jail for 560 days waiting for their appeals." Freeman was supported by Charles Mason, who reported that the Massachusetts legislature had recently added such a court to the state system at the recommendation of a commission headed by Professor Archibald Cox, and that "[m]y impression is that it works very well [in reducing appellate backlog]." Delegate Simmons argued that an intermediate court might be needed to prevent economic inequality, because although poor people might wait in jail for an appeal, "if you've got money, power, and status, you don't languish. You do get your case expedited." The two-tier system would therefore disadvantage "high visibility minorities and poor people."

The only opposition expressed to the Freeman amendment came from delegates who were troubled by the idea of reopening any issue that had already been decided once on the floor, and from Delegate Janette Harris, a member of the Committee on the Judicial Branch, who reiterated that some witnesses before the Committee had stated that an intermediate court would not reduce backlog. The amendment received the two-thirds vote necessary for passage on a second reading, and perfecting amendments that clarified the jurisdictional relationships among the various levels of courts were then adopted.[6]

With respect to the judiciary, the delegates also focused on judicial selection and retention. Some delegates would have preferred a system of elected judges to the appointive system that the Committee on the Judicial Branch had recommended. Instead, aware that they did not have the votes for an elective system, these delegates proposed that the judges, though appointed by the governor, would have to submit to periodic retention elections at which the voters would either keep them in office or remove them. Delegates argued that a retention system would prevent the judiciary from being "too controlled by lawyers," get citizens involved in reviewing sitting judges and strike a balance between independence and accountability. Opponents of retention elections claimed that judges facing election might be influenced by the press when deciding cases involving individual rights, that the existing judiciary might campaign in Congress against statehood because this clause would so threaten sitting judges, and that special interest groups would campaign against judges who had resolved policy issues in a way inconsistent with their views. By a narrow vote, a provision was added to the constitution requiring judges to stand for election after three years of service, and periodically thereafter.[7]

THE EXECUTIVE BRANCH

When the report of the Committee on the Executive Branch reached the floor, the delegates concentrated their attention on which constitutional officers would be established, and on whether the appointing authority of the governor would be qualified by limitations against appointing all members of boards and commissions from the same political party. The principal issue was whether the constitution would provide for a lieutenant governor.

The Committee on the Executive Branch had recommended the establishment of four elected officers: a governor, lieutenant governor, secretary of state, and attorney general.[8] On the floor, Delegate Brian Moore moved to strike the office of lieutenant governor, arguing that the office would be an unnecessary expense for a small jurisdiction that had no need for an essentially ceremonial office. He proposed instead that the constitution define the duties of the secretary of state to "include the combined functions normally carried out by a lieutenant governor found in larger states." The Committee responded that the new state needed an ideologically compatible substitute for an ill or absent governor, and that a secretary of state elected for technical proficiency might not agree with the governor's policies. Despite the Committee's arguments, the Moore motion carried. Here, too, the convention had second thoughts; on second reading, the office of lieutenant governor was restored, and the position of secretary of state abolished.[9]

The unusual political makeup of the District of Columbia contributed significantly to the other textual change in the article on the executive branch. The District's overwhelmingly Democratic electorate made the convention's few Republicans apprehensive that all appointed officials in the new state would forever be Democratic, freezing out Republicans from virtually any participation in state government. Accordingly, one of the Republicans proposed, apparently at the Republican Party's request, that each board or commission be required to include minority party representation. Opponents of this concept argued that it would politicize otherwise professional commissions, and that no governor would ignore a minority party. Notwithstanding these arguments, the proposal was adopted on a voice vote.[10]

SUFFRAGE

The principal issue of floor debate concerning suffrage involved the question of voter registration. The Committee on Suffrage proposed that the new state's board of elections be authorized to close voter registration for a period of up to thirty days before elections.[11] Several delegates took issue with this plan, and proposed instead that prospective voters be permitted to cast ballots simply by showing proof of residence when they went to vote. They pointed out that the District, like most jurisdictions, had a high percentage of unregistered but otherwise potentially eligible voters, and that as of 1982 five states permitted voting upon presentation of a local driver's license at the polls.

In the debate that followed, what appeared to separate the two sides were different assumptions about why otherwise eligible voters failed to participate in the electoral process. Proponents of "same-day" registration believed that the administrative burden of registering in advance, before the election was fully focused, was excessive. They argued that nonparticipation had cultural, educational, and financial underpinnings, and that the D.C. Board of Elections had historically made so many errors that citizens were discouraged from registering and voting. Those who preferred to let the legislature close registration in advance acknowledged the history of voting problems in the District, but claimed that they would get worse if officials were not given a quiet period in which they could sort out the voters before election day. They also believed that massive forgery of voter identification would take place, and that candidates would purchase votes on election day. More important, the opponents of same-day registration did not believe that the election machinery itself bore much responsibility for low participation. Instead, they suggested that those who did not vote were alienated from the process because they did not understand "the reasons and the importance of voting." In the end, the same-day registration proposal was narrowly defeated by the convention.[12]

THE LEGISLATIVE BRANCH

One of the most vigorously contested battles of the convention was the fight over the structure and size of the legislature. On the surface of this debate, three issues were interwoven: The name of the legislative body or bodies, their number, and their size. As in the Committee on the

Legislative Branch, however, the real issue involved the delegates' competing conceptions of how "professional" a legislature they wanted.

This underlying issue was reflected in the fact that the name of the legislature was hotly contested; the name became a symbol for each side's view of the kind of legislature it wanted. The Committee on the Legislative Branch, which had recommended a one-house legislature, had proposed calling it the "Senate."[13] As two Committee members explained it on the floor, the title of "Senator" is "prestigious [and] traditional," and the new state's unicameral body should be called a Senate because it would be the highest lawmaking body in the state.

A proposal to change the term to "House" or "House of Delegates" was put forward because, in the view of some delegates, a "House" is "generally considered the people's body," whereas a "Senate" has traditionally been "far more elitist, . . . the bastion of privilege [and] wealth." This proposal failed, because although a majority of the delegates opposed the name "Senate," some of them also disliked the name "House" because its members could be confused with the new state's United States Representative.[14]

Before the name of the state legislature was fully resolved, the more central issue of unicameralism or bicameralism arose. The delegate who launched the challenge to the Committee's recommendation first explained that a two-house legislature was needed for a system of checks and balances, but she soon made clear that the "more fundamental" problem was that a unicameral legislature was more likely to be composed of "professional and full-time people" which "takes away the ability of regular, everyday citizens to actually have a decisionmaking role in forming legislation." This concern was later echoed by a delegate who worried that full-time legislators were "removed from the world that the rest of us inhabit, with the normal concerns and worries that we have."

Curiously, the argument against elitism was also made in favor of the unicameral approach. One of its most outspoken supporters argued that the concept of an upper house was designed in England "to provide an undue advantage to the money interests," and that even the American Revolution was led by the "rich landowners." A two-house body would necessarily include an upper house, he noted, asking, "Whose checks are we trying to balance?" Most of the supporters of unicameralism based their defense, however, on more traditional grounds: that a one-house body would concentrate political responsibility, preventing leaders in each house from trading responsibility for killing popular legislation; that keeping the legislative process simple enough to be followed by the citizenry was desirable; that a unicameral system was familiar to D.C. residents; and that a unicameral system would be less costly. Those opposed to what they saw as an inevitably elitist professional legislature were particularly unmoved by the cost argument. They argued that nonprofessional, citizen legislators could be paid relatively little; one delegate mentioned a range of $2,000 to $3,000 a year.[15]

Initially, the convention voted for a bicameral system. The next day, however, during a lengthy debate about the size of the legislature, it reversed itself.[16] The Committee had recommended a total of twenty-four legislators, but individual delegates proposed a large number of alternatives. Supporters of the Committee proposal argued, in addition to the lower cost of a relatively small body, that it would prove politically impossible ever to reduce the size of the legislature if it should prove to be too large. They further argued that if the number of legislators became much larger than twenty-four, and districts correspondingly smaller, it would be impossible ever to unseat incumbents, because the number of swing voters would be small enough for the incumbent to affect through personal influence. Finally, Committee proposal supporters argued that if the public believed that the convention was creating jobs for politicians, the constitution would not be ratified.

Challengers of the Committee proposal again framed the issue in terms of the probability that the legislature would be more likely to vote higher salaries to fewer people, enabling members to spend full time on legislative duties. This was perceived as a strongly negative influence by some delegates, who reminded the others, to two bursts of applause, that "it is the professionals who brought you Ronald Reagan. It is the professionals that brought you a 100% increase in defense spending, because that's best for industry. And it is the professionals in our city that in fact cannot deliver services adequately to our neighborhoods . . . . I am much happier to allow my laws to be written by folks like you or I . . . ." The Committee's proposal was defeated, twenty-two to ten, and the convention decided on a legislature of forty members.[17]

Despite the success of this challenge to the Committee's concept of a smaller legislature, the convention rejected a more direct attempt to prohibit the legislature from becoming too "professional." Many state constitutions limit the number of days during which the legislature may sit each year, and a motion was made to limit the time that the new state's legislature could meet to 120 days per annual session. One delegate responded to this motion in the strongest possible terms:

> All I need to do is look at those two pathetic examples of statehood on either side of us, Maryland and Virginia, with their hectic, chaotic sessions, which meet your approximate criteria every year—ill-devised, ill-advised, ill-enacted legislation—to see all the ills and evils of what you're trying to perpetrate on us. . . ."

The proposal received only a single vote.[18]

ECONOMIC DEVELOPMENT

The proposals of the Committee on Economic Development, like those of the Committee on the Bill of Rights, were among the most controversial of the convention. Some of the disagreement involved particular provisions, but to a significant extent, the issue dividing the delegates was the question of whether economic proposals belonged in a constitution at all. This issue was joined at the outset of the debate when Delegates Wesley Long and William Cooper, two members of the Committee on Economic Development, introduced a minority report that would have substituted a single sentence in the place of all six proposed articles drafted by the Committee.

Their substitute would have empowered the legislature to pass laws for the general welfare, including laws relating to labor, health, the environment, and utilities. The sponsors of the substitute believed that the articles proposed by the Committee seemed to create new and sometimes controversial rights of dubious economic merit—"red flag[s]" that might put the constitution in jeopardy. They also claimed that Committee deliberation was inadequate and that the Committee had exceeded its authority:

> [W]e are all aware of the high-handedness that some delegates can serve [sic]. I think we are all aware of how many delegates vote in unison, how many delegates don't give an objective view to what is before us. . . . We [who served on the pre-convention Committee on Committees] certainly did not expect the Committee on Economic Development to come out with such an extraneous document. This was not their purview.

Supporters of incorporating economic policy judgments in the constitution acknowledged that to do so was controversial, but argued that "the Continental Congress was controversial," that the convention should not ignore the "issues of vital interest" and that the convention should defer to the work that the Committee had done. They responded to the argument that the economic provisions might make the adoption of the constitution more difficult by asking, "Why should I, for the sake of getting out of jail, contract myself to be bound and stocked in the public center? Now if to secure statehood, we have to encumber ourselves to the economic interests for the sake of their own gains, rape and rob and prostitute the citizens of the city, then let them keep statehood." The minority substitute was defeated easily.[19]

Although the six articles proposed by the Committee embraced literally dozens of regulatory topics, four of these topics attracted most of the attention of the delegates. The Committee had proposed language to make it the "policy," a word changed on the floor to "responsibility," of the state to "protect . . . the environment." The proposal had gone further by specifying that it would do so "by . . . preventing pollution or degradation of the air, land and water; contamination of indoor air and drinking water; and the creation of unnecessary noise, hazardous wastes or other threats to the public's right to health and enjoyment of its surroundings." The inclusion of what became known as this "laundry list" provoked a classic ideological battle between environmentalist absolutists and cost-benefit analysts.

A motion was made to strike the laundry list, and although that proposed amendment need not have raised the question of taking costs into account in making environmental decisions, the delegates read that issue into the wording. Delegate Oulahan, a lawyer, claimed that the words "right to health" in the list could imply a right enforceable in court and said that the drafters had not estimated the cost of implementing that right. The convention's counsel, commenting not especially on the laundry list but on the inclusion of environmental protection language in general, conceded that "the courts will decide ultimately . . . what this section means " The possibility that some of the language of the section might frighten off cost-conscious delegates aroused the absolutists. One argued:

> It is also fascinating to me that the issue of cost of protecting our environment comes up. Do we talk about the costs of the right to vote? Well, what is the right to vote if the environment exists that you can't exist in it?

Another performed a thumbnail balance:

> It costs much more to put people in hospitals, and when you get right down to it, the cost of human services is an awful lot of money in this city and I think the money ought to be spent to make you comfortable.

By a narrow margin, the laundry list was removed.[20]

The second issue that generated intense controversy involved a proposed section which provided that:

> Each person has the right to a clean and healthful environment, and a corresponding duty to refrain from environmental impairment. Each person may enforce these rights and duties against any party, public or private, through appropriate legal proceedings, subject to reasonable limitations and regulations as provided by law.[21]

Again, Delegate Oulahan claimed that the concept was flawed. He noted that the first clause was stated in absolute terms, but that it was in fact impossible to assure an absolutely clean or healthful environment. Therefore, each person's right to such an environment necessarily would be violated. Because this would give rise to a cause of action under the second clause, Oulahan argued that the provision would become "the single most important source of litigation in our state." Other delegates feared that previously innocuous behavior might be declared unlawful under the proposed section. For example, one delegate noted that she might be sued for smoking, one wondered whether she might be liable if she stopped cutting her grass and one recalled that he used to keep "a ewe and a little ram" which might attract the attention of litigious neighbors.

In response, supporters of the clause pointed out that the District of Columbia suffers from extremely bad pollution and that the clause empowered the legislature to impose reasonable limitations on the right to sue. The language was approved by a margin of sixteen to twelve.[22]

The third controversy arose from a Committee proposal to include a provision in the constitution stating that utility "rates shall not be so excessive for the service rendered as to take rate-payers' property."[23] The concept of a taking of property obviously originated in the United States Constitution's guarantee against governmental takings without just compensation. The link between that context and the Committee's proposal lay in the claim, sometimes made by utilities, that if governmental regulatory bodies did not permit them a sufficient rate of return on their investment, the utilities' property was being "taken" by the government. The proposed clause was thought to give consumers of utility services a "corresponding property right" that would enable them to "force utilities to accrue costs in the most efficient manner."[24]

Though it appeared from the Committee's report that its real intention was to strengthen the public's hand as against *inefficient* utilities, the language chosen by the Committee did not relate only to inefficiency but added the phrase about the taking of property. This additional phrase might be interpreted, at some later time, to preclude charging consumers (or at least those consumers who were down to their last dollars, or perhaps their last discretionary dollars) for electricity, gas, or telephone service. The problem was compounded by the fact that a noncontroversial part of the same provision stated that utility services shall be provided at the "lowest reasonable" rates. One delegate questioned how any charge for utility service could be construed as a taking of property if rates were already at their lowest reasonable level.[25]

Maurice Jackson

The chair of the Committee on Economic Development vigorously defended the Committee's language. He noted that utilities were "private monopol[ies]" with "a constitutional right to a rate of return. The consumer has no constitutional right. What we are trying to do is provide the consumer with a constitutional right." Many of the other delegates spoke on this issue, most of them supporting the Committee's language based on a sense that public utilities were charging excessive rates and needed additional constraints. An amendment to delete the reference to a taking of ratepayers' property was defeated, but the Convention ultimately settled upon a compromise in which a phrase barring "unreasonably high rates on excessive capital investments" was substituted for the "takings" clause.[26]

The final major controversy on the economic articles raised the question of whether, and under what conditions, public employees would have the right to strike. The Committee had debated this controversial issue extensively, and in the end had sought to construct a balance between the right to strike and protection of the general welfare.[27]

Under the Committee's compromise, public employees' right to strike "shall not be abridged unless it serves a compelling governmental interest, is narrowly drawn so as to serve that interest, and it is clear that no alternative form of regulation is possible which does not abridge such right." Some delegates, for whom Delegate Maurice Jackson was the principal spokesperson, did not think that this limited recognition of public workers' rights went nearly far enough. Jackson proposed to substitute an absolute right to strike, and he explained the reasons in one of his major addresses to the convention:

> Labor is a commodity, bought and sold in the market every day. For those who are lawyers and whatnot, it goes to the highest bidder; for those who are like me and have nothing, in many cases it goes to the highest, in some cases it goes to the lowest. But it is still all we have . . . . [The right to strike is missing in the U.S. Constitution because] not a single black person—which means one out of six people in this country . . . —passed this Constitution. . . . And if there is anything in society that I know I will do, it is stay poor, stay black, work my tail off, pay taxes, and die . . . . My labor is something to die for, and I will put this on the line right now.

Other delegates were equally impassioned. One spoke of her father, who had been attacked by dogs and hosed down by water hoses in three-degree weather walking a picket line. Another reminded delegates pointedly that there had once been an implicit bargain under which public employees enjoyed greater job security than private employees and in return gave up the right to strike, but that the deal had been broken by government layoffs by the Reagan Administration.

Opponents to the Jackson substitute combined pragmatic and emotional arguments. They asserted that an absolute right to strike would be an easy target for opponents of statehood, and that Congress would have particular concerns about the possibility of police strikes in the state surrounding the federal enclave that would remain the nation's capital. They also asked the delegates to view the issue not only from the perspective of the worker, but also from the perspective of the recipient of public services: "If you had a relative who had a heart attack, or if you had a relative who had been shot, like I had a few weeks ago, if you had your house burn down with children in it, how would you feel if the police were on strike, and you couldn't do anything about it?" The Jackson substitute was ultimately defeated by a vote of sixteen to fourteen, and the Committee proposal was approved by a wide margin.[28]

FINANCE AND TAXATION

The proposed article on finance and taxation was one of the most technical portions of the Constitution, and the debate was relatively subdued. The Committee's proposal that the legislature be required to approve a "balanced" operating budget for the state was questioned, but after a Committee member explained that this did not really require operating within a balanced budget, but only submission of such a budget subject to later amendment, the Committee's position was sustained.[29]

The Committee recommendation that was most thoroughly debated was its proposal to prevent the legislature from granting real property exemptions to any entity except "real property used exclusively for religious purposes or as required by federal law." Barring the legislature from granting tax exemptions to such other traditionally exempt nonprofit entities as universities or charities was not a drafting oversight. The Committee's report conceded that most state constitutions take exactly the opposite tack, constitutionally exempting from state taxation all organizations that are exempt from income taxation under section 501(c)(3) of the Internal Revenue Code. But the Committee had chosen to avoid granting exemption "to those institutions which do not promote and serve the public interest of the citizens," perhaps because "currently almost 50 percent of the land" of the District was exempt from taxation.[30]

Shortly before the proposed article was to be acted upon by the convention, the Committee had second thoughts, and sought to amend the draft to permit, though not require, the legislature to exempt property used for "nonprofit, educational, or charitable purposes." The wording of this amendment led to much confusion. A delegate questioned whether the word "nonprofit" modified "charitable" as well as "educational" and was told by a member of the Committee that it modified neither, implying that nonprofit institutions could be exempted even if they were neither educational nor charitable. The President of the Convention noted that if the word "nonprofit" stood alone, then educational institutions could qualify for a tax exemption even if they were profit-making in nature. The convention's general counsel was asked to comment, and he stated that despite the comma between "nonprofit" and "charitable," and the explanation by a Committee member, the Committee must have meant the words to be interpreted as though no comma was present; that is, as though the sole purpose of the word "nonprofit" was to modify both "educational" and "charitable." A delegate moved to amend the Committee's amendment by striking the comma. Before the amendment was voted upon, the Committee chair confirmed that the Committee had intended, contrary to what one of his members had said earlier, that the word "nonprofit" modified both "educational" and "charitable." The delegate who had offered the amendment to strike the comma apparently heard this as a decision to eliminate the controversial comma by consensus and withdrew his amendment. Other delegates suggested that the list of institutions that the legislature might validly desire to exempt should be broadened to include, for example, scientific and cultural endeavors or consumer cooperatives. The issue became further confused by a complex parliamentary tangle over how many proposed amendments were simultaneously on the floor and by some doubt as to the precise wording of what had been offered by the Committee. With so many matters before it, the convention apparently lost sight of the question of the comma. The convention voted narrowly to adopt the Committee amendment, permitting exemptions for "nonprofit, educational, or charitable purposes." The comma was never actually removed, and it remained in the constitution.[31]

EDUCATION

The major policy decision made by the Committee on Education was the decision to continue the District's practice of assigning governance of the educational system to an elected school board, rather than to an appointed official or commission. This policy decision was not questioned on the floor of the convention.[32] Three minor issues did, however, become the focus of significant debate.

The first of these issues involved a catchall phrase at the end of the clause on equal educational opportunity. The Committee's proposed text, as amended slightly on the floor, stated: "The State shall guarantee equality of educational opportunity in the public schools and other public educational institutions to all residents regardless of race, sex, religion, color, national origin, citizenship, condition of disability and other individual characteristics and may be sued for default of this guarantee." The catchall was intended to include "all other personal characteristics," and the examples given by the Committee were personal appearance, excessive weight, and sexual orientation. Some delegates, however, suggested that the words of the catchall phrase were broad enough to prohibit making distinctions on the basis of aptitude or achievement tests, thereby requiring the state university, or any specialized secondary schools, to admit applicants randomly rather than on the basis of "individual characteristics" that these tests would measure. Others opposed catchall phrases as a matter of principle, because they did not know what would later be read into them. The Committee suggested, however, that no problem existed, because the section applied only to equal educational opportunity (that is, the right to apply for education), and not to education itself, and that no individual characteristics could justify denying children the right to go to school. The Committee's language was sustained.[33]

The second issue for debate concerned the ages for compulsory education. At the time of the convention, schooling was compulsory to the age of sixteen or high school graduation, if that was achieved earlier. The Committee proposed to impose a constitutional requirement of education to the age of eighteen unless graduation had earlier been achieved. Some delegates opposed this change, arguing that to force a person to go to school after the age of sixteen "is infringing upon the right of the teenage person to make a free choice," that the age of compulsory education was a detail best left to the legislature and that providing the additional schooling might impose too great a financial burden on the new state. But Committee members supported the constitutional provision strongly. Delegate Nixon, the youngest delegate, made an appeal from his recent personal experience:

> I graduated at age 16 and . . . could not find a job, and I don't think that the labor market is really taking anyone at the age of 16 . . . . Some [16-year-olds] just walk out because they have an opportunity at age 16 just to go . . . . If we keep them in school until they are 18, I think they will be finished by [that] time.

Delegate Simmons, a member of the School Board, was equally emphatic, saying that "to throw kids out at 16 with no job is to guarantee them penalization in a penal institution or mental institution, and incarceration therein is much more expensive than education." A motion to retain the ceiling of sixteen years was easily defeated.[34]

Conflict also emerged over a proposal by the Committee to require *all* elementary and secondary schools in the state to meet the "same standards for instructors, instruction and student achievement as may be imposed by the State Board of Education on the public schools." Some delegates were concerned that this proposal would defeat the whole purpose of alternative education and would straight-jacket the private and parochial schools because it could be read to require all private schools to modify their curricular or personnel requirements if the School Board imposed a foreign language requirement on the curricula of public schools, or required all public school teachers to have degrees in education, whether or not the School Board even intended this effect. The convention's general counsel also questioned the proposal, asking, "What about the rights of a parent to make choices regarding his or her child's education? ... What about the role that certain 'experimental' private schools have played in making a contribution to the direction of public school systems, where change is often effected more slowly due to regulations and bureaucracy?"[35] Accordingly, an amendment was offered to change the provision to permit the state to establish "minimum standards, including equivalent alternatives" that all schools would have to meet.

The Committee opposed the amendment on the ground that if private schools did not have to meet standards identical to those set for the public schools, "you will get—and they are cropping up by the thousands all over the country—little fly-by-night schools, intended to make money for their owners, which will have no standards at all ... and will teach them nothing with instructors who are incapable of teaching...." In making this objection, the Committee was particularly referring to "so-called Christian academies." The Committee chair further objected that the level of education obtainable by children should not depend on the level of their parents' affluence; the standards should be identical "so that our children, regardless of which [schools] they have to go to or are able to go to, public or private, will be afforded the same opportunity and the same curriculum." The amendment was narrowly defeated, but with the Committee's support, the convention added the word "minimum" after the word "same," and authorized the Board of Education to establish equivalent alternatives (for both types of schools) for its educational standards. The result, apparently, is that if the Board imposes, for example, a foreign language requirement as a "minimum standard" for the public schools, that requirement must also be imposed on the private schools, although the Board may be able to designate such a requirement for the public schools as something other than a "minimum standard" to avoid its application to alternative school systems.[36]

LOCAL GOVERNMENT

The Committee on Local Government, which had replaced its original plan for a three-tiered system of local government with a proposal under which the legislature was directed to hold referenda on chartering a plan for local government, met relatively little resistance to its concept. The convention did, however, change the proposal in two respects. It deleted the Committee's requirement that if the voters disapproved the chartering plan put forward by the legislature, the legislature would be required to resubmit a new plan every other year for sixteen years. The convention also deleted the section in which the Committee had proposed that local government units, once established, would have the right to receive appropriations in lieu of centrally provided services, and to provide those services themselves. Opponents of this section argued that if some neighborhoods opted out of delivery of services by the state government, provision of those services, per capita, to the remaining neighborhoods might be prohibitively expensive.[37]

HEALTH, HOUSING AND HUMAN SERVICES

As the article on health, housing and human services arrived on the floor, it appeared that a significant policy dispute would arise in connection with the Committee's decision that certain levels or types of public assistance would be "guaranteed" by the constitution of the new state. The Committee's draft, for example, proposed to guarantee "assistance to its residents unable to maintain standards of living compatible with decency and good health care," to grant them a "right" to a clean and healthful environment, and to "guarantee" public health by the establishment of a network of comprehensive health facilities.[38] But the Committee itself drew back from its proposed language, which could well have invited lawsuits from citizens who did not believe that they had received all that the constitution had promised. The Committee proposed instead that the right to a healthful environment be deleted, and that the state be given "the power to provide for assistance" and "the power to provide for the establishment and maintenance of a network of comprehensive health facilities." The convention accepted these Committee-sponsored changes readily, but the issue of whether the constitution should mandate the provision of specified social services or only authorize the legislature to provide them reemerged in connection with the issue of day-care centers.[39]

As written by the Committee, the state would "have the power to provide and maintain public day care centers." Immediately before this section was debated on the floor, however, the convention discussed another section offered by the Committee, pursuant to which the state would be given the power to provide for the maintenance and support of prisons. A delegate moved to amend that section to require rather than enable the state to establish prisons. She explained that she wanted "to be sure that these . . . institutions shall be maintained. I am not interested in the 'power to do' if people are not disposed to do it. I want to demand that this exist." The convention's approval left it in the uncomfortable position of having mandated the establishment of prisons but not of humanitarian services, and although it was too late, given the convention's restrictive rule against reconsideration, to require the state to provide welfare or health care, the section on day care had not yet been approved. Accordingly, an amendment was offered to require the state to establish day-care centers, and the chair of the Committee supported it on the ground that "if we can find money to build new jails, then we can find money to provide for our children." The day-care amendment was approved, sixteen to thirteen, and became part of the constitution.[40]

THE BILL OF RIGHTS

The last subject considered on the floor, and the most controversial, was the bill of rights.[41] The proposed article that the Committee on the Preamble and Bill of Rights presented to the Committee was moderate in comparison to the list of possible clauses that it had circulated at its public hearing, but nevertheless guaranteed many liberties not addressed in the Federal Bill of Rights. The sections raised literally dozens of issues on which many delegates held relatively strong views. Furthermore, its orientation was such that one delegate termed it a "bill of lefts."[42]

The first controversy that arose was atypical, in that the Committee's proposal was defeated by the convention. The Committee had included among its proposed rights a "reporter's privilege," defining freedom of the press to include protection of the press from "searches, seizures or compulsory testimony to discover the identity of confidential sources or information provided by such sources." Opposition to this provision was based in part on the ground that unnecessary controversy should be avoided in the bill of rights, but the most forceful ground of attack involved delegates' distrust of the *Washington Post*. A few months before the convention, the *Post* had printed a story by one of its reporters about a child who had become a heroin addict. The story had been challenged by community leaders, but the *Post* had refused to require the reporter to identify her sources. After the story was recommended for a Pulitzer Prize, it was revealed to be a hoax, and the reporter was fired. The incident was cited by delegates as evidence that the press in Washington might well abuse a reporter's privilege, and that, in the process, communities could be "tarnish[ed]." The vote against the privilege was nineteen to seventeen.[43]

A second area of controversy involved criminal procedure. The Committee had proposed to allow criminal defendants access not only to exculpatory evidence in the state's possession or to evidence to be used against them at a trial, but to "the discovery of all evidence possessed by the state." This was opposed on the ground that it might require disclosure even prior to indictment, and that the disclosure might involve the names of confidential witnesses, whose identity would be needlessly revealed in cases that were never prosecuted. An attempt to delete the Committee's proposal, however, was narrowly defeated.[44]

Another aspect of criminal law—the issue of preventive detention of accused criminals—also divided the delegates. The Committee's draft language on bail included a clause stating that "bail is a right whose sole purpose is to assure the presence of the accused at trial." Some delegates read this sentence as a guarantee to accused persons that they would have a right to have bail set for them until the date of their trial, and could not be detained in prison, or even have limitations imposed on their activity until convicted. Some delegates were particularly concerned that known recidivists and murderers would be freed pending trial and would commit additional crimes.

The Committee defended the provision in two different ways. Some members believed that the state constitution should bar preventive detention legislation. They argued that "you are innocent until proven guilty," and that if preventive detention were permitted, "all groups of people, all classes of people, all colors of people—can be picked up and put in jail for some reason and never, my dear, be released." In support of the Committee, Delegate Simmons asserted that "we've got lots of political prisoners in this country now incarcerated, and it isn't for crimes that have been proven . . . [Y]ou could charge anybody with anything." Other Committee members, however, advocated the view that the Committee's proposed language did not preclude the legislature from providing for preventive detention. They argued that the language only prohibited the legislature and the courts from misusing bail for this purpose, by setting bail at excessive levels when defendants appeared to be dangerous.

The latter rationale did little to allay the concerns of those who saw a need for preventive detention in some cases, and the issue had to be settled by a compromise. The reference to a "right" to bail was struck by common consent from the Committee's language, but a statement that the "sole" purpose of bail was to assure the presence of the accused at trial remained in the Constitution. The convention voted down amendments that would have permitted denying bail to accused murderers and would have authorized "nonfinancial conditions of bail" to be set in the interest of "the safety of the community."[45]

The provision on discrimination also produced division among the delegates. In fact, fifteen to twenty amendments to the Committee's draft were introduced. The essence of the controversy lay in the Committee's decision not to base the state constitution's anti-discrimination clause in the language of the fourteenth amendment to the Federal Constitution, but rather, in a more modern vein, to try to list encyclopedically and more specifically the kinds of discrimination that were prohibited. Accordingly, the principal clause of the Committee's draft provided that "[e]very person shall have a fundamental right to be free from historic caste discrimination, public or private, based on factors such as race, color, creed, citizenship, national origin, sex, sexual orientation, poverty or out-of-wedlock birth . . . . All persons shall also have the right to be free from all forms of discrimination on account of age."[46]

The convention dealt with this language in two ways. First it considered a suggestion to substitute the Federal Constitution's equal protection clause for this list of more explicit rights, and for additional explicit protections that followed in later parts of the anti-discrimination section. This suggestion was unacceptable to the convention, however, in view of the fact that courts had not interpreted the equal protection clause to offer full equality to all the groups (such as the poor, women, and homosexuals) listed by the Committee, and had not interpreted the clause to apply to discrimination by private parties, as opposed to discrimination by the government. The suggestion received so little support, in fact, that it was withdrawn by its sponsor.

On the other hand, although the convention supported the Committee's approach in general, it was evident that the proposed text raised many legal problems. The convention's counsel listed several of them in a written report, in which he had noted that "the more sparse the bill of rights, the more judicially enforceable a document it becomes, thus providing real protection for the individual."[47] The convention therefore turned to the Committee's text on a line-by-line basis. The convention included an equal protection clause in addition to the list of prohibited types of discrimination, changed "caste discrimination" to "group discrimination," and deleted the phrase "factors such as" that had preceded the list, on the ground that it was too vague. "Religion" was added as a form of prohibited discrimination, although, by a single vote, the convention defeated a proposal to add "marital status, parentage, age, family responsibilities, political affiliation, physical handicap, income or lack thereof, place of residence or business, appearance or other individual characteristics." "Out-of-wedlock birth" was changed to "parentage." Constitutional protection against age discrimination was limited to adults, and further limited to discrimination in housing or employment.[48]

The Committee's recommendations that the constitution include the right of a woman to free choice on abortion and the right of consenting adults to be free from official restrictions on private sexual behavior were not controversial.[49] The most significant policy dispute of the convention, however, developed from the Committee's proposal that the constitution include a right to employment.

The Committee had proposed that people in the new state be given "the right, within the state's ability to provide, to . . . a job." When this recommendation reached the floor, Delegate Harris, who had been presiding, stepped down from the chair and moved, as a substitute, that "[e]very person shall have the right to employment or if unable to work, an income sufficient to meet basic human needs." The substitution was quickly accepted by the Committee on the Preamble and Bill of Rights, but several delegates recognized that the substitute deleted qualifying language that would have given the legislature an opportunity to regulate the degree of responsibility that the state would have for the provision of jobs. The elimination of the qualifying language, they pointed out, seemed to convert the provision from a policy goal to a judicially enforceable individual right, perhaps a right to demand public employment if private employment could not be found.

"The way the wording stands now, the state must provide employment for everyone who asks for a job," one delegate said, "and I believe it is just plainly impractical." Another said, "[W]e might want the government to be the employer of last resort. Maybe that someday will be the case as it is in a national situation. But on the local level, I don't think that we have the revenue or the ability to provide for that. And besides, . . . everybody will move here."

An amendment was offered to restore the Committee's original qualifying phrase. In a relatively rare descent from the rostrum to address the convention from the floor, President Cassell spoke at length against this amendment:

> I think it would be practical and it would not be difficult at all . . . . No state has ever had difficulty providing the number of police or law enforcement officers that are decided by the state at any time to be needed, never . . . . No state has ever had any problem providing a sufficient militia . . . . The Federal Government [has had no trouble] . . . providing full employment for the United States Army, the United States Navy, the Air Force and the Marines. There is always money for that because the state wants to.

And another delegate asked, "why is it the right of Pepco [a public utility] and other companies to make millions and millions and billions and trillions and whatever is after that, but my young black children don't have a right to a job?" The amendment was defeated, and the unqualified right to employment became part of the constitution.[50]

THE NAME OF THE NEW STATE

The convention left for last its decision on a name for the new state. It had charged the Committee on the Preamble and Bill of Rights with the duty of making a recommendation. The Committee took a limited public survey, in which the name "Columbia" received forty-seven votes, "North Potomac" received twenty-eight, and "South Potomac" received twenty-two. The Committee added the votes for the two "Potomac" choices and it recommended the name "Potomac." From the floor, delegates proposed, as alternatives, the names "Columbia" and "Anacostia," the latter a reference to an Indian tribe that had once been located in the region, a tributary of the Potomac River that empties into the Potomac in the District of Columbia, and the part of the District east of the tributary, one of the least affluent sections of the city. In addition, a delegate proposed naming the state "Utopia," "for all the far-out things that our people have said." But one by one, motions to adopt each of these names were defeated, although Anacostia only failed by a single vote.

It became clear that no one name was likely to obtain a majority over the aggregate of all possible names. The convention therefore reverted, for purposes of choosing a name, to the run-off method that it had used for electing its officers. On this second attempt, the name of "New Columbia" was added to the list of candidates by Delegate Warren, and it won on the second ballot.[51]

CLOSING CEREMONIES

On Saturday, May 29, 1982, the delegates assembled for what was technically the third reading of the proposed articles of the constitution. In fact, the occasion was ceremonial because amendments at this stage would have required a three-fourths vote to be approved, and there was little likelihood that any effort to change the substance of the document could be successful; besides, television cameras were present for the first time since the opening ceremonies. To minimize the likelihood that lingering policy differences would be aired on television, the convention decided, by a nearly unanimous vote, not to vote on an article-by-article basis (which would have encouraged the offering of amendments, at least on the issues that had been highly contentious), but to read the entire constitution aloud, and then to hold a final vote on the complete document. At the end of the oral reading, most of the delegates made short statements explaining the reasons for the final vote that they planned to cast. When these statements had been made, the roll was called, and by a vote of thirty-seven to two, with four abstentions, the constitution of the State of New Columbia was approved.[52]

1. Revised Rules, § 3.3.

2. The three exceptions were authorization for an intermediate appellate court, establishment of a position of lieutenant governor, and a change in the name of the legislature.

3. Transcript, Apr. 26, 1982, pp. 90-110.

4. Judiciary Committee Proposal, Apr. 19, 1982, § 3.1 (two tiers), § 3.5 (en banc).

5. Transcript, Apr. 27, 1982, pp. 46-49; Transcript, Apr. 28, 1982, pp. 86-113.

6. Transcript, Apr. 30, 1982, pp. 202, 208 ("not workable"), 223 (first reading); Transcript, May 22, 1982, pp. 166-68 (Delegate Freeman), 174 (Delegate Charles Mason), 176 (Delegate Simmons), 179 (Delegate Talmadge Moore) and 172 (Delegate Cooper) (opposed to reopening), 171 (Delegate Harris), 181 (vote on second reading); Const., art. IV, § 2(A).

7. Transcript, Apr. 28, 1982, pp. 176 (Delegate Thomas, quoting other delegates) (prefer elected judges), 175 (propose retention election), 184 (Delegate Rothschild) ("too controlled"), 187 (Delegate Garner) (citizens involved), 192 (Delegate Jordan) (strike balance), 182-83 (Delegate Clarke) (influenced by press, campaign against statehood), 187 (Delegate Eichhorn) (special interest groups), 199 (vote); Const., art. III, § 10.

The subsequent elections are to be held every ten years for supreme court judges and every six years for superior court judges.

8. Committee on the Executive Branch Proposal, SC1-3A-0003, Apr. 24, 1982.

9. Transcript, May 3, 1982, pp. 46-49 (Delegate Brian Moore), 53 (Delegate Simmons) (need for Lt. Governor), 56 (first vote); Transcript, May 26, 1982, pp. 120-42 (second reading).

10. Transcript, May 4, 1982, pp. 124 (Republican Party request), 106 (minority party representation), 114 (Delegate Shelton) (politicize), 116 (Delegate Simmons) (Governor not ignore), 127 (vote); ; Const., art. III, § 8(C).

11. Committee on Suffrage Proposal, SC1-104-0009, Apr. 28, 1982, § 1(e).

12. Transcript, May 5, 1982, pp. 64-76 (14-12 vote).

13. Committee on the Legislative Branch Proposal, SC1-2A-0017, May 1, 1982, § 1.

14. Transcript, May 11, 1982, pp. 15-16 (Delegates T. Moore and Warren) (Senate prestigious), 9-10 (House people's body, Senate elitist), 24 (House proposal fails); Transcript, May 11, 1982, p. 14 (confusion over new state's U.S. Representative).

On the first reading, the name "Legislature" defeated the name "Senate" by one vote. The Legislature was eventually renamed the House of Delegates on second reading. Const., art. II, § 1.

15. Transcript, May 11, 1982, pp. 29-30 (Delegate Nahikian) (need for two-house legislature), 58 (echoing concern about professional politicians), 55-56 (Delegate Jordan) (rich landowners, checks balanced), 31 (concentrate responsibility), 59 (not trade responsibility), 31-32 (simpler and more familiar), 32-33, 53-54 (less costly), 58 ($2,000 to $3,000).

16. Transcript, May 11, 1982 p. 66 (bicameral vote); Transcript, May 12, 1982, p. 96 (reversal).

17. Committee on the Legislative Branch Proposal, SC1-2A-0017, May 1, 1982, § 2 (committee recommendation); Transcript, May 11, 1982, pp. 90-148; Transcript, May 12, 1982, pp. 14-96 (alternative proposals); Transcript, May 12, 1982, pp. 40 (lower cost, impossibility of reduction), 41 (size of constituency), 44 (ratification concern), 49, 51 (applause), 50 ("professionals"), 67 (committee proposal defeated), 86 (forty members); Const., art. II, § 2.

18. Md. Const. art. III, § 15(1), S.D. Const. art. III, 6, Texas Const., art. III, § 40 (states limiting days); Transcript, May 13, 1982, pp. 139 (motion), 139 (Delegate Kameny) (response), 151 (vote).

19. Transcript, May 14, 1982, p. 51 (minority report); Transcript, May 17, 1982, pp. 23-24 (Delegate Long) ("red flags"), 29 (Delegate Cooper) ("extraneous document"), 26 (Delegate Coates) ("Continental Congress, vital interest"), 27 (Delegate Holmes, asking for deference to committees, stating "if we didn't want the committees, we shouldn't have put the ten together"), 32 (Delegate Coates) (response to adoption of constitution concern) (the record shows that the speech was applauded, suggesting more than isolated support for Delegate Coates' views), 35 (vote, 25-5).

20. Committee on Economic Development Proposal, SC1-9A-0011, Apr. 29, 1982, § 1; Transcript, May 14, 1982, pp. 129 ("responsibility"), 117 ("laundry list"), 119 (motion to strike), 120 (Delegate Oulahan), 121 (convention's counsel), 122 (Delegate Marcus) ("right to vote"), 122-23 (Delegate Jones) ("cost of human services"), 123 (15-12 vote).

21. Committee on Economic Development Proposal, SC1-9A-0011, Apr. 29, 1982, § 3.

22. Transcript, May 14, 1982, pp. 138 (Delegate Oulahan), 141 (Delegate Eichhorn) (smoking), 152 (Delegate Jones) (cutting grass), 144 (Delegate Jordan) (ewe and ram), 139, 150-51, 155 (D.C. pollution), 140-41, 146, 153 (reasonable limits on suits), 158 (vote).

23. Committee on Economic Development Proposal, SC1-9A-0012, Apr. 29, 1982, § 2(a).

24. Report of the Committee on Economic Development, Apr. 30, 1982.

25. Transcript, May 14, 1982, p. 180 (Delegate Schrag).

26. Transcript, May 14, 1982, pp. 185 (Delegate Croft) (chairman defends proposal), 198-225 (debate), 211 (amendment defeated), 228 (Const., art. X, § 2(a) substituted).

27. Report of the Committee on Economic Development, April 30, 1982; Committee on Economic Development Proposal, SC1-9A-0013, Apr. 29, 1982, § 1.

28. Transcript, May 15, 1982, pp. 110-11 (Delegate Jackson), 117 (Delegate Nahikian) (speaking of father), 121 (Reagan Administration breach), 115 (easy target), 119, 128 (police strikes), 130 (Delegate H. Mason) (heart attack or fire), 140 (Jackson substitute defeated), 171 (22-8 vote).

29. Transcript, May 17, 1982, pp. 48-50.

30. Committee on Finance and Taxation Proposal, SC1-5A-0004, May 7, 1982; Report of the Committee on Finance and Taxation (undated).

31. Transcript, May 17, 1982, pp. 171-214; Const., art. VII, § 7(c).

32. Committee on Education Proposal, SC1-7A-0018, May 12, 1982, § 2(B); Transcript, May 19, 1982, pp. 86-92.

33. Committee on Education Proposal, SC1-7A-0018, May 14, 1982, § 1(B); Report of the Committee on Education, May 17, 1982 (examples given by committee); Transcript, May 19, 1982, pp. 43-67; Const., art. VI, § 1(B).

34. Committee on Education Proposal, SC1-7A-0018, May 14, 1982, § 2(A); Transcript, May 19, 1982, pp. 70-74.

35. Memorandum to Delegates from Ralph C. Thomas, III, General Counsel, May 19, 1982.

36. Committee on Education Proposal, SC1-7A-0018, May 14, 1982, § 2(I); Transcript, May 19, 1982, pp. 135-198; Const., art. VI, § 2(I).

37. CLGIRT Proposal, SC1-6A-0019, May 14, 1982, § 2; Transcript, May 20, 1982, pp. 194-215.

38. CHHHS Proposal, SC1-8A-0020, May 21, 1982, § 8.1 (health care), § 8.2 (environment), § 8.4 (health facilities).

39. Transcript, May 22, 1982, pp. 23 (environment right deleted), 8 (power to provide for assistance added), 41 (health facilities provision), 23, 24, 50 (acceptance of committee-sponsored changes).

40. CHHHS Proposal, SC1-8A-0020, May 21, 1982, § 8.7 (day care centers), § 8.8 (prisons); Transcript, May 22, 1982, pp. 72 (require, not enable;

"demand that this exist"), 75-76 (approval of prison requirement), 72-73 (Delegate Jackson) ("The state must take care of you if you're in jail, but the State doesn't have to provide day care or maternity and so on, or education"), 80 (amend day care section), 86 (Delegate Paramore) (committee chair), 90 (vote on day care requirement); Const., art. XI, § 3(C).

The impact of the change was softened somewhat by a subsequent amendment which added the words, "as provided by law." Transcript, May 22, 1982, p. 93. The level of day care service is, therefore, apparently a matter of legislative discretion.

41. Delegate Courts Oulahan has written about the bill of rights article in much greater detail than the description given here. *See* Oulahan, "The Proposed New Columbia Constitution: Creating a 'Manacled State'," *American University Law Review*, v. 32 (1983) p. 635.

42. Transcript, May 24, 1982, p. 57 (Delegate Long).

43. Committee on Preamble and Bill of Rights Proposal, SC1-1A-0021, May 21, 1982, § 2; Maraniss, "Post Reporter's Pulitzer Prize is Withdrawn," *Washington Post*, Apr. 16, 1981, p. A1 (discussing *Post* article); Transcript, May 24, 1982, pp. 81-87 (debate and vote).

44. Committee on Preamble and Bill of Rights Proposal, SCl-1A-0021, May 21, 1982, § 6; Transcript, May 24, 1982, pp. 168-70 (vote, 17-15); Const., art. I, § 7.

45. Committee on Preamble and Bill of Rights Proposal, SCI-1A-0021, May 21, 1982, § 8; Transcript, May 24, 1982, pp. 201, 203, 208, 231-32 (right to bail, no detainment or limitations until conviction), 200 (recidivists), 218-19 (murderers), 201 (Delegate Kameny) ("innocent until proven guilty"), 205 (Delegate Jackson) ("never . . . be released"), 221 (Delegate Simmons), 203 (Delegate Marcus) and 209 (Delegate Freeman) (language not preclude preventive detention), 216 ("right" struck), 218-22 (voting down denial of bail to murderers), 240 (voting down "nonfinancial conditions"); Const., art. I, § 9.

46. Committee on Preamble and Bill of Rights Proposal, SCI-1A-0021, May 21, 1982, § 17.

47. Memorandum to Delegates from Ralph C. Thomas, III, May 24, 1982.

48. Transcript, May 25, 1982, pp. 218-43 (consideration of equal protection clause); 245 ("group discrimination"), 258 (delete "factors such as"), 266 ("Religion"), 282-87 (failure of "marital status"), 290 ("parentage"), 330-31 (age discrimination).

49. A motion to strike the right to abortion was defeated by a vote of 28-5, transcript, May 25, 1982, p. 386, while a motion to strike the right to be free from official restrictions on private sexual behavior was defeated by a vote of 21-4. *Ibid.* p. 404.

50. Committee on Preamble and Bill of Rights Proposal, SCI-1A-0021, May 21, 1982, § 20; Transcript, May 26, 1982, pp. 15 (Harris substitute), 16 (committee acceptance), 16 (Delegate Long) ("impractical"), 21 (Delegate Rothschild) (lack of revenue, incentive to move), 18-19 (President Cassell), 25 ("Pepco"), 27, 31 (defeat of amendment to restore qualifying language); Const., art. I, § 20.

The entire floor debate concerned the desirability of including a right to employment in a state constitution, so the record offers little guidance in construing section 20. It is unclear, for example, whether the state may provide the alternative "income sufficient to meet basic human needs," an amount that is presumably at welfare levels (substantially below the minimum wage) to those "unable to work" because of general economic conditions, or whether the phrase "unable to work" refers only to individual physical or mental disabilities. The former, broader reading was supported by one delegate during a brief discussion on second reading. Transcript, May 27, 1982, p. 84. This broader reading would obviously require a much higher additional public outlay, especially for a state that already has a general assistance program for the poor.

Similarly, the convention did not clarify whether a person from another state could claim his or her right to employment immediately upon arrival in the state. After the section was adopted, President Cassell tried to offer an amendment to limit the right to "citizens" of the state, but he was told that it was too late. Transcript, May 26, 1982, p. 61.

Finally, it is not even certain that the right to employment is a judicially enforceable individual right to be employed, for although nearly every speaker, on both sides of the issue, assumed that it was, one key delegate (Jerry Moore, who chaired the Committee on Preamble and the Bill of Rights) treated the clause as setting a goal, not creating a right: "[C]onstitutions are broad goals toward which a society works. To say that you have a right does not mean that it is going to be fulfilled tomorrow morning. . . . [T]he goals and the ideals should be lofty . . . [w]hether it takes 20 years or 50 years, 100 years or more to accomplish these ends is really the important question. . . . We are setting a standard. We are establishing goals. We are drafting the broad perimeters [sic] for a new society. . . . " *Ibid.* p. 23.

51. Transcript, May 24, 1982 pp. 98-180.

52. Revised Rules, § 3.3(F)(4) (three-fourths vote on third reading); Transcript, May 29, 1982, pp. 14-16 (vote on entire document), 101-30 (short statements), 139-42 (vote of approval).

CHAPTER 10

The Floor: People in Combat

After months of committee work, it is finally coming together. We are scheduled to begin settling on the actual language of the constitution for a new state. To be sure, our first taste of this process is only the preamble. But it's the real thing, at last.

At the president's request, the convention's new general counsel steps to the front of the room to give his own analysis of the draft preamble that the Committee on the Preamble and Bill of Rights has submitted. He is somewhat critical. He says that the phrase "'free and sovereign state' doesn't really add any power [and] could possibly cause some opposition," and that "the phrase 'We have determined to control our collective destiny,' does not add any powers and might cause some fears."

The general counsel is interrupted in the middle of his report. His "personal opinion" has no business in the Convention, a delegate objects. Another delegate complains about receiving opinions from counsel at all, "unless I know that this is a constitutional lawyer of the highest order. . . . He is not Thomas Jefferson."

President Cassell tries to defend the lawyer, who seems to be wondering what kind of pit he has just fallen into. Casell asks the delegates to be courteous, apologizes to the attorney, and requests that he continue. But the interruptions have had their effect; future commentary will probably be more guarded.

The preamble is opened to amendments. Oulahan tries to offer a substitute, but the man managing the floor debate on behalf of the Committee is its chair, Jerry Moore, who by day is both a member of the Council and, more importantly, a preacher. He begins an oration, as though from his pulpit. "I have a serious reservation about any delegate who undertakes to become a committee and report to the convention. . . ."

From the floor of the convention there are shouts of "Amen."

"However eloquent, however well-meaning, however astute may be the intention," he continues, his voice cadenced.

Shouts of "All right."

"I do not believe that that which he recommends takes precedence over the long, weary hours—"

"Yeah!"

"—that this Committee has spent."

The room bursts into cheers and applause.

"Therefore, as chairman of this Committee," Moore continues, "I stand for the eight members who have shouldered the burden with me in the heat of the day and ask you to turn back this proposed amendment."

Around me, amidst the applause, there are cheers, whistles, and shouts. I do not participate, and I am disturbed by the event. After the convention's retained counsel was intimidated for trying to offer views that had been requested of him, a delegate's amendment is being turned aside, not through any consideration of its merits, but, at best, because of an appeal to loyalty to the sponsoring Committee. It's worse than that, really, because the *manner* in which Oulahan's motion is being swept away is not merely a product of a speech appealing to support for the work of the Committee. Oulahan is being outclassed, out-styled; nothing he could say could compete with the participatory, revivalist sermon that Moore has just delivered. Oulahan bravely replies that "being the butt of laughter does not bother me a bit because I am just as equal as any other member of this convention." My heart goes out to him, but I think he has picked the wrong issue on which to make a stand; the Committee's draft preamble is not important enough, nor flawed enough, to fight. His substitute is trounced, thirty-four to six, and I vote with the Committee despite my disapproval of Jerry Moore's tactic.[1]

* * *

The article on the judicial branch is the first substantive portion of the constitution to come before us. The amendments are all fairly routine, fairly technical; much of the Convention's time is spent arguing, as we have from the beginning, about the application of our own rules of procedure. When we come to the section on the method for choosing judges, though, Absalom Jordan rises to offer a substitute. Jordan is one of the most independent and unpredictable of delegates. A large man with a goatee, he has taken some radical positions on both issues. For example, he has been quoted in the press for his sponsorship of a constitutional provision to prohibit gun control legislation. On the other hand, in our work together in the Committee on Local Government, his views always seemed balanced, and he and I voted together, as part of the more cautious bloc in that Committee, more often than not.

Jordan's amendment would accept gubernatorial appointment of judges, as the Committee has recommended, but he would also require each appointed judge to go before the voters in a retention election after three years, and every few years thereafter—appellate judges every ten years and trial judges every six years. This strikes me as a bad idea, for although several states use this system, it would be seen by the judges in the District, who never have had to face an election, as a major step backward. They might work strenuously to block statehood in order to resist it. In fact, a few weeks earlier I had discussed the convention with a judge of the District's court of appeals. He had told me that the judges would strongly oppose any constitution that made reappointment any more difficult than it now was. I asked why he and his fellow judges had not made their views known to the Committee on the Judiciary, either informally or in the public hearings. He gave several reasons for their failure to respond to the Committee's invitation. First, several of the court of appeals judges received letters from the convention addressed to them as "Superior Court" judges; they felt that any convention that made a basic error of this sort must "really be rinky-dink." Second, the convention had given them only four days' notice of the public hearing, and had asked them three times, within that four-day period, to testify. "It looked as though they didn't really care whether or not we showed up," he told me, "but that they just wanted to make a record that we had been asked." Finally, they did not want to seem to endorse the idea of statehood by appearing to participate in the convention. So they had decided not to try to help shape the constitution, but to reserve their right to oppose it in Congress if they did not like its terms.

I am unable to report this on the floor. The judge wants his identity kept secret, and in any event, his information would enflame the convention against the judiciary. So I listen helplessly to the speeches about whether the Jordan amendment would excessively undermine the independence of the judiciary, hoping that the votes are present to defeat it. Looking around the room, I think there are, but it is going to be close. It is almost eleven o'clock at night. Many delegates have gone home. Terrell, sitting next to me, wants to leave. I ask him to stay for this vote, but he cannot. Jordan himself brings up the underlying political issue. He says that if his motion is passed, the judges may well lobby on Capitol Hill against statehood, but "we've had to fight this battle before, with the judges coercing and intimidating and never subjecting themselves to the will of the people." And he says that he might not have proposed his amendment "had any of the judges [seen] fit to accept an invitation of a committee to appear before it."

The amendment's supporters ask for a roll-call vote. The chair of the Committee on the Judicial Branch votes against Jordan, as I do, and I am not surprised at the source of many of the other negative votes: the Masons, Oulahan, Clarke, and some of the more conservative blacks such as Harry Thomas and Samuel Robinson. But there are two surprises on the affirmative side: Cassell and Baldwin, the two most senior officers of the convention, both support Jordan. The Jordan proposal carries by one vote, fifteen to fourteen.[2]

The phones are busy the next day. Gloria Corn tells me that she passed on the first round of voting during the roll call to see how the lawyers voted; when she saw that all four of the convention's lawyers had voted against Jordan, she had decided to support him. Harry Thomas, a member of the Committee on the Judicial Branch, tells me, "I never should have voted for Cassell for president. I didn't really understand what I was doing when I voted against Hilda, and we made a mistake. The whole thing was racial, and it never should have been. I am for a constitution that isn't loaded up with a bunch of junk. I never understood until now what that election was all about."

Thomas and I spend the day calling delegates and trying to garner support for reconsideration. We are allies now, full circle from that awful last meeting of the pre-convention Rules Committee, when he denounced me for not wanting to continue the Committee's life. The *Post* has

Absalom Jordan

reported the vote on the Jordan amendment, and Baldwin finds himself acutely embarrassed by the outcome, and by his own contribution to it; he himself is willing to make the motion to reconsider, and he will ask Cassell to support the motion as well. Such a motion could well carry, since only two-thirds of the delegates had been present when the vote was taken, and a different constellation of voters might produce a different result. Unfortunately, we have written the convention's rules to make reconsideration nearly impossible. With leadership support for reconsideration, however, and the fact that Cassell had said on the record, after the vote, that "you can ask for reconsideration," there is still a chance.[3]

Our strategy is to get our troops to the meeting on time, and to bring reconsideration up at the beginning of the meeting. Timing is important, because many of the opponents of retention elections for judges are scheduled to go to a political dinner later in the evening and will have to leave the convention early.

Unfortunately, there is a diversion. Simmons moves that the Convention go into "executive session," excluding the court reporter and the *Washington Post*. This appears to be prohibited by our rules, and several delegates object. Simmons eventually withdraws the motion, but the hour is getting late and many delegates want to leave. It is all I can do to keep them in the hall.[4]

Finally, Baldwin makes his motion to reconsider. There is some debate on it; Coates urges a negative vote because "we ought not to hold this convention hostage to pedestrian and fragmented opposition." On a roll-call vote, the motion to reconsider passes, twenty to eighteen. I feel relieved, because if everyone stays in the room, the new, reconsidered vote on Jordan's amendment is likely to go exactly the same way.

But Jordan is alert, and he objects that the action we have just taken is unlawful because our rules prohibit reconsideration of constitutional provisions except by a two-thirds vote when they come before the convention on second reading. Cassell reads the rule twice, and he says that Jordan is correct. Wesley Long counters with a rather weak reply, but it is the best that can be mustered under the circumstances: Our rules also say that when the rules are silent, Robert's Rules will govern the convention, and Robert's Rules allows reconsideration. The problem is that our rules are not silent on this point, and Long's appeal of the ruling of the chair, which under our rules requires a two-thirds vote, does not even obtain a majority.

Now Harry Thomas is really mad. The package that the Committee had presented to the convention was a delicate, interconnected whole; this change will require a reworking, on the floor, of several other sections of the article, which had assumed that the judges would be appointed for long terms of office. "There's no way in the world I could spend every night here working on something that got fouled up in this convention the way that it has," he says. "I think we've been treated very badly on the whole situation, and I cannot serve on that committee again." To dramatize his resignation from the Committee on the Judicial Branch, he leaves his Committee seat at the front of the room and takes a new seat in the rear. Oulahan follows him to the back of the room.[5]

Together with a few other delegates, I spend the rest of the evening, and the next, making the article more traditional in other ways to compensate for the political problems that the Jordan amendment will cause. In view of the system of retention elections, the convention agrees to give the judges lifetime appointments, to create an appointed commission that will publicly review their qualifications prior to retention elections, and to make all of the seats on the judicial nominating commission appointive rather than elective. I even get a private commitment from Jordan that when the article returns to the convention on second reading, he and I will cosponsor an amendment to make the trial judges run in retention elections every ten years, rather than every six years as our text currently provides.

The work is tedious and technical, and it is frequently interrupted by procedural debate. We are constantly threatened by the possibility that we will lose our quorum, and the ultimate threat arrives at about 10:30, when the elevator operator tells us that she has not been paid to work after 10 p.m. We are put to the choice of ending the meeting in the middle of a debate over composition of the judicia nominating commission, or walking down the nine flights of stairs. One of the delegates, essential for the quorum, says that she cannot walk the stairs again. Creatively, the delegates pass a hat and take up a collection to pay the elevator operator to work another hour, a tradition that is destined to continue.[6]

Harry Thomas calls me the next morning, still fuming. Jordan has called him, he says, and is willing to take the retention elections for judges out of the constitution if Harry will support a constitutional right to bear arms. Thomas has refused to play.

*   *   *

Convention hours are long and meetings often take place at unusual times. Everyone gets hungry. The closest source of nourishment is a McDonald's, and during the committee phase of the convention, delegates could often be seen with a pencil in one hand and a Big Mac in the other. Some delegates specialized in french fries, some in hot apple pies; I dabbled in hot fudge sundaes.

For the convention's Saturday afternoon plenary meetings in March and April, more ambitious arrangements were made. Nahikian began a practice of passing around menus from her cooperative's food catering service, collecting money from delegates at the beginning of the meetings, and delivering hot lunches to them at 2:30 in the afternoon.

But now that we are meeting every night as well as Saturdays, Nahikian's catering service has been overtaken by a new institution. A woman named Thelma Blackwell has set up an impromptu food service for delegates in an anteroom adjacent to the hall in which we meet. There she lays out salads and desserts and cooks main courses in an electric skillet, and she sells dinners to the delegates for about two and a half dollars.

But Thelma Blackwell is as much at the mercy of the elevator operators as are the delegates. We have finished with the article on the judicial branch; Saturday the first of May is a day on which we expect to push forward to the next article. But when we convene at 1:15, Cassell

Harry Thomas

tells us that no one has arranged for the elevator operators to be paid after two o'clock, and because the court reporter's recording equipment must be carried by elevator, the session must end at that time.[7] There is only time to read aloud the article on the executive branch. At two o'clock the delegates rush for the elevators. In the anteroom, Thelma Blackwell sits behind her spread of watermelons, salads, and breads, her urns of coffee, her casseroles of lasagna. Today she has not made a single sale.

* * *

"Home" for this month of plenary debate is a large rectangular room with four windows along one side, the main doorway on the opposite side (in which the smokers among us stand during the debates), and a smaller doorway in the rear from which the smells originating in Thelma Blackwell's skillet waft their way to us. The walls are white, broken by a series of leftover Bicentennial posters—sketches of Thomas Paine, Sam Adams, Jefferson, Washington, John Adams, Madison, and Franklin. The delegates sit in molded plastic chairs at parallel rows of tables, facing the front of the room. Three of these rows are formica-topped work tables, but there are not enough work tables to go around, so the fourth and final row of delegates sit at eight small cafe tables strung together. On these tables can be found, in addition to copies of the articles and amendments on which the delegates are working, a large assortment of coffee cups, soft drink cups with McDonald's advertising, cans of Pepsi and Sunkist orange drink, books, newspapers, hats, and pocketbooks.

At the front of the room, still on the convention's floor, is a row of tables behind which sit six to nine delegates who face the others; these are the members of the committee presenting its draft. And behind them, on a raised dais with an unused piano off to one side, is still another table, behind which sits our senior leadership: Cassell, Baldwin, Harris, Freeman, and Cooper. They are flanked by United States and District of Columbia flags, and over their heads runs an enormous banner proclaiming: "D.C. Statehood Constitutional Convention."

The windows are kept open, for there is no air conditioning, and the late spring nights are already oppressively warm. Fragments of jazz arrive from the street as a counterpoint to our motions and amendments.

In this setting, we begin our race through the month of May. The judiciary article took four working days to mark up and approve, and if each of the remaining nine articles takes only two-thirds as long, we will not make the ninety-day limit. Realizing this, Cassell pushes us through the article on the executive branch. Decisions that a legislature might take weeks to study and debate, such as the issues of whether the governor's power to pardon should be delegable and whether a parole system should be constitutionally established, must be disposed of in five minutes.[8]

With the pace intensified, the convention is even less willing than it had been to show patience with Gloria Corn. Throughout the debates on the preamble and judiciary article, Corn and Brian Moore have offered numerous amendments that were debated at length but received almost no support. There is now a sense in the air that the convention can ill afford to take time with amendments that have little chance of being approved, but Corn clearly has a right to offer them, and she can usually count on Moore to give her a second. Furthermore, she continues to be among the most argumentative of delegates when it comes to rulings by the chair, and though she may often be correct, the impression is that she is being dilatory. Accordingly, delegates begin to demand that the chair "keep her quiet and maintain decorum," and "catcalls" interrupt her speeches. Clearly, a showdown is coming.[9]

Another casualty of our working conditions is political accountability. Cassell reports that the court reporter's recording of a roll-call vote consumes "three to eight pages" of transcript, at $2.25 per page, or about "$35" [sic] per roll-call vote. He recommends that "we limit roll-call votes to nil, unless its something that is very essential" in order to save money, and the delegates honor this request.[10] Perhaps the effect on political accountability is only marginal, because the *Washington Post* has not at any point reported how individual delegates voted on an issue.

* * *

The debate on Brian Moore's motion to require the legislature to set up a system of same-day voter registration is as elegant and informative as any I have heard in the convention. Moore has done his homework; he has called a dozen or so delegates during the day and made the case to them on an individual basis, so that his concept does not hit the floor as a last-minute off-the-cuff idea. A few delegates have little patience with it; Janette Harris says that "I didn't think that it would be necessary tonight to entertain and discuss this motion because you canvassed me, along with you say fifteen other people, today to see how we thought about it. . . . I think what you are proposing is ludicrous." But Moore finds some converts, including Jordan. The vote is closer than I expected, and Moore loses by only a two-vote margin.[11] During the show of hands, I notice that Theresa Jones votes no; this is a surprise, because I can rarely recall her disagreeing with her fellow delegate from Ward Eight, Absalom Jordan. I walk over to her and ask why. She refuses as a matter of principle, she tells me, to vote for anything that Brian Moore proposes.

I am still mulling over this dominance of personal pique—presumably a result of the time that the convention consumes in debate about amendments proposed or seconded by Moore—over political principle when, the next day, I am hit with it myself. We are debating the article on the use of the initiative, and I have a technical amendment to offer, an improvement in the wording that will not change the meaning of the clause that the Committee on Suffrage has proposed. I write out my amendment and carry it to Richard Bruning, who is sitting at the committee table. Bruning looks it over. It's fine, he tells me. It's a definite improvement on the Committee's wording. I suggest to him that it will save the convention a lot of time if he or some other member of the Committee moves it, as opposed to my moving it from the floor; official sponsorship will smooth the way. He can't do that, he tells me, because Jones is a member of the Suffrage Committee, and she will oppose anything that I have written, a scar from our many battles in the Committee on the Legislative Branch. He's sorry, he tells me, but he has to be able to continue to work with her.

Personal pique and political principle 5 May 1982

page 209

Brian Moore

*   *   *

One evening, as I am waiting for other delegates to arrive, I wander down to the end of the hall where the convention's small staff of research assistants and secretaries work in a large open area. I strike up a conversation with one of the research assistants, who is so angry that I can almost see the smoke rising from his head. The staff has been working for six weeks, he tells me, and has not yet received its first paycheck. "They keep giving us different reasons why they can't pay us. The latest claim is that the time sheets that we turned in were all stolen yesterday."

The staff is also upset about working conditions, he reports. The staff's executive director has ruled that no staff members can be paid for time in which they work out of the office, even though office conditions are so noisy, office equipment so frequently broken, and telephone lines so rarely available that it is almost impossible to work on the premises. She has also just laid down the rule that staff members, who are paid by the hour, may not be paid for more than forty hours of work per week; he worked fifty-nine hours last week and can never be paid for the nineteen extra hours.

There is talk of a strike, he says, though he hopes that the staff can be paid and a strike avoided. But he can't continue to work for the convention without compensation; the gas at his house has already been disconnected because he was unable to pay the bill.

*   *   *

Suspicion of lawyers has never been very far beneath the surface of this convention. We are debating a proposed amendment that would require a referendum on holding a new constitutional convention; its sponsor has proposed that this referendum be held ten years after "the date of adoption of this constitution." Just after the amendment is approved, Kameny points out that "adoption" of the constitution might be interpreted to mean ratification by the voters, which could take place many years—even more than ten years—before statehood is achieved. I offer that substituting the phrase "entry into force" for the word "adoption" will solve this problem, and because the amendment has already been approved, and is beyond further amendment or reconsideration, I ask unanimous consent that we make this change.

Theresa Jones objects. "I have a gut feeling about what it's actually going to mean when it actually gets interpreted and what's going to happen to us as a state," she says. "I'm not a lawyer. I'm just a person from the community. Therefore, entry into force can mean one thing with you and one thing with me. I could be tricked because I don't know."

I try to calm her. "If Congress says 'You are a state as of January 2, 1984,' then that's the moment of entry into force. . . . [I]t's the precise date . . . that all the provisions of the Constitution go into effect."

But she is not satisfied. "[P]eople like me who just come out of the community, we don't understand what you mean. And that thing has the meaning—it's like the witches when they were saying certain things, you know, all those double meanings. We'd be the ones boiling in the pots."

The convention is amused, but I am not, as the flawed language remains in the convention's draft, and I am left to mull over the fact that one of my few campaign slogans was to help write "a Constitution that you don't have to be a lawyer to understand." At least Jones didn't quote that back to me on the convention floor.[12]

* * *

While the convention takes a short recess, I chat with the court reporter who has been making the record for about half of the sessions. I tell her that I expect to write about the convention, and that I hope that the transcript she is preparing from her tapes will be verbatim. To my horror, she tells me that as she has been typing up the transcript, she has not always made a verbatim record, but has paraphrased some of the delegates' by-play in parentheses.[13]

But the convention's history is more than its formal debates, I remonstrate. The delegates' outbursts at each other, what they really say, are an equally important aspect of what is happening here.

She was a sociology major in college, she tells me, and she sympathizes with my point of view. But court reporters are trained, she says, to make the judge look good and the defendant look bad. She used to be a court reporter in the United States Supreme Court, and she recalled that one of the Justices "always left his microphone on and said stupid things to the Justices next to him. They appeared on my tape, but not in my transcript."

That is very different, I tell her, because delegates who are arguing vigorously with each other do not intend their remarks to be private. Whatever they say should go onto the written record. She nods, and it is apparent that she is torn between her professional training and her respect for history.

* * *

I am seated, for a change, behind the barricade, a member of a reporting committee, facing the other delegates. The convention's officers are somewhere above and behind my head; somehow, because I cannot see them, I trust them less. The convention appears strikingly different from this vantage point. I have never before noticed Norman Nixon wearing a Walkman during the debates.

We always expected a floor fight on the issues of unicameralism and a relatively small legislature, and it erupts on schedule. There is an initial skirmish about the name of the legislature. Then we tackle the more fundamental question of unicameralism.

Our Committee has recommended a one-house body; as expected, a motion is made to substitute a bicameral legislature. It's going to be a close question, and both Masons are occupied at a night session of the District's Council. A vote on this issue, by show of hands, produces a nineteen to sixteen vote in favor of bicameralism, but Terrell quickly demands a roll-call vote. Cassell complains that he "question[s] the wisdom of spending the money [on a roll call], but nobody listens to the will of the chair."

The roll is called. Alexa Freeman is talking with others in the back of the room; when her name is called, she asks, "What are we voting on?" Then, a moment later, she says, "I'm voting for a bicameral." The vote count continues, while Freeman talks with other delegates. When all of

Alexa Freeman

the delegates' names have been called, but before the tally is announced, Freeman calls out that she wants to change her vote. Cassell says he sees no provision in our Rules, or in Robert's Rules, which supplement ours, for changing a vote in the middle of a roll-call. He asks Cooper to announce the result, and Cooper reveals that the motion to have a bicameral legislature has passed on a vote of eighteen to seventeen.

An appeal is lodged against Cassell's decision to hold Freeman to her vote, and the appeal is supported by a majority of the delegates, but once again we are haunted by a relic from the days in which the convention was divided by racial distrust: Our rules require a two-thirds vote to overrule the chair.

Cassell asks Terrell to continue to present proposed sections of the Committee's proposal, but the Committee's entire legislative plan was premised on unicameralism, and Terrell is unable to continue. Cassell takes over; he substitutes himself for Terrell and reads the next section of Committee language. A delegate objects that this procedure is irregular, and in the resulting confusion, the delegates vote themselves a recess.[14]

There is much yelling during the break. Freeman searches through Robert's Rules for a section that would permit her to change her vote before the results are announced. Paul Valentine, the *Washington Post*'s reporter, finds it for her, and Anita Shelton, who had voted for bicameralism, admonishes him for interfering in the work of the convention. Valentine loses his cool and calls Shelton a fascist. Cassell grabs the microphone of the convention's public address system and begins screaming, "Do I hear the *Washington Post* calling one of our delegates a fascist?" Valentine scowls at him.

The recess over, delegates return to their quarrel. Though Freeman sporadically tries to raise again her right to change her vote, Cassell insists that we continue with the size of the legislature. The Committee, presuming a unicameral legislature, had recommended that it have twenty-four members. Jones moves to give the two houses, together, thirty-two members. Nahikian moves a substitute: Forty-eight members for the lower house and sixteen for the upper house. After extended debate, the Nahikian motion fails on a tie vote, whereupon she offers another substitute: Thirty-two members in the lower house, and eight in the upper house. To this set of numbers, a further amendment is proposed to give the lower house thirty-six members and the upper house twelve.[15]

Sitting behind the barricade, I feel helpless in the face of this array of proposals. Freeman was correct all along; she had a right to change her vote, and then we would have the much simpler task of dealing with a unicameral body. The Committee decided early in the process that the legislature should have one house, and all of the other Committee proposals, such as the procedure for passing legislation, are premised on that decision.

Terrell and I discuss the situation, and we come up with a plan. I announce it to the convention: "Vote for the Jones amendment [which is the closest to our original conception]. Then, when the entire section is up for approval, Chairman Terrell will recommend that you vote against the entire section, deleting [it. Then he will move to] replace it with a 32-member unicameral legislature."

Cassell says that my suggestion "doesn't seem to be that germane." I don't know whether he fails to follow its logic or is working for a bicameral legislature, which he supported on the original roll call. Nixon offers still another variant, sixteen and thirty-two members, which is accepted by consent of the maker of the most recent motion on the table. A vote is held on that set of numbers, but Cassell and Cooper get into a series of arguments over the count, and several recounts are necessary. Finally, Cassell gives up trying to get an accurate count, and asks for a roll-call vote. Although the proposal failed on all of the earlier efforts to count hands, it is approved, nineteen to sixteen on the roll-call tally.

By this time it is 10 p.m., and tempers are higher than normal. A motion is made to adopt the section as a whole, and this is the last chance to recover the day for unicameralism, for only by defeating the section, with its two-house legislature, can we go back and start from scratch. On a show of hands, though, the delegates vote, seventeen to sixteen, to adopt the section.

There is still one last desperate shot. The delegates have reversed themselves in a roll-call on the number of legislators, and they might also do so on the number of houses in the legislature. I ask for a roll-call vote, and other supporters of unicameralism back me up.

But Harris who, like Cassell, voted for bicameralism, moves to adjourn, and Cassell backs her right to do so over my protest that even that privileged motion cannot be made in the middle of a vote. Now I am truly sunk, for if the convention has demonstrated anything, it is that the body will never muster the two-thirds vote necessary to overrule the chair. But there is a surprise: Harris' motion to adjourn is defeated by one vote, and I renew my demand for a roll-call vote.

Before Cassell can deal with this, however, Freeman is recognized on a point of order, and she uses that recognition to move that the convention permit her to change her vote on bicameralism. Suddenly, Corn becomes very active, arguing against Freeman. Bruning yells at her, "Sit down, Gloria," but Corn remains on her feet, ready to continue the argument. I try to raise a point of order, for my demand for a roll-call vote is being forgotten. But I am ignored. Freeman argues for her right to change her vote. There is increased commotion on the floor. Corn is on her feet screaming, "Point of order, Mr. President. Point of order." Bruning walks up behind her, puts his hands on her shoulders and shoves her into her chair.

"What is the matter with you?" Corn screams at him. "Have you lost your mind? Get your hands off of me. You'll be lucky if I don't sue you for assault and battery."

Through the chaos, Cassell tries to restore some order. He admonishes Bruning for having "exerted some degree of physical violence on another delegate" and asks him to apologize.

"Oh it's more than an apology," Corn says. "He will get a medical bill and a lawsuit."

Cassell calls for a vote on Freeman's motion. My roll call is getting buried deeper.

"Richard, that was the most sexist thing I could ever think of," Corn yells, "when a man uses physical violence on a woman. You humiliated

Richard Bruning

me in front of this whole body. I'm going to sue you for this. . . ."

Cassell takes the microphone. "The chair, unable to restore order in the assembly, declares that the meeting is adjourned."[16]

* * *

The next meeting starts on a more sober note. Word has spread around the convention that Corn had long suffered from back ailments, and that I had taken her to the hospital from the Convention floor. Bruning apologizes to an absent Corn, and Cassell announces that an apology by the *Washington Post* reporter will not be necessary. During the day, Freeman has called around to try to put together a coalition in favor of a unicameral legislature and a large number of legislators; it is not clear whether she has succeeded. Cassell seems to accept the notion that, with my roll-call demand left hanging, we have not yet adopted the section that includes a bicameral legislature, and we begin by voting again on that section. The composition of tonight's assembly is somewhat different from what it was before, and the outcome could be different.

In fact, it's not even close. The motion to adopt the section, which appeared to pass by one vote last night, now fails by a vote of twenty-two to six. Terrell puts forward the Freeman compromise: A unicameral legislature with thirty-six members.

There is a motion to amend that to thirty-two members, so that the number of members will be divisible by eight, the number of existing political subdivisions in the District of Columbia. And there is a counter motion to make the number twenty-four. My head is starting to spin again. It is not fun to be sitting at the committee table. We are incredibly hemmed in, my fellow member of the Committee on the Legislative Branch and I. There is no room in which to spread out papers. There's all this action out there on the floor, but from behind the table it's impossible to get up, circulate among delegates, try to change some votes. Furthermore, I'm hemmed in politically as well as physically; I feel duty bound to support the Committee's position, to preserve the narrow majority that prevailed there, and to oppose any amendments from the floor, no matter how sound they seem.

A fan of bicameralism moves that the section be amended to create two houses once again, and we are off into a debate about whether such a motion is in order. It is not.

The proposal for twenty-four legislators—the Committee's original recommendation—is easily defeated. Before we vote on thirty-two or thirty-six, there is a new motion, for a legislature with forty members. To my surprise, it carries, seventeen to fourteen. There are further motions, including attempts to restore bicameralism, but the debate has now gone for so many hours that the body is anxious to move on to the other issues. Through a process of voting as complex as any in this procedurally intricate convention, delegates have determined that the legislature of our new state shall be a unicameral body with forty members.[17]

* * *

The punishing schedule of nightly plenary meetings is taking its toll. Under doctor's orders, Vice-President Baldwin misses about half of the sessions. Cassell, too, has missed nearly half of the meetings. Attendance is rarely above thirty delegates, and often hovers just above a quorum of twenty-three; on any given evening, several delegates come early and leave early, while others arrive later and stay until adjournment.

I am very tired. I get home from the convention every night at a quarter to twelve. I glance at the mail and try to work off some of the steam of the evening, but it's not so easy. I get about six hours of sleep and drag myself out of bed at seven. By the time I stumble down to breakfast, my fifteen-year-old son David has already left for school, so I don't see him all week long. I have been coughing for nearly two months, and people tell me that I look pale.

The schedule is driving all of us nuts. Some delegates cope by missing meetings. I do not want to miss a meeting, since almost all of the committee drafts have some technical irregularities or inconsistencies, and I have been able to fix many of them in the plenary meetings, working quietly with the committee chairs and with a few other delegates. And my two absences from meetings of the Committee on Local Government were both near-disasters for me.

* * *

The leaders of the Convention realize that chances are good that we will not meet the ninety-day deadline. We are so contentious that we take four days to debate articles that they expected would require only a few hours. With seventeen days to go, Cassell and Baldwin raise the question that we argued over at the very beginning of this process—whether to ask the Council to pass a law giving us more time in which to do the job.

Baldwin recommends that the convention vote to ask the Council for a one-week extension, and from the floor another delegate suggests a two-week request. Several delegates speak against any extension; they point out that much of the time of the convention is already wasted, that some of them have other commitments in June, and that they are already physically exhausted. Both motions to ask for more time are defeated.

Cassell is infuriated by this turn of events, and he lectures the delegates. "[T]here's been discussion and charges about wasted time. About people who have not attended. About the fact that the meetings have started late. . . . It's too much ingrained into us that we can finish this on May the 29th. . . . [W]hat you've done today is to vote that you do not care to finish within the allotted time. . . . [Y]ou'll be laughing stocks." Cassell's lecture is to little avail, for we are instinctually aware of the original Peter Principle: Work expands to fill the time available, and extending the time limit will only prolong the agony. We do agree to start our daily meetings at 4 p.m. instead of 6 p.m., but I have inner doubts about our ability to muster a quorum at that hour.[18]

* * *

For twenty-four hours, when it appeared that the legislature might be bicameral, I started to wonder about what duty I owed to the convention if the constitution included provisions that I believed harmful to the cause of statehood and therefore did not support. I have been spending my daytime hours on the telephone with committee chairs, proposing perfecting amendments that they might accept by consent and thereby strengthen their articles. The delegates I call are often initially suspicious of amendments that I suggest, and rightly so, for although I am trying to make the text as technically sound as possible, I am a delegate, not a staff member. I do have policy views of my own, and I am not surprised when a delegate is unsure about which hat I am wearing. Should I continue to knock myself out as an informal editor if provisions are adopted that make my support for the final product unlikely?

Similarly, I am spending many hours in the Style and Drafting Committee, helping to edit the text grammatically after it has been approved on the floor. This work involves hours of tedious argument with Committee members about whether the use of a near synonym, or the inversion of a phrase, changes the meaning of a section. When it rains, the work is even less pleasant, for the room in which Style and Drafting meets has a hole in the ceiling through which water drips onto our heads. Do I owe it to the body to put in this extra work on behalf of a document if it appears that I cannot support it in the end? Do I owe it to my Ward Three constituents not to help dress up a constitution that includes provisions they will very much dislike, such as a three-fold increase in the size of the District's legislature? I keep on working, and try to avoid making a judgment on the document until it is closer to a finished product.

Courts Oulahan, on the other hand, tells me that he has reached a tentative decision. I give him a ride home one night, and he tells me that he plans to vote against the constitution, citing the forty-member legislature, the retention elections for judges, and various clauses in the preamble. I ask him whether he would be inclined to vote against the constitution if the text was exactly as it is, but he felt procedures for its debate and adoption had been fair, the body deliberative, and his views considered. He thinks for a moment and then tells me that if the process were more orderly and deliberative, the outcome so far would not seem bad enough to justify his opposition.

*　　*　　*

We plod our way through the less dramatic issues about the functioning of the legislature—qualifications, terms of office, public access. Corn offers two amendments to a section dealing with how the legislature selects its officers. Annoyed that they have not been consolidated, Kameny tells her, "Don't save up your motions," and she responds, "Shut up, Frank."

Barbara Maguire is offended. She says that under parliamentary procedure, "if a delegate, after three times being corrected about how she speaks to the delegation and her behavior, if she does not conform to the wishes of the body or the chair, the body can direct her to be removed from the hall." She asks Baldwin, who is presiding, to warn Corn of the possibility of removing her, and Kameny suggests that Bruning do the removal.

Other delegates sense that the sanction of removal is too extreme, for it would deprive a ward of one of its representatives, and the convention has no alternates. But the next time Corn speaks out, calling Baldwin "a very uneven-handed chair [who doesn't] know the rules that well," Theresa Jones reacts by moving that Corn be censored and deprived of the right to speak for one session.

Asked whether the convention has the power to impose these sanctions, Baldwin says that it does, and Corn reacts by standing up and heading for the door. "I hereby resign the chair of Style and Drafting," she yells over her shoulder. "You can do your own work."

"Gloria, stay here," Ken Rothschild urges.

"I am not staying. I have been beaten up by that bully. And then listen to this crap? No way, there is no way." And out she goes.

Despite her departure, Baldwin instructs the Convention to vote on Jones' motion to impose sanctions. Much as I would like to stay out of this fracas, I feel some responsibility to my constituents not to permit the convention to disenfranchise one of their representatives. I suggest that in view of Corn's absence, the motion is moot, and although Baldwin disagrees, he sees that it is not in anyone's interest to create trouble unnecessarily. He suggests to Jones, successfully, that she withdraw her motion.[19]

We go back to our business, and complete the article on the legislative branch, but no one maintains the illusion that the episode is closed.

*   *   *

Some other committee's article is the target, and I am out from behind the barricade. How good it feels to be a back bencher, to be able to circulate on the floor of the convention, walk in and out, whisper with other delegates. The Committee on Economic Development has proposed that utility rates not be so high that they would amount to a "taking of rate payers' property."[20] This phrase seems odd, confusing, perhaps even embarrassing to the constitution, because any rate whatever that is charged for utility service will obviously take away some of the property of those who are customers. I move to strike it. Since Corn has already moved to strike an even larger chunk of the section, my proposal becomes a substitute for hers. A lengthy debate ensues, and it is clear that some, perhaps many, of the delegates don't understand that my point is a relatively technical one; the debate is cast largely in terms of whether the speaker is for the utility companies or against them.[21] My amendment is defeated on a vote of eleven to nine. That's a close enough margin—worth another try. Quickly, I draft another amendment. This time I try a better tactic. Instead of moving simply to strike the Committee's language, I move to substitute for the language about "taking" a phrase drawn from a Committee member's explanation as to what the Committee intended— that "unreasonably high rates based on excessive capital investment shall not be permitted."

After more debate, my second effort carries, on a vote of twelve to nine. But a delegate points out that all we have done is to amend Corn's amendment; we have not adopted the amendment, as amended. This will be a problem, because the mere fact that Corn's name is attached to the motion on the floor may cost a vote or two, and a switch of two votes will bring down the motion.

In fact, when delegates raise their hands to vote, eleven delegates support it, and eleven raise their hands in opposition. The amended Corn amendment appears to fail. But there stands Oulahan, with his hand raised in opposition to my effort! I rush to the back of the room to talk to him; if I can get him to abstain, the motion will carry. Two delegates who oppose the motion try to block my path, but I outflank them to the right and get to Oulahan.

Meanwhile, there is a disturbance; Jones announces that the elevator is about to stop running. The interruption causes Freeman, who is now chairing the meeting, to lose track of the count, and she starts again. By now Oulahan has explained to me that he doesn't like the whole article on public utilities, and he wants to make it read as poorly as possible to encourage votes against the entire article. I attempt to persuade him, quickly, that this strategy will not succeed, because after spending hours on the article, the delegates will have so much invested in it that they will never vote it down. Oulahan changes his vote on Freeman's recount, and the amendment carries, twelve to ten.

The supporters of the "taking" clause are furious. "There is nothing that allows members to lose on the first vote and then go to the back of the room and lobby," one says. But Freeman says that she called for a second count because she was confused, and the adjournment necessitated by the elevator's impending shut-down seals the issue in favor of the amended language.[22]

* * *

There are only two weeks to go, but just four of the ten committees have completed the first readings of their articles. An extension seems out of the question; not only have the delegates voted down making a request, but action by the District's Council would have to be effected by emergency legislation, which would require a two-thirds vote, a margin probably unattainable as the constitution that is being drafted becomes increasingly controversial.

Yet exhaustion prevents us from achieving the efficiency we need. It is Saturday morning. The plenary meeting has been called for 10 a.m., but at a few minutes after 11 a.m., only fourteen delegates are present. The absentees include the president and all three vice-presidents, and the delegates are angry at those who have frustrated the possibility of holding a session. Their hostility is directed particularly at the leadership, which is accused of taking "a laissez-faire attitude about coming to these plenary sessions." "We can recall some of these people, and put somebody else up there," says a delegate who voted for the black caucus' slate, and his remarks are applauded.[23] Terrell is sitting next to me and I ask him why he went along with the caucus during the early weeks of the convention. "They seemed to know what they were doing," he tells me. "They seemed very sure of themselves."

* * *

Early in the life of the convention, the delegates were given, with much fanfare, "official" parking passes for their cars. These did not entitle us to park illegally, we were told, but they did permit us to park in officially reserved spaces during convention sessions. For weeks, we have been parking in the reserved spaces adjacent to the FBI building without incident, but just in the last day or two, delegates using those spaces have been peppered with parking tickets. The problem erupts during a session of the convention.

"Mr. President," Kameny calls out. "A number of us have begun receiving parking tickets. . . . We have been told repeatedly that you would take care of these and cause the cessation of the issuance of the tickets. What are you going to do about it?"

"[T]his is the first I've heard of this," Cassell says.

"Well, remember, these double after 15 days, so action has to be taken fast."

Delegates have been complaining so bitterly about the ticketing that they have a hard time believing that Cassell has not heard about it. By now, Cassell is facing a sea of pink paper being waved at him by dozens of delegates on the floor. He tells the delegates to give their tickets to the staff's executive secretary. "We'll write a letter to the proper authorities," he tells the convention, "and maybe we'll ask one of our delegates who knows how to fix tickets, or whatever."[24] The delegates submit their tickets, but they do not seem to have a great deal of confidence in the process.

* * *

Several committees are not yet ready to report their articles for First Reading, and the convention will have to waste precious time waiting for them unless it finds other necessary work to do. Fortunately, the Style and Drafting Committee has already finished its editorial work on the article on the judicial branch, and the convention agrees to take it out of order and to commence Second Reading on that article.

Corn, however, is dissatisfied with the editing job to which the rest of the Committee on Style and Drafting has agreed. She wants to make certain additional stylistic changes "to make this a cleaner document, easier to read, better organized." Baldwin, who is chairing the meeting, rules that a dissenting member of the Style and Drafting Committee does not have the right to propose editorial changes that were not accepted by the Committee, and he is sustained by the convention, twenty-three to three. He asks "Graham and her committee" to step forward, and Corn protests that "[she is] the chair."

There is more than a small stir on the floor; the delegates are eager to see how this gets worked out. Baldwin says that Corn resigned the chair on the record, and that he had accepted her resignation subject to a possible reversal by Cassell of that acceptance. Cooper, the secretary, argues that only the president can remove the chair of an operating committee. Cassell is in the hall, and he indicates that he is ready to respond.

Cassell still has some loyalties to Corn for electing Harris as second vice-president; perhaps he also knows that the Committee is producing under Corn's leadership a well-drafted product despite the grumbling from members of Style and Drafting about the excessive length and contentiousness of that committee's meetings. He waffles, saying that before he acts on the proffered resignation, he would like to have a recommendation from the Style and Drafting Committee itself. Baldwin asks the Style and Drafting Committee to go out into the hall to come up with a recommendation.

In the hallway, there is much yelling and confusion. Corn is screaming that her resignation was not official because she did not put it in writing; besides, it was made in the heat of anger, and she telephoned Cassell that very night to rescind it. Most of the members of the Committee are delighted that Corn has handed the convention the opportunity to depose her from the chair. They have found her excessively argumentative both in Committee and on the floor, and they have long been annoyed by what they perceive as an arrogant attitude. One delegate says that on an elevator, she said she had come to the convention "to sabotage and not to work for statehood," and another quotes her as saying that no one on the committee can write with her expertise, and that the entire convention will go down in disgrace if she is removed.

On the other hand, there is no need to butcher ourselves. Why should the members of the Committee have to take responsibility for undercutting one of their fellow members? Isn't this really a matter between Corn and Cassell? Hilda Mason and I insist that it is not up to us, no matter what Cassell would prefer, to decide whether or not Corn is correct that her resignation was never effective. The furthest we should go, we suggest, is to tell Cassell that it is his responsibility to determine whether a vacancy exists, and to tell him that if one does, Graham is our choice to fill it.

The Committee goes along with this plan. Cassell declares that the chair is vacant, and he appoints Graham to fill it. The Committee moves to the front bench to preside over the second reading of the judicial branch article.[25] Corn does not come with us, but sits at one of the back benches and glares.

We begin to work on the article but hit a snag almost at once. Harris, a member of the Committee on the Judicial Branch, points out the changes that Style and Drafting has made, and claims that they are changes in meaning rather than style. As the chair of the Style and Drafting Subcommittee which edited the judiciary article, I believe that she is in error.[26] But she is not reassured either by my explanations of what Style and Drafting did, and why, or by the protestation of her own chair that "Schrag and I kept in constant contact during the whole time that [editorial] work was being done on this article, and I can assure the . . . delegates that no substantial change was made. . . ." Most of the delegates are unsettled by the charge that their meaning has been altered. There is no easy way for them to check the situation for themselves, for there is no single official mark-up showing what the convention did in its first reading, and the reporting service has not yet transcribed the record of the session in question. The convention passes a resolution asking that the Style and Drafting and Judicial Branch Committees remain after the meeting to go over the edited draft.[27] Corn watches and smirks.

Unable to continue with the agenda until the two Committees can meet together, the delegates clear out of the hall before nine o'clock, and another evening is wasted, with only eleven days to go. I stay behind, along with most of the members of the Style and Drafting Committee. But most members of the Committee on the Judicial Branch, including its chair, do not attend our joint meeting, which boils down to a debate between Harris and myself, moderated by Baldwin. Harris moves through the many editorial changes that we have made, one by one, and I show, in each instance, that what we have done is a rearrangement, or a stylistic improvement, or the elimination of redundancy, or a clearer rendering of the convention's intention. Harris and I, once again—it is like the old pre-convention Committee on Rules and Calendar.

But there is a difference. Baldwin, who once had chaired the black caucus and now slightly outranks Harris in the hierarchy of this convention, is following our argument carefully, and he is satisfied that on each point, no substantive change was made by the Style and Drafting Committee. We lose two hours in pointless bickering, but it appears clear that the Committee on Style and Drafting did an honest job. But is it clear to Harris? She does not seem convinced, or any less suspicious.

*   *   *

When I get home from my boxing match with Harris, Barbara Maguire calls, very troubled by how fractured the convention is, with so much still to do and so little time left. She says she needs a brief vacation and is not planning to attend the following evening's debate on the article on education. I urge her to come, because so many issues are decided by a single vote, and I tell her of how I had urged Terrell to remain the night that Jordan's system of retention elections for judges had been approved by one vote. Still, she says that she does not think she can attend; she needs some relief from the constant crisis.

During the day, I study the article on education. It is fairly straightforward, with one major oddity, a section providing that any standards for instructors or instruction that the Board of Education imposes on the public schools must also apply to private and parochial schools in the new state.[28] This seems at odds with the very concept of private schools, which are designed to be experimental, and free of officially imposed bureaucratic requirements such as the standard rule that public school teachers must have degrees in education. But what a terrible issue to have to take on in the convention! Private schools are fairly unpopular in the District of Columbia, in general, because they tend to drain off the children of parents who are affluent, or white, or both, and make racial and economic integration of the public school system nearly impossible. This convention will be particularly hostile to private school education, because many of the delegates work in the public school system; the chair of the Committee on Education is even the spouse of a Board of Education member. And I am especially the wrong person to make an issue of this point, because my children attend private schools.

So there is every reason to try to get this section altered by agreement of the Committee, as I have done with other sections of the constitution. The Committee's chair tells me that this particular provision was written by Frank Kameny, and I will have to deal with him on it. That's a bit of a relief; Frank is from Ward Three, and we have done quite a lot of work together. Furthermore, his constituents include many private school parents who would share my concern. But when I call him, he is unbending. His concern is that substandard or even standardless Bible schools will move into the state, and that because of their status as private or parochial schools, they will be able to persuade the legislature or the School Board to exempt them from any demands of intellectual rigor, unless the constitution forecloses this opportunity. They will, for example, grant creationism at least equal air time with evolution in their school curricula.

After many hours on the telephone with Frank, I persuade him to accept an amendment to this language that would permit the state to "establish minimum standards, including equivalent alternatives," for curriculum, instructors, and so forth. It's not the language I would have preferred—indeed, perhaps no constitutional language about private and parochial schools would be best—but at least it eliminates the requirement that standards for the two school systems need be the "same."

Debate on the education article begins, with Harris in the chair. A Committee proposal to guarantee equal educational opportunity to people regardless of "race, sex, religion," several other listed factors and "other individual characteristics" gives rise to questions early in the debate.[29] This catch-all phrase is troublesome because the new state's school system will include a university and perhaps also special high schools for academically or artistically talented children; such schools frequently deny admission on the basis of "individual characteristics" such as aptitude and achievement.

So I jump into the debate and propose to add, after "other individual characteristics," the phrase "that are not related to ability to learn." This qualification, I suggest to my fellow delegates, will distinguish between relevant and irrelevant characteristics and will permit the state to impose admissions tests if it so desires.

What a firestorm flares up around me! One delegate says she has "grave problems with the implication of the words" I have offered. Another calls my phrase "dangerous." Before too long, I find out what the problem is; I have accidentally stumbled upon a phrase with current racist connotations. I redden as Bob Love explains on the floor why my proposal must be defeated: because "several psychologists . . . are claiming that people of the black race are not able to learn the same things that people of the white race are able to learn" and that my inclusion of this phrase in a constitution could provoke a court test of whether these psychologists are correct. It does not matter whether the other delegates are jumpy about legal language that might be interpreted to have racial implications or whether my amendment reflected insensitivity to a major concern of the convention; when a black delegate asks to "join that bandwagon of speakers who are bitterly against" my proposal, I hasten to withdraw it.[30]

After this gaffe, I sit quietly through most of the evening, worried even more about having to stand up for the rights of private schools and their students in this crowd. But I am the only delegate exercised about that clause, so I have to raise it; perhaps with Kameny's support my change will presumably not be that controversial.

When the time comes, I offer my amendment, and in the course of discussing it, I mention that the particular language that I am suggesting is language that I worked out on the telephone with Kameny.[31] But to my surprise, Kameny "rise[s] in the strongest objection and opposition" to my motion: "[I]f you have private schools which are not required to meet the same standards that the public schools do, you will get . . . little fly-by-night schools . . . which have no standards at all." A delegate sees a racial twist in my phrase about "equivalent alternatives:" "[P]eople come up with this black English, black math, and these concepts which in many cases have deprived young black minds of uniform ways of learning." It is going badly, and I am deeply grateful to Hilda Mason, a former teacher and now the chair of the Council's Education Committee, when she speaks for my proposal. At the elementary school at which she taught, she says, they got permission to hire scientists instead of regular teachers. That's the meaning and importance of substitution of equivalent alternatives for Kameny's uniform standards.

A delegate provokes laughter when, after referring to my afternoon's negotiation with Kameny, he says, "I'm glad that I didn't talk with Dr. Kameny this afternoon." The convention's mood lightens slightly, and he, too, supports my idea, because he would not want "to replicate an educational system which is the slowest institution of change in society. . . . Along comes a novel idea and the first thing an educator does is get some extermination fluid. . . ." Delegates are looking around the floor for facial hints of how others are going to vote; what looked like a certain loser is actually going to be very close.

Harris calls for a vote, and we raise our hands. Fourteen delegates line up on each side; with Barbara Maguire resting up, my amendment is about to lose on a tie vote. But there is always that one last chance that someone's vote will change during a different sort of count, one in which the delegates will be on record. There is nothing to lose, in any event, so I ask for a roll-call vote.

Franklin Kameny

Harris understands. "Delegate Schrag, because the vote is so close, there is no reason paying $35 or $50 for a roll-call vote," she lectures me. "It is just uncalled for. There was no question in the counting."

Harris tries to move on to the next section, but Brian Moore reminds her that there was a request for a roll call. I am not at all sure that the result will change, but I am certain that I can muster the four supporting delegates that will give me the right to have the roll called. The convention's rules provide that all votes shall be by voice or by a show of hands "unless a delegate requests a roll call vote and is supported by at least four other delegates," and that "a roll call may be requested before, during, or immediately following the announcement of the results of the vote by voice or by show of hands."[32]

Harris ignores Moore; both he and I call a point of order. But she goes on, calling for discussion on the next section of the article, and not recognizing either of us to state our point of order. I can't believe what is happening. Our presiding officers have often been unsure about the interpretation of some of our rules, but Harris seems to be flaunting them entirely, for our practice has been for the presiding officer to ask, after a request for a roll call, whether four other delegates support the request.[33] Never has a presiding officer totally ignored a delegate who said the magic words, "point of order."

I say the words again, with no effect. She pretends not to see or hear me. Perhaps she is getting even, after her failure to upset the editorial changes that I had helped to make on the judiciary branch article. In any event, she is depriving me of my ultimate right as a delegate, the right to insist that the convention follow its rules. I am entitled to my roll-call vote, or at least to an inquiry as to whether four other delegates support me.

But she goes on, and there is only one course open to me: disruption. I am entitled to say the words, "point of order" without recognition, until I am recognized to state the point, and say them I do, again and again, loudly.

Despite the fact that the convention cannot continue over the sound of my protest, she continues to ignore me, and Brian Moore takes up the call again. "There is a point of order, Madam Chair, and you did not recognize it in the proper manner."

"I do not have to recognize it."

"You do too have to recognize it," he says. "A point of order has to be recognized."

"Point of order," I call.

"You're violating every rule in the book in this Convention," Moore says.

"Point of order, Madam Chair," I add.

The chair of the convention's Education Committee says, "I refuse to go through this, through this abuse."

"Please preside in a correct manner and recognize the point of order and let's get on with it," Wesley Long says.

But Harris just keeps pressing on with the debate, as if nothing were happening. "Point of order" is all I say.

Still she will not recognize me, and I can sense that while most delegates know that I am right to insist on recognition, my tactic is alienating them quickly. It occurs to me that one further tactic is available to me besides disruption, and that is exit. I conspicuously gather my papers and head for the elevator.

Half a dozen delegates follow me into the hall, pleading with me to come back. "I'd be glad to come back," I tell them, "but I'm entitled to have Harris canvass support for a roll-call vote." The elevator arrives, and I step into it. Three delegates come in with me, and Hilda Mason orders the elevator operator not to take me down.

The elevator doors shut, but the astounded operator makes no move to descend. Behind the closed doors of the cabin, delegates beg me to take my place on the floor. "First, a roll call," I tell them.

I am really of two minds. I am disgusted, and I really want to get out of there. But these delegates, Mason, Sandra Johnson, Chestie Graham, Terrell, have become my friends and allies during this convention. We respect each other. And they are not pleading with me to accept defeat; they are asking that I return to fight the issue.

I allow myself a half-way step. I will return to the hall, but not to the floor. I will not accept the humiliation of permitting Harris to treat me as if I do not exist. I will sit in the spectators' area while they argue the issue, and if Harris calls the roll, I will take my seat again.

From the back of the room, the convention seems a million miles away; Harris is a distant figure on the horizon. Before those who were on the elevator with me can speak, the issue of procedural regularity is raised by Absalom Jordan. "[T]here is going to be some question raised about the validity of some actions that will be taken," he warns, "and I'm saying that consideration ought to be at least taken under advisement by the chair."

"I would like for the sake of the convention that we recognize the point of order that was brought by some of the members on the floor," Graham adds.

Talmadge Moore weighs in, the retired Army colonel who contributes relatively more because he speaks relatively less. "Madam Chair, I think you could operate in a better atmosphere if you would comply with the rules and regulations as set down previously. . . ."

Hilda Mason gets to the point, and asks Harris to "entertain the roll call which was requested before the chaos took place." But Harris sweeps by her, saying that beside myself, only one other person had called for a roll call. She sidesteps the fact that she did not ask for a showing by other supporters.

Sandra Johnson persists. "It seems as though you're ignoring the question. . . ."

Harris again presses on, and in urging the delegates to continue substantive debate, she rules Johnson out of order. Frustrated, Johnson appeals. From my distant vantage, I know at once that this is a fatal error; an appeal from a ruling of the chair has always been a hopeless maneuver in this convention. It not only requires a two-thirds vote, but even worse, it transforms the issue from one of construction of the rules to one of the convention's confidence in its presiding officer, a kind of personal loyalty test. Any other procedural challenge, even a motion to table debate on the article until the roll-call issue is resolved, would have been better than this one.

Sandra Johnson

When the chair is sustained, I return to the elevator, quietly this time, and alone. During the drive home, I try to figure out what posture to take with respect to the convention. I consider resigning, but that might seem to my friends like disloyalty, and would deprive me of any opportunity to try to repair this section and others if the constitution is rejected by the voters and we reconvene in a year to amend our work. At the same time, the combination of the fight with Harris on the judiciary branch article, the insinuations that my efforts to fix the section on "individual charac-teristics" were rooted in racism, and the battle over the roll call do not make me anxious to hurry back. Other questions, too, are forming in my mind: If the press should ask me for a statement about tonight's walkout should I speak to them? And what should I do about this constitution that is becoming increasingly cluttered with provisions—the retention elec-tions, the forty-member legislature, the new provisions on private schools—that I fought against? At what point do I say "no" to the package? And if I don't vote for the constitution in the convention, is it my duty in the fall to go on the road to urge voters to turn it down? These questions are too weighty, and the only one that has to be decided right away is whether I should be available to the press. I decide that I should not, and I leave the rest for the week to come.

* * *

In the morning, despite the news that the convention ultimately included both Kameny's requirement that all schools have the "same" standards and my language about "equivalent alternatives,"[34] I continue to feel discouraged, and I still entertain thoughts of resignation. But David Koplow, my closest colleague on the Georgetown University Law Center faculty, urges me to follow, instead, one of his favorite courses, a declaration of victory. With his help, I draft a letter to all the delegates, in which I state with great precision, even with section numbers, the rules that Harris did not follow, and I urge that "particularly at a time such as this, when the press of urgent business invites us to disregard the procedures we have put into place, it is of utmost importance that each of us remembers that respect for one another . . . requires respect for—and strict adherence to—the Convention's Rules, and particularly the rules regarding recognition of delegates, which protect the right of each of us to express ourselves to each other." Though Harris counters with a letter asserting that "[i]t was the opinion of the presiding officer at the session in question that Delegate Schrag's action was improper and dilatory," the point is made, and I resume my convention activities.[35]

So do the others; we begin again our daily grind through constitutional text. The feeling on the floor is one of profound discouragement; with nine days to go, three articles have yet to have their first readings, and the bill of rights people are still drafting their proposed article for submission to the convention. Cassell says on the floor that "we're simply not going to make it. I hate to say that." Baldwin concurs. The delegates are so distracted that when the central section of the article on local government comes up on a routine voice vote, it is defeated, only to be approved by a two-to-one margin when the presiding officer insists on a show of hands. "Now, if that is not a lesson to listen to the chair when the chair is announcing that we are voting on something, then nothing is a lesson," Freeman tells us.[36]

* * *

Desperately searching for ways in which to speed up the process, Cassell asks the Style and Drafting Committee to meet with him. How can drafts be turned around more quickly, he asks. Why aren't the Committee's edited drafts coming back to the Convention right away?

For the first time, Cassell learns of some of the mechanical bottlenecks that have been slowing down production of the Constitution: The lack of enough word processing capability, particularly in the peak period of the final ten days, and particularly the lack of sufficient copying machinery. Cassell tells us that at this point in the convention, we can have anything we ask for. We make one request: That the convention's very capable research director, Dr. Bobby Austin, who has been working with us, be given an authority that has previously been withheld—the right to use the one and only Xerox machine. In recognition of true emergency, our extraordinary wish is granted.

* * *

The judiciary branch article comes up on second reading. Jordan has agreed to my suggested amendment of his provision for retention elections; he is willing to space them every ten years for all judges, rather than to require trial judges to face the voters every six years. Indeed, he is willing to sponsor the amendment himself, so this proposal stands a chance of getting the two-thirds vote it needs on second reading.

But when the meeting begins, Jordan is absent. If he does not speak for it, its chances will be much diminished. Baldwin, chairing, asks me to read it in Jordan's absence.

I make a little speech in favor of "a more independent judiciary" and a slower transition to a new system for judicial tenure. There is some argument on either side, but then Harry Thomas, who should have been counted on as a supporter in view of his vote against having retention elections at all, says that he's going to vote against it. "I got the word that Mr. Jordan had to put this amendment in for political reasons," he says. "Mr. Schrag [has] 'pull' in this convention as far as this article is concerned. It isn't right."

I have no idea what he means. I wish Jordan were there to say that I had suggested the idea to him, as a compromise that might enable the voters and the Congress to swallow retention elections a little more easily, but that the idea that I have any hold on him is absurd. Jordan, however, has still not arrived, and in his absence, the amendment bearing his name is defeated.[37]

* * *

With only five days to go, a rumor sweeps the convention that the staff's executive secretary has resigned because Cassell has directed her to let Dr. Austin use the Xerox machine. She is said to have closeted herself in her office all day; Austin can't get in to see her to find out from her that he really can use the machine. If she leaves, it will be still harder to finish on time, because only she knows the location of certain critical documents. And all those parking tickets, which are still on her desk, will never get fixed.

Eventually, the rumor proves unfounded, and photocopying resumes.

* * *

The bill of rights comes before us at last. The proposal is not as unusual or as controversial as it might have been; many of the most extraordinary proposals, such as a draft proposal to require the press to print both sides of public issues, have disappeared in the process of Committee review. Many of the provisions that are novel when measured by the standards of other state constitutions are little more than reflections of the liberal *zeitgeist* of the 1980's: the abolition of capital punishment, the right to abortion, an equal rights provision for women, a gay rights clause, and the like. There are, nevertheless, a few provisions that seem extreme even to one who regards himself as a civil libertarian, and two of these, though challenged strenuously on the floor, are sustained by the convention. These two sections involve a right of suspected criminals to the discovery of "all" evidence possessed by the State, which David Clarke argues could "hurt a lot of innocent people" (presumably by jeopardizing the identities of confidential informants), and a ban on the use of evidence unlawfully seized by "private persons."[38]

I never expected to approve of every clause in the constitution we are writing, and no one provision alone gives me so much trouble that I can't support the document, but the cumulative impact of several dubious provisions continues to concern me. Voting against the constitution was unthinkable just a week or two ago; assuming that we somehow make the deadline, it now has become an option to consider. Unfortunately, if I, as a delegate from Ward Three, were to vote against the constitution, my action would certainly be misinterpreted as a vote against statehood, reflecting the views of the ward on that subject, and I am not desirous of boosting the anti-statehood cause. An abstention is possible, too, and is explicitly authorized by the Convention's rules, but to abstain seems like an abdication of responsibility after all these months of work and judgment.

I call a couple of moderate black delegates to ask what they plan to do. They are in the same quandary. They are under a lot of pressure to join with the overwhelming majority of delegates who are pleased with the way the product is shaping up. On the other hand, particular provisions do not sit well with them. One of them tells me that he plans to vote for the constitution in the convention but to speak against ratifying it in the fall. He doesn't think that it should be approved, but he believes that the voters, rather than himself, should make that determination, and that he should vote for it merely to send it on to the next stage of consideration.

*   *   *

Passions run higher over sections in the bill of rights than they did over most provisions in the constitution. Council Member David Clarke, who made his name as a civil rights lawyer before running for office, is an active player in many of the bill of rights debates, though other duties, including his campaign for the Council presidency, have caused him to miss most sessions of the convention. Clarke's last-minute emergence as an active delegate is not well-received by the convention. At one point, he offers an amendment orally, though the convention has earlier adopted an informal tradition of submitting proposed amendments in writing. "If you would show up and show up on time regularly," Cassell snaps at him, "you would know that the rules require that you must write it out and submit it to the Chair." Cassell explains the procedure in detail, adding, "You're a lawyer and I should think you could easily retain these things." Another delegate, arguing against Clarke's amendment, calls him a "slick Philadelphia lawyer."[39]

Most of the sections of the bill of rights are hammered out in a marathon session that runs from 5 p.m. until three in the morning, the convention's ultimate solution to its deadline problem. No funds are available to pay for building security or an elevator operator after 11 p.m., so all of the delegates are locked into the building to complete their work, and the sense of pressure increases measurably.

In this atmosphere, I am somewhat reluctant to stick my neck out again, but the draft section on discrimination is terribly awkward.[40] It outlaws "private" as well as official discrimination, with no exceptions of the type normally found in civil rights legislation, suggesting that a church might have to hire an atheist as a minister, or that men could not be barred from employment as attendants in women's restrooms. It prohibits public and private discrimination on grounds of "poverty," perhaps implying that the state must permit indigents to ride without charge on the buses and subways, or even that stores would have to give their merchandise without charge to those who can't afford to pay. It includes phrases whose meanings are unclear or obscure, such as its prohibition on "historic caste discrimination." It bars discrimination on grounds of age without making an exception for minors, inviting a possible lawsuit to strike down child labor or liquor laws.

I have, I think, a fairly easy solution. Simply replace the rather lengthy section developed by the Committee with the one-sentence equal protection clause of the Federal Constitution, augmented by a clause authorizing the legislature to pass appropriate legislation, including affirmative action legislation.

I no sooner make my suggestion, and my critique of the Committee's draft, when the roof again falls in on me. "I am black and have been discriminated against," Jackson says, implying that a white could not possibly understand the subject we are now discussing. "What we want," he continues,

> is the justice for black people, the justice for the group in here to exercise the freedom that they have so long been denied. . . . [W]hat am I guaranteed [by the U.S. Constitution] 300 years after slavery? Not one deep thing. . . . [The equal protection clause is just] two or three simple words that give me nothing but more of the same. Madam Chair, I cautiously urge everyone to vote against Mr. Schrag's amendment, to keep the status quo status quo. It does nothing for me, for my children, for my wife, for my old, old mother, for my young, young child, nothing.

The applause for this rhetoric is deafening and prolonged, and Jackson's statement is followed by speeches from other delegates who also intimate that my proposal is a plot to deny them freedom. "I will go to my grave," Croft says, "my daughter will go to her grave, her children to their grave, and every member of my family who has ever lived, will indeed go to the grave asking the question: What does it mean to be free?"

Harris adds that she has read my proposed substitute "three or four times [and] I have found there's nothing in it. There's no guts in it," and a delegate who directs the District's Office of Human Rights says that "as the struggle for Civil Rights has gone forward, the rights of blacks are still unheard of in the District of Columbia."

By this point in the convention, I know when I am licked, and there is no point in allowing my proposal to become a vehicle through which every black delegate in the convention argues that I don't know anything about discrimination. My proposal is obviously not helpful to the convention, for instead of encouraging the delegates to focus on the particular deficiencies of the Committee's draft, it has caused them to overlook them, and to use the debate as a clash of two symbols, the allegedly inadequate Federal Constitution against the improvements that the Committee on the Bill of Rights has attempted. I hasten to withdraw my proposal before I can be attacked further, angry at the black delegates for their escalation of the rhetoric, but angrier at myself for not realizing, especially after what happened to my "ability to learn" amendment, that in the context of this convention, my proposal was absurd.[41]

* * *

The faculty at the University where I teach is scheduled to discuss a report that I have helped to write, and I am compelled to be late for a plenary session of the convention. What a session to miss! The convention has put a section into the bill of rights giving every person in the new state a right to employment; it has even adopted an amendment offered by Harris that struck from this provision the qualification that the right existed only "within the state's ability to provide."[42] As soon as I hear the news, I know that it's a disaster for me; I had been considering not voting for the constitution, but the choice has been withdrawn. I cannot vote for it now. The section could be interpreted otherwise, for example, as a goal, but the normal interpretation of the word "right" in a bill of rights is that the subject of that right is judicially enforceable against the state. If this "right" were really enforced, this provision would have extraordinary tax consequences for the citizens of the new state, and perhaps particularly for those in the ward that I represent.

A few other delegates are also troubled. One of them approaches me with a plan. David Clarke tells me that the bill of rights has moved the constitution off the deep end. He understands that Baldwin is looking for a way out, and he has one to suggest. He requests that I draft up an alternative bill of rights, based on the bill of rights of the Federal Constitution, which could be offered as a substitute when the entire bill of rights comes up on Second Reading.

I tell him that the effort is pointless because it would not stand a chance. He says that Baldwin will make the motion, and that he thinks a lot of people will support it, because they know that the bill of rights that we have marked up will be so controversial that it may drag down the constitution.

I can still feel the pain from trying to substitute the Federal Constitution's equal protection clause for the one drafted by the Committee on the Bill of Rights, and I tell Clarke that I would be willing to help out as a technician, but that I will not sponsor or speak for such an effort, and I do not want to be associated with it in a public way. That's good enough for him; when I've written up the substitute, he says, just put it in an envelope and leave it in Baldwin's mailbox.

I find a typewriter and a United States Constitution, and in an hour, the job is done: A state constitution's bill of rights, as ordered, which is almost word-for-word based on that of the Federal Constitution. I follow Clark's delivery instructions, and surreptitiously drop the envelope in Baldwin's box. Only in this convention would a person have to carry around the Federal bill of rights in a plain, unmarked wrapper.

*   *   *

When the bill of rights comes up for its second reading, Baldwin is not in the hall. Clarke will need a two-thirds vote to amend the bill of rights at this stage; indeed, because he has not obtained a waiver from the Committee's chair, he needs a two-thirds vote to suspend the rules even to permit consideration of a substitute. He moves for suspension of the rules, and a voice rings out, "Who is he to come in here like this at the last minute?" And when Clarke attempts to explain what he wants to do, and why, a delegate objects with a point of order: A motion to suspend the rules is not debatable. Clarke's motion is defeated quickly when it gains a majority but falls short of two-thirds.[43]

*   *   *

In these last three days, I am working around the clock to help put the convention's work into final form. The Style and Drafting Committee is not only editing the articles in preparation for second readings on the floor, but also proofreading the final product, ordering the articles within the constitution, preparing a cover, and performing a myriad of other tasks. I feel it to be my duty to continue to work as hard as I can to get the job finished, but I am immensely sad. I have devoted half a year to this project, and I can almost, but not quite, support the result. In the final hours, since I decided that I cannot vote for the constitution, I have become much less active on the floor, though I am working harder than ever in the editing room.

Torn by my general sympathy for the project and my sense that a few clauses render the final product irresponsible, I have decided to abstain. A negative vote would be too strong an indictment. I begin to work on a detailed statement for the record that will explain an otherwise incomprehensible cop-out. I am tremendously relieved that, at last, it is almost over.

*   *   *

The convention's failure to cancel its delegates' parking tickets, or even to ascertain definitively whether or not it is legal to park in the reserved spaces across the street, has become a symbol of its distance from reality. At last, two days before the end, the convention's executive director interrupts a meeting of the Style and Drafting Committee to say that she has achieved a breakthrough on the problem. No new parking tickets will be issued until the convention ends. I have been paying a garage, but on the second-to-last-day, I at last avoid the four dollar garage fee and park in the reserved area to attend the final meeting of the Style and Drafting Committee. At four in the afternoon, Jeannette Feely goes to McDonald's and returns with a fistful of parking tickets for me and all of the other members of the Committee.

*   *   *

The last issue to be settled by the Style and Drafting Committee is the form of the signature page. If the line above the signatures says that the signatories "approve" the text or "recommend" its ratification, the signature page becomes a kind of loyalty oath, and only those who vote for the constitution should sign it. If the signatories merely certify the authenticity of the document, all forty-five of us should, in principle, be able to affix our names. Kameny is a tiger for "approval," but I would prefer a neutral page, so that I, too, can sign it; I have no desire to be seen as an oddball by the delegates or by the voters in my ward who will, for the most part, support my abstention.

In the end, only Kameny insists on signatures that mean approval. I am sent out of the room to type up the more neutral signature page, a small last-minute satisfaction.

*   *   *

The final day of the convention. I arrive to discover television lights have been set up, and cameras are rolling. All but two delegates are present.

I have copies of the statement explaining my vote for all of the delegates, and I distribute them.[44] Then I take my seat at the front of the room, where the members of the Style and Drafting Committee are sitting at the first table, presenting the constitution on the third reading as they did on the second. But I'm not too comfortable being photographed at the front table; it could be misinterpreted in Ward Three as support for the constitution.

Barbara Lett Simmons beckons me over to speak with her. Why am I sitting at the front table, she wants to know, in view of my decision to abstain? I tell her that I have continued to carry out my responsibility, as a member of the Style and Drafting Committee, to finish the job, even though I cannot vote for it. She tells me that she thinks it is improper for me to sit at the front in light of my decision. It all fits together, then: My own discomfort with being pictured as though I were responsible, my desire to avoid still another argument, and, most important, the symbolic appeal of finishing the convention as a back bencher, the role I've enjoyed most all along. I move to the rear of the room.

The television reporters pick up my statement from a delegate and ask me to read it on camera. I decline, for this day belongs to those who support the constitution wholeheartedly, and I do not want to upstage them. I hand my statement to the court reporter for inclusion in the record, but I do not join the other delegates in oral expressions of their views.

* * *

The roll is called for the last time. Corn votes no "on behalf of Ward Three." Kameny votes yes, "especially on behalf of the people of what is presently Ward Three." Corn interrupts, "Considering I had twice the vote count he did. . . ." The delegates laugh. I announce my abstention without any comment. The constitution is adopted by the convention.[45]

Notes to Chapter 10

1. Transcript, Apr. 26, 1982, pp. 60-66 (general counsel), 87-102 (Oulahan amendment).

2. Transcript, Apr. 28, 1982, pp. 186-99.

3. Valentine, "Statehood Meeting Backs Elected Judiciary System," *Washington Post*, Apr. 29, 1982, p. B1 (*Post* report); Revised Rules, § 4.2(O) (reconsideration rules); Transcript, Apr. 28, 1982, p. 200 (Cassell remark).

4. Transcript, Apr. 29, 1982, pp. 7 (Simmons motion), 9-17 (delegates object), 17 (Simmons withdraws); Revised Rules, § 5.6 (prohibiting rule).

5. Transcript, Apr. 29, 1982, pp. 23-52.

6. Transcript, Apr. 30, 1982, pp. 8-47 (appointed commission for public review); Transcript, Apr. 29, 1982, pp. 86-94 (lifetime appointments), 105-07 (appointive seats), 137-39 (elevator operator).

7. Transcript, May 1, 1982, pp. 13, 39.

8. Transcript, May 3, 1982, pp. 101-11.

9. Transcript, Apr. 26, 1982, pp. 118A-26, Transcript, Apr. 28, 1982, pp. 86-113, Transcript, Apr. 30, 1982, pp. 56-67 (Corn); Transcript, Apr. 28, 1982, pp. 93-102 and 157-62 (Moore); Transcript, May 4, 1982, p. 82 ("keep her quiet"), 168 (catcalls); Transcript, Apr. 26, 1982, p. 94 ("I am going to call 911 if you [Corn] speak again. [Laughter and Applause]").

10. Transcript, May 5, 1982, p. 8.

From April 26 to April 30, the convention took eight roll-call votes. But after Cassell's request on May 5, the convention took only ten roll-call votes, other than the votes on the name of the state and the final, formal vote on May 29 to adopt the constitution.

11. Transcript, May 5, 1982, pp. 66-76.

12. Transcript, May 8, 1982, pp. 20-28.

13. Transcript, Apr. 26, 1982, pp. 109 ("[Uproar, untranscribable]"), 113 (["Many voices exhort Delegate Corn to be seated]"); Transcript, May 12, 1982, p. 53 ("[Comment by Delegate Love not transcribed]").

14. Transcript, May 11, 1982, pp. 9-47 (name of legislature), 51-75 (unicameralism).

15. Transcript, May 11, 1982, pp. 85, 131, 139 (Freeman attempts), 95-115 (proposed number of members).

16. Transcript, May 11, 1982, pp. 117-48.

As for the Bruning-Corn incident, the court reporter noted that "(A disturbance occurred in the body)".

17. Transcript, May 12, 1982, pp. 4-94; Const., art. II, § 2.

18. Transcript, May 12, 1982, pp. 128-55.

19. Transcript, May 13, 1982, pp. 163-74.

20. Committee on Economic Development Proposal, SC1-9A-0012, Apr. 29, 1982, § 2(a).

21. Transcript, May 14, 1982, pp. 186-99. One delegate argued, "[I]n my block alone, which has over a hundred houses in it, and if everybody pays $25 for fuel, for coal to give them some electricity, then you count every house and see how much the utilities are getting . . . and I think we should have some kind of protection."

22. Transcript, May 14, 1982, pp. 177-229; Const., art. X, § 2(a).

23. Transcript, May 15, 1982, pp. 2A-52.

24. Transcript, May 17, 1982, p. 264.

25. Transcript, May 18, 1982, pp. 42-58.

26. Her errors were of two types. In some cases, her personal records of what had been done on first reading were apparently incomplete. For example, she objected to the phrase "to the extent provided by law," which Style and Drafting had included in the grant of jurisdiction to the Supreme Court with respect to matters *other* than appeals from decisions of the superior court, though this phrase

had allegedly been deleted on the floor. Transcript, May 18, 1982, p. 86. The original proposal had, however, included that phrase with respect both to appeals from superior court decisions and to other matters, and it had been deleted by the convention only with respect to appeals from superior court decisions to grant those appeals as of right. Transcript, Apr. 28, 1982, p. 127.

The second type of error was that Harris apparently did not always understand the reason for the Committee's editorial changes. She objected, for example, to the Committee's insertion of the word "initially" in the grant of supreme court jurisdiction to hear appeals from "decisions initially made by the Superior Court." Transcript, May 18, 1982, p. 86. The Committee had inserted this word because the convention's intention had been to guarantee one appeal as of right, not create an unqualified right to appeal to the supreme court even from appellate decisions of the superior court in cases initially decided by statutorily-created inferior courts. Transcript, Apr. 28, 1982, p. 126.

27. Transcript, May 18, 1982, pp. 85-107.

After this fracas, the convention's research director, Dr. Bobby Austin, was asked to make an official mark-up as amendments were approved.

28. Committee on Education Proposal, SC1-7A-0018, May 14, 1982, § 2(I).

29. *Ibid.* § 1(B).

30. Transcript, May 19, 1982, pp. 43-49.

31. The following events are recorded in the Transcript, May 19, 1982, pp. 135-85.

32. Revised Rules, § 5.3(A), § 5.4(A).

33. Transcript, May 15, 1982, p. 169.

34. Const., art. VI, § 2(I).

35. Letter to Delegates from Philip G. Schrag, May 20, 1982; Letter to Delegates from Janette Hosten Harris, May 21, 1982.

36. Transcript, May 20, 1982, pp. 152-87.

37. Transcript, May 24, 1982, pp. 5-13.

38. Const., art. I, § 7 (discovery of all evidence); Transcript, May 24, 1982, p. 168 (Delegate Clarke); Const., art. I, § 6 (ban on use of evidence).

39. Transcript, May 24, 1982, pp. 228-34.

40. Committee on Preamble and Bill of Rights Proposal, SC1-1A-0021, May 21, 1982, § 17.

41. Transcript, May 25, 1982, pp. 219-41.

The convention did consider the proposed section on a line-by-line basis, and it corrected most of the problems that had been identified in the critique. *Compare* Committee on the Preamble and Bill of Rights Proposal, SC1-1A-0021, May 21, 1982, § 17, *with* Const., art. I, § 3.

42. *See* Transcript, May 26, 1982, pp. 3-32.

43. *See* Transcript, May 27, 1982, pp. 2, 107 (Baldwin absent); Revised Rules, § 3.3(D)(4) (two-thirds vote); Revised Rules, §§ 3.3(D)(3)(a), 4.2(H) (consideration of substitute); Transcript, May 27, 1982, pp. 99-108 (convention action).

44. Letter to Delegates to the Statehood Constitutional Convention from Philip G. Schrag, May 29, 1982.

45. Transcript, May 29, 1982, pp. 86-139.

CONCLUSION

Despite extraordinary external and internal obstacles, the District of Columbia Statehood Constitutional Convention wrote a constitution within the time period permitted by law. However one judges the particular decisions reached by the convention, the achievement of this task must be reckoned a surprising political success. The convention began its life with more apparent strikes against it than any state constitutional convention in modern history. The very idea was conceived by a fringe political group which had never been able to obtain support from a majority of the legislature and therefore had to resort to an initiative campaign. Initial opinion among the business and political elite ranged from indifference, through skepticism, to hostility. The District's Council, presented by the results of the statehood initiative with a *fait accompli*, provided the convention with a minimal appropriation, far smaller than that authorized by the voters or expended in other jurisdictions. At the same time, the Council imposed a strict ninety-day limitation on the life of the convention, without providing, as other jurisdictions had done, for any preparatory commission to lead the way.[1]

In addition, delegate selection did little to increase the visibility of the imminent convention. The election timetable required circulation of nominating petitions many months before the election of delegates, at a time when the press was not paying any attention to the statehood issue. As a result, only people already involved in the statehood movement were likely to declare their candidacies in time to run. The Mayor did not run, nor did he designate a close aide or associate as his stand-in, despite the fact that in other jurisdictions, active participation by the chief executive officer made the difference between success and failure.[2] Only three members of the legislature sought roles as delegates, and although all three were elected, only one attended most of the committee meetings and plenary sessions. In addition, only four of the forty-five delegates were lawyers, and all four of them were among the convention's racial minority.[3]

Furthermore, the convention's beginning was a near-disaster. For two months, the delegates were deeply divided along racial lines, and voting on issues relating to control and structure of the convention was bitter, often following these racial divisions. The formation of a black caucus caused most of the white delegates to fear that they were being shut out of any important role in the convention, and this racial division, more than any other factor, made it appear very unlikely that the convention could succeed. Lawrence Guyot, a black resident of the District who had worked with Martin Luther King and had helped to found the Mississippi Freedom Democratic Party, told the convention in despair that

> In all my study of the attempt at black empowerment, never, from John Walker's *One Continual Cry* to *My Soul is Rested* by Howard Raines, there is not a single incident of political consequence to black people in which blacks had a mathematical majority and then organized a black caucus. I want to state publicly that I think this is political suicide.

Guyot identified two groups of black delegates in the Convention, the 'builders,'

> who use [power] consistent with the needs of the people [and the] 'breakers' whose position is based on negation, on the inability of the system to deliver. . . . [Certain delegates] are political individuals who have rested their political careers on negation, nihilism and hate . . . and . . . at this moment, have political control, and racist control, of the Constitutional Convention.[4]

Finally, the convention's work repeatedly came close to failure through a series of unique internal factors. The budgeting process lagged, so that weeks passed before the convention was able to acquire even minimal supplies such as copies of other states' constitutions. It was required to limp along for its entire life with a single copier that was wholly inadequate to the task and periodically launched its own sit-down strike. The hastily assembled staff found cause for grievances in the wages and working conditions. Delegates lacked the luxury enjoyed by their counterparts in some other jurisdictions who had been able to devote full time to the convention during its sessions.[5] Most delegates had to fit their convention work into the evenings after working at a full-time job. Most delegates took the rules of procedure very seriously, and although this had some beneficial consequences, a large fraction of convention time was devoted to parliamentary argument. And some delegates used more than what most other delegates regarded as their fair share of floor time, resulting in occasional suspicion that they were trying to use up time so that the convention would not meet its deadline.

The convention managed to complete its task by turning some of its liabilities at least partially into assets, and by confining its racial divisiveness to issues of power rather than policy. The scant attention that the public gave the convention before and during its life may have isolated the delegates from mainstream thinking about some of the issues that they were considering, but it also freed them from pressures by corporate and other lobbyists who traditionally seek out contact with legislators. The fact that so few legislators were delegates may have produced a convention that was, on some issues, more idealistic than practical, but it saved the convention from the classic split between incumbent politicians and reformers that has characterized other conventions. The crisis atmosphere created by the strictness of the ninety-day limit probably helped to pull delegates together in the final two weeks; had the timetable been easy to extend, there might well have been greater difficulty in obtaining and holding a quorum.

The racial division that threatened to consume the Convention and to doom it to failure dissolved under the pressure of the business of constitution-writing. The black caucus ceased to meet after the rules were adopted and the officers and committee chairs chosen; once the committees began to meet, new divisions formed, and they were not primarily racial in nature. Analysis of political alignments in the convention is seriously impeded by the convention's having honored its president's request to refrain from voting by roll call,[6] but the roll calls that were held reflect the shift from racial to ideological voting patterns as the convention shifted from organizational to policy issues.[7]

Table VIII reveals this shifting pattern.

TABLE VIII: Convention Votes by Race on 8 Key Issues*

STRUCTURAL VOTES

	Feb. 2 Secret Balloting[8]		Feb. 4 Removal of Officers[9]		Feb. 11 Election of President[10]	
	Yes	*No*	*Yes*	*No*	*Cassell*	*Mason*
Black	2	25	3	20	23	5
White	15	1	16	0	0	16
TOTAL	17	26	19	20	23	21

POLICY VOTES

	April 28 Retention Elections[11]		May 11 Bicameralism Issue[12]	
	Yes	*No*	*Yes*	*No*
Black	10	5	12	9
White	5	9	6	8
TOTAL	15	14	18	17

	March 11 Proposal for 48 Legislators[13]		*May 15 Unqualified Right to Strike[14]*		*May 27 Consider Substitute Bill of Rights[15]*	
	Yes	*No*	*Yes*	*No*	*Yes*	*No*
Black	13	9	10	7	9	10
White	6	7	4	8	8	3
TOTAL	19	16	14	15	17	13

*Although 45 delegates were elected, often fewer than that number attended meetings. Hence the varying voting totals here and elsewhere.

The table summarizes the voting on the three primary roll calls on structural issues and the five primary roll calls on policy issues held during the convention. It shows a high correlation between race and voting on issues involving control over the convention's mechanisms, but significantly less correlation on policy issues once the issues of control had been determined. On policy votes that were closely contested within the convention as a whole, both blacks and whites tended to divide somewhere between evenly and a two-to-one margin, although they had split in an entirely lopsided fashion for purposes of organizing the convention. The author's own observation of floor voting by show of hands, and of alliances and divisions within committees, confirmed this tendency away from racially divided voting as the convention progressed.

On the other hand, Table VIII also suggests that race was not altogether irrelevant to the voting patterns. In all five of the primary roll calls on closely divided policy questions, blacks as a group and whites as a group voted in opposite ways. A majority of black delegates voted to require judges to run in retention elections, to establish a two-house legislature, to have forty-eight members of the legislature, to give public employees an unqualified right to strike, and to reject suspension of the rules in order to consider a substitute for the bill of rights that had been approved on first reading. A majority of white delegates preferred the opposite conclusion on each occasion. In each instance, the position preferred by a majority of the black delegates might be said (independently of knowledge as to which delegates tended to support it) to be the more "progressive" position, suggesting that black delegates as a group tended to be more progressive than white delegates as a group, although neither group was sufficiently cohesive as to imply voting by racial blocs once the organizational phase of the convention had ended.

Ideological tendencies can be observed for some of the individual delegates as well. Delegates Croft and Feely, for example, voted for the more "progressive" position on each of the five key policy votes for which they were present; Delegates Eichhorn, Maguire, Talmadge Moore, Oulahan, Schrag, and Thomas consistently voted the other way. Most delegates, however, did not vote so predictably, and in any event, individual political outlooks on key dividing issues do not reveal very much about why the constitution is shaped as it is. They reveal relatively little about the general framework of the constitution, as opposed to the particular outcomes on highly visible issues. Thus, it is necessary to step back from the roll-call voting in order to ascertain the broader influences on the convention.

Ironically, the most important among these broad influences is precedent. Despite its innovative trappings, the convention drafted a constitution essentially quite similar to the constitutions of the existing fifty states. Although it would have been open to the convention to establish a different sort of state government—one with a parliamentary structure, rather than separate legislative and judicial branches, for example, or a tricameral legislature, or a lay judiciary, or a legislature selected by proportional representation—no radically different system of government was ever considered seriously by the convention, either in a committee or on the floor.[16] If the fifty-first state is brought into existence by the Congress, its basic structure will be that of its sisters. Its sole structural innovation—the unicameral legislature—is perhaps its only concession to its uniquely urban character, and even that feature has a precedent in the constitution of Nebraska.

While the fifty state constitutions (and the Federal Constitution) are a general precedent on which the constitution of New Columbia is based, more particular precedents can also be cited. Despite the ideological resistance of some delegates to the National Municipal League's Model State Constitution, that short volume was in the possession of virtually every delegate, and it certainly had an impact on the drafting process. Of the Convention's ten committees, for example, eight (all but Economic Development and Health, Housing and Human Services) correspond to substantive articles of the Model, and only the civil service article of the Model did not have a convention counterpart. The Committee on the Legislative Branch used the Model explicitly, as a checklist of items to be covered, while adopting its particular language only occasionally, and particular sections of the Model were used by individual delegates as the basis for their floor amendments.[17] In addition, particular provisions of the constitution of New Columbia may be traced to sections of certain other state constitutions—the provision on recall elections of judges to the Alaska constitution, for example, and the bill of rights' section on the right to change to the constitution of Maryland.[18]

Another important influence on the shape of the constitution was the advice of trusted experts. The orientation seminars sponsored by universities were important in acquainting delegates with a sense of the boundaries of their discretion. They also qualified their speakers as experts who could be and often were called back to consult with particular committees. In addition, because Washington, D.C., has so many centers for policy analysis, convention committees were easily able to call upon volunteer experts in nearly every field of government. Every committee began its work by consulting with a small number of people from the field in which it was to draft an article, and some committees, such as the Committee on the Executive Branch, remained in touch with its consultants throughout the drafting process.

Floor debate was also a significant determinant of outcome. It has been reported elsewhere that the constitutional conventions are unlike ordinary legislatures in the degree to which the content of floor speeches is likely to influence the outcome of issues.[19] The District's statehood convention suggests why this is true. With respect to major issues whose identity could be anticipated well in advance, such as the decisions on unicameralism, or the Governor's term in office, or how judges should be selected, the delegates might form their opinions over a period of weeks or even months, and floor debate might not be a significant determinant. But writing an entire constitution involves literally hundreds of much smaller, interstitial decisions as well.

Many of these smaller issues are ones that most delegates could not possibly anticipate in advance, because they are presented by amendments offered on the floor, or even by amendments to those amendments. Even if delegates could have anticipated the Jordan amendment to require retention elections for judges, for example, they could not have expected that in the wake of its passage they would have had to make immediate decisions on whether a review commission would be empowered to publish commentaries on the judges' work before each such election, or whether, if such a commission were so empowered, review would be mandatory or optional.[20] Even some of the constitution's major provisions, such as the establishment of an intermediate appellate court, the duties of the Attorney General, and the right to be free from electronic surveillance were written entirely on the floor, depriving delegates of such notice and opportunity to deliberate as may have resulted from the inclusion of a provision in the committee drafts.[21] Under these circumstances, and with only a few minutes between the introduction of an idea and the vote on virtually final approval, it is not surprising that persuasive speeches by a few delegates—the only resource available on the spot to the large group of delegates who had not previously considered the newly introduced issue—were significant influences on votes.

While delegates' floor speeches appeared to be influential, at least on interstitial issues, vote trading and log rolling did not appear to play a major role in convention decisionmaking. This proposition is not easy to document, but the author was aware of only one offer by any delegate to trade a vote on one issue for a vote on another, and that one instance may have been at least in part a jest.[22] As in Hawaii in 1968, "[n]either individual delegates nor committee chairmen were in a position to tie together the fate of proposals, and the convention's more fluid structure and the limited sanctions of its formal leadership discouraged attempts at trading or otherwise lining up support."[23] But a more subtle kind of trading may have been at play on a personal rather than an ideological or political basis, as when a delegate withheld her vote on an issue because she refused to support anything proposed by its sponsor.

No catalogue of influences on the outcome could be complete without reference to the impact of particular convention institutions, such as rules and structure. Foremost among these factors was the decision to have ten substantive committees, a decision motivated primarily by the need to devise a plan that would deny the convention's president the opportunity to appoint members and chairs of committees, but which had the effect of insuring that the constitution would include regulatory articles that were not legally necessary for the formation of a valid document: Education; health, housing, and social services; finance and taxation; and the articles (banking and corporations; land and the environment; labor; and public services) that emerged from the Committee on Economic Development. By the time that the committees to which these subjects were assigned had completed two months of research and writing, it was unthinkable, as Arnold Leibowitz had told the delegates at the outset, that the convention would reject their work altogether by not including articles on these subjects.

A second major technical influence was the rule that made reconsideration virtually impossible. This rule may have saved the Convention, given the fact that the body barely finished within its ninety-day time limit, but the rule did tend to make final almost any decision the delegates made on their first pass, whatever the results of more sober reflection might have produced. On at least one occasion, the rule against reconsideration prevented a majority of delegates from asserting its will.[24]

Finally, a word should be added about a factor which did not appear to constitute a major influence on the policy decisions made by this convention: The role of the president. In some state constitutional conventions, the president has played a very large role in shaping the document. In Maryland, for example, "on the entire process of constitutional revision . . . the imprint of H. Vernon Eney is marked," and "[p]ossibly the principal determinant of the character and style of Alaska's constitution-making process was the man chosen as president."[25] President Cassell, on the other hand, did not attempt to point delegates in any particular directions, either on the record or informally. His constant exhortations to the delegates to keep making progress suggest that all of his energies were consumed by keeping the convention on course, and although he voted like any other delegate and occasionally descended from the rostrum to speak on an issue, he was not closely identified with a particular philosophy of government for the new state. The delegates in this grass roots convention were no more "bossed" by their own leadership than they were by the District's political establishment, which was no more involved in the life of the convention than it had been in its creation.

* * *

The statehood initiative required the constitution to go before the voters for ratification by majority vote.[26] This process required voters to make a single decision aggregating three types of preferences, for a vote in favor of ratification was, simultaneously, a vote to advance the process of statehood, a vote to accept the structure of state government that the convention had devised, and a vote to include in the new state's Constitution the civil and economic rights that had been embodied in the bill of rights and the non-structural articles, such as those on labor, education, and land and the environment.

The constitution was approved by the convention at the end of May 1982, but with one exception, the ratification campaign did not really begin until September, with the vote scheduled for November. The exception involved Delegate Courts Oulahan, who had voted against the constitution and became a leading spokesperson for the opposition in the fall campaign.[27] In June, Oulahan testified before the House Subcommittee on District of Columbia Appropriations. He noted that the statehood initiative authorized the appropriation of funds to the Statehood Commission (whose members had been appointed by the convention) so that the Commission could "educate, advocate, promote and advance the proposition of statehood for the District of Columbia within the District of Columbia and elsewhere."[28] The Council of the District of Columbia had appropriated $100,000 pursuant to this authorization, but like all District appropriations, this one had to be reviewed and approved by Congress. Oulahan asked the Congress to "tie some strings" to the appropriation. Specifically, Oulahan asked that Congress require that the Statehood Commission's funds be used to mail to every voter a copy of the constitution, together with arguments for and against adoption of each article, and prohibit any part of the appropriation from being used to distribute any statement for or against ratification.[29] Congress acceded to the essence of this request, once again changing significantly a law approved in the District, and in the process further energizing the supporters of statehood, who saw in the congressional action additional proof of the need for full self-determination.[30]

Oulahan's maneuver effectively neutralized what might have been a campaign for ratification, at public expense, organized by the Statehood Commission. But there were further problems for the proponents of ratification. Initial newspaper commentary on the constitution was almost uniformly negative, and in September, the District's Republican Party formally opposed ratification. The focus of the opposition was neither the concept of statehood nor the structural provisions of the constitution; the opponents focused almost exclusively on the economic provisions and particularly on the right to a job and the right of public employees to strike.[31]

In the face of these problems, several delegates who had voted for the constitution favored withdrawing it from the ballot; sixteen of twenty-nine delegates surveyed by the *Washington Post* supported withdrawal. "That way, we could iron out some of the rough spots," Delegate Harry Thomas said. Most members of the District's Council said that they were willing to pass legislation taking ratification off the November ballot, but only if the convention requested such action.[32]

Under these circumstances, President Cassell convened an "emergency meeting" of the convention, "to consider recommendations . . . for wording and format of the [issue on the ballot]."[33] At the meeting, Delegates Hilda Mason and David Clarke, who were also Council members, floated the idea of having the Council withdraw the matter from the ballot to save it from defeat, but the convention voted instead to request the Board of Elections to use a "Hawaiian ballot," the device employed successfully to secure ratification of amendments to Hawaii's constitution after the constitutional convention of 1968. A Hawaiian ballot would have required voters to cast separate ballots for or against each of the constitution's proposed articles: only those receiving a majority would have become part of the document. Because the bill of rights and labor articles were receiving most of the criticism, the procedure might have resulted in approval of the bulk of the constitution, without one or both of those articles.[34]

Through the Statehood Commission, the convention made its request to the Board of Elections at the Board's October 6, 1982, meeting. But the Board's General Counsel rendered his opinion that the statehood initiative, which mandated submission of the constitution to the voters "for their adoption or rejection," did not permit other than a straight up-or-down vote.[35]

The Board's rejection of a middle option left the convention with only two alternatives: Put the measure to a vote and thereby risk its rejection, or ask the Council to withdraw it. As public officials began to comment on the constitution, the former course seemed increasingly problematic. The Mayor, the Chair of the Council, and the District's Delegate in Congress all said that they favored approval, but that they would not speak for it in public. David Clarke, who had just defeated the incumbent Council Chair in the Democratic primary and was running unopposed for the position in the November election, said that he would vote against ratification, but he too declined to speak about it in public forums.[36]

President Cassell called a second emergency meeting, ostensibly to review the budget of the Statehood Commission, but also to cope with the emerging sense of crisis. On the day that he mailed notice of this meeting, the *Washington Post* reported that nine of the thirteen Council members favored taking the issue off the ballot. Three of them, in addition to Clarke, said that they would oppose ratification as well. And the Greater Washington Board of Trade, the principal business organization of the District, called for defeat of the measure. On the day that the delegates gathered once again to consider the question, the *Post* editorially called upon the Convention "to withdraw the proposal and improve on it. . . ."[37]

At the convention meeting, Brian Moore made the inevitable motion to withdraw the constitution from the ballot to permit redrafting. The motion was debated extensively. Its proponents argued that there was at least a very substantial risk that the constitution would be defeated. Opponents of the motion countered that Martin Luther King had never turned back in the face of adversity, that the minority of delegates that had not voted for the constitution in May were attempting to have their way without a vote by the public, that the people were entitled to express their preference either way, and that removal of the question from the ballot would be a concession to the voices of reaction, innuendo, and subtle racism. The motion was defeated by a vote of nineteen to twelve.[38]

At the very end of this meeting, Clarke made one further motion—a move which may be of great importance in the ultimate history of D.C. statehood. He noted that even if the Constitution were approved by the people of the District, such endorsement need not mean that the public was satisfied with every clause in the document. Further, it was clear that Congress would be skeptical of some of the provisions. The convention had taken account of this and had included in the constitution a provision permitting its amendment prior to its entry into force. Amendments would have to be proposed either by the convention itself or by a two-thirds vote of the District's Council, and would have to be adopted by the voters in a referendum.[39] Because the source of the constitution's legitimacy was the statehood initiative, however, Clarke doubted that the constitution could itself give the voters the power to adopt amendments. He urged the convention to request that the Council pass parallel legislation amending the initiative to authorize the procedure contemplated by the constitution. His motion was approved on a voice vote.

The *Washington Post* reacted to the delegates' decision not to request withdrawal by terming that move the "kiss of death for statehood." In the *Post*'s view, the constitution was "so larded with political prickles that even some of the strongest advocates of statehood won't touch it." The paper cited the right to work and right to strike clauses in particular, and it concluded that voter approval of the constitution "would be a shaky statement at best—and certainly not a solid foundation for a new state government."[40]

Hilda Mason continued to see the Hawaiian ballot as the way to save the constitution. The Board of Elections could interpret its authority as it wished, but the Council could alter its mandate by legislation. Mason drafted a bill to require article-by-article voting, but Board of Elections officials testified that new ballots could not be printed in the two weeks remaining before the election, and Mason's bill was laid aside.[41]

In the wake of this defeat, Mason turned to the device that the convention itself, on Clarke's motion, had recommended. She introduced a bill to permit the Council to offer amendments to the constitution before it became effective, giving voters the opportunity to vote in favor of the document in the hope that it would be improved before statehood became a reality. This proposal had some appeal for Council members who had not played a major role in the statehood effort, because it tended to give them, rather than convention delegates, control over the content of the constitution that might someday become a reality. As the *Post* put it, "[M]any city leaders who oppose some sections of the constitution believe it should be passed to avoid sending the constitution back to the statehood convention for possible revision. . . . It would be better for the constitution to be handled by the Council and Congress now." The proposal was approved by the Council on its first reading, but it was never given final approval, and consequently died at the end of the Council term. It could, of course, be revived at any time.[42]

While all of this legislative maneuvering was taking place, a quiet political campaign was under way in the District's neighborhoods. The Statehood Commission was forbidden by Oulahan's appropriations rider from advocating an affirmative vote, but it did mail 300,000 copies of the constitution, with brief statements for and against ratification, to the city's voters, and it placed 5,000 "Vote Statehood Constitution" posters on the city's lampposts. It also launched a $10,000 radio campaign to get out the vote. Though the commentary in the radio spots was neutral, as Congress had required, the Commission targeted the spots by playing them on stations most frequently listened to by blacks. "We are playing very heavily to where much of the support for statehood is," said Ed Guinan, who had become staff director of the Statehood Commission. "That is not west of the [Rock Creek] Park [in Ward Three]."[43]

Individual delegates and other citizens were not fettered by legal restrictions. An organization called "FOR the Statehood Convention" was formed which circulated a leaflet urging voter support for the constitution. Delegate Joel Garner became treasurer of "Citizens for a Better Constitution," which published an opposing leaflet. Delegates and Statehood Commission members engaged each other in a series of forums and debates sponsored by civic organizations and Advisory Neighborhood Commissions. In general, however, citizen participation in the ratification process was at a low level and the forums were sparsely attended.[44]

Ten days before election day, the *Post* weighed in with its final judgment: Vote no. "[T]o accept this politically charged and poorly worded document could cause irreparable damage to the cause," the paper warned. "[L]ocal officials are acknowledging its flaws by promising to clean it up if only the voters will hold their noses and vote to approve it." Delegate in Congress Walter Fauntroy, on the other hand, urged approval. He acknowledged that the constitution contained "many crippling provisions" and referred to two in particular. The right to a job was, he said, "unworkable," and the expanded constitutional rights of criminal defendants "run counter to a clear and discernible trend toward providing greater victim and witness protection." Nevertheless, Fauntroy concluded, rejection of the constitution would send it back for redrafting to the very people who were satisfied with it, while approval would send it onward to Congress, which could insist that certain objectionable features be removed as a condition to statehood.[45]

On November 2, 1982, the voters of the District of Columbia ratified the constitution. Fifty-three percent of those voting approved the measure, which carried in all but two wards and lost by a significant margin only in Ward Three. Table IX shows the distribution of the vote by ward.[46]

TABLE IX: Total Vote by Ward on Ratification of the Constitution[47]

	Votes Against	Votes For	Percentage For
Ward 1	4,734	7,079	59.9%
Ward 2	6,470	6,112	48.6
Ward 3	16,379	3,952	19.4
Ward 4	7,485	12,240	62.0
Ward 5	7,037	10,462	59.8
Ward 6	5,677	7,484	56.9
Ward 7	5,213	9,342	64.2
Ward 8	1,910	4,762	71.4
TOTAL	54,905	61,433	52.8

Not surprisingly, proponents and opponents of ratification interpreted the results differently. Oulahan and Garner cited the substantial negative vote as a "mandate to change the document," while Cassell said that he expected any modifications to be minor.[48] In the wake of ratification, the factions began to skirmish over the issue of how any changes would be proposed. David Clarke, now Chair-elect of the Council, embellished the constitution's plan by offering an amendment to the Mason bill when it came before the Council for final approval. Under the Clarke amendment, which passed on a nine to three vote, if the convention and the Council proposed inconsistent amendments, only those approved by the Council would go onto the ballot for voter approval. Clarke's proposal further amended the Mason bill by permitting a simple majority, rather than two-thirds of the Council, to propose amendments for voter ratification.[49] Mason was among the dissenters to this modification of her legislation, and although her proposal was amended over her opposition, her unwillingness to accept it was sufficient to prevent final passage by the Council. Accordingly, no legislation authorizing the Council to propose amendments was approved in the Council term that ended in 1982, nor has such legislation been passed as of this writing in March 1984.[50]

* * *

For advocates of D.C. statehood, the road ahead seems clearer than ever, although the project may take many years to complete, if it is achievable at all. Congress is likely to remain skeptical about D.C. statehood, but probably not because of particular provisions in the constitution. Congressional reluctance to make the District a state will probably center on the issues on which it has always centered: Doubt that such a small geographical area merits equal treatment with other states; reluctance to upset a delicate political balance by suddenly adding two probably Democratic Senators to the upper House; fear of encouraging secessionist movements in other municipalities; uneasiness about the continued reliability of police and fire protection of federal property if Congress releases its ultimate authority over the District; and, in the case of the legislators from Maryland and Virginia, perhaps an unwillingness to permit what is now the District to have the authority, inherent in states, to tax the incomes of those who earn money there but live in neighboring states.[51] Within days after the convention approved the constitution, Senator Alphonse D'Amato, Chairperson of the Senate's District of Columbia Appropriations Subcommittee, said that the District was a "long way from statehood."[52]

Unless there appears to be a prospect of a statehood application from a jurisdiction that would supply two balancing Republican Senators, the best bet for New Columbia's admission to the Union is probably the route that led to home rule and to congressional approval of the D.C. Voting Representation Amendment to the Constitution: Political pressure on behalf of self-determination in a jurisdiction that is primarily black. As Delegate in Congress Walter Fauntroy put it,

> It is no accident that Strom Thurmond led the full voting representation fight in the Senate. The simple fact was that he was up for reelection in a state where one-third of the electorate was black and in a state where the blacks enjoyed kicking Cain with John L. McMillan. . . . I asked him if he was up for reelection, and he said yes. I asked him if he knew a gentleman by the name of Ravenel, a young Yalie with plenty of money, who was very attractive to the black community in South Carolina. He said, 'How many votes do you need?' And I said, 'I need 19.' He said, 'I can't get 19.' I said, 'I have to go to South Carolina and talk to my friends then.' He went and got Goldwater [who became his 19th vote].[53]

It is by no means impossible that D.C. statehood, which offers a real possibility of sending two blacks to the U.S. Senate, could become a significant national civil rights issue, and one that would be all the easier for members of Congress to support because it would not require the establishment of a bureaucracy or the appropriation of federal funds.

But if statehood is a serious possibility, care should be taken not to impose unnecessary, artificial obstacles. The right to employment clause of the constitution of New Columbia is such an obstacle.[54] At the least, it offers skeptical members of Congress an easy excuse to dismiss statehood on the ground that New Columbia could not implement this clause and remain economically viable; at worst, if it entered into force and were not interpreted merely as a goal, it could bankrupt the state rapidly. A few other clauses of the constitution may also be more harmful to the cause of statehood, or to the residents of the new state, than they are helpful. Before a major political effort is mounted for the admission of New Columbia, a few changes need to be made in the new state's proposed charter.

Delegate Clarke's amendments to the Mason bill are the wrong place to start. The Council rather than the convention should propose amendments, because the constitution needs editing by a body attuned to pragmatic politics and responsible to voters in periodic elections. But there is no need for Clarke's proposal to give ballot precedence to amendments originating in the Council rather than the convention. The convention has served its purpose; despite the three-year terms of its members, it is quite dead and will not propose amendments to its product. Its appropriation has been spent; it has neither staff nor supplies; it has lost possession of its headquarters in the Pepco Building. Even if it could reach consensus on amendments, which is highly doubtful, it could not even retain a court reporter to transcribe the meeting at which they were debated.[55] By declining to appropriate new funds to the convention, the Council can ensure that it will control the amendment process; it need not insult the delegates and appear to arrogate new power to itself by enacting the precedence provisions of the Clarke proposal.

Similarly, it would be preferable that legislation empowering the Council to propose amendments require a two-thirds vote of the Council, as in the Mason bill, rather than a majority, as in the Clarke amendment. A two-thirds provision would track the language of the constitution, which the voters have approved, and would therefore enjoy greater legitimacy. More important, a two-thirds rule would preserve the concept that the constitution, developed not by the Council but by an extraordinary process, is not ordinary legislation, that can be amended by a routine law, and it would help to ensure that only the serious excesses of the constitution would be addressed. This protection of the document is important not only because of the special steps that have been taken to bring it to the point it has reached, but also because if the Council were to conceive its task as rewriting the constitution from start to finish, the effort could easily take many years. And there is no promise whatsoever that the resulting product would be a net improvement. Indeed, constitutions are usually written by conventions, rather than by legislatures, in part to protect the public against a charter that might otherwise lean too strongly in the direction of serving the interests of incumbent politicians.

Once it adopts a two-thirds rule, the Council should hold public hearings and make a strenuous effort to encourage participation in those hearings by all segments of the District's population. The convention lacked the time and resources to make the witness lists at its hearings fully representative, and some significant institutions, such as the judiciary, boycotted the events. This can be redressed, at least in part, by more extensive Council hearings. Meanwhile, the Mayor should informally ask that Congress take no action on statehood admission.

When the Council has presented proposed amendments to the voters and the electorate has decided which of them to adopt, the political campaign for statehood can begin in earnest. Even then, the constitution need not be regarded as in final form; further amendments could be added in the course of months or years of discussions with congressional committees. Congress could demand particular amendments as at least a temporary condition of admission to the Union, or even require the District to conduct new elections, hold a new convention, and write and ratify a new constitution before becoming a state. Despite the fact that the constitution of New Columbia may never enter into force in precisely the form in which it was approved by the voters, it represents an important political step on the road to statehood. Particularly in light of the problems and crises that attended the convention from commencement to conclusion, the consititution of New Columbia stands as a remarkable contribution from people who were neither lawyers nor politicians to the constantly developing mosaic of American law.

Notes to the Conclusion

1. *See* John Wheeler & Melissa Kinsey, *Magnificent Failure: The Maryland Constitutional Convention of 1967-68* (New York: National Municipal League, 1970) pp. 16-33 (description of the activities of Maryland's preparatory commission, which held 140 committee meetings and 25 plenary meetings before the convention began). The leading text on state constitutional revision takes the view that "[i]t is a serious error for a convention to begin meeting without some kind of advance provision for research material." Elmer Cornwell, Jay Goodman & Wayne Swanson, *Constitutional Conventions: The Politics of Revision* (New York: Praeger Press, 1974), p. 10.

2. Active leadership by Gov. Raymond P. Shafer, former Gov. William W. Scranton, and Lt. Gov. Raymond J. Broderick was important in Pennsylvania, and significant roles were also played by Gov. John Burns of Hawaii, Gov. Winthrop Rockefeller in Arkansas, and Gov. Millard Tawes in Maryland. E. Cornwell, J. Goodman & W. Swanson, p. 10.

3. This is a smaller fraction than in other state constitutional conventions.

4. Testimony of Lawrence Guyot, Before the Committee on Economic Development of the District of Columbia Statehood Constitutional Convention, Apr. 13, 1982, pp. 22-23.

5. The Alaska Statehood Convention was isolated on a university campus in a "remote locale," and only a few Fairbanks delegates tried to keep up on their other work during the convention. Victor Fisher, *Alaska's Constitutional Convention* (Fairbanks: University of Alaska Press, 1975), p. 187.

6. The convention took 34 votes by roll call, only 10 of them involving policy issues that were decided after the president implored the delegates to save money by avoiding roll calls. By contrast, the Maryland convention of 1967 took 672 roll-call votes. J. Wheeler & M. Kinsey, p. 55.

7. The author had to use some judgment in determining which roll calls on policy issues were primary. He included in this compilation all policy roll calls that were closely divided (*e.g.*, where the difference between the sides was equal to or fewer than four votes) except (1) a vote on whether the tenure commission's public review of judges' performance (prior to retention elections) was to be mandatory rather than optional with the judge in question, Transcript, Apr. 30, 1982, p. 23, and (2) a vote limiting property tax exemptions to religious, charitable, and educational entities, Transcript, May 17, 1982, p. 216. The first of these two exclusions was made because the issue was relatively trivial; the second because only 7 of the 17 white delegates voted.

8. J. Moore proposal to elect officers by secret ballot rather than by roll-call vote. Transcript, Feb. 2, 1982, p. 116.

9. Clarke proposal to limit officers' terms of service to one year and to permit the convention to remove officers by two-thirds vote. Transcript, Feb. 4, 1982, p. 174.

10. Transcript, Feb. 11, 1982, p. 83.

11. Jordan proposal to require judges to run in periodic retention elections. Transcript, Apr. 28, 1982, pp. 193-99.

12. Barnes proposal to make the legislature bicameral. Transcript, May 11, 1982, pp. 64-66.

13. Bruning proposal for 16 senators and 32 delegates in the legislature. Transcript, May 11, 1982, pp. 129-30.

14. Jackson proposal for an unqualified rather than a qualified right to strike. Transcript, May 15, 1982, p. 139.

15. Clarke motion to suspend rules to permit him to offer a substitute bill of rights. Transcript, May 27, 1982, pp. 106-08. This vote may be a less significant measure of ideological attitude than the others, in that some delegates might have been willing to permit Clarke to offer his substitute (*e.g.*, in the spirit of open consideration of ideas) while planning to vote against the substitute on the merits.

The motion received majority but not two-thirds support, so the second vote was not held.

16. Delegates Brian Moore and Kenneth Rothschild occasionally made sweeping proposals, but their suggestions were brushed aside. Transcript, Apr. 27, 1982, pp. 115-62. Of course, a novel system of neighborhood government was considered seriously by the Committee on Local Government, but it was ultimately rejected by that Committee.

17. *Compare National Municipal League, Model State Constitution*, § 11.02(b) (1968) *with* Const. art. I, § 6 (electronic surveillance). Transcript, May 26, 1982, p. 439 (Delegate Graham).

18. Ala. Const. art. IV, § 6; Md. Const. Declaration of Rights, art. 1.

19. Norman Meller, *With An Understanding Heart: Constitution Making in Hawaii* (New York: National Municipal League, 1971), pp. 142-43.

20. Transcript, Apr. 30, 1982, pp. 8-16.

21. Transcript, May 22, 1982, pp. 166-200 (approval of legislative power to establish intermediate appellate court and rewriting on the floor of the jurisdiction of the supreme court); Transcript, May 4, 1982 pp. 191-95 (Attorney General); Transcript, May 25, 1982, pp. 436-39 (electronic surveillance).

22. Jordan's reported offer to change his view on retention elections for Thomas' vote on gun control.

It is hard to see how Jordan could have delivered at the time that the offer was allegedly made, since his amendment had already been approved and reconsideration was not permitted.

23. N. Meller, p. 142.

24. Transcript, Apr. 29, 1982, pp. 39-40 (proposed reconsideration of judicial retention elections).

25. J. Wheeler & M. Kinsey, p. 17; V. Fischer, p. 190.

26. D.C. Sess. Law 3-171, § 4(b) (1980).

27. Oulahan had served notice on the delegates who supported the constitution that he intended to oppose ratification in the fall. Transcript, May 29, 1982, p. 121.

28. D.C. Sess. Law 3-171, § 6(b) (1980).

29. Hearings before the House of Representatives Subcomm. on District of Columbia Appropriations of the House Comm. on Appropriations, 97th Cong., 2d Sess., pp. 3171-80 (June 24, 1982).

30. Pub. L. No. 97-176, § 114(a), 96 Stat. 1186, 1193 (1982).

31. Associated Press, "Alas, D.C. Won't Be Utopia," *Baltimore Sun*, May 30, 1982, p. C2; Editorial, "Utopian," *Baltimore Sun*, June 7, 1982, p. A10; Leavitt, "The Funding Fathers," *Baltimore Sun*, Aug. 18, 1982, p. A6 (negative press); "Proposed D.C. Constitution Is Opposed," *Washington Post*, Sept. 17, 1982, p. A27 (formal opposition); Clines, "Bold Document for a City-State," *San Francisco Chronicle*, July 26, 1982, p. 48 (characterizing economic sections as "radical").

32. Valente and Sherwood, "Most Delegates Support Vote on Statehood," *Washington Post*, Oct. 8, 1982, p. C1.

33. Letter to Delegates from Charles I. Cassell, Sept. 24, 1982.

34. By this time, the convention had completely exhausted its funds; no transcript of this meeting was made, nor were minutes circulated. The information in the text was given to the author by Delegate Robert Love in a conversation on Sept. 29, 1982.

For a description of the Hawaii procedure, *see* N. Meller, pp. 123-28.

35. Memorandum to the author from Sal Mungia, a law student research assistant who observed the meeting, Oct. 7, 1982; D.C. Sess. Law 3-171, § 4(b) (1980).

36. Sherwood, "Some Officials Lukewarm Toward D.C. Constitution," *Washington Post*, Oct. 5, 1982, p. C1.

37. Sherwood, "Support Grows to Remove Statehood Issue From Ballot," *Washington Post*, Oct. 6, 1982 p. C1 (nine of thirteen favor removal); Valente, "D.C. Board of Trade Aims a Broadside at Statehood Constitution," *Washington*

Post, Oct. 15, 1982, p. B3; Sherwood, "Support Grows to Remove Statehood Issue From Ballot," *Washington Post*, Oct. 6, 1982, p. C1; Editorial, "Hold Off That Statehood Vote," *Washington Post*, Oct. 9, 1982, p. A18.

38. No transcript was made of this meeting. The information in the text is based on the notes of the author, who was present. *See also* Sherwood, "Statehood Delegates Stand Firm," *Washington Post*, Oct. 10, 1982, p. B1.

39. Const., art. XVIII, § 9.

40. Editorial, "A Kiss of Death for Statehood," *Washington Post*, Oct. 12, 1982, p. A12.

41. Sherwood, "Council to Vote on D.C. Constitution Ballot Plan," *Washington Post*, Oct. 13, 1982, p. C3; Sherwood, "Council Keeps Yes-No Vote on Constitution," *Washington Post*, Oct. 14, 1982, p. B5.

42. Sherwood, "Council Gets Authority to Amend Constitution," *Washington Post*, Oct. 20, 1982, p. C1 (quoting critic of constitution).

43. Sherwood, "Voters Get Copies of D.C. Constitution Draft," *Washington Post*, Oct. 26, 1982, p. C2.

44. The author attended three such events, the audiences for which were 9, 4, and (for the debate in Ward Three) 55.

45. Editorial, "Ballot Decisions in the District," *Washington Post*, Oct. 23, 1982, p. A2; Walter E. Fauntroy, Letter to the Editor, *Washington Post*, Oct. 28, 1982, p. A22.

46. The author voted in favor of ratification, as he had announced he would a week earlier at a forum in his ward. In casting an affirmative vote, he accepted the reasoning of long-time statehood advocate Sam Smith, who said that while there were "serious flaws" in the constitution, "rejection will send the matter back to the Constitutional Convention, which has a tendency to prefer impressive rhetoric to legislative pragmatism [and] will be viewed in some quarters as a rejection of statehood," while a vote could be cast for the constitution "with the hope that following passage the city council will immediately move to present proposed amendments. . . ." Editorial, D.C. Gazette, reprinted in *Washington Post*, Oct. 17, 1982, p. B8.

47. D.C. Board of Elections and Ethics, Election Results for Nov. 2, 1982, pp. 1-137. The totals given in this table were derived by adding the official precinct totals. Unaccountably, the D.C. Board of Elections and Ethics' official District totals vary slightly from the numbers generated by this process. The official District-wide totals are 61,405 votes for the constitution and 54,964 votes against.

48. Sherwood & Milloy, "D.C. Voters Approve Statehood, Constitution and Nuclear Freeze," *Washington Post*, Nov. 3, 1982, p. C1.

49. Pianin, "Council Votes Itself Final Authority On Statehood Constitutional Changes," *Washington Post*, Nov. 17, 1982, p. C4.

50. Despite the Council's failure to facilitate amendments to the constitution, Mayor Marion Barry transmitted it to Congress on Sept. 9, 1983, along with the petition of the District of Columbia for admission to the Union as a new state. Teeley, "D.C. Statehood Languishes on Hill with Little Chance Seen for Passage," *Washington Post*, Nov. 8, 1983, p. B2. Three days later the District's Delegate in Congress, Walter E. Fauntroy, introduced a bill for admission into the Union of the State of New Columbia. H.R. 3861, 98th Cong., 1st Sess. Fauntroy had earlier predicted that a subcommittee of the House Committee on the District of Columbia would hold hearings on D.C. statehood during the fall of 1983. Fauntroy, Foreword to District of Columbia Statehood Constitution, Ser. No. S-1, Committee on the District of Columbia, 98th Cong., 1st Sess. (July 4, 1983). But he realized that "[i]f we brought it to a vote today, it would have a snowball's chance in July in Florida of passing." Teeley, "Barry Ready to Submit Petition for Statehood," *Washington Post*, Sept. 28, p. B1. Accordingly, in the fall of 1983 he sent letters to his colleagues on Capitol Hill asking for suggested amendments to the constitution which he would then forward to the Mayor and the Council. Teeley, "D.C. Statehood Languishes on Hill with Little Chance Seen for Passage," *Washington Post*, Nov. 8, 1983, p. B2.

51. Transcript, May 8, 1982, p. 104 (remarks of Delegate in Congress Walter Fauntroy to the convention). Congress could require, as a condition of admission, that the new state include a prohibition on commuter taxes (or any other desired clause) in its constitution. But it could not constitutionally prevent the state from amending its constitution after admission to the Union to achieve the result that Congress wanted to avoid. *See* Coyle v. Smith, 221 U.S. 559, 572 (1911).

52. Clines, "Bold Document for a City-State," *San Francisco Chronicle*, July 26, 1982, p. 48.

53. Transcript, May 8, 1982, pp. 106-07.

54. Const., art. I, § 20.

55. The convention was not able even to tape record its emergency meetings in the fall of 1982.

APPENDICES

APPENDIX A

The Delegates to the District of Columbia's Statehood Constitutional Convention

The Elected Members of the District's Constitutional Convention

(NAMES OF THE 28 BLACK DELEGATES ARE PRINTED IN **bold type**, THOSE OF THE 17 WHITE DELEGATES IN *italic type*.)

	Political Party	Sex	Occupational Status in 1982	Prior Elective Office
WARD 1:				
Richard Bruning	Statehood	M	D.C. Gov't employee	none
Maurice Jackson	Communist	M	Political organizer	none
Robert Love	Democratic	M	Psychologist	none
Marie Nahikian	Democratic	F	D.C. Gov't employee	ANC
Anita Shelton	Democratic	F	D.C. Gov't employee	none
WARD 2:				
Alexa Freeman	Democratic	F	Student	none
Wesley Long	Democratic	M	D.C. Gov't employee	ANC
Barbara Maguire	Democratic	F	Waitress	none
Brian Moore	Democratic	M	Unemployed	ANC
Kenneth Rothschild	Democratic	M	Taxi driver	ANC
WARD 3:				
Gloria Corn	Republican	F	Unemployed	ANC
Joel Garner	Democratic	M	Federal Gov't employee	ANC
Franklin Kameny	Democratic	M	Retired	none
Courts Oulahan	Republican	M	Attorney	none
Philip Schrag	Democratic	M	Professor	none
WARD 4:				
William Cooper	Republican	M	Unemployed	none
Jeannette Feely	Democratic	F	D.C. teacher*	none
Janette Harris	Democratic	F	D.C. professor**	none
Charles Mason	Statehood	M	D.C. Council employee	none
Victoria Street	Democratic	F	Retired	Board
WARD 5:				
Michael Marcus	Statehood	M	Professor	none
Talmadge Moore	Democratic	M	Retired	ANC
Norman Nixon	Democratic	M	Student	none
Samuel Robinson	Democratic	M	D.C. Gov't employee	none
Harry Thomas	Democratic	M	Federal Gov't employee	ANC

* In the District's public school system.   **In the District's public university.

Prior Elective Office:

ANC = Advisory Neighborhood Commissioner
Board = Member of Board of Education of the District of Columbia
Council = Member of the Council of the District of Columbia

	Political Party	Sex	Occupational Status in 1982	Prior Elective Office
WARD 6:				
Howard Croft	Democratic	M	D.C. professor**	none
Janice Eichhorn	Democratic	*F*	D.C. Gov't employee	ANC
Chestie Graham	Democratic	F	D.C. teacher*	ANC
Charlotte Holmes	Democratic	F	Federal Gov't employee	ANC
Geraldine Warren	Democratic	F	D.C. Gov't employee	none
WARD 7:				
James Baldwin	Democratic	M	Retired	none
David Barnes	Democratic	M	Computer specialist	none
William Blount	Democratic	M	D.C. teacher*	ANC
Sandra Johnson	Democratic	F	D.C. administrator*	none
James Terrell	Democratic	M	Professor	none
WARD 8:				
James Coates	Democratic	M	Minister	Board
Theresa Jones	Democratic	F	D.C. Gov't employee	ANC
Absalom Jordan	Democratic	M	D.C. Gov't employee	none
Mildred Lockridge	Democratic	F	Retired	none
Gwendolyn Paramore	Democratic	F	D.C. teacher*	none
AT-LARGE:				
Charles Cassell	Statehood	M	Concert promoter	Board
David Clarke	Democratic	M	Elected D.C. official	Council
Hilda Mason	Statehood	F	Elected D.C. official	Council & Board
Jerry Moore	Republican	M	Elected D.C. official	Council
Barbara Lett Simmons	Democratic	F	Elected D.C. official	Board

SOURCES:
For ward from which elected: Program for Installation and Opening Session of the Convention, January 30, 1982.
For party: interviews with Delegates James Baldwin (a member of the D.C. Democratic State Committee) and Richard Bruning (Statehood Party Secretary); and T. Sherwood, "45 to Draft Charter for Statehood," *Washington Post*, November 8, 1981, p. B1.
For race and sex: author's observations.
For occupation and prior elective office: interview with Delegate James Baldwin, First Vice President of the Convention, February 27, 1983, supplemented by interviews with Janice Eichhorn and Brian Moore, February 27, 1983.

The Constitution of the State of New Columbia

WE, THE PEOPLE OF THE FREE AND SOVEREIGN STATE OF NEW COLUMBIA, *seek to secure and provide for each person: health, safety and welfare; a peaceful and orderly life; and the right to legal, social, and economic justice and equality.*

We recognize our unique and special history and the diversity and pluralism of our people, and we have determined to control our collective destiny, maximize our individual freedom, and govern ourselves democratically, guaranteeing to each individual and the people collectively, complete and equal exercise and protection of the rights listed herein.

We reach out to all the peoples of the world in a spirit of friendship and cooperation, certain that together we can build a future of peace and harmony.

Therefore, being mindful that government exists to serve every person, we do adopt this Constitution and establish this government.

Article I: BILL OF RIGHTS

Section 1:
FREEDOM OF ASSOCIATION, ASSEMBLY, EXPRESSION, AND PETITION

Freedom of association, assembly, press, speech, and other forms of expression, and petition for redress of grievances shall not be abridged.

Section 2:
FREEDOM OF RELIGION
The State shall establish no religion nor interfere with the free exercise thereof. No person shall be denied any right or privilege because of religious belief or the exercise thereof.

Section 3:
FREEDOM FROM DISCRIMINATION
Every person shall have a fundamental right to the equal protection of the law and to be free from historic group discrimination, public or private, based on race, color, religion, creed, citizenship, national origin, sex, sexual orientation, poverty, or parentage. Affirmative action to correct consequences of past discrimination against women, and against racial and national minorities, shall be lawful.

Persons with disabilities shall have the right to be treated as equal community members and the right to the services as defined by law provided in a way that promotes dignity and independence and full community participation.

Youth and seniors shall have the right to the enjoyment of health and well-being and to the services as provided by law necessary for their development and welfare. No adult shall be discriminated against in housing or employment on the basis of age, except that services limited to senior citizens may be provided.

It shall be unlawful to commit or incite acts of violence against persons or property based on race, color, religion, creed, national origin, sex, or sexual orientation.

Equality of rights under the law shall not be denied or abridged in the State or any of its subdivisions because of sex.

This Section shall be self-executing and shall be enforced by appropriate legislation.

Section 4:
PRIVACY

The right of the individual to decide whether to procreate or to bear a child is inviolable, as is the right to noncommercial private, consensual, sexual behavior of adults. Those who exercise or advocate these rights have, in addition, the right to be free from all forms of discrimination.

Political surveillance is contrary to democratic principles. Therefore, unless relevant for prosecution of past, present, or imminent crime, information on any person's exercise of freedom of religion, expression, association, assembly, or petition for redress of grievances, shall not be collected surreptitiously under color of law.

Individual privacy with respect to personal bank accounts, health, academic, employment, communications, and similar records, the disclosure of which would constitute an invasion of privacy of the individual concerned, is a right, the protection of which shall be provided by law. However, the name, salary, and place of employment of each employee of the State and of any of its agencies or local government units is a matter of public record and shall be available to the public.

Section 5:
DUE PROCESS

The State shall not deprive any person of life, liberty, or property without due process of law. The right of all persons to fair and just treatment in the course of legislative and executive investigations shall not be abridged.

Section 6:
SEARCHES AND SEIZURES

Privacy is a fundamental right. Therefore, the people shall be free from unreasonable searches and seizures of their persons, homes, businesses, vehicles, papers, and effects. This right extends to all places and for all circumstances in which the individual has a reasonable expectation of privacy. The fruits of unlawful intrusions, including intrusions by private persons, shall not be used by the State for any purpose in any judicial or administrative proceeding against any individual, whether or not the individual was the target of an unlawful search or seizure, and whether or not the expectation of privacy of that individual was violated.

No search will ensue except under the authority of a valid warrant issued by a judicial officer; such warrant shall be issued only upon probable cause and must be supported by oath or affirmation describing with particularity the place to be searched and the persons or items to be seized. This Section does not preclude warrantless searches or seizures in the following circumstances: searches incident to a valid arrest; exigent circumstances under which officials conducting the search or seizure have no time to secure a warrant; inadvertent discovery of illegal material pursuant to the execution of a valid search warrant; searches and seizures conducted at international borders or their functional equivalent; administrative searches of pervasively regulated businesses pursuant to a general plan; and searches upon the consent of the individual who is the subject of the search or seizure, provided that the individual had been fully informed of the right to withhold consent, and no other exception to this Section is present. The official conducting the search bears the burden of proving fully informed consent.

The right to be secured against unreasonable interception of telephonic, telegraphic, electronic, and other forms of communication and against unreasonable interception of oral and other communications by electronic methods shall not be violated. No such interception shall occur except following issuance of a warrant. No orders of warrants for such interceptions shall be issued but upon probable cause supported by oath or affirmation that evidence of crime may be thus obtained, and particularly identifying the means of communication and the person or persons whose communications are to be intercepted. Evidence obtained in violation of this paragraph shall not be admissible in any court against any person.

Section 7:
RIGHTS OF ARRESTEES AND DEFENDANTS
In all criminal matters, all persons have the right to the assistance of competent counsel from commencement of a custodial interrogation, during trial and appeal, and whenever they are subject to a deprivation of liberty. When arrested they shall be informed of their right to consult with counsel. Persons charged with a crime have the right to receive an explicit statement of the nature and cause of the accusation, to the discovery of all evidence possessed by the State, and to the presumption of innocence until proven guilty beyond a reasonable doubt. Convicted persons shall have the right to judicial review.

Section 8:
GRAND JURY
All persons have the right to be free from unwarranted or arbitrary prosecutions. The grand jury shall not engage in fishing expeditions. Grand jury indictments are required for all offenses carrying authorized prison sentences of one year or more. Grand jurors shall be drawn from a cross-section of the community. All grand jury witnesses shall have the right to assistance and presence of counsel, to be informed of the privilege against self-incrimination, and to be advised if they are, or may become, targets of prosecution. Criminal defendants are entitled to grand jury transcripts in a timely fashion.

The grand jury shall appoint and the State shall pay nongovernmental counsel for independent advice. Indictments shall be issued only on probable cause and shall, upon motion, be dismissed for violations of this Section.

The House of Delegates shall determine the manner of grand jury selection and operation.

Section 9:
BAIL
The sole purpose of bail is to assure the presence of the accused at trial. Bail shall not be excessive and may take the form of a cash or property guarantee.

Section 10:
TRIAL BY JURY

Every person accused of a criminal offense is guaranteed the right to: a speedy, public, and fair trial; compulsory attendance of witnesses; confrontation with adversary witnesses; and trial by a jury of 12 persons. Conviction may be based only upon a unanimous jury verdict finding the accused guilty beyond a reasonable doubt.

Section 11:
PUNISHMENT

The State shall not require excessive fines, nor impose cruel, corporal, or unusual punishment, or sentence of death. Penal administration shall be based upon the principle of reformation with the objective of restoring the offender to a useful role in community life. Convicted persons shall not be denied any rights specified in this Constitution except as shall be reasonably necessary for the security of a penal institution or the State and its citizens.

Section 12:
IMPRISONMENT FOR DEBT

No person shall be imprisoned for inability to pay a debt.

Section 13:
DOUBLE JEOPARDY

No person shall be tried more than once for the same offense; further, the State shall try in a single trial all charges, actual and potential, arising from the same facts and circumstances. Trial of a person for an offense in any jurisdiction of the United States and subsequent trial under the jurisdiction of the State for the same offense based on the same set of facts and circumstances shall constitute double jeopardy under this Section.

Section 14:
BILLS OF ATTAINDER AND EX POST FACTO LAWS

Bills of attainder and ex post facto laws are prohibited.

Section 15:
HABEAS CORPUS

The writ of habeas corpus shall be available promptly at all times, successively, and without limit in all cases of unlawful detention, conviction, or sentencing, whether or not the petitioner is in custody.

Section 16:
ABOLITION OF COMMON LAW CRIMINAL OFFENSES

Every crime shall be defined with specificity in a statute enacted by the House of Delegates, and no person shall be accused, arrested, tried, or convicted for any act not expressly defined as an offense by such statute. This Section shall take effect after the expiration of a time period to be specified by law.

Section 17:
ABOLITION OF SOVEREIGN IMMUNITY

Unless otherwise provided in this Constitution, the State and any of its subordinate levels of government, and any branch, agency, and office thereof, and any officer or agent thereof in both official and personal capacity, shall be amenable to suit and liability in the courts of this State or of the United States, with respect to official acts both of commission and omission, including the failure, inability, or refusal by law enforcement agencies of the State to provide reasonable protection to individuals from crimes of violence; except that, no judge of any court may be sued with respect to a decision rendered in any case, but may be questioned and required to testify as to issuance of any warrant.

Section 18:
SLAVERY AND INVOLUNTARY SERVITUDE
   Slavery and involuntary servitude are prohibited.

Section 19:
CIVIL SUITS
   The right to a jury trial in a civil suit shall remain inviolate. The House of Delegates shall assure access to courts for those litigants unable to pay. Court costs shall not be required of any litigant unable to pay.

Section 20:
RIGHT TO EMPLOYMENT
   Every person shall have the right to employment, or if unable to work, an income sufficient to meet basic human needs.

Section 21:
EQUAL PAY
   All employees shall be guaranteed equal pay for equal work and equal pay for comparable work.

Section 22:
THE RIGHT TO CHANGE
   The State with its institutions belongs to the people who inhabit it. Whenever a government fails to serve its people, they may exercise their inalienable right to alter, reform, or abolish it.

Section 23:
UNENUMERATED RIGHTS
   The enumeration in this Constitution of certain rights possessed by the individual or limitations upon the government shall not be construed to disparage nor deny other rights or limitations not enumerated.

Section 24:
SELF-EXECUTION
   All Sections of this Article shall be self-executing.

ARTICLE II: THE LEGISLATIVE BRANCH

Section 1:
LEGISLATIVE POWER
   The legislative power of the State shall be vested in the legislature, which shall be called the House of Delegates.

Section 2:
COMPOSITION OF THE HOUSE OF DELEGATES

The House of Delegates shall have one chamber composed of 40 members who are elected from single-member legislative districts. By majority vote of the Delegates present and voting, the House of Delegates shall elect a President from among its members.

Section 3:
QUALIFICATIONS OF MEMBERS

A candidate for the House of Delegates must be a citizen of the United States. To become a Delegate, a candidate must receive the highest number of votes on the designated day of election from the qualified voters of the legislative district.

A Delegate must be at least 18 years old, a resident of the State for at least three years, a resident of the legislative district for at least 18 months, and a registered voter of that district. Every Delegate must reside in the legislative district while in office.

Section 4:
DISQUALIFICATIONS

While in office, no appointed or elected Delegate may hold any other federal or state elected or appointed public office, position of profit, or employment. During the term of office, no member shall be elected or appointed to any public office or employment which shall have been created, or the salary or benefits of which shall have been increased, by legislative act during such term. This Section does not apply to Delegates seeking re-election, or election to a constitutional convention.

Section 5:
TERM IN OFFICE

A Delegate shall be elected for a four-year term.

Section 6:
TIME OF ELECTION

In general elections, half the Delegates will be elected in every even-numbered year. Following their election, winning candidates shall assume office on the second Monday of January.

Section 7:
VACANCIES

Legislative vacancies shall be filled as provided by law.

Section 8:
COMPENSATION OF MEMBERS

The members of the House of Delegates shall receive annual salaries and such allowances as may be prescribed by law. However, any increase or decrease in salary or allowances shall not apply to a Delegate serving in the House of Delegates which enacted the increase or decrease until the re-election of that Delegate.

The Governor shall appoint, subject to the advice and consent of the House of Delegates, members of a five-member commission. Every four years, this commission shall report to the public the level of legislative compensation that is appropriate, taking into account comparable compensation in the public and private sectors. The members of the commission shall hold no other public office. Procedures for the establishment and operation of the commission shall be established by law.

Section 9:
SESSIONS

The House of Delegates shall be a continuing body during the term for which Delegates are elected; however, all unapproved pending bills shall expire automatically on the second Monday in January of each odd-numbered year. The House of Delegates shall meet in regular sessions annually, as provided by law. It may also be convened by the Governor, subject to the conditions of Article III, or by the President of the House of Delegates at the written request of a majority of all Delegates.

Adequate advance notice of all meetings of the House of Delegates and of its committees shall be published. The notice shall include the agenda. All meetings of the House of Delegates and its committees shall be open to the public, to the press, and to radio and television coverage. However, meetings involving confidential discussions of specific staff personnel may be closed by a two-thirds vote of the House of Delegates or the committee.

Section 10:
ORGANIZATION AND PROCEDURE

The courts shall be the final judge of the election and qualifications of Delegates. The House of Delegates shall prescribe its rules of procedure which shall be consistent with this Constitution. It may compel the attendance of absent members, discipline its members and, with the concurrence of two-thirds of all members, expel a member for cause. It shall have power to compel the attendance and testimony of witnesses and the production of books and papers either before the House of Delegates as a whole or before any of its committees.

Section 11:
LEGISLATIVE IMMUNITY

For any speech or debate in the House of Delegates, Delegates shall not be questioned in any other place.

Section 12:
TRANSACTION OF BUSINESS

A majority of all Delegates shall constitute a quorum to do business, but a smaller number may adjourn from day to day and compel the attendance of absent members. The House of Delegates and its committees shall keep journals of proceedings. Each journal shall be available to the public and shall also be promptly published. The journal shall contain all motions made and the votes on those motions. A record vote, with the yeas and nays entered into the journal, shall be taken in the House of Delegates on any vote deciding final passage or defeat of a bill, on any vote to defer consideration of a question indefinitely, and on any vote on the demand of four members. In committee, upon demand of any member, or on any vote deciding final approval of a report, the yeas and nays shall be recorded and entered into the journal.

A verbatim or electronically produced record of proceedings of the House of Delegates and of standing committees shall be made available to the public on request.

Section 13:
C OMMITTEES

The House of Delegates may establish committees necessary for the conduct of its business.

Section 14:
BILLS

The House of Delegates shall enact no law except by bill. The subject of every law shall be clearly expressed in its title. Each law shall have an enacting clause as follows: "Be it enacted by the people of the State of New Columbia." No bill embracing more than one subject shall be passed except appropriation bills which shall include only appropriations and bills for the codification or revision of the laws. All laws shall be published. Whenever a law or section of law is amended, it shall be re-enacted and republished. Every law shall be plainly worded.

Section 15:
PASSAGE OF BILLS

No bill shall become law unless

a) a majority of the entire House of Delegates has approved it in identical form on two occasions at least 13 calendar days apart and the bill had been printed and distributed at least three calendar days in advance on both occasions; or

b) the Governor has certified that prompt passage, precluding a time lapse of 13 days, is essential, and a majority of all Delegates approve the bill.

Section 16:
APPROVAL OR VETO

All bills approved by the House of Delegates, except those relating solely to legislative procedure, shall be presented to the Governor for signature or for veto. The Governor may, by veto, strike items in appropriation bills. The Governor shall veto other bills only as a whole. The Governor shall promptly return any vetoed bill or item of appropriation to the House of Delegates with a statement of objections. A bill shall become law if the Governor either signs it or does not veto it within 15 days of presentation.

Section 17:
LEGISLATIVE ACTION UPON VETO

Upon receipt of a veto, the House of Delegates shall promptly reconsider passage of the vetoed bill or appropriation item. Such a bill or item requires only one reading. A vetoed bill shall become law by the affirmative votes of two-thirds of all Delegates, except that a veto of an appropriation bill or item shall be overridden by the affirmative votes of two-thirds of the Delegates present and voting.

If the House of Delegates is not in session when a bill or item is vetoed, the House of Delegates may consider the bill or item at its next regular or special session.

Section 18:
EFFECTIVE DATE OF LAWS

No law shall take effect earlier than 90 days after enactment except laws declared to be emergency laws and laws which under this Constitution are not subject to referendum. An emergency law shall contain a preamble setting forth the facts constituting the emergency and a statement that the law is necessary for the immediate preservation of the public peace, health, safety, or convenience. A separate recorded vote shall be taken on the preamble, and unless the preamble is adopted by two-thirds of the members of the House of Delegates present and voting, the law shall not be an emergency law.

Section 19:
AUDITOR

The House of Delegates shall appoint an auditor to serve for six years or until a successor has been appointed. By a two-thirds vote of all Delegates, the House of Delegates at any time may remove the auditor from office for cause. Each year the auditor shall conduct a thorough audit of all State government accounts and operations and shall submit these audit reports to the Governor and to the House of Delegates. The House of Delegates shall make available these reports and distribute summaries to the public.

Section 20:
IMPEACHMENT

Any executive official elected or appointed with legislative consent is subject to legislative impeachment for cause as may be provided by law.

Impeachment shall originate in the House of Delegates and must be approved by the affirmative votes of two-thirds of all Delegates.

The motion for impeachment shall state the reasons for the proceeding.

Trial on impeachment shall be conducted by the House of Delegates in accordance with procedures provided by law. A Justice of the Supreme Court shall preside at the trial.

Conviction requires the affirmative votes of two-thirds of all Delegates.

The judgment on conviction may not extend beyond removal from office and disqualification to hold and enjoy any state office of honor, trust, or profit but shall not prevent proceedings in the courts on the same or related charges.

Section 21:
CODE OF ETHICS

The House of Delegates shall enact conflict-of-interest legislation which shall apply to all elected and appointed State and local candidates for and officials in the executive, legislative, and judicial branches of government. The conflict-of-interest legislation shall include, but not be limited to, requirements for mandatory annual disclosure by public officials of economic interests and sources of income. A Delegate who has personal or private interests, as defined by law, in any proposed or pending bill, shall disclose this fact to the presiding officer and shall not vote on that bill.

ARTICLE III: THE EXECUTIVE BRANCH

Section 1:
EXECUTIVE POWER VESTED IN THE GOVERNOR
The executive power of the State shall be vested in the Governor, who shall be responsible for the faithful execution of the laws.

Section 2:
THE LIEUTENANT GOVERNOR
There shall be an elected Lieutenant Governor whose primary duties shall be prescribed by law.

The Lieutenant Governor shall serve as Governor during any period of gubernatorial disability as determined by the Supreme Court. The Lieutenant Governor shall exercise only those administrative duties necessary for the continued and efficient functioning of the State until the Governor either resumes office or is replaced in a special election.

Section 3:
THE ATTORNEY GENERAL
There shall be an Attorney General appointed by the Governor, with the advice and consent of the House of Delegates, for a term of four years. The Attorney General shall be the chief legal officer of the State and shall have responsibility for advising the Governor on legal questions, prosecuting offenders, and representing the State in all legal matters.

Section 4:
ELECTION OF GOVERNOR AND LIEUTENANT GOVERNOR
(A) *Election* The Governor and the Lieutenant Governor shall be elected by direct popular vote at the regular elections in Presidential election years. Their term shall be four years, beginning on the second day of January following their election.

(B) *Voting* Candidates for Governor and Lieutenant Governor shall run in pairs for whom a single vote shall be cast.. The pair of candidates having the highest number of votes shall be elected Governor and Lieutenant Governor. In case of a tie between two or more pairs of candidates, a runoff election shall be held.

(C) *Re-election* A person who has served two consecutive terms of office as Governor or as Lieutenant Governor shall be ineligible for re-election to the same office for the term immediately following.

(D) *Qualifications* The Governor and the Lieutenant Governor must be at least 30 years old upon assumption of office, citizens of the United States, and residents of the State for at least five years. They shall hold no other public office or regular employment.

Section 5:
POWERS OF THE GOVERNOR
(A) *Administration* The Governor shall control the administration of the Executive Branch. With the advice and consent of the House of Delegates, the Governor shall appoint the heads of all principal departments, and administrative offices and agencies whose appointment or election is not otherwise provided. The Governor may at any time require information, in writing or otherwise, from the officers of any administrative department, office, or agency concerning any subject relating to their offices. The Governor may remove any gubernatorially appointed official of the Executive Branch.

(B) *Commander-in-Chief* The Governor shall be Commander-in-Chief of the armed forces of the State, and may call out such forces to execute the laws.

(C) *Executive Clemency* The Governor shall have power to grant reprieves, commutations, and pardons, after conviction, for all offenses, subject to such procedures as may be prescribed by law. A parole system shall be provided by law.

(D) *Legislative Power* On extraordinary occasions, the Governor may convene the House of Delegates by a proclamation which shall state the purposes for which the session is convened. When so convened, the House of Delegates shall not legislate on any subject not specified in the proclamation, except to provide for the expenses of the session and other incidental matters. The Governor may convene the House of Delegates at some other place if the security of the seat of government is threatened.

The Governor shall present a message to the House of Delegates at the beginning of each session. At other times the Governor may inform the House of Delegates of the affairs of the State and may submit legislative recommendations.

(E) *Judicial Powers* The Governor shall appoint Justices and Judges as provided for in this Constitution.

Section 6:
BUDGET

At a time fixed by law, the Governor shall submit to the House of Delegates a budget for the next fiscal period.

Section 7:
PRINCIPAL DEPARTMENTS

(A) *Limitation* All offices and agencies of the Executive Branch shall be allocated by law among not more than 20 principal departments which shall be grouped as far as practicable according to major purposes. For this limitation the offices of Governor, Lieutenant Governor, Attorney General, and the governing bodies of institutions of higher education provided for in this Constitution shall not be counted.

(B) *Reorganization* The Governor may make changes in the organization of the Executive Branch or in the assignment of functions among its units in order to improve the administration of government. If such changes require amendments to existing law, they shall be set forth in Executive Orders, which shall be submitted to the House of Delegates at least 60 days before the end of the regular session, shall have the force of law, and shall become effective 60 days after submission, unless specifically modified or disapproved by a resolution concurred in by a majority of all the members of the House of Delegates.

Section 8:
BOARDS AND COMMISSIONS

(A) *Appointments* With the advice and consent of the House of Delegates, the Governor may appoint members of boards and commissions. The terms of office and procedures for removal of such members shall be as prescribed by this Constitution or by law.

(B) *Establishment* Boards and commissions may be established by law unless otherwise provided in this Constitution.

(C) *Membership* Not all members of any board or commission shall be members of the same political party.

Section 9:
ADVICE AND CONSENT TO APPOINTMENTS

An appointment subject to the advice and consent of the House of Delegates requires a majority vote of all members of the House of Delegates.

Section 10:
VACANCIES

(A) *State Officials* The Governor may make an interim appointment to fill a vacancy occasioned by the death, resignation, suspension, or removal of an appointed or elected officer, other than a legislative or judicial officer, until the officer is reinstated or the vacancy is filled in the manner prescribed by law or this Constitution. A person whose appointment to an office has been disapproved by the House of Delegates, shall not be eligible for an interim appointment to that office.

(B) *United States Senators* In the event of a vacancy in the office of United States Senator or Senator-elect, the Governor may appoint a person who possesses the necessary qualifications to hold the office until the next regularly-scheduled general election at which the vacancy can practicably be filled or the expiration of the term, whichever is sooner.

(C) *Implementation* The House of Delegates shall implement this Section by appropriate legislation.

Section 11:
COMPENSATION

The Governor and the Lieutenant Governor shall each receive the compensation provided by law in full payment for all services performed and expenses incurred during their terms of office. Such compensation shall not be diminished during the term of office.

Section 12:
EXECUTIVE RESIDENCE

A suitably furnished executive residence may be provided within the State for the use of the Governor. The Governor shall receive an allowance for its maintenance as provided by law.

Section 13:
SUCCESSION TO THE GOVERNORSHIP

(A) *Governor* If the Governor dies, resigns, is removed from office, or is determined by the Supreme Court to be permanently disabled, the Lieutenant Governor and other persons in a sequence prescribed by law shall become Governor for the remainder of the term of the Governor.

(B) *Governor-elect* If the Governor-elect dies, or is determined by the Supreme Court to be permanently disabled, the Lieutenant Governor-elect, and other persons in a sequence prescribed by law shall become Governor at the commencement of the term of the Governor-elect.

Section 14:
GREAT SEAL

There shall be a Great Seal of the State, which shall be kept and used officially by the Lieutenant Governor as prescribed by law.

ARTICLE IV: THE JUDICIAL BRANCH

Section 1:
JUDICIAL POWER

The judicial power of the State shall be vested in a unified judicial system, consisting of a Supreme Court, a Superior Court, and such inferior and appellate courts as may be established by law. All such courts shall be courts of record.

Section 2:
SUPREME COURT

(A) *Jurisdiction* The Supreme Court shall have jurisdiction of appeals from final decisions of the Superior Court or, alternatively, of appeals from final decisions of an intermediate appellate court, if one has been established. The Supreme Court shall also have jurisdiction of other matters, including

1) appeals from decisions of the Superior Court that are not yet final, as may be provided by law;
2) appeals from appellate decisions of the Superior Court, as may be provided by law;
3) appeals from determinations regarding disability of the Governor and of the Governor-elect;
4) appeals from gubernatorial and other executive branch orders and decisions, as may be provided by law; and
5) such other jurisdiction as may be provided by law.

(B) *Composition*: The Supreme Court shall consist of a Chief Justice and eight Associate Justices, who shall sit en banc and not by division or panel when determining the merits of appeals. The Chief Justice shall be designated by the Judicial Nomination Commission from among the Justices in regular active service. The Chief Justice shall serve as Chief Justice for a term of four years or until a successor is designated. The Chief Justice shall be eligible for redesignation as Chief Justice.

Section 3:
SUPERIOR COURT

(A) *Jurisdiction* The Superior Court shall have jurisdiction of civil actions or other matters, at law or in equity, brought in the State; criminal proceedings under any statute of the State; and such other jurisdiction, including appellate jurisdiction of cases decided by inferior courts, as may be provided by law.

(B) *Composition*: The Superior Court shall consist of a Chief Judge and 43 or more Associate Judges, as provided by law. The Chief Judge of the Superior Court shall be designated by the Judicial Nomination Commission from among the Judges in regular active service and shall serve as Chief Judge for a term of four years or until a successor is designated. The Chief Judge shall be eligible for redesignation as Chief Judge.

Section 4:
QUALIFICATIONS
(A) *Qualifications* A person nominated as a Judge or Justice must be

1) a citizen of the United States;
2) an active member of the Unified State Bar who has been engaged in the practice of law in the State for five years preceding nomination but who has not served within the two preceding years as a member of the Judicial Nomination Commission or the Commission on Judicial Disabilities and Tenure; and
3) an actual resident of the State for at least five years immediately prior to nomination.

(B) *Disqualifications* No Judge or Justice shall hold any other State or Federal paid office, position of profit, or employment. Upon becoming a candidate for any elective office, or upon ceasing to reside in the State, a Judge or Justice shall forfeit judicial office.

Section 5:
VACANCIES IN THE OFFICE OF JUDGE OR JUSTICE
The Governor shall fill any vacancy in any office of Judge or Justice by appointing one of two or more persons nominated by the Judicial Nomination Commission.

Section 6:
SALARY OF JUDGES AND JUSTICES
The salary and benefits of a Judge or Justice may not be reduced during the term in office of the Judge or Justice.

Section 7:
JUDICIAL NOMINATION COMMISSION
The Judicial Nomination Commission shall consist of nine members, each of whom shall serve for six years and until a successor has been appointed. Each member shall be a citizen of the United States, shall have been an actual resident of the State for at least five years prior to appointment, and shall maintain residency in the State.

Section 8:
JUDICIAL NOMINATION COMMISSION MEMBERSHIP
Members of the Commission shall be selected as follows:

a) Six members shall be appointed by the Governor, with the advice and consent of the House of Delegates. Two of them shall have been engaged in the practice of law in the State for at least five successive years preceding appointment. The other four shall not be lawyers.
b) Two members shall be appointed by the Board of Governors of the Unified State Bar and shall have been engaged in the practice of law in the State for at least five years preceding appointment.
c) One member shall be appointed by the House of Delegates and shall be a lawyer or a retired Judge or Justice of the State.

Members shall receive compensation as provided by law. The Commission shall choose annually from among its members its chairperson and such other officers as are deemed necessary.

Section 9:
TENURE OF JUDGES AND JUSTICES

Judges of the Superior Court and Justices of the Supreme Court shall be appointed for life, subject to removal by the voters and to removal, suspension, or involuntary retirement by the Commission on Judicial Disabilities and Tenure, as provided for in this Article.

Section 10:
RETENTION ELECTIONS

In a manner provided by law, each Judge or Justice shall be subject to retention or removal by the voters, on a nonpartisan ballot, at the first general election held more than three years after initial appointment. An additional retention election shall be held every ten years for a Supreme Court Justice, and every six years for a Superior Court Judge.

Not less than eight months prior to a retention election, a Judge or Justice may file with the Commission on Judicial Disabilities and Tenure a request for official evaluation. If a request is filed, this Commission shall prepare, not less than 90 days prior to the date of the election, a written evaluation of the performance and fitness for continued service of the Judge or Justice, including a rating on a scale established by law. In evaluating the Judge or Justice, the Commission shall collect relevant information from a representative sample of judges, lawyers, scholars, litigants, and jurors familiar with the work of the Judge or Justice. The Commission shall makes its report and rating available to the Judge or Justice, the press, and the public. If no request for evaluation is filed, the Commission shall report that fact.

Section 11:
COMMISSION ON JUDICIAL DISABILITIES AND TENURE

(A) *Qualifications* The Commission on Judicial Disabilities and Tenure shall consist of five members, each serving for a term of six years. A member must

> a) be a United States citizen who is not an officer or employee of the State government or of the legislative branches of the federal government; and
> b) have been an actual resident of the State for at least five years immediately prior to appointment.

(B) *Selection* Two members shall be lawyers appointed by the Board of Governors of the Unified State Bar. Two members, one of whom shall not be a lawyer, shall be appointed by the Governor with the advice and consent of the House of Delegates. One member shall be appointed by the House of Delegates, and shall not be a lawyer. Members who are lawyers shall have the qualifications prescribed for persons appointed as Judges of the Superior Court.

(C) *Procedure* The Commission shall choose annually, from among its members, a chairperson and such other officers as it may deem necessary. It may adopt any necessary rules of procedure. It may conduct studies regarding administration of the Judiciary. It may require the Governor to furnish such records, information, services, and other assistance and facilities as may be necessary to enable it to perform its functions properly, but information so furnished shall be treated by it as privileged and confidential. The Commission shall act only at meetings called by the chairperson or by a majority of the members after notice to all members.

Section 12:

REMOVAL, SUSPENSION, AND INVOLUNTARY RETIREMENT OF JUDGES AND JUSTICES

A Judge or Justice of a court shall be removed from office upon the filing in the Supreme Court by the Commission on Judicial Disabilities and Tenure of an order of removal certifying the entry, in any court within the United States, of a final judgment of conviction of a crime which is punishable as a felony under federal law or which would be a felony in the State. A Judge or Justice shall also be removed from office upon affirmance of an appeal from an order of removal filed in the Supreme Court by the Commission on Judicial Disabilities and Tenure (or upon expiration of the time within which such an appeal may be taken) after a determination by that Commission of willful misconduct in office, willful and persistent failure to perform judicial duties, or any other conduct which is prejudicial to the administration of justice.

A Judge or Justice shall be involuntarily retired from office when the Commission on Judicial Disabilities and Tenure determines that the Judge or Justice suffers from a mental or physical disability, including habitual intemperance, which is or is likely to become permanent and which prevents, or seriously interferes with, the proper performance of judicial duties, and that Commission files in the Supreme Court an order of involuntary retirement and the order is affirmed on appeal or the time within which an appeal may be taken has expired.

A Judge or Justice shall be suspended without salary upon proof of conviction, which has not become final, of a crime which is punishable as a felony under federal law or which would be a felony in the State, or upon the filing of an order of removal which has not become final. A Judge or Justice shall also be suspended without salary upon the filing by the Commission on Judicial Disabilities and Tenure of an order of suspension in the Supreme Court. Suspension for either of these reasons shall continue until termination of all appeals. If the conviction is reversed or the order of removal is set aside, the Judge or Justice shall be reinstated and shall recover the salary and all rights and privileges of office.

A Judge or Justice shall be suspended from judicial duties with any retirement salary to which the Judge or Justice is entitled, upon the filing by the Commission on Judicial Disabilities and Tenure of an order of involuntary retirement in the Supreme Court. Suspension shall continue until termination of all appeals. If the order of involuntary retirement is set aside, the Judge or Justice shall be reinstated and shall recover all judicial salary less any retirement salary received and shall be entitled to all the rights and privileges of office.

A Judge or Justice shall be suspended from all or part of the Judge or Justice's judicial duties, with salary, if the Commission on Judicial Disabilities and Tenure, upon concurrence of four members, orders a hearing for the removal or retirement of the Judge or Justice pursuant to this Section and determines that the suspension is in the interest of the administration of justice, and files an order of suspension in the Supreme Court. The suspension shall terminate as specified in the order (which may be modified, as appropriate, by the Commission) but in no event later than the termination of all appeals.

Section 13:

ADMINISTRATION

The Chief Justice of the Supreme Court shall be the administrative head of all courts of the State. The Chief Justice may assign Judges and

Justices for temporary service in any court. With the approval of the Supreme Court, the Chief Justice shall appoint an administrative director to serve at the pleasure of the Supreme Court and to supervise the administrative operations of the judicial system of the State.

Section 14:
FINANCING

Before each fiscal period, the Chief Justice of the Supreme Court shall submit to the Governor a budget for the judicial system, including detailed estimates of necessary appropriations and expenditures, full-term operating and capital improvements projections, and a qualitative and quantitative description of court activities. The Governor shall transmit the proposed budget to the House of Delegates without changing it, but may make recommendations with respect to it. The Governor shall not be required to propose revenues to fund the entire submission but must propose revenues to finance that portion of the proposed budget recommended for acceptance by the House of Delegates.

Section 15:
RULEMAKING

The Supreme Court shall make and promulgate rules governing the administration of all courts, including rules governing practice and procedure. These rules may be changed by law.

Section 16:
VACANCIES IN JUDICIAL COMMISSIONS

Persons appointed to fill vacancies arising for a reason other than expiration of a prior term on the Judicial Nomination Commission or the Commission on Judicial Disabilities and Tenure shall serve only for the remainder of the unexpired term. Any vacancy shall be filled in the manner in which the original appointment was made.

Section 17:
DEFINITION

The term "practice of law" as used in this Article means the active practice of law, service on the faculty of a law school, or employment as a lawyer by the state government or by the federal government.

ARTICLE V: SUFFRAGE

Section 1:
VOTING ELIGIBILITY

Every citizen of the United States is eligible to vote in any election and to circulate and sign nominating, initiative, referendum, recall, and other petitions authorized by law, provided that the person

(a) resides or is domiciled in the State or the National Capital Service Area as defined in this Constitution and does not claim voting residence or the right to vote in any other state, territory, or country;

(b) will be at least 18 years old on the date of the election;

(c) is not mentally incompetent as determined by a court of competent jurisdiction;

(d) is not incarcerated in a correctional institution as a result of conviction in the United States of a crime which would be a felony in the State; and

(e) has registered to vote at the time of the election or by the time the petitions are filed.

An eligible person may register at any time except that the House of Delegates may prescribe a period of delay of up to 30 days between the date on which a person registers and the date on which that person becomes eligible to vote.

Section 2:
ELIGIBILITY OF RESIDENTS TEMPORARILY OUT-OF-STATE

No person shall be deemed to have lost residence or domicile in the State solely because of temporary absence from the State while serving in the service of the United States, while serving as an officer or member of the crew of a merchant vessel, or while attending an educational institution outside the State.

Section 3:
ABSENTEE VOTING

The House of Delegates shall provide for absentee voting.

ARTICLE VI: EDUCATION

Section 1:
PROVISION FOR EDUCATION

(A) *Preamble* Recognizing the distinct and unique heritage of its diversified population, the State is committed in its educational goals to the preservation of cultural integrity and to the promotion of equality of opportunity for every individual to develop fully.

(B) *Equal Educational Opportunity* The State shall guarantee equality of educational opportunity in public educational institutions to all residents regardless of race, sex, religion, color, national origin, citizenship, condition of disability, and other individual characteristics. The State may be sued for default of this guarantee. The House of Delegates shall provide penalties for any individual who violates this guarantee.

Section 2:
PRIMARY AND SECONDARY EDUCATION

(A) *Primary and Secondary Schools* The State shall provide for the establishment, financing, and control of a uniform, high-quality, statewide system of free public primary and secondary schools, including specialized schools, for all residents. Education to standards established by the State Board of Education shall be compulsory for all residents between the ages of 6 and 18, except those who have already completed all secondary school requirements. All public schools shall be free of sectarian or religious instruction. Children of Diplomatic Corps members may attend public schools, as provided by the State Board of Education.

(B) *State Board of Education* The general control and supervision of the public school system shall be vested in a State Board of Education consisting of nine voting members. Eight members shall be elected from separate electoral districts varying by no more than three percent from the average population of all districts, and one shall be a student representative who shall be enrolled in a public senior high school and elected by the public senior high school student population. The duties, qualifications, compensation, term of office, and manner of election of the State Board of Education and the electoral district boundaries shall be as provided by law and by this Constitution.

(C) *State Superintendent of Public Instruction* The State Board of Education shall appoint the State Superintendent of Public Instruction and shall prescribe the length of term, compensation, powers, and duties of the Superintendent.

(D) *Budget* The State Board of Education shall prepare and submit to the Governor detailed estimates of expenditures and appropriations necessary for the maintenance and operation of all primary and secondary schools. For each fiscal period, the House of Delegates shall appropriate a total budget sum for the State Board of Education, but not in a line-item manner. This budget shall include full-term operating and capital improvements projections and qualitative and quantitative descriptions of school activities. The expenditure of this money shall be under the exclusive control of the State Board of Education.

(E) *Title to Property* Any property titled in the name of the District of Columbia or of the State and used by or acquired for the use of the Board of Education of the District of Columbia or of the State Board of Education shall henceforth be deemed to be titled in the name of the State Board of Education.

(F) *Control of Property* The State Board of Education shall control the leasing and renting of its buildings and lands. With the advice and consent of the House of Delegates the State Board of Education may sell and purchase buildings and lands.

(G) *Public Involvement in Schools* To the maximum extent possible, the State Board of Education shall promote parental, administrative, community, teacher, and student involvement in local schools.

(H) *Libraries* Public libraries and other such institutions may be used to enhance public school programs relating to the history and culture of the State.

(I) *Minimum Standards* All private elementary and secondary schools shall be required to meet the same minimum standards for instructors, instruction, and student achievement as may be imposed by the State Board of Education upon the public schools. The State Board of Education may establish equivalent alternatives to the above standards.

Section 3:
HIGHER EDUCATION

(A) *System of Higher Education* The State shall provide for the establishment, financing, and control of a public system of higher education which shall constitute a public trust and shall consist of the State University and such other institutions of higher learning as may be established by law. This system shall be supervised by the Board of Higher Education which shall be a body corporate. The Board of Education shall have general supervision of all state institutions of higher instruction, direction and control of all funds and appropriations, and other powers and duties as prescribed by law.

(B) *Board of Higher Education* The Board of Higher Education shall consist of

(1) eight voting members, of whom one shall reside in each State Board of Education electoral district, who shall be appointed by the Governor, with the advice and consent of the House of Delegates, and who shall serve for staggered terms of six years;

(2) three voting members representing alumnae, alumni, and students, of whom one shall be selected by the body of alumnae and alumni, one shall be a graduate student selected by the entire graduate student body, and one shall be an undergraduate student selected by the entire undergraduate student body; and

(3) three ex-officio members without the right to vote: the Governor, the President of the House of Delegates, and the Superintendent of Public Instruction.

(C) *Compensation and Tenure* Members of the Board of Higher Education

(1) shall receive no salary, but may be reimbursed for expenses incurred in the discharge of their duties; and

(2) shall not be removed except for cause and by due process of law.

(D) *Budget* The State Board of Higher Education shall prepare and submit to the Governor detailed estimates of expenditures and appropriations necessary for the maintenance and operation of its entire system. The budget for the State Board of Higher Education shall include all State colleges and universities and the institutions subject to its control. For each fiscal period, the House of Delegates shall appropriate a total budget sum for the State Board of Higher Education but not in a line-item manner. This budget shall include full-term operating and capital improvements projections and qualitative and quantitative descriptions of school activities. The expenditure of this money shall be under the exclusive control of the State Board of Higher Education.

(E) *Title to Property* Any property titled in the District of Columbia or in the State and used by or acquired for the use of the Trustees of the University of the District of Columbia, or any of its predecessor institutions, or of the State Board of Higher Education shall henceforth be deemed to be titled in the name of the State Board of Higher Education, which shall control the leasing and renting of these properties.

However, no such buildings or lands shall be sold or purchased, except with the consent of the House of Delegates.

Section 4:
RESTRICTIONS ON FINANCING OF NON-PUBLIC EDUCATION

(A) *Prohibition of Financial Support to Schools* The State shall provide no financial support, either directly or indirectly, unless earmarked for a program of public service, to any sectarian, denominational, or religious school, or to any pre-elementary, elementary, secondary, or post-secondary school which is not owned and exclusively controlled by the State.

(B) *Prohibition of Support for Students or Employees* Except as otherwise provided in this Section, the State shall provide no payment; credit; tax benefit, exemption, or deduction; tuition voucher; or subsidy, grant, or loan of public monies or property, in any way, either directly or indirectly,

(1) to support the attendance of any student at any pre-elementary, elementary, or secondary school or other institution at those levels, which is not owned and exclusively operated by the State; or

(2) to pay the salary of any employee at any non-public school or institution where instruction is offered in whole or in part to non-public school students at any level.

(C) *Students with Disabilities* The State may pay the private school tuition of a student with a disability which renders the student unable to receive an education in the public schools.

(D) *Federal Funding* Nothing in this Section shall restrict the acceptance of funds from the government of the United States, nor the expenditure of those funds in accordance with the terms under which they are accepted.

ARTICLE VII: FINANCE AND TAXATION

Section 1:
FISCAL PERIOD
The fiscal, accounting, and budget periods of the State shall be 24 months which shall commence and terminate as provided by law.

Section 2:
THE BUDGET
At a time established by law, the Governor shall submit to the House of Delegates a balanced operating budget estimate for the next fiscal period. It shall state all anticipated expenditures and income for the State and for all its departments, agencies, and subdivisions. At that time, the Governor shall also submit a general appropriation bill or bills authorizing all anticipated expenditures and a bill or bills to raise all necessary revenues.

From time to time, the Governor may prepare and submit to the House of Delegates such supplemental or deficiency budget recommendations as in the judgment of the Governor are necessary to serve the public interest.

The proposed budget shall include a budget message, which shall contain multi-year plans for all departments, agencies, and sub divisions of the State, and for capital improvements. The period of the multi-year plans and their specific contents shall be defined by law.

The budget of the Governor shall be available and summaries shall be distributed to the public.

The House of Delegates shall establish an independent agency to project revenue estimates for the next fiscal period. These projections shall be published and made available to the public.

Section 3:
ADOPTION OF THE BUDGET
After receipt of the proposed budget from the Governor and within a time period established by law, the House of Delegates shall adopt and transmit to the Governor a balanced operating budget for the State.

Section 4:
EXPENDITURES

No money shall be withdrawn from the Treasury except in accordance with appropriations made by law, nor shall any obligations for the payment of money be incurred except as authorized by law. The appropriation for each department, agency, or subdivision of the State shall specify distinctly the sum appropriated and the general or specific purpose for which it is made.

Section 5:
BORROWING

The State may incur indebtedness only by authorization of the House of Delegates and only by issuing general obligation bonds for capital projects, revenue notes in anticipation of revenues, and negotiable notes to meet appropriations.

The House of Delegates shall set an overall debt limit for indebtedness through general obligation bonds.

All indebtedness, except general obligation bonds for capital projects, must be retired within the same fiscal period or within the succeeding fiscal period.

Section 6:
DEBT SERVICE LIMITATIONS

Long-term debt shall not be incurred to the extent that it requires debt service of more than 14 percent of the revenues during any biennial fiscal period.

Section 7:
TAXATION

(A) *Taxing Power* The State House of Delegates shall have the power to tax. This power shall never be surrendered, suspended, or contracted away, except as provided in this Constitution.

(B) *Tax Exemptions—Retail Sales* The State House of Delegates shall not have the power to tax purchases of retail groceries and prescription drugs and other medicines. These terms shall be defined by the House of Delegates.

(C) *Tax Exemptions—Real Estate* Tax exemptions on real property not owned and controlled by the State or its political subdivisions and not used exclusively for a public purpose may not be granted by the House of Delegates except with respect to real property used exclusively for non-profit, religious, educational, or charitable purposes or as required by the United States Constitution. Private leaseholds, contracts, or interests in land or property owned or held by the State, or its political subdivisions, shall be taxable to the extent of the interests.

(D) *Tax Bills* No tax shall be levied, except as provided by law, and every law imposing a tax shall be addressed in a separate bill. No matter not immediately relating to and necessary for raising revenue shall be blended with or annexed to a bill for imposing taxes.

Section 8:
EARMARKING

Except as required by participation in federal programs or interstate compacts or as needed to secure authorized debt, the State shall not authorize the earmarking of funds for longer than two fiscal periods.

Section 9:
LIMITATIONS ON APPROPRIATIONS
No appropriation shall ever be made from any public fund in aid of any religious creed, church, or sectarian purpose, or to help, support, or sustain any private school, academy, seminary, college, university, or other institution of learning controlled by any religious creed, church, or sectarian denomination, unless earmarked for a program of public service. No grant or donation of personal property or real estate shall ever be made by the State or any of its political subdivisions for any religious creed, church, or sectarian purpose.

ARTICLE VIII: BANKING AND CORPORATIONS

Section 1:
STATE BANKING COMMISSION
The House of Delegates shall establish a State Banking Commission to regulate State chartered financial institutions and to perform such other functions as may be provided by law.

Section 2:
STATE DEPOSITORS INSURANCE FUND
The House of Delegates shall establish a State Depositors Insurance Fund System.

Section 3:
STATE ECONOMIC DEVELOPMENT BANK
The House of Delegates shall establish a State Economic Development Bank. Its primary responsibility shall be to provide loans to those individuals, corporations, partnerships, limited partnerships, cooperatives, or other businesses and establishments that are unable to obtain loans from any private bank, savings and loan association, or credit union within the State.

Section 4:
CORPORATIONS
The House of Delegates shall provide by law for the organization, regulation, and qualification of all corporations, credit unions, unincorporated enterprises, mutual and cooperative companies and associations, and foreign corporations doing business in the State.

ARTICLE IX: LAND AND THE ENVIRONMENT

Section 1:
LAND
(A) *Comprehensive Plan*

(1) *Plan* Every ten years within a time period fixed by law, the Governor shall submit to the House of Delegates and the public a ten-year comprehensive land use plan. The objective of the plan shall be

the use and development of land in a manner consistent with the public welfare. The neighborhoods of the State shall serve as the foci for the development of the plan. A summary of the plan shall be distributed to the public.

(2) *Citizen Advisory Planning Commission* In order to ensure citizen participation in the development of the land use plan, the Governor shall establish a Citizen Advisory Planning Commission. The Governor shall determine the size of the Commission and appoint its members including at least one resident from each legislative district. The House of Delegates shall determine the terms of office of members of the Commission and establish their rate of compensation, if any.

(3) *Adoption* Within a time period fixed by law, after receiving the proposed comprehensive plan and conducting public hearings on it, the House of Delegates shall consider it, make any necessary changes, and upon adoption transmit the approved plan to the Governor. The plan shall guide the actions of all State agencies and commissions.

(B) *Eminent Domain* Private property shall not be taken or damaged for public purposes without just compensation. Private property shall not be taken in order to transfer it to another private use for profit unless the taking serves a compelling public purpose that clearly cannot be achieved by any alternative means.

(C) *Public Land Acquisition* The State may acquire interests in real property to control future growth, development, and land use.

(D) *Zoning* The House of Delegates shall establish a Zoning Commission to protect the public health and welfare, protect property, and secure the public safety.

Section 2:
ENVIRONMENT

(A) *Public Policy* It is the responsibility of the State to protect, restore, and enhance the quality of the human environment for this and future generations.

(B) *Preservation* The State shall provide for the preservation and development of open green space and of sites, objects, and properties of historical or cultural value.

(C) *Rights of Individuals* Each person has the right to a clean and healthful environment and has a corresponding duty to refrain from environmental impairment. Each person may enforce these rights and duties against any party, public or private, through appropriate legal proceedings, subject to reasonable limitations and regulation as provided by law.

(D) *Legislative Responsibility* The House of Delegates shall establish an agency and enact other appropriate legislation to carry out the policies of this Section.

ARTICLE X: PUBLIC SERVICES

Section 1:
TRANSPORTATION
Public Transportation performs a function essential to the general welfare of the State. It is a policy of the State to provide convenient access to effective means of public transportation at reasonable rates for all of its geographical communities.

Section 2:
UTILITIES
The general welfare of the State requires effective regulation of public utilities through consumer participation and the protection of consumers from excessive rates. To advance these goals,

a) it is hereby declared that utility service shall be provided at the lowest reasonable rates sufficient to assure adequate, efficient, and reasonable services; and that unreasonably high rates based on excessive capital investment shall not be permitted;

b) the House of Delegates shall establish one or more commissions to regulate public utilities and provide for the conservation of energy resources within the State, as provided for by law; and

c) there shall be an Office of People's Counsel to represent consumers before the regulatory commission or commissions.

Section 3:
PUBLICLY OWNED UTILITIES
Utilities are works of public necessity and importance the services of which the State may itself provide. The State may acquire, own, or operate public utilities and provide their services to consumers.

ARTICLE XI: HEALTH, HOUSING, AND SOCIAL SERVICES

Section 1:
HEALTH
(A) *General Provisions* The State shall provide for the protection and promotion of public health. The State shall have the power to assist residents unable to maintain standards of living compatible with decency and good health care.

(B) *Disabled Persons* As provided by law, the State shall provide treatment, care, and training, including education to their fullest potential, for persons suffering from mental illness, physical disability, or retardation.

The State shall have complete administrative control of state hospitals and other state institutions and centers established to assist these persons and shall administer other programs as provided by law.

As provided by law, the State shall regulate private institutions established to assist these persons.

There shall be a Chief Administrator of Mental Health who shall be responsible for regular, systematic visitation and inspection of all public and private institutions used for the care and treatment of mentally disabled persons.

(C) *Public Health Facilities* The State shall have the power to provide for the establishment and maintenance of a network of comprehensive health facilities which provide for the prevention, treatment and care of illnesses and health-related problems.

(D) *State Board of Health* There shall be a State Board of Health whose responsibilities shall include enforcing, overseeing, and maintaining decent health and nutritional care, and maintaining the vital statistics necessary to improve the health of the people.

The House of Delegates shall determine the size and composition of the Board.

Section 2:
HOUSING

The State shall have the power to provide low and moderate income families with assistance in obtaining decent, sanitary, and safe housing and to develop or rehabilitate substandard areas. The exercise of this power is deemed for public use and purpose.

Section 3:
SOCIAL SERVICES

(A) *Unemployment and Workers Compensation* The State shall have the power to provide an adequate system of unemployment compensation and workers compensation benefits for employees, including provisions for compensating employees absent from work because of pregnancy, childbirth, or the need to care for newborn or young children.

(B) *Public Sector Jobs and Welfare* The State shall have the power to create jobs and to provide transfer payments for the purpose of meeting basic human needs.

(C) *Day Care Centers* The State shall provide and maintain public day care centers as provided by law and shall establish standards for publicly and privately operated day care centers.

(D) *Youth Offenders and Criminals* The State shall provide for the maintenance and support of institutions for the detention of youth offenders and persons charged with or convicted of crimes. Rehabilitation programs shall be developed and maintained for the transition of persons from these institutions to the community, as provided by law.

(E) *The Elderly* The State shall have the power to establish and promote programs to assure the economic and social well-being of the elderly, including provision for their health, security, and access to public buildings. The State shall regulate private and public nursing homes for the elderly and the disabled, as provided by law.

(F) *Cultural Resources* The State shall have the power to preserve and enhance the cultural, creative, and traditional arts of its people and shall maintain an appropriate facility for this purpose. The State shall preserve historical sites and landmarks.

ARTICLE XII: LABOR

Section 1:
COLLECTIVE BARGAINING

Persons in private and public employment shall have the right to organize and bargain collectively, through representatives of their own choosing. The right to strike is fundamental and is an inherent part of the right to organize and bargain collectively. The right of public employees to strike shall not be abridged unless the abridgement serves a compelling governmental interest and is narrowly drawn so as to serve that interest, and it is clear that no alternative form of regulation is possible.

Section 2:
MINIMUM WAGES, EQUAL PAY, HEALTH AND SAFETY

The House of Delegates shall provide for minimum wages, equal pay for equal work and equal pay for comparable work, and a safe and healthy workplace. Minimum wages established shall apply to all employees covered thereby. The House of Delegates may enact other laws to enhance and promote the dignity and general welfare of labor, but no laws shall be enacted which impair the ability of collective bargaining organizations to carry out their lawful functions.

Section 3:
ADMINISTRATION OF LABOR RELATIONS

The House of Delegates shall establish an agency or agencies within one of the principal executive departments to administer and enforce all laws, regulations, and programs concerned with collective bargaining and the general welfare of labor.

ARTICLE XIII: LOCAL GOVERNMENT UNITS

Section 1:
AUTHORITY

The House of Delegates shall permit areas of the State to elect local officers and to exercise such local authority, other than the authority to tax, zone land, or enact legislation, as it may by law provide. The House of Delegates shall have the ultimate authority for establishing standards and for determining whether the proposed local government unit meets those standards.

Section 2:
CHARTERS

The House of Delegates shall establish procedures to permit an area to petition for the election of a Charter Commission. A charter shall include provisions for a charter amendment process and for a process by which neighboring areas may later be considered for inclusion in the local government unit. The House of Delegates shall provide that the charter drafted by the elected Commission be submitted to the voters of the proposed unit for approval before submission to the House of Delegates.

Section 3:

SPECIAL DISTRICTS

The House of Delegates shall have the power to create special districts for public purposes.

Section 4:

ADVISORY NEIGHBORHOOD COMMISSIONS

Advisory Neighborhood Commissions shall exercise the authority which they had at the time the State entered the Union, and any additional authority subsequently provided by law. The House of Delegates may modify this structure but shall always provide for elected advisory neighborhood mechanisms in unchartered areas of the State.

Section 5:

IMPLEMENTATION

A law implementing this Article shall be passed by the House of Delegates within two years of the convening of the first House of Delegates and shall be subject to the approval of the voters of the State.

ARTICLE XIV: APPORTIONMENT

Section 1:

REAPPORTIONMENT OF LEGISLATIVE DISTRICTS

The State shall be apportioned into 40 legislative election districts of substantially equal population. As soon as practicable after the results of each decennial census are reported, but in any event not later than the calendar year following the taking of the census, these districts shall be revised to maintain districts of substantially equal population. The Reapportionment Commission established by this Article shall conduct the reapportionment, which shall be subject to judicial review upon the application of any qualified registered voter of the State.

Section 2:

REAPPORTIONMENT COMMISSION

(A) *Membership* The reapportionment of legislative districts shall be carried out by a Reapportionment Commission consisting of five members appointed by the Governor in January of the year before the year in which the decennial census is conducted. No member may hold any other public office. The State Committee of each of the three political parties having the highest number of votes in the most recent gubernatorial election shall submit to the Governor a list of three names of registered voters who are members of that party for the consideration of the Governor. The President of the House of Delegates shall also submit to the Governor the names of three registered voters, regardless of party affiliation. The Governor shall appoint Commission members from the combined list of 12 names. No more than two of the five appointees shall be members of the same political party. Any independent candidate receiving one of the three highest totals in the most recent gubernatorial election shall be treated as a state committee for purposes of this Section.

(B) *Additional Duties* In addition to establishing legislative districts, the Commission shall establish any districts required for the members of the United States House of Representatives representing this State, establish appropriate single-member districts for any other elective office, and participate with the United States in joint preparations for the decennial census.

(C) *Term* The Reapportionment Commission shall continue in office until the completion of the reapportionment relevant to all offices as a result of the decennial census, including the final adjudication of all appeals.

Section 3:
APPORTIONMENT STANDARDS

Each district shall have a population which varies by no more than three percent from the average population of all districts. Each district shall respect neighborhood integrity, be contiguous, and be as compact as possible. In reapportioning the State, the Commission may take into account natural features and open spaces, such as rivers and parks, but shall not take into account the addresses of incumbent elected officials, the political affiliations of registered voters, the results of previous elections, or demographic information other than the actual number of persons found by the most recent census to reside in each census tract or other geographical area. No reapportionment shall be effected for the purpose of favoring or harming any political party, incumbent public official, or other person or group.

ARTICLE XV: INITIATIVE, REFERENDUM, AND RECALL

Section 1:
RIGHT TO INITIATIVE, REFERENDUM AND RECALL

Although the legislative power of the State is vested in the House of Delegates, the people reserve to themselves the power to propose, adopt, and repeal laws and constitutional provisions. The people also reserve to themselves the power to remove from office elected State and local government officials.

Section 2:
INITIATIVE PROCEDURES

(A) *Definition, Presentation, and Limitations* Initiative is the power of the voters to propose laws and amendments to the Constitution and to adopt or reject them.

An initiative may be proposed by presenting to the Lieutenant Governor the text of the proposed law or constitutional amendment.

The proposed law or amendment to the Constitution shall embrace a single subject and related matters.

(B) *Obligation and Responsibilities* Upon receipt of an initiative, the Lieutenant Governor shall submit it immediately to the Attorney General.

Within 20 calendar days, the Attorney General shall provide the proponents of the initiative an advisory opinion on its clarity and whether or not it meets the requirements of this Article for placement on the ballot.

The proponents shall then resubmit the proposal, revised or unchanged, to the Lieutenant Governor.

Within 20 calendar days, the Lieutenant Governor shall prepare an accurate title and summary statement for use on the petition form.

(C) *Certification and Circulation* Upon the receipt of petitions signed by qualified voters equal in number to five percent, in the case of a law, and ten percent, in the case of a constitutional amendment, of the votes cast for all candidates for Governor in the most recent gubernatorial election, provided that the respective percentages for each type of initiative must have been met in at least two-thirds of the legislative districts of the State, the Lieutenant Governor shall submit the measure at the next election held at least 120 days after it qualifies.

The circulation period allowed for an initiative petition shall be 180 days after the proponents receive a title and summary from the Lieutenant Governor.

(D) *Effective Date* An initiative approved by a majority of the voters shall take effect 30 days after certification by the Lieutenant Governor.

(E) *Limitations* No proposal shall be the subject of any initiative if it relates to the appointment, qualifications, tenure, removal, or compensation of Justices or Judges; to the powers, jurisdiction, creation, or abolition of courts or any rules thereof; to the appropriation of any money other than new revenues created and provided thereby; or to the diminishment of the rights and protections of any persons as enumerated in this Constitution or provided by law.

(F) *Conflicts* If provisions of two or more initiatives approved at the same election conflict, those of the measure receiving the highest affirmative vote shall prevail.

(G) *Amendment and Repeal* The House of Delegates may amend or repeal an initiative law during a two-year period following its enactment only by a three-fourths majority vote of the Delegates present and voting. Repeal of an initiative by another law shall become effective only when approved by the voters unless the law adopted by initiative permits repeal without their approval.

Section 3:
REFERENDUM PROCEDURES

(A) *Definition* The referendum is the power of the voters to approve or reject newly enacted laws or parts of laws.

(B) *Requirements* A referendum may be proposed by a voter to the Lieutenant Governor, within 90 days after the enactment of the law which is the subject of the referendum, provided that the petition contains the required number of signatures of voters.

A petition must be signed by registered voters in number not less than five percent of the statewide votes cast for all candidates for Governor at the most recent gubernatorial election, provided that the signature percentage requirement shall have been met in at least two-thirds of the legislative districts of the State.

The petition shall ask that a law or a part of a law be submitted to the voters.

(C) *Implementation*

(1) Upon verification of the petition signatures, the Lieutenant Governor shall submit the referendum to the voters for approval or disapproval.

(2) The referendum election shall be held 60 days after verification of requirements.

(3) The Governor may call a special statewide election.

(D) *Limitations* A referendum petition may not be filed with respect to a law or part of a law that provides human rights or protections or relates to appointment, qualifications, tenure, removal, or compensation of judges; the powers, creation, or abolition of courts; the appropriation of money for the current or ordinary expenses of the State or for any of its departments, boards, commissions, or institutions. Any capital project may be the subject of a referendum, except for capital projects for public education.

(E) *Effective Date* The result of a referendum election takes effect immediately after the official declaration of the vote by the Lieutenant Governor.

(F) *Exception* Except in the case of an emergency law, the timely filing of a referendum petition and verification by the Lieutenant Governor that it complies with the requirements of this Article shall suspend the operation of the law which is the subject of the referendum unless the Lieutenant Governor finds that it does not comply with all the requirements of this Article.

A majority affirmative vote shall put the law into effect; a negative vote shall render it null and void. An emergency law remains in effect unless there is a majority vote against the law, in which case it shall become null and void.

Section 4:
PUBLICITY

The House of Delegates shall provide methods of publicizing all initiative or referendum measures referred to the voters with statements for and against the measures so referred. The Lieutenant Governor shall undertake distribution of the measures to ensure that voters shall have an opportunity to study the measures prior to the election.

Section 5:
RECALL PROCEDURES

(A) *Definition* Recall is a process by which voters may remove an elected State or local government official.

(B) *The Petition Process* The Lieutenant Governor shall supervise the petition process including certification of the required number of signatures. A maximum of 90 days is allotted for the collection of signatures.

(C) *The Petition Statement* The recall petition shall contain a concise statement alleging the reasons for recall. The wording of the statement shall be determined by the petitioners in cooperation with the Attorney General.

(D) *Petition Signature Requirements* A recall petition shall contain at least 25 percent of the total number of all votes cast in the most recent election for the position in question. In the case of a statewide office, this 25 percent requirement must be met in at least two-thirds of the legislative districts.

(E) *Initiation of Recall* Recall cannot be initiated within the first six months or the last 12 months of the term of an elected official nor upon more than one occasion during that term.

(F) *Time of Recall Election* A recall election shall be held no less than 60 days nor more than 120 days after certification of the signed petitions.

(G) *Votes Required for Recall* A simple majority vote shall remove the official from office.

(H) *Reimbursement* Within limits set by the House of Delegates, recall expenses incurred by the official, if retained, shall be paid by the State.

(I) *Filling a Recall Vacancy* When an official is recalled, the vacancy shall be filled by a special election held no more than 90 days after the recall certification or at the next regularly scheduled election if it occurs within 150 days.

(J) *Local Government Units* Any local government unit shall have the power to provide in its charter for recall of its elected officials.

Section 6:
ENABLING LEGISLATION
This Article is self-executing, but enabling legislation may be enacted.

ARTICLE XVI: INTERGOVERNMENTAL RELATIONS

Section 1:
BOUNDARIES OF THE STATE
(A) The boundaries of the State shall be subject to the approval of the Congress of the United States and the voters of the State. The State shall include, however, at least all of the territory of the District of Columbia which is not included within the boundaries of the National Capital Service Area as defined in this Section.

THE OUTER LIMITS OF THE BOUNDARIES OF THE NATIONAL CAPITAL SERVICE AREA ARE:

BEGINNING AT THE NORTHWEST POINT on the present Virginia-District of Columbia boundary, running due east to the eastern shore of the Potomac River;

THENCE generally south along the shore at the mean high water mark to the northwest corner of the Kennedy Center;

THENCE east along the north side of the Kennedy Center to a point where it reaches the E Street Expressway;

THENCE east on the expressway to E Street Northwest and thence east on E Street Northwest to Eighteenth Street Northwest;

THENCE south on Eighteenth Street Northwest to Constitution Avenue Northwest;

THENCE east on Constitution Avenue to Seventeenth Street Northwest;

THENCE north on Seventeenth Street Northwest to Pennsylvania Avenue Northwest;

THENCE east on Pennsylvania Avenue to Jackson Place Northwest;

THENCE north on Jackson Place to H Street Northwest;

THENCE east on H Street Northwest to Madison Place Northwest;

THENCE south on Madison Place Northwest to Pennsylvania Avenue Northwest;

THENCE east on Pennsylvania Avenue Northwest to Fifteenth Street Northwest;

THENCE south on Fifteenth Street Northwest to Pennsylvania Avenue Northwest;

THENCE southeast on Pennsylvania Avenue Northwest to John Marshall Place Northwest;

THENCE north on John Marshall Place Northwest to C Street Northwest;

THENCE east on C Street Northwest to Third Street Northwest;

THENCE north on Third Street Northwest to D Street Northwest;

THENCE east on D Street Northwest to Second Street Northwest;

THENCE south on Second Street Northwest to the intersection of Constitution Avenue Northwest and Louisiana Avenue Northwest;

THENCE northeast on Louisiana Avenue Northwest to North Capitol Street;

THENCE north on North Capitol Street to Massachusetts Avenue Northwest;

THENCE southeast on Massachusetts Avenue Northeast so as to encompass Union Square;

THENCE following Union Square to F Street Northeast;

thence east on F Street Northeast to Second Street Northeast;

THENCE south on Second Street Northeast to D Street Northeast;

THENCE west on D Street Northeast to First Street Northeast;

THENCE south on First Street Northeast to Maryland Avenue Northeast;

THENCE generally north and east on Maryland Avenue to Second Street Northeast;

THENCE south on Second Street Northeast to C Street Southeast;

THENCE west on C Street Southeast to New Jersey Avenue Southeast;

THENCE south on New Jersey Avenue Southeast to D Street Southeast;

THENCE west on D Street Southeast to Canal Street Parkway;

THENCE southeast on Canal Street Parkway to E Street Southeast;

THENCE west on E Street Southeast to the intersection of Canal Street Southwest and South Capitol Street;

THENCE northwest on Canal Street Southwest to Second Street Southwest;

THENCE south on Second Street Southwest to Virginia Avenue Southwest;

THENCE generally west on Virginia Avenue to Third Street Southwest;

THENCE north on Third Street Southwest to C Street Southwest;

THENCE west on C Street Southwest to Sixth Street Southwest;

THENCE north on Sixth Street Southwest to Independence Avenue;

THENCE west on Independence Avenue to Twelfth Street Southwest;

THENCE south on Twelfth Street Southwest to D Street Southwest;

THENCE west on D Street Southwest to Fourteenth Street Southwest;

THENCE south on Fourteenth Street Southwest to the middle of the Washington Channel;

THENCE generally south and east along the midchannel of the Washington Channel to a point due west of the northern boundary line of Fort Lesley McNair;

THENCE due east to the side of the Washington Channel;

THENCE following generally south and east along the side of the

Washington Channel at the mean high water mark, to the point of confluence with the Anacostia River, and along the northern shore at the mean high water mark to the northernmost point of the Eleventh Street Bridge;

THENCE generally south and east along the northern side of the Eleventh Street Bridge to the eastern shore of the Anacostia River;

THENCE generally south and west along such shore at the mean high water mark to the point of confluence of the Anacostia and Potomac Rivers;

THENCE generally south along the eastern shore at the mean high water mark of the Potomac River to the point where it meets the present southeastern boundary line of the District of Columbia;

THENCE south and west along such southeastern boundary line to the point where it meets the present Virginia-District of Columbia boundary; and

THENCE generally north and west up the Potomac River along the Virginia-District of Columbia boundary TO THE POINT OF BEGINNING.

(B) Where the National Capital Service Area is bounded by a street, the street and its sidewalks shall be included within that Area.

(C) The District Building shall, however, be part of the State.

Section 2:
COOPERATION WITH OTHER GOVERNMENTS

With the consent of the House of Delegates, the Governor may enter into agreements or compacts for any public purpose with other governmental entities including other states and the United States. At the request of the United States and with the consent of the House of Delegates, the Governor shall negotiate contracts with the United States to provide police, fire, sanitation, and other services to foreign embassies and chanceries and to federal buildings and other federal property located in the State or in the National Capital Service Area.

Section 3:
ACCEPTANCE OF FEDERAL FUNDS

No taxes shall be imposed by the State upon any property now owned or hereafter acquired by the United States, unless the property becomes taxable because the United States disposes of it or consents to taxation. The State may accept from the United States grants and other payments, including payments in lieu of tax revenues that would be collected were the federal property in the State subject to taxation.

ARTICLE XVII: AMENDMENT AND REVISION

Section 1:
INTRODUCTION

Amendments to this Constitution may be proposed by the House of Delegates, an initiative, or a constitutional convention.

Section 2:
THE HOUSE OF DELEGATES

The House of Delegates may propose an amendment by the

affirmative votes of two-thirds of all members. The Lieutenant Governor shall distribute the proposed amendment no less than 90 days before the next appropriate election.

The Lieutenant Governor shall then place the proposed amendment on the ballot.

The amendment shall take effect immediately after certification that it received a majority vote, unless otherwise provided in the amendment.

Section 3:
THE INITIATIVE

The voters of the State may propose an amendment by initiative as prescribed by this Constitution.

Section 4:
THE CONSTITUTIONAL CONVENTION

(A) *Call* The voters of the State may, by the initiative, call for a constitutional convention at any time. The convention may propose amendments or revisions to the Constitution. The Lieutenant Governor shall distribute the proposed amendment or amendments no less than 90 days before the next appropriate election. The Lieutenant Governor shall then place the amendment or amendments on the ballot. The proposed amendment or amendments shall take effect immediately after certification of a majority vote.

(B) *Decennial Review* If within ten years following the date this Constitution enters into force the people do not file an initiative to call a constitutional convention, the Lieutenant Governor shall place on the ballot at the next general election a referendum consisting of the question: "Shall there be a constitutional convention?" Thereafter, the same requirement shall hold for every succeeding ten-year period.

(C) *Preparatory Commission* After an affirmative vote to hold a constitutional convention, the Governor shall provide for a preparatory commission to assemble information on constitutional issues and to organize administrative support for the convention.

(D) *Delegates* Each legislative district shall elect an equal number of delegates to the constitutional convention.

Section 5:
CONFLICTING AMENDMENTS

If provisions of two or more amendments approved at the same election conflict, those of the amendment receiving the highest affirmative vote shall prevail.

Section 6:
DISAPPROVAL OF AMENDMENTS

If an amendment is disapproved neither that amendment nor any substantially similar amendment shall be submitted to the voters for a period of two years.

Section 7:
ENABLING LEGISLATION

This article shall be self-executing, but enabling legislation may be enacted.

ARTICLE XVIII: TRANSITION

Section 1:
EFFECTIVE DATES

The provisions of Sections 1 through 3 of this Article, providing for the establishment of the first government of the State, shall enter into force on a date specified in the federal legislation admitting the State to the Union. The State shall come into being and the remainder of this Constitution shall enter into force at 10:00 A.M., Eastern Standard Time, on the second day of the tenth full month after that date.

Section 2:
INITIAL APPORTIONMENT AND ELECTIONS

(A) *Commission* Immediately following the enactment of legislation admitting this state to the Union, the Mayor of the District of Columbia shall initiate appointment of a Commission and the Council of the District of Columbia shall provide election procedures. The Mayor of the District of Columbia shall issue a Proclamation and shall promptly appoint, with the advice and consent of the members of the Council, nine members of a Commission of Initial Apportionment, including at least one member from each of the eight wards of the District. The members and staff of the Commission shall be compensated as provided by law. The Commission shall, within thirty days after its last member is appointed, apportion the State into 40 legislative districts in a manner consistent with Section 3 of Article XIV of this Constitution.

(B) *First Elections* By law, the Council of the District of Columbia shall provide for the election of the House of Delegates, Governor, and Lieutenant Governor of the State. Regular or special primary and general elections shall be held for these offices within 120 days after the initial apportionment plan enters into force, except that these elections shall not take place during July or August or before September 15th. The 120-day limitation may be extended, if necessary, in order to avoid having to hold these elections during those months.

Section 3:
INITIAL TERMS OF OFFICE OF DELEGATES, THE GOVERNOR, AND LIEUTENANT GOVERNOR

(A) *Staggered Terms for Delegates* At a public drawing within five days after the initial apportionment plan has entered into force, the Chair of the Commission on Apportionment shall select, at random, half of the legislative districts to be Group A districts. The initial terms of office of members of the House of Delegates elected from Group A districts shall begin 20 days after the date of certification of their elections and shall expire on the second Monday in January of the second odd-numbered year following their election. The initial terms of office of members of the House of Delegates elected from other districts shall begin 20 days after the date of certification of their election and shall expire on the second Monday in January of the first odd-numbered year following their election; except that if this provision would result in a term shorter than one year, their terms shall expire on the second Monday in January of the third odd-numbered year following their election.

(B) *Governor and Lieutenant Governor* The terms of office of the first Governor and the first Lieutenant Governor shall begin 20 days after certification of their elections and shall expire on the second day of January following the date of the next Presidential election. If this provision would result in terms shorter than one year, their terms shall expire on the second day of January of the year after the second Presidential election year following their election.

(C) *Holdover Term for Mayor* If the first election for Governor of the State has not been held by the date that the State comes into being, or if for any other reason a Governor cannot assume office on that date, the Executive power of the State shall be exercised temporarily by the person last elected as Mayor of the District of Columbia prior to the effective date of this Section of the Constitution.

(D) *Holdover Term for Council Members* If the first election for State Delegates has not been held by the date that the State comes into being, or if for any other reason the members of the House of Delegates cannot assume office on that date, the legislative power of the State shall be exercised temporarily by the persons last elected as members of the Council of the District of Columbia prior to the effective date of this Section of the Constitution.

(E) *No Interim Elections* No new election for Mayor or Council shall be held after this Section of the Constitution becomes effective. If such an election would ordinarily be scheduled between the date when this Article of the Constitution becomes effective and the date when the other Articles of the Constitution become effective, the Mayor and the Council shall hold over.

(F) *Eligibility for Re-election* The first term of the Governor and Lieutenant Governor shall count as a full term for the purposes of determining eligibility for re-election only if it is of fouryear duration or longer.

Section 4:
JUDICIARY AND OTHER OFFICERS

(A) *Judges* The Chief Judge and Associate Judges of the Court of Appeals of the District of Columbia on the date when this section enters into force shall become the Chief Justice and Associate Justices of the Supreme Court of the State. The Chief Judge and Associate Judges of the Superior Court of the District of Columbia on that date shall become the Chief Judge and Associate Judges of the Superior Court of the State. At the general election held in the final year of their terms, such judges shall be subject to retention or rejection by the voters in accordance with the provisions of Article IV. Retired Judges of the Court of Appeals of the District of Columbia and of the Superior Court of the District of Columbia shall become Retired Justices of the Supreme Court of the State and Retired Judges of the Superior Court of the State, respectively. They may be assigned by the Chief Justice for temporary service.

(B) *Judicial Nomination Commission* The terms of seven of the members first appointed to the Judicial Nomination Commission shall be shorter than six years, as provided by law, so that terms of members will expire on a staggered basis. The Governor of the State and the Board of Governors of the Unified State Bar shall determine, for their initial appointments, which appointees shall serve which terms.

(C) *Commission on Judicial Disabilities and Tenure* The persons first selected as members of the Commission on Judicial Disabilities and Tenure shall begin to serve their terms upon the expiration of the terms of corresponding incumbent members of the Commission on Judicial

Disabilities and Tenure established by Section 431 of the District of Columbia Self-Government and Reorganization Act (Dec. 24, 1973, 87 Stat. 792).

(D) *Marshals* By agreement between the State and the United States, the United States Marshal may provide services to the courts of the State until the State has appointed its own officers to provide these services.

(E) *Other Officers* Except as otherwise provided in this Constitution, all other officers filling any office by election or appointment shall continue to exercise their duties, according to their respective commissions or appointments, until their offices shall have been abolished or their successors have assumed office.

Section 5:
EXISTING LAWS, RIGHTS, AND PROCEEDINGS

(A) *Laws and Regulations* All laws and regulations of the District of Columbia not inconsistent with this Constitution shall continue in force until they expire by their own limitation or are amended or repealed.

(B) *Congressional Legislation* Legislation passed by Congress applicable only to the District of Columbia and not inconsistent with this Constitution is hereby adopted as state law, subject to amendment or repeal by the House of Delegates.

(C) *Legal Continuity* All existing writs, actions, suits, judicial and administrative proceedings, civil or criminal liabilities, prosecutions, judgments, sentences, orders, decrees, appeals, causes of action, contracts, claims, demands, titles, and rights shall continue unaffected except as modified in accordance with the provisions of this Constitution. The State shall be the legal successor to the District of Columbia in all matters.

(D) *Residence and Qualifications* Residence, citizenship, or other qualifications under the District of Columbia may be used toward the fulfillment of corresponding qualifications required by this Constitution.

(E) *Debts, Assets, and Records* The debts and liabilities of the District of Columbia, as of the date that the State comes into being, shall be assumed by the State, and debts owed to the District of Columbia shall be collected by the State. Assets and records of the District of Columbia shall become the property of the State.

Section 6:
UNITED STATES SENATORS AND REPRESENTATIVES

(A) *Senators-Elect and Representatives-Elect* The Senators-elect and Representatives-elect chosen by the people prior to admission of the State to the Union shall serve as United States Senators and Representatives in Congress until their successors have assumed office.

(B) *First Elections* New elections for these offices shall be held at the first general election which occurs in an even-numbered year after this Constitution becomes effective.

(C) *Staggered Terms for Senators* At that time, one Senator shall be elected for the long term and one Senator for the short term. Each term shall begin on the third day of the following January and shall expire on the third day of January in an odd-numbered year to be determined by authority of the United States.

Section 7:
AGENCIES WITH FEDERALLY-APPOINTED OFFICERS

Boards, commissions, or other agencies of the District of Columbia, the duties of which are consistent with this Constitution and the membership of which includes persons who hold office because they also hold or were appointed by persons who hold federal office, shall continue to function without those Federally-appointed officers. No vacancies shall be deemed to be created by the abolition of the Federal positions.

Section 8:
TRANSFER OF MATTERS TO THE ATTORNEY GENERAL

Upon assuming office, the Attorney General of the State shall assume control of all matters formerly handled by the Corporation Counsel of the District of Columbia.

When the Attorney General is prepared to handle legal matters of the type previously handled by the United States Attorney for the District of Columbia, the Attorney General shall arrange with the United States Attorney for the orderly transfer of such matters to the Office of the Attorney General. The House of Delegates may limit the time within which matters shall be transferred.

The Attorney General may agree with the United States Attorney to enable the United States Attorney to continue to handle any case or category of cases, including any case arising after this Constitution becomes effective, so that responsibility over these matters is transferred in an orderly manner. To facilitate continuity, the Attorney General may also agree to permit the United States Attorney to complete any case.

Until a matter is transferred at the request of the Attorney General, it may be handled by the United States Attorney as if it had been transferred to the Attorney General.

Section 9:
AMENDMENTS BEFORE THE CONSTITUTION ENTERS INTO FORCE

After the voters have approved it and before Article XVII enters into force, amendments to this Constitution may be adopted by the voters of the District of Columbia after affirmative recommendation by a District of Columbia Statehood Constitutional Convention or by a two-thirds vote of the Council of the District of Columbia. This Section shall take effect when the Constitution is approved by the voters.

*The Delegates
to the District of Columbia Statehood Constitutional Convention
assembled, at the University of the District of Columbia,
in Washington, D.C., do hereby certify
that this Constitution was adopted by the Convention
this 29th Day of May 1982.*

INDEX

Delegates elected to the Statehood Constitutional Convention of the District of Columbia are indicated in **boldface**. The complete list of delegates appears on pages 254 and 255.